THE AUTHOR

Jonathan Barnes is Fellow and Tutor in Philosophy at Oriel College, Oxford, and Lecturer in Philosophy at the University of Oxford. He was educated at the City of London School and at Balliol College, Oxford, where he read Mods and Greats. He has taught in America, both at the University of Chicago, and at the University of Massachusetts at Amherst. He has also been Visiting Fellow of the Institute for Advanced Study at Princeton. His publications include *The Ontological Argument* (Macmillan, 1972) and *Aristotle's Posterior Analysis* (Clarendon Press, 1976).

THE PRESOCRATIC PHILOSOPHERS

Volume 2   Empedocles to Democritus

The Arguments of the Philosophers

EDITOR: TED HONDERICH
Reader in Philosophy, University College London

The group of books of which this is one will include an essentially analytic and critical account of each of the considerable number of the great and influential philosophers. Each book will provide an ordered exposition and an examination of the contentions and doctrines of the philosopher in question. The group of books taken together will comprise a contemporary assessment and history of the entire course of philosophical thought.

Already published in the series

Plato	J. C. B. Gosling
Meinong	Reinhardt Grossman
Santayana	Timothy L. S. Sprigge
Wittgenstein	R. J. Fogelin
Hume	B. Stroud
Descartes	Margaret Dauler Wilson
Berkeley	George Pitcher
Kant	Ralph Walker

THE PRESOCRATIC PHILOSOPHERS

Volume 2
Empedocles to Democritus

Jonathan Barnes

Fellow of Oriel College, Oxford

Routledge & Kegan Paul
London, Henley and Boston

First published in 1979
by Routledge & Kegan Paul Ltd
39 Store Street,
London WC1E 7DD
Broadway House,
Newtown Road,
Henley-on-Thames,
Oxon RG9 1EN and
9 Park Street,
Boston, Mass. 02108, USA
Photoset in 11/12 pt Garamond by
Kelly and Wright, Bradford-on-Avon, Wiltshire
and printed in Great Britain by
Lowe & Brydone Printers Ltd
Thetford, Norfolk
© Jonathan Barnes 1979

British Library Cataloguing in Publication Data

Barnes, Jonathan
The Presocratic philosophers.
Vol. 2: Empedocles to Democritus.—(The arguments
of the philosophers).
1. Philosophy, Ancient
I. Title II. Series
182   B188   78–40272

ISBN 0 7100 8861 2

Contents

CONTENTS

EPILOGUE

Prefatory Note

This volume is intimately linked to volume 1, the two volumes forming a unitary whole. Nevertheless, the reader of volume 2 should find a coherent history between its covers, and he will not often require to look back at volume 1.

The Preface printed in volume 1 applies to the work as a whole; and it records the prejudices which informed its conception and the debts which were incurred in the course of its execution. It would be extravagant to reprint that Preface here: instead, let me iterate, in general form, my gratitude to the many people who have offered me advice and assistance; and let me ask the reader who wants a proper Preface to turn to volume 1.

JB

Note on Citations

Quotations of and allusions to ancient texts will often carry more than one reference; e.g. '1: Diogenes Laertius, I.24 = **11 A 1**'.

A bold arabic numeral accompanies the more important quotations, which are inset from the margin: that numeral documents the position of the text in this book. Thus the quotation labelled '**1**' is the first text of substance that I quote.

The source of every citation is specified: usually the author's name alone is supplied, and further information must be gleaned from Diels-Kranz; fuller details are given for more familiar authors (e.g., Plato and Aristotle), and also in cases where the citation is not printed in Diels-Kranz. Full citations follow the usual canons; and abbreviations of all book titles are explained in Appendix A. (But note here that 'fr.' abbreviates 'fragment'; that titles of the Greek commentaries on Aristotle are abbreviated by prefixing '*in*' to the abbreviated titles of Aristotle's works; that *SVF*, in citations of the Stoics, refers to H. von Arnim's *Stoicorum Veterum Fragmenta*; and that *FGrH*, in citations of certain historians, refers to F. Jacoby's *Fragmente der Griechischer Historiker*.) Thus 'Diogenes Laertius, I.24' refers to Chapter 24 of Book I of Diogenes' only work, the *Lives of the Philosophers*.

Almost all the texts I refer to are printed in the standard source book on early Greek philosophy, *Die Fragmente der Vorsokratiker* by Hermann Diels and Walther Kranz. References to Diels-Kranz, in bold type, cite chapter, section, and item (but the chapter number is omitted wherever it can be divined from the context of the citation). Thus '**11 A 1**' refers to the first item in section **A** of Chapter **11**, 'Thales'. Chapters in Diels-Kranz are usually divided into two sections: section **A** contains *testimonia*; section **B** contains fragments. Sometimes, where no fragments survive, **B** is missing; sometimes a third section, **C**, contains 'imitations'. In the case of Chapter **58**, 'The Pythagorean School', a different principle of division is adopted. Readers should be warned that the **B** sections contain many texts whose status as genuine Presocratic fragments is disputed. (Citations bearing on Heraclitus, Empedocles, Melissus and Zeno sometimes carry an additional bold figure reference: those references are explained in the notes to the chapters in which they are used.)

Finally, where a numeral in plain type is suffixed to a bold type reference, it serves to indicate the line (or occasionally section) of the text in question. Thus '**31 B 115**.9' refers to line 9 of **31 B 115**.

All this is, I fear, somewhat cumbersome; and it makes for unsightliness. But I can discover no more elegant method of citation which is not annoyingly inconvenient.

PARADISE REGAINED

I

The Ionian Revival

(a) A few depressing facts

If the Eleatics are right, scientists may as well give up their activities: *a priori* ratiocination reveals that the phenomena which science attempts to understand and explain are figments of our deceptive senses; the scientist has little or nothing to investigate—let him turn to poetry or to gardening.

Fortunately few Greeks reasoned in that way; and some of the brightest gems of Greek philosophical science were polished in the generation after Parmenides. Empedocles, Anaxagoras, Philolaus, Leucippus, Democritus, Diogenes of Apollonia, all pursued the old Ionian ideal of *historia* despite the pressure of the Eleatic *logos*. And these neo-Ionian systems contain much of interest and much of permanent influence. How far they were genuine answers to the Eleatic metaphysics, and how far they were obstinate attempts to follow an out-moded profession, are questions which I shall later discuss. First, I shall offer a brief and preliminary survey of the main neo-Ionian systems which will, I hope, indicate the connexions between these men and their early models, show the respects in which their new systems must lead to conflict with Elea, and uncover the novelties of thought and argument by which they hoped to win that conflict.

This section, however, will concern itself primarily with a few issues of chronology. I begin with Anaxagoras: his dates are remarkably well attested, and we know he lived from 500 to 428 BC (Diogenes Laertius, II.7 = **59 A 1**); between his birth in Clazomenae and his death in Lampsacus he enjoyed a thirty-year sojourn in Athens, during which time he is said to have 'taught' Pericles and Euripides (e.g., Diogenes Laertius II.10; 12 = **A 1**) and to have been

3

condemned on a charge of impiety brought against him by Pericles' political opponents (e.g., Diogenes Laertius, II.12 = **A 1**). The dates of that sojourn are uncertain: the period from 463–433 seems not improbable.[1] A charming though doubtless apocryphal story has it that as he lay dying the rulers of Lampsacus asked him how he would like to be commemorated, 'and he said that every year the children should be allowed a holiday in the month of his death' (Diogenes Laertius, II.14 = **A 1**).

The dates of our other philosophers are less certain. Empedocles was 'not much younger' than Anaxagoras, according to Theophrastus (Simplicius, **31 A 7**) and he died at the age of sixty, according to Aristotle (fr. 71 R[3] = **A 1**). A perplexingly ambiguous phrase in the *Metaphysics* (984a11) says that Anaxagoras was *tois ergois husteros* than Empedocles: I agree with those scholars who give *husteros* its literal sense of 'later', and I suppose that Empedocles wrote before Anaxagoras.[2] If the question is controversial, it is also unimportant; for I see no evidence of any interaction between the two philosophers.

Of Philolaus' life and dates we know little. A passage in Plato's *Phaedo* (61 E) and a scholiast's note upon it (**44 A 1 a**) suggest that as a young man Philolaus, a Pythagorean, escaped the persecutions of his sect and left South Italy in about 450 BC to reside in Thebes. He appears to have lived on into the fourth century. A working career spanning the years 450 to 400 will not be wildly inaccurate.[3]

The Atomists, Leucippus and Democritus, are shadowy figures: 'I came to Athens,' Democritus allegedly said, 'and no one knew me' (**68 B 116**); and Epicurus, who is said to have studied under Leucippus, is also reported to have denied that Leucippus ever existed (Diogenes Laertius, X.13 = **67 A 2**). A strong tradition says that Leucippus was a 'pupil' of Zeno (Diogenes Laertius, IX.30 = **A 1**; Clement, **A 4**; etc.); and a late report makes him, interestingly, a student of Melissus (Tzetzes, **A 5**). Simplicius observed that

> Leucippus the Eleatic or Milesian—for both titles are given
> him[4]—having shared in the philosophy of Parmenides, did not
> follow the path of Parmenides and Xenophanes about what exists
> but, it seems, quite the opposite path (**193: A 8**; cf. Epiphanius,
> **A 33**).

Democritus came from Abdera; and he was a 'companion' or 'pupil' of Leucippus (Diogenes Laertius, IX.34 = **68 A 1**; Suda, **A 2**; etc.). He is also said to have 'heard' Anaxagoras (ibid.). By his own account he was a young man in Anaxagoras' old age, perhaps forty years his junior (Diogenes Laertius, IX.34, 41 = **A 1**); and that puts his birth in 460 BC. His major work, the *Mikros Diakosmos* or *Little World-Order*, was published, so he said, 730 years after the capture of Troy (Diogenes Laertius, IX.41 = **A** 1). Alas, we do not know to what year Democritus dated the fall of Troy; but if we think of the period of 440–400 as his working life we shall not be far wrong.[5]

Those sparse, dry facts are of little intrinsic interest; I mention them in the hope of throwing light on the relations between the Eleatics and their neo-Ionian opponents. But hope is illusory. Parmenides' work, we may be sure, antedated all these neo-Ionian inquiries; but the relationships between Melissus and the neo-Ionians, and between Zeno and the neo-Ionians, which are of much greater interest, must remain dark. Melissus' dates are unknown; and we can say little better for Zeno. Did any of the neo-Ionians know and study Melissus' prose system of Eleatic metaphysics? Did any of them puzzle over Zeno's paradoxes? The chronological data I have listed are far too scanty to encourage an answer to these questions: the dates we have are compatible with several competing answers. Nor will internal evidence help us: it is, of course, frequently appealed to, but in contradictory senses. Thus some scholars find evidence in the fragments that Empedocles knew and attempted to answer Melissus' views on motion; others are equally certain that Melissus attacks Empedocles' doctrine of the four roots. Again, many scholars find in Anaxagoras a clear knowledge of Zeno's views of infinite divisibility; but others see, if anything, an opposite influence.

The moral is negative: we cannot hope to chart in any detail the course of fifth-century philosophical thought. We may speak generally of 'answers to the Eleatic challenge'; and one or two particular connexions between neo-Ionian fragments and the verses of Parmenides can be discerned. Beyond that, all is speculation. When we study the history of seventeenth-century thought, our philosophical and our historical appetites are whetted and satisfied together; we consider, say, Locke's attack on innate ideas, and Leibniz' defence. As philosophers, we are keen to decide whether the Leibnizian defence breaks Locke's attack; and as historians we can enter the fray with dates and personalities, for we know that Leibniz' *Nouveaux Essais* were written as a commentary upon Locke's *Essay*. The intellectual excitement of the fifth century BC must have been no less intense than that of the seventeenth AD, and the cut and thrust of debate was doubtless as violent and as personal in Greece as it was later in enlightened Europe: when Greek meets Greek, then comes the tug of war. But we cannot recover and relive those Olympian games; and if the handbooks on ancient philosophy make us think we can, they are deceptive. We must reconcile ourselves to ignorance of the historical wars and be content to investigate the abstract battles of ideas. The prospect is sad, but not appalling: men are less permanent than thought.

(b) Empedocles' cosmic cycle

This section is purely expository. I shall state what I take to have been the Empedoclean world-view; and I shall briefly sketch the basic positions of Anaxagoras, of Philolaus, and of the Atomists. I shall have little more to say about Empedocles' cosmology, which is philosophically unrewarding; but some of my remarks on Empedoclean psychology in a later chapter will refer back to his 'cosmic cycle'. Anaxagoras, Philolaus and the Atomists will receive detailed treatment later on; and Diogenes of Apollonia will get a chapter to himself.

Everything connected with Empedocles' cosmology is now controversial: there is what may be called the traditional view of his theory, which I shall expound and which I believe to be in all essentials true; and there are various heterodoxies, recently advocated with great scholarly power and ingenuity. I shall not enter into any of these issues; and the reader should be warned that my exposition here is more than usually one-sided.

The main text is **31 B** 17.1–13[6] (most of its contents are repeated, sometimes verbatim, in **B 26** and **B 35**):

I shall tell a double tale; for at one time they[7] increased to be one thing alone
from being many; and then again they grew apart to be many from being one.
And two-fold is the generation of mortal things, two-fold their disappearance;
for the one[8] the collocation of everything both brings to birth and destroys,
and the other is nourished and flies apart[9] as they again grow   5
apart.
And they never cease from continuous interchange,
now by Love all coming together into one,
now again each carried apart by the enmity of Strife.
[Thus in so far as they have learned to become one from being many][10]
and as the one grows apart they become many,   10
thus far do they come into being and there is no stable life for them;

6

but in so far as they never cease from continuous interchange, thus far do they exist forever changeless in the cycle (**194**).

The fragment has as its subject the four elemental stuffs or, as Empedocles call them, 'roots (*rhizômata*)': earth, air, fire, water (cf. **B 6**; **B 21**.3–8). According to Aristotle, fire had a place of special importance in Empedocles' system (*GC* 330b20; *Met* 985b1 = **A 36–7**; cf. Hippolytus, **A 31**); but that is not apparent from the fragments. Nor need we pay any heed to the doxographical assertion that the roots had an atomic or corpuscular substructure (e.g., Aëtius, **A 43**).[11] The roots are eternal (cf. **B 7**); they are obliquely characterized in **B 21** and given divine appellations in **B 6**.[12]

The roots are involved in a never-ending cycle of change (**194**. 6; 12–3; cf., e.g., Aristotle, *Phys* 187a24 = **A 46**). One part of the cycle is dominated by the agency of Love (**194**. 7), during which the elements gradually commingle into one mass; another part is dominated by Strife (**194**.8), during which the elements gradually separate out into four distinct masses. The ontological status and the causal functions of these two cosmic powers will be discussed in a later chapter. When Love is supreme, a homogeneous Sphere is formed in which all the roots promiscuously interpenetrate (**B 27**; **B 28**; cf., e.g., Philoponus, **A 41**; Simplicius, **A 52**); and the Sphere is at rest for a period of time.[13] Then the force of Strife grows again; the Sphere breaks up (cf. Eudemus, fr. 110 W; Aristotle, *Met* 1092b6); and the elements eventually become completely separated. It appears that this state, when Strife is totally dominant, is instantaneous.

As for the four roots 'run through one another, they become different in aspect' (**B 21**. 13), and their interminglings form the cosmos and everything in it:

> For from these comes everything that was and is and will be—
> trees sprang up, and men and women,
> and beasts and birds and water-dwelling fish,
> and long-lived gods who are first in honour (**195: B 21.** 9–12).

The creative process is described in a pleasant analogy:

> As when painters decorate offerings—
> men well trained in their craft by skill—
> they grasp the many-coloured pigments in their hands,
> mixing in harmony more of some and less of others,
> and from these they make forms resembling all things,
> creating trees, and men and women,
> and beasts and birds and water-dwelling fish
> and long-lived gods who are first in honour

7

—so let not your mind be conquered by the falsehood that from
anywhere else
is the spring of all the myriad mortal things that are plain to see;
but know this clearly, hearing the tale from a god. (196: B 23; cf.
Galen, A 34).

From a few primary colours painters make an imitation world: in the
same way, the mixing of the four elements produces the natural
world, one proportion making bone (B 96), one blood (B 98), others
other stuffs (Aëtius, A 78; Simplicius, *ad* B 96).

The natural world and its production were described in detail in
Empedocles' poem *Concerning Nature*: there was a cosmogony, an
astronomy, a meteorology; a zoogony; a biology and a botany;
remarks on embryology and anatomy, on physiology and psychology—
in short, a detailed and often novel natural science in the grand
Ionian tradition.

The cosmic cycle rolls on endlessly; a partial map of it may have
looked like this:

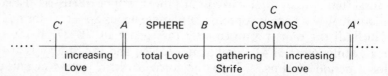

AA' represents one complete cycle: identical cycles are repeated
infinitely often. $AB = BA'$: during AB, for just half the cycle, the
elements are homogeneously commingled into the Sphere. At B the
hold of Love is relaxed: Strife gradually regains its powers, separating
the elements until, at C, they lie completely distinct, arranged about
one another in concentric hollow spheres. Then Love increases again,
until the Sphere is reformed at A'. C, the point of total Strife, is
midway between B and A'.

BC and CA' are mirror images of one another: take any point P on
BC and construct P' on CA such that $PC = CP'$; then the state of
the world at P is qualitatively indistinguishable from its state at P'.
We live in BC the period of increasing strife (Aristotle, *GC* 334a5 =
A 42): our world is doomed to destruction; but after that destruction
another world will be created, a perfect reflexion of our own. And
before and after these twin worlds there have been and will be
infinitely many others.

Empedocles' system may have had less order and symmetry than I
have ascribed to it; for my account has idealized in some places and
ignored serious controversy in others. But few would deny the cosmic
cycle a subtle aesthetic fascination; and Empedocles' poetical

style—grand, formulaic, repetitive, hierophantic—adds to that seductive power.[14] Poetry and reason do not always cohabit; and Empedocles has frequently been held to have lost in ratiocinative capacity what he gained in poetical talent. Thus according to Aristotle, 'anyone who says this should not simply state it—he should also give the explanation of it, and not posit it or lay down some unreasoned axiom but bring either an induction or a demonstration' (*Phys* 252a22–5; cf. *GC* 333b22–6). A modern scholar has generalized Aristotle's criticism: 'Imaginative vividness took hold of [Empedocles] with more persuasiveness than did logical consistency, and he inevitably baffles minds not constituted like his own. The important thing in understanding him is to stop thinking at the right moment'.[15]

That criticism is harsh, but not wholly unfair: certainly, we shall look in vain for any argument in favour of Empedocles' cycle; it is a construction of great 'imaginative vividness', but it lacks all rational support. I do not say that it is inconsistent, only that it was, so far as we can now tell, unreasoned. And what holds of the general scheme holds of many of its particular parts: we look in vain for argument, either inductive or deductive. Thus Empedocles confidently gives us a recipe for making bone: it is patent that he never tested his own recipe—a poor intellectual cook. Or again, he says much about the activity of Love and Strife; yet he nowhere explains why Love and Strife are the two active principles in the cosmos, or why they do what they are alleged to do.

But it would be wrong to dismiss Empedocles as a mere fantastic, a writer of versified science fiction. There are fragments which contrive to be both descriptive and illuminating, genuine contributions to natural science; the two long similes about the structure of the eye (**B 84**) and about the nature of respiration (**B 100**) are only the most extended examples of that. And there are one or two fragments containing philosophical argument. These philosophical fragments, which I shall quote below, are Eleatic in tone and content: though Empedocles never mentions Parmenides, the many echoes of Eleatic verse in his poem prove that he knew his great predecessor's work;[16] and since Empedocles' cycle is patently un-Eleatic, it is hard to avoid the conclusion that he was consciously striving to answer the Eleatic challenge and to restore Ionian science to its high intellectual place.

So much for Empedocles. Let me now describe in barest outline the other major neo-Ionian systems.

Anaxagoras' cosmology differs considerably from Empedocles'; but in Elea the differences would have seemed trifling. Anaxagoras' world begins in an undifferentiated mass of stuffs, comparable to

Empedocles' Sphere. An active principle, Mind, then stirs the mass into rotatory motion; and that rotation produces our world, the different stuffs in the primordial mass commingling and separating in different amounts and proportions. Like Empedocles, Anaxagoras raised a full Ionian science on these foundations; the doxography preserves much of the detail, even though we have almost nothing of it in Anaxagoras' own words. Anaxagoras' cosmogony ends with the creation: his variegated world did not finally break apart into its elements; nor did the original mass ever reform; nor, consequently, did Anaxagoras follow Empedocles in postulating an infinite sequence of worlds.[17]

Anaxagoras' system is less strange than Empedocles'; and it was expounded in plain prose. Moreover, it was in a strong sense a rational structure: the fragments contain a quantity of argument; and it is clear that Anaxagoras was not content to state, but strove to prove. Much of that argument will be investigated in the next chapter. Finally, observe that in Anaxagoras no less than in Empedocles there are clear traces of Eleatic influence.

Philolaus was a Pythagorean; and some will object to my calling him 'neo-Ionian'. My excuse is simply this: he offered a cosmogony and an astronomy, as all good Ionian scientists did; and he paid some attention to Eleatic arguments, as all good neo-Ionians must. His system was sensibly different from those of Anaxagoras and Empedocles in all other respects: Philolaus has cosmic 'principles', two in number, but they have curiously abstract and immaterial names. From the union of those principles our world was somehow formed and made intelligible; and the union was carried out under the auspices of Harmony, a force eminently comparable to Empedocles' Love (which indeed is sometimes called Harmonia: e.g., 31 B 27). That brief sketch will hardly inspire excited anticipation; but I hold out the promise that Philolaus' cosmogony will prove stimulating.

The Atomists 'say that the full and the empty are elements, calling the one "being" and the other "not being"' (Aristotle, *Met* 985b5 = 67 A 6). Apart from 'the full and the empty', atoms and the void, there is nothing. The atoms, which differ from one another in shape and size, move perpetually through the infinite void. The movement occurs by necessity (67 B 2); and in its course the atoms knock against, and sometimes adhere to, one another. Sometimes those adhesions increase in size and complexity; and our own universe is the result of a vast set of such atomic collisions. Not merely the formation of the world but everything else is ultimately explicable in terms of atomic structure: macroscopic qualities and relations rest upon microscopic form and arrangement; macroscopic changes are but the phenomenal results of microscopic motions.

With the Atomists' adoption of 'the void', and their assertion that 'what is not is', we meet the most far-reaching challenge to the Eleatic philosophy that the Presocratics produced; with the Atomists' thoroughgoing corpuscularianism, and their self-conscious and systematic development of its implications, we meet the most impressive achievement of Presocratic science. The Atomists are often regarded as the *élite* of the Presocratics; of all the early thinkers their thought was nearest to our own—and hence, of course, most rational.

Here, then, are the neo-Ionian systems. That they clash, obviously and fundamentally, with the doctrines of Elea, is a plain fact. And it is plain too that, to some extent at least, their proponents were conscious of the clash.

(c) *Four blind alleys*

The success of the neo-Ionian attack on Elea cannot be judged until its nature has been determined; and since there are several popular misconceptions of the nature of the attack, I begin by mentioning four routes along which the neo-Ionians did not march.

First, it is frequently said that Empedocles' Sphere or *Sphairos* corresponds to the ball or *sphaira* to which Parmenides likened 'what is'. Parmenides 'One' is spherical, homogeneous, and motionless: Empedocles' *Sphairos* is also homogeneous and motionless. After describing the 'One', Parmenides gives an account of the plural, changing world of Mortal Opinion: from the *Sphairos* Empedocles generates the plural, changing world of natural science. Empedocles, in brief, replaces the logical relation between the Way of Truth and the Way of Opinion by a chronological relation between the time of the Sphere and the time of the Cosmos; and thus he 'perpetuates Parmenides' insight', while reconciling it with common sense'.[18]

There are literary links between Parmenides' *sphaira* and Empedocles' *Sphairos*; and perhaps psychologically Empedocles was influenced by Parmenides here. But it is perfectly plain that the Sphere in no way 'perpetuates Parmenides' insight', nor does it marry Eleaticism with science. Even if Parmenides was a spherical monist he would have scorned the *Sphairos*: the *Sphairos* generates the natural world; the *Sphairos* is no more real than the plural world it produces; the *Sphairos* is not sempeternal; nor is it changeless—it lasts for a fixed period of time and then gradually breaks up into the world we know. A silly person might attempt to reconcile Zeno and Antisthenes by urging that for half of his time in the stadium the

11

runner really is at rest, and that for the other half he moves. Such a reconciliation is ludicrous. No less ludicrous is the suggestion that Empedocles' stable *Sphairos* 'reconciles' Parmenidean metaphysics with Ionian science. I do not believe that Empedocles could have imagined anything so foolish.

The *Sphairos* is irrelevant to the neo-Ionian answer to Parmenides. I suppose that no one will suggest that Anaxagoras' primordial mass, or Philolaus' originative elements, or the little bodies of the Atomists, have any conciliatory tendencies.

Second, it is often observed that the neo-Ionians were, so to speak, axiomatic pluralists: they made it an initial posit that there is a plurality of things or stuffs. Thus Empedocles lays it down that there are four originative and ungenerated 'roots'; Anaxagoras has an indefinite variety of stuffs in his primordial mixture; Philolaus starts from a pair of principles; the atomists begin with an irreducible infinity of bodies. Parmenides, it is then said, observed the old Ionian systems, and found an impossibility in the suggestion that their single primordial stuff should give rise to a plural world. And against Parmenides the neo-Ionians reasoned thus: 'Parmenides was right in denying that a plurality could ever be derived from an ultimate unity; but what if there was no ultimate unity, but a plurality of primary entities which had always existed?'[19] Parmenides, in short, rejects the move from one to many; the neo-Ionians concur, but they counter the argument by presenting cosmogony as a move from many to many: a derived manifold is possible, for all that Parmenides has said, provided only that it derives from a primitive manifold.

It would be tedious to set out all the confusions and inaccuracies in that account of the central feature of Presocratic philosophy; and the account can be rejected by a quick and easy observation. Parmenides objects, not to the generation of a manifold from a unity, but to generation *tout court*. He does not argue, specifically, that nothing can be derived from a unity; he argues, quite generally, that nothing can be derived at all. The account I have just reported ascribes the grossest *ignoratio elenchi* to Empedocles and his fellows; I see no reason to suppose that they had misunderstood Parmenides' message in so crude a fashion. Indeed, on that point at least they were fully aware of the force of the Eleatic argument.

The word '*homoios*' signposts the third alley. Empedocles' roots are 'always utterly homogeneous' (**31 B 17.35**); for 'all these are fitting to their own parts' (**B 22.1**). Any parcel of a given elemental stuff has all and only those qualities possessed by any other parcel. In a similar way, Anaxagorean stuffs are 'homoiomerous': the precise

12

sense of that controversial appellation will be investigated later (see below, pp. 18–20); here it is enough to say that homoiomereity imparts some measure of homogeneous stability to Anaxagoras' world.

The Eleatics argued that the world was *homoios*, homogeneous. The neo-Ionians accepted the argument, but to a limited extent: the elemental stuffs of the world, they admitted, are *homoia*; but that admission is consistent with change and decay. Plainly, that constitutes no answer to Elea: just as the postulation of a temporary Sphere does not reunite science with the Eleatic ban on change, so the admission of homogeneous elements does not unite scientific truth with the assertion that the whole universe is homogeneous. I do not think that Anaxagoras and Empedocles can have seriously supposed that their references to homogeneity constituted an answer to Elea; and I turn to the fourth and final alley.

It is drawn only on the map of Empedocles' thought. In **194**.9–13 (= **B 26**.8–12) Empedocles explains how, in one respect, things 'come into being and there is no stable life for them', while in another respect 'they exist forever, changeless in the cycle'. The language is reminiscent of Parmenides; and we may suspect that Empedocles is offering an answer to Elea. Roughly, Empedocles' position is this: *within* any cosmic cycle there is constant change—birth and decay, alteration and locomotion; but viewed from a higher vantage point the cosmos exhibits an eternal fixity—there is nothing new in the world; each event has occurred already infinitely many times, and will recur infinitely often. There is local change but global stability; for the local changes occur in accordance with unalterable global laws. Thus the Empedoclean universe is, at a global level, Eleatic: its laws do not change; its grand cycles are forever fixed. But that Eleatic stability can be reconciled with the changes observed by the scientist; for the stability itself governs and accounts for those changes.

Now as an answer to Parmenides, that is plainly futile: if Parmenides is right, there is no possibility of change, either at a global or at a local level. Eleatic arguments work, if they work at all, across the board; and if we suppose that Empedocles failed to see that fact, we accuse him of a wretched blindness: as well say that astronomy can be harmonized with Zenonian immobility by the reflexion that the stars always return to their starting points. And in fact, **194**.9–13 is not to be construed as an answer to Elea at all: rather, it makes, in somewhat picturesque language, a perfectly sane and sober point. Empedocles is saying, in effect, that the choppings and changings of the phenomenal world do not remove that world from the domain of rational science, whose first postulate is the existence of some system and stability in the phenomena; for the choppings and changings, though they may seem careless or random, are in fact the manifestations of eternal regularities; behind the phenomena lie stable and strong laws. That is not an original thought in Empedocles, although in 194 it has an idiosyncratically Empedoclean twist; but it is a comprehensible and a true thought—and a thought that has no bearing on the problems raised for science by Eleatic metaphysics.

(d) Five through roads

If those four alleys are blind, where are we to go? There are, I think, five main lines of contact between the Eleatics and the neo-Ionians; together they constitute the framework within which the new scientists tried to pursue their craft without falling foul of old Parmenides. First, the neo-Ionians agree with the first theorem of Eleatic metaphysics: generation, the absolute coming into being of real entities, is an impossibility. But, second, they hold that the alteration (in some sense) of existing entities is a possibility; and, third, they believe that locomotion is also possible. Then, fourth, they supply a 'moving cause' which will explain and account for the changes that the world contains; and finally, they reinstate, in a guarded fashion, the methodology of empirical observation. Generation goes, but locomotion stays; locomotion is causally explicable and in turn will account for alteration; and perception, the first instrument of science, will reveal what locomotions and what alterations take place.

Scientifically speaking, the final point is crucial: in order to return to the rich pastures of Ionian science, the neo-Ionians were obliged to rescue the senses as instruments of discovery and signposts to truth. The complex and ingenious hypotheses of Empedocles, of Anaxagoras, of Philolaus, and of the Atomists are designed to organize and to explain 'the phenomena'; such hypotheses are chimerical if the phenomena have no objective status but remain, as they are in Elea, dreams and delusions of the human fantasy; and the phenomena can only be granted a decent scientific status if our senses, by which the phenomena are apprehended, have some claim to be regarded as dispensers of truth.

Philosophically, the third point is crucial: locomotion must be saved at all costs; for it was, as we shall see, primarily by their defence of the possibility of locomotion that the neo-Ionians hoped to rehabilitate the world of science. Generation and destruction, they believed, could, with some important reservations, be left in the Eleatic hell of nonentity; and they were surprisingly nonchalant in their attitude towards alteration. But on locomotion they were adamant: *pace* Elea, things can move; and they do move. In that way science gains a toehold in reality, and it can again dare to ascend the lofty cliffs of truth.

Such, I believe, is the essential doctrine of the neo-Ionian counter-reformation. Different thinkers developed it in different ways, and it is their differences which, being intrinsically fascinating, are generally held up for inspection and admiration. Yet it is important to grasp in a general and abstract way the common *nisus* that guided their diverse efforts to escape from the narrow and blinkering tenets of Elea. That *nisus* had nothing to do with the desire to balance periods of change against periods of stability, nor with the hope of securing phenomenal pluralities on the basis of elemental multiplicity. It had everything to do with the possibility of locomotion.

In the next three chapters I shall look into the different systems proposed by the neo-Ionians. The discussion will lead away from the common core of neo-Ionian doctrine. But the core must not be forgotten; and I shall take occasion later to examine it in more detail and to assess its power to defend Ionia against Elea.

II

Anaxagoras and the Nature of Stuffs

(a) *Outlines of Anaxagoreanism*

Anaxagoras' book was available at the *bouquinières* in the Athenian agora (Plato, *Apology* 26E = **59 A 35**). Some infer that it was 'read and understood without much difficulty';[1] if that is so, times have changed: of all the Presocratics Anaxagoras is the most difficult. Thanks to Simplicius, we possess substantial portions of the first part of Anaxagoras' work *Concerning Nature*;[2] and there is a rich doxography. But Anaxagoras' views are of considerable complexity, his arguments subtle in conception; and his thought is often (or so I at least find) of a peculiarly elusive character.

I shall begin by offering a crude statement of what I take to be Anaxagoras' fundamental tenets about the nature of the physical world. I shall first set them down, and then quote the several fragments in which I claim to find them expressed. The fundamental tenets are three:

(A) In the beginning, everything was mixed together.
(B) There is no smallest portion of anything.
(C) Now, everything is mixed together.
(Note that 'mind (*nous*)' is not included in 'everything' here: I shall leave *nous* out of the discussion in this chapter; it is readily separated from Anaxagoras' physical theories, and separation makes for easier exposition.) I find these three theses in the following fragments:

> All things were together [= A], unlimited both in quantity[3] and in smallness; for the small too was unlimited [= B]. And since all things were together [= A], nothing was clear by reason of the smallness. For air and aether contained[4] everything, both being unlimited. For these are the greatest items present in all things, both in quantity and in magnitude (**197: B 1**).

16

For neither of the small is there the least [= B], but there is always a less (for what is cannot not be)—but of the great too there is always a greater, and it is equal in quantity to the small. And in relation to itself each is both great and small (198: B 3).

These things being thus, it is necessary to suppose that there are many things of every sort in everything that is conjoined [= C], and seeds of all things having various aspects and colours and tastes (199: B 4a).⁵

And men were compounded, and the other animals that have a soul (*psuchē*). And these men possess inhabited cities and cultivated fields, as we do; and they have a sun and a moon and the rest, as we have; and the earth grows for them many and various things, the most beneficial of which they gather into their dwellings and use. This, then, have I said about the separation— that it would have been separated not only by us but elsewhere too (200: B 4b).

Before these things were separated off, since everything was together [= A], not even any colour was clear; for this was prevented by the commingling of all things [= A]—of the wet and the dry and the hot and the cold and the bright and the dark, there being much earth present and seeds unlimited in quantity and not like one another. For of the other things none is like any other. And these things being thus, it is necessary to suppose that all things are present in everything [= C] (201: B 4c).

And since too there are equal portions of the great and the small in quantity, for this reason too everything is in everything [= C]; nor can they exist separately, but everything shares a portion of everything [= C]. Since the least cannot be [= B], things cannot be separated nor come to be by themselves, but as in the beginning [= A], so now too everything is together [= C]. And in all things there are many even of the things that are separating off, equal in quantity in the greater and in the smaller (202: B 6).

The things in the one cosmos have not been separated from one another [= C], nor have they been cut off by an axe—neither the hot from the cold nor the cold from the hot (203: B 8).

In everything there is present a portion of everything [= C], except mind; and in some things mind too is present (204: B 11).

17

These are the central fragments bearing on Anaxagoras' theory of physical nature. Thesis (B) is stated clearly enough; in the various statements of (A) and (C) I assume a synonymy among 'everything is *together*', 'everything *is* (*present*) *in* everything' and 'everything *has a portion of* everything'. My first task is exegetical: what does Anaxagoras mean by 'things'? The question is, surprisingly, difficult and controversial; and it calls for a section to itself.

(b) *The nature of things*

'All things were together': *homou panta chrêmata ên*. With those words Anaxagoras began his book (Simplicius, *ad* **B 1**). The Greek word '*chrêma* (thing)' gives nothing away; and in any case Anaxagoras sometimes simply uses the pronoun 'everything, (*panta*)'. The delicious suggestion that by 'all things' Anaxagoras meant literally 'all things' is, alas, untenable: 'all things are in all things' will then imply that Anaxagoras is in my typewriter and Clazomenae in its keys; and those idiocies were evidently no part of Anaxagorean physics.

We might start by considering Anaxagoras' examples of 'things'. They are: air, fire (**197**); wet, dry, hot, cold, bright, dark, earth (**201**); hair, flesh (**B 10**); thin, thick (**B 12**); cloud, water, stone (**B 16**). The doxographers add such things as: gold, blood, lead (Simplicius, **A 41**); white, black, sweet (Aristotle, *Phys* 187b5 = **A 52**). We do not, of course, know whether these latter examples actually occurred in Anaxagoras' text.

Do the examples suggest any generic determination for the notion of a 'thing'? Two suggestions have been widely canvassed. First, it is suggested that the Anaxagorean things are in fact the opposites: hot and cold, light and dark, wet and dry, and so on. Where we ordinarily speak of something's being hot, philosophically-minded men may say that a thing has the property of heat or hotness, or that heat or hotness or 'the hot' resides or inheres in the thing. And it is those properties which Anaxagoras had in mind when he talked about 'all things'. Such at least is the suggestion. But it is palpably false: hair and flesh, water and stone, are not properties or 'opposites'; but they are used by Anaxagoras himself in illustration of his theory. A modified version of the suggestion has it that if X is in Y, then X, but not Y, is an 'opposite'. That version fares no better: earth, according to **202**, is 'in' things; and in any case, the formula 'everything is in everything' shows that if X is in Y then Y is in X. Specific talk of the opposites may profitably be dropped from the discussion of Anaxagoras' theory of nature.

The second suggestion, far more complicated and influential, goes back at least to Aristotle:

> But Anaxagoras says the opposite [to Empedocles]; for [he makes] the homoemeries elements (I mean, e.g., flesh and bone and each of those things), and air and fire mixtures of these and of all the other seeds; for both of these are put together from all the invisible homoemeries (205: *Cael* 302a31–b3 = A 43).

The passage raises several questions: I want first to single out the 'homoemeries' for attention; and I shall consider the simple suggestion, implicit in Aristotle and repeated *ad nauseam* by the doxographers, that Anaxagoras' things are in fact homoeomeries.

Aristotle explains the term 'homoeomerous' in another passage:

> For he [sc. Anaxagoras] posits the homoiomeries as elements—e.g., bone and flesh and marrow and the other things whose part are synonymous (206: *GC* 314a18 = A 46).

Thus an F is homoiomerous if the parts of F are themselves synonymous with the whole, i.e. if they are F: flesh is homoiomerous because parts of a lump of flesh are themselves flesh; hands are not homoiomerous, because parts of hands are not hands.[6]

It is not clear precisely what Aristotle means to ascribe to Anaxagoras. Most generously, we might imagine him to offer Anaxagoras the *term* 'homoiomerous', so that some lost part of Anaxagoras' book will have said: 'By "thing" I mean homoiomerous thing'. But there is no special reason to interpret Aristotle so strictly; and it seems, on linguistic grounds, improbable that Anaxagoras would have coined a word like '*homoiomerês*'.[7] Most pinchingly, we might imagine that Anaxagoras gave no general description at all of his things: Aristotle read through his examples, saw that they were all what *he* would call homoiomeries, and hastily concluded that Anaxagoras meant to include all and only homoiomeries under his umbrella of things. There is a slight difficulty with this view: Anaxagoras' examples include opposites or properties, and Aristotle more than once uses that fact in criticism of Anaxagoras' theory (*GC* 327b21; *Phys* 188a6 = A 52; *Met* 989b3 = A 61). Now properties are not homoiomerous in Aristotle's mind; and it is therefore a trifle hard to suppose that Aristotle eyed Anaxagoras' examples and judged them all to be homoiomeries. The difficulty is not great; but it is enough to give some plausibility to a third way of understanding Aristotle's ascription: Anaxagoras, we may suppose, did give some general characterization of his things, and that characterization seemed to Aristotle to fit his own notion of a homoiomery. Indeed, there is no reason why Anaxagoras should not have said something like this: 'All things—I mean air and fire and flesh and blood and everything where the part is like the whole . . .'

Thus the notion of a homoiomery may point in a genuinely Anaxagorean direction; but the value of the pointer is modest. For the notion itself is neither as clear nor as precise as it appears to be. How are we to define homoiomereity? A first attempt might read:

(D1) A property P is homoiomerous if and only if if a has P then some part of a has P.

That is too weak: it will allow benches and buildings, swarms and schools, to be homoiomeries; and it is plain that they should not be included in the class. A stronger definition is:

(D2) A property P is homoiomerous if and only if if a has P then every part of a has P.

Now that, I suspect, does answer to Aristotle's thought; but for us it is far too strong: it makes all Aristotle's paradigmatic homoiomeries anhomoiomerous; for it is not the case that *every* part of a piece of flesh is itself flesh, since the atomic parts of mundane stuffs do not share their properties.

(D2) can be emended—adding the word 'macroscopic' before 'part' might do. But it is better to abandon (D2) and to ask, more laxly, what sort of thing Aristotelian homoiomeries are supposed to be. The answer is plain: homoiomeries are *stuffs*; homoiomeries relate to substances as matter to formed individuals; the homoiomeries are the material of which substances are composed (e.g., Aristotle, *Meteor* 389b27; *GA* 715a11).

Thus I propose that we read Anaxagorean 'things' as stuffs; and I claim that the proposal is fundamentally Aristotelian.[8] What of the obvious objection, that 'the hot', 'the cold', 'the wet' and so on are not stuffs?[9] Here again I side with Aristotle: according to him, Anaxagoras mistakenly treats properties, like 'the hot', as substances; the criticism seems to me to be just, for the fragments reveal Anaxagoras doing exactly that. Moreover, Anaxagoras was not the only early thinker to substantialize qualities; on the contrary, such substantiation was, notoriously, a common feature of Greek thought (for a nice example see [Hippocrates], *Nat hom* 3). In short, the occurrence of the opposites among the examples of Anaxagorean things shows not that those things are not stuffs but that Anaxagoras misidentified the opposites as stuffs.

I have not provided much argument for the suggestion that Anaxagoras, like his Ionian predecessors, has an ontology of stuffs. The proof of the suggestion must come in my exposition of his arguments.

(c) *The seeds of the world*

Before turning to those arguments there are some preliminary questions to be raised about Anaxagoras' third tenet, that everything is now mixed together or that 'everything has a portion of everything'. That tenet can now be expressed as follows:

(C*) For any pair of stuffs, S, S': in every piece of S there is now a portion of S'.

In what sense can a portion of S' be in a piece of S? The obvious suggestion is that the lump of S contains, scattered through its volume, particles of S'; those particles will be invisible to gross observation (for S does not wear the aspect of S'), and they will be multitudinous, or even infinite (for they permeate every part of S). Such a particulate view of matter is traditionally ascribed to Anaxagoras; and it seems to make sense. The ascription is supported by four props.

The first prop is the word 'seed (*sperma*)'. Aristotle talks of the homoiomeries 'and all the other seeds' (*Cael* 302b2 = **A** 43); and the word *sperma* is Anaxagorean: 'seeds of all things' 'seeds unlimited in quantity' are present in the primordial mass (**199**; **201**).[10] It is easy to imagine that 'seeds' of S are (minimal) particles of S: the original mass contains everything inasmuch as little seed-particles of every stuff are suspended in it like pollen in the summer air.

That is a tempting interpretation, but not an obligatory one. *Sperma*, in Greek, is as much a biological as a botanical term: where the word 'seed' suggests particles to us, the word *sperma* would not have done so to a Greek. The language of seeds does not imply a particulate theory of stuffs; and to say that X contains seeds of Y need mean no more than that Y may grow from X.[11]

The second prop for particles is the word 'unlimited'. According to Aristotle, Anaxagoras 'says that the principles (*archai*) are unlimited (*apeiroi*)' (*Met* 984a13 = **A** 43; cf. *Phys* 187a25 = **A** 52); Theophrastus repeated the assertion, with reservations (Simplicius, **A** 41); and it is a doxographical commonplace. Must not these 'unlimited principles' be an infinite set of minimal particles or atoms?

No. Aristotle, as his context shows, is thinking not of an infinity of particles, but of an infinity of kinds of stuff. Moreover, we almost certainly possess, in **197**, the words that Aristotle is here interpreting: 'All things were . . . unlimited both in quantity (*plêthos*) and in smallness'. The sentence plainly does not refer to an infinity of corpuscles, and Aristotle rightly did not so construe it; rather, he took Anaxagoras to mean that there was an unlimited quantity of kinds of thing: earth, air, stone, flesh, bone, blood, etc. Aristotle's negative

21

point is correct; but his positive interpretation is not. By '*S* is unlimited in smallness' Anaxagoras means: 'For any *n* and *m*, where *m* < *n*, if there is a portion of *S* of magnitude *n* units, then there is a portion of *S* of magnitude *m* units.' Thus if *S* is 'unlimited in smallness' it follows that the *portions* of *S* are unlimited in number; for if two portions have a different magnitude, they cannot be identical. And that, I suggest, is precisely what Anaxagoras means by '*S* is unlimited in quantity': for any *n* and *m*, where *m* > *n*, if there are *n* portions of *S*, then there are *m* portions of *S* (see below, pp. 33–7). That doctrine does not commit Anaxagoras to infinitely numerous discrete atoms of *S*; it does not commit him to an Aristotelian infinity of stuffs;[12] it does not commit him to the view that some portion of *S* is infinite in size—for *S*'s infinitely numerous portions may all be happily nested inside one another.

Third, consider Anaxagoras' language when he talks of the composition of things and stuffs: things are 'commingled' (*summignusthai*: **B 17**) or 'conjoined' (*sunkrinesthai*: **199**) or 'compounded' (*sumpêgnusthai*: **200**; **B 16**). Those words surely suggest the amassing of discrete particles of stuff. Similarly, Anaxagoras uses 'separate off' (*apokrinesthai*: **B 2**; **201**; etc.) and 'separate out' (*diakrinesthai*: **B 5**; **B 12**; etc.) to denominate the discrimination of sensible stuffs from the rough primordial mass; and such terms suggest an effluxion of particles.

Against that I have little to say but Boo: commingling and separating do not suggest to me the confluence or effluence of particles.[13]

The fourth prop for the view that Anaxagorean stuffs are particulate in structure is the strongest. The doxographers, who follow Aristotle in stressing the imperceptibility of Anaxagorean stuffs in the original world-mass, also follow Aristotle in explaining that imperceptibility in terms of the smallness of the stuff-particles. Stuffs, in the neat and anachronistic phrase of Aëtius, are composed of 'intellectually contemplatable parts (*moria logôi theôrêta*)' (**A** **46**).[14] We can imagine, but we cannot perceive, the fine particulate structure of chalk and cheese.

Here too we need not rely on doxographical interpretation: we have, again in **197**, the original words in which Aristotle and his followers replied:

> And since all things were together, nothing was clear by reason of the smallness. For air and aether contained everything, both being unlimited. For these are the greatest items present in all things, both in quantity and in magnitude.

'Nothing was clear by reason of the smallness.' It is natural to explain the word 'smallness' by way of its first occurrence in **197**: there it indicated small *portions* of stuff; here, accordingly, it is naturally taken in the same way, and the Aristotelian interpretation seems to be confirmed. But a portion of S is not a part of S; and portions, however small, need not be conceived of as particles. Moreover, we can find a better interpretation for the sentence 'nothing was clear by reason of the smallness'.

Consider the word 'greatest' in the last sentence of the fragment. Anaxagoras' point here is fairly straightforward: if we look about the world today we see that two stuffs, air and aether, are vastly more extensive than any others; consequently, Anaxagoras invites us to infer, air and aether must, in the original mixture, have 'contained' or dominated everything else. The 'greatness' of air and aether lies in the fact that the total amount of air and aether in the world is greater than that of any other stuff. Similarly, the 'smallness' of, say, gold, consists not in its being divided into minute particles but rather in the simple fact that there is very little gold in the world.

In the original mixture the proportion of gold or flesh was so small that it made no perceptible difference, as a glass of wine thrown into the sea makes no perceptible difference to the brine. (That, of course, is why the original mass has no colour (**201**): air and aether, themselves colourless, are large enough to absorb the colours of all the other stuffs commingled with them. A glass of Burgundy will not make the green one red.)

I conclude that we have no binding reason for ascribing to Anaxagoras a particulate theory of matter. Moreover, there is one excellent reason for denying him such a theory.[15] If *every* piece of S contains a particle of S', and if every piece of a piece of S is a piece of S, then every piece of S is wholly composed of particles of S'—which is absurd. The inference is easy enough to grasp; and even if Anaxagoras had no notion of it (which I doubt), we must deny him particles if we are to give him a theory of matter consistent with his tenet (C*). Anaxagorean stuffs contain portions of all other stuffs; but those portions are not located at one or more points within the parent lump—they are mingled smoothly and regularly throughout its body. Any stuff contains every stuff; but the contained stuffs are not present by virtue of a mechanical juxtaposition of particles; they are present as the items in a chemical union.[16] Every cloud contains a little silver; but the silver is not spread out as a lining: there is no part of the cloud which is pure, or even impure, silver.

A rough analogy may help. Artists may make a patch of their canvas seem green in either of two ways. First, and unusually, they

23

may adopt a *pointilliste* technique, setting minute dots of blue next to minute dots of yellow: from a distance the effect is green; from close up we see adjacent spots of blue and yellow. Alternatively, they may mix masses of blue and yellow on their palette and apply the mixture to the canvas: the effect from a distance is green; and however closely we look at it, the effect is still green. No part of the canvas, however small, is painted blue; and no part yellow. For all that, the green on the canvas 'contains' blue and yellow; they are its constituents, and some chemical technique might, for all I know, be capable of 'extracting' some of the yellow from the artist's green. Atomists are physical *pointillistes*: their world is made up of microscopical dots, individually indistinguishable to the eye. Anaxagoras was a painter of the traditional type: his world is made of stuffs mixed through and through, its components as invisible to the microscope as to the naked eye.

That conclusion allows us to solve a little puzzle in Anaxagorean scholarship. Anaxagoras' theory of matter, it is said, 'rests on two propositions which seem flatly to contradict one another. One is the principle of homoiomereity: a natural substance such as a piece of gold consists solely of parts which are like the whole and like one another—every one of them gold and nothing else. The other is: "There is a portion of everything in everything".'[17] That criticism misinterprets the principle of homoiomereity: the principle says, not that every part of a lump of gold is 'gold and nothing else', but that every part of a lump of gold has the same material constitution as the lump itself. If 'everything is in everything', then the lump of gold contains a portion of every other stuff. Hence every part of that lump contains a portion of every other stuff. Is there a contradiction, flat or curvaceous, here? Not, I think, if Anaxagorean stuffs are non-particulate. The view is certainly strange; but I see no logical inconsistency in it. In short, given a non-particulate theory of matter, Anaxagoras may safely maintain both (C*) and a principle of homoiomereity.

(a) *Elements and compounds*

Green is a compound colour; blue and yellow are simple or elemental. Are the stuffs in (C*) limited to elemental stuffs? Does Anaxagoras distinguish between elements and non-elemental stuffs? The doxography is clear enough: the homoiomeries are standardly called 'elements' (*stoicheia*: e.g., *Cael* 302a32 = **A 43**) or 'principles' (*archai*: e.g., *Met* 984a13 = **A 43**). If that does not quite suffice to distinguish elemental from non-elemental *stuffs*, two texts take that further step: the *de Caelo* asserts that 'air and fire' are not elements but 'mixtures of the homoiomeries' (302b1 = **A 43**); and elsewhere Aristotle says that 'they [sc. the Anaxagoreans] [say] that these [i.e. the homoiomeries] are simple and elements, and that earth and fire and water and air are compounds' (*GC* 314a24 = **A 46**). The former passage, as its context makes clear, is relying on **197**. **197** does give a special status to air and aether (which Aristotle interprets as fire); but it surely does not imply that air and aether are compounds and not elemental. The second Aristotelian passage is, I suspect, no better based: Aristotle carelessly assumes that what, in his opinion, holds of two of the Empedoclean roots must hold for all four. At all events, I can find no fragment which clearly supports Aristotle's view, or makes any distinction between elemental and non-elemental stuffs.[18]

'But surely Anaxagoras must have realized that some stuffs are compounds of others: that bronze is made from copper and tin; that wine is a mixture of water, sugar, alcohol, and so on. Then why need his original mass contain bronze *in addition to* copper and tin, wine *in addition to* water, sugar and so on? At best such additions are otiose; at worst they are confused. In general, then, the original mass will contain only those stuffs which science shows not to be compounds of other stuffs.'

But what does that suggestion really amount to? If the original mass contains a portion of green then it contains, *eo ipso*, portions of yellow and of blue; and equally, if it contains a portion of yellow and a portion of blue, it contains a portion of green.[19] It is easy to deny that; but the denial rests on an unconscious adherence to a particulate theory of stuffs: we imagine, wrongly, that the blue and the yellow must, as it were, be located in determinate parts of the mass and that they will produce green only if their locations happen to be related in one out of innumerable possible ways. But blue and yellow are not located in any such fashion; they are smoothly mixed throughout the mass of stuff. What more could possibly be required for us to say that the mass contains green? Does the mass contain green *in addition to* blue and yellow? It contains yellow and it contains blue and it contains green; and that is that. I conclude that Anaxagoras' theory takes no stand on the question of elements: it has no peculiar resistance to them; and it provides no special place for them. The contrast between element and compound is of secondary interest to the theory.[20]

But is that theory coherent? It is sometimes argued that theorem (C*) implies that there are no 'pure' stuffs and hence that we cannot intelligibly talk of such stuffs, let alone say that they occur in different proportions in different places. Anaxagoras' theory is self-stultifying: it is a theory about stuffs; but its main tenet is inconsistent with the existence of stuffs.[21]

I shall approach that argument obliquely. The end of **B 12** reads thus:

> And there are many portions of many things; but nothing is altogether separating off or separating out, one from another, except mind. And all mind is homogeneous (*homoios*), both the greater and the smaller. But nothing else is homogeneous,[22] but each single thing is and was most clearly those things of which most are present in it (**207**; cf. **301**).

The last sentence is adequately glossed by Aristotle: 'Things seem different and are given different names from one another on the basis of what especially preponderates in quantity in the mixing of the unlimited [stuffs]. For there is no whole which is purely white or black or sweet or flesh or bone; but the nature of the thing seems to be that of which it contains the most' (*Phys* 187b2–7 = **A 52**). Simplicius puts it bluntly: 'that is gold in which there is much gold, though many things are in it' (**A 41**; cf. Lucretius, **A 44**); and we have already come across an Anaxagorean illustration of the point in **197**: the original mixture, since it contains more air and aether than anything else, is, or wears the aspect of, air and aether. Dig up a spadeful of stuff from your back garden: you can be sure that it will not be a spade of any pure stuff; it will contain countless impurities of every sort. But you are, for all that, warranted in calling it earth; and you may properly surmise that it contains a dominant proportion of earth—which accounts for its earthy aspect.

Here the charge of incoherence shows its teeth: 'How can you know that the dominant stuff in your spadeful is earth? How can you even speak sensibly of "earth"? It will not do to define earth by way of **207**, saying that a is earth if and only if a is a lump of stuff in which earth predominates. Such a definition is vainly circular. And if we evade the circle by putting subscripts to the term "earth"—"a is earth$_1$ if and only if a is a lump of stuff in which earth$_2$ predominates"—then "earth$_2$" remains unexplained. If earth$_2$ is elemental, it cannot be explained in terms of any components; and since, by (C^*), earth$_2$ is never present in the world, we cannot learn the meaning of earth$_2$ by "ostensive definition". In short, "earth", or "earth$_2$" if you prefer, is a bogus term: it has no use in science.'

That argument constitutes a serious challenge to Anaxagoras, whether or not we ascribe to him a distinction between 'earth$_1$' and 'earth$_2$'. Moreover, it poses, I think, a more general difficulty: every schoolboy chemist learns that all the sample elements he uses in the laboratory are impure; no process will guarantee the removal of every impurity from a bottle of stuff. Now the chemist needs and uses the notion of (pure) hydrogen. Yet he lives in an impure world, and he experiments on impure samples of hydrogen. How can Anaxagoras and the modern chemist speak intelligibly of earth or of hydrogen? How can Anaxagoras seriously say that most of the stuff on my spade is earth? How can the chemist determine that most of the stuff in the test-tube is hydrogen?

A part of the answer to those questions runs, I think, like this. We begin by observing, crudely, that different lumps of stuff have different qualities: two buckets of stuff look and smell and feel and taste different; they act and behave differently; and we give them different names—'sand', say, and 'sea'. Evidently, the buckets do not contain pure samples of sand and sea; for we can see plainly that the sea is sandy, and we can feel the wetness of the sand. For all that, we can distinguish sand from sea, and begin some quasi-scientific tests. Various observations and experiments will associate one set of properties with buckets of sand and another set, largely non-overlapping, with buckets of sea. And we may now define the 'scientific' notion of 'pure' sand as 'the stuff—whatever its structure may be—that supports *those* properties'; and sea as 'the stuff—whatever its structure may be—that supports *those* properties'. Such definitions are dangerous and indeterminate: they are dangerous because they suppose that some single structure is common to all our buckets of sand; and closer, microscopic, observation might falsify that supposition (whales and dolphins are not, after all, fish; mercury is a metal). They are indeterminate because the batch of properties they assemble and refer to may well change in the course of time and further investigation. For all that, definitions of such a type do allow us to get a grip on the notion of a 'pure' substance, even though all our buckets of sand and sea are impure.

Do those definitions import new senses for our stuff names? or do they make old senses more precise? Does 'water' have two senses, one of which is explicable by the chemist in terms of H and O, the other of which is explained by pointing to rivers and seas? And does Anaxagoras mean to suggest that stuff names like 'earth' are ambiguous between 'earth₁' and 'earth₂'? I see no hint of ambiguity in Anaxagoras;[23] I see no good reason to suppose an ambiguity in English; and I find nothing of interest in the question.

However that may be, as science advances our investigatory techniques are improved. Let us leave the seaside and enter the laboratory. We have a jar of gas which we know is predominantly oxygen. The next question is: can we discover *how much* oxygen the jar contains? How can we determine the *degree* of impurity in the gas if we can never extract *all* the impurities? Now our techniques will have developed a process of separating H from a predominantly O mixture, and another process of extracting O from a predominantly H mixture. Take a jar of predominantly O gas: by the first process, extract *n* units of predominantly H gas, leaving *m* units of predominantly O gas. Now apply the second process to the *n* units and the first to the *m* units; and so on. Applications of those processes will always provide results; for though we may purify our H we can never produce pure H—you cannot cut H off from O with an axe. Yet it is not hard to see that the continued applications of the two processes will enable us to give ever closer approximations to the proportion of H to O in the original jar. No doubt

> of the things that are separating off one does not know
> the quantity either by reason or in fact (**208: B 7**)—

but one can make an indefinitely close approximation to knowledge.[24]

My argument here has been, I fear, somewhat jejune: to consider the issue at full length would call for a chapter on its own. Yet the issue is important enough: if the objection I have been considering is correct, then Anaxagoras' physical theory (and with it modern chemistry) is blown up. I do not think the objection has any such explosive powers.

(e) *Inherent powers*

Some of the difficulties in (C*) have now been aired; and I turn to the connexion between that tenet and the other parts of Anaxagoras' system. I begin by asking why Anaxagoras put forward his first tenet, that 'in the beginning, everything was in everything'. That tenet can be expressed by:

(A*) For any pair of stuffs S, S' : in every piece of S there originally was a portion of S'.

Discussion may start from a passage in Aristotle:

> They [the Anaxagoreans] say that everything was mixed in everything because they saw everything coming to be from everything (**209**: *Phys* 187b1 = **A 52**).

Simplicius gives a somewhat breathless gloss:

> Seeing, then, everything coming to be from everything, if not immediately at least serially (*kata taxin*)—for air comes from fire,

and water from air, and earth from water, and stone from earth, and fire again from stone; and though the same food, e.g., bread, is applied, many different things come into being, flesh bones veins muscles hair nails—and perhaps wings and horns—even though like is increased by like: for these reasons he supposed that in the food—in water, if that is what trees feed on—there is wood and bark and fruit; and that is why he said that everything was mixed in everything, and that coming to be comes about by virtue of a separating out (**210: A 45**).

No extant text of Anaxagoras contains precisely that argument, and it has been supposed a Peripatetic rationalization.[25] But I am inclined to go along with Aristotle's interpretation; for the alternative is baffled silence, an unendurable fate. Nor do the fragments bear no relation to the Peripatetic argument. **B 16** reads as follows:

> From those things as they separate off is compounded earth; for from clouds water separates off, and from water earth, and from earth stones are compounded by the cold, and these are further distant from water (**211**).[26]

The fragment reveals an interest in what Simplicius calls 'serial' generation: A come from B serially if A comes from C_1 and C_1 comes from C_2 and . . . and C_{n-1} comes from C_n and C_n comes from B. An anecdote in Diogenes runs as follows: 'they say that when someone asked him if the mountains in Lampsacus would ever be sea, he said: "If time doesn't give out"' (Diogenes Laertius, II.10 = **A 1**).

But such remarks are Presocratic commonplaces. The Peripatetic argument requires us to ascribe to Anaxagoras the thesis that 'everything comes from everything'. By 'everything' is meant 'every stuff'; and I take 'S comes from S'' to mean 'from any quantity of S' a quantity of S is extractable'. Thus 'Water comes from cloud' means: 'From any bit of cloud you can extract a drop or two of water'; 'Flesh comes from bread' means: 'From any lump of bread you can extract a piece of flesh'; 'Fire comes from flint' means: 'From any flint stone you can extract a spark of fire'. Then to say that 'everything comes from everything' is to assert:

(1) For any pair of stuffs S, S': from any piece of S there is extractable a piece of S'.

On the Peripatetic interpretation, proposition (1) is the logical foundation-stone of Anaxagorean physics, more fundamental even than the three tenets, (A)—(C), which I set out at the start of this chapter. (The proposition uses the word 'extract' in a highly general sense, to cover all cases in which one stuff is wrung from another.

What particular process of extraction is appropriate in any given case is a matter for experiment: thus ice is extracted from water by refrigeration (cf. **211**); flesh from bread by digestion; salt from brine by evaporation; cheese from milk by compression; fire from stone by concussion; and so on.)

Why should Anaxagoras have embraced (1)? According to Aristotle, on the basis of empirical evidence: he 'saw' that 'everything comes from everything'. **211** suggests that a part of that evidence derived from the stock-in-trade of the old Ionian scientists: the familiar meteorological processes provide clear and repeated evidence for the serial generation of the main world-masses from one another. Biology provides another area of observation: Simplicius, in **210**, refers to the phenomena of nutrition; and the reference is repeated (e.g., Lucretius, **A 44**; Aëtius, **A 46**). A further testimony points to the allied phenomena of reproduction, where from a seed there develops an embryo with its complement of flesh and bones and hair (**B 10**, see below). There are close connexions between Anaxagoras and the fifth-century doctors;[27] and there is biological terminology in the fragments: it is tempting to conclude that the study of biology and medicine led Anaxagoras to his philosophical position. That conclusion is conjectural, and I suspect that it is exaggerated. But it is plausible to suppose that Anaxagoras was as impressed by biological as by meteorological changes: if flesh and blood and bone may come from bread and milk and cheese, then surely anything may come from anything?

Proposition (1), then, may stand as an Anaxagorean hypothesis. Like the cosmological hypotheses of the Milesians, it is strong and simple; and it is supported by a mass of empirical evidence. It has a further dialectical advantage: it stands in the strongest possible contrast to the stability of Elea. If (1) can be defended against Eleatic attack, then any weaker hypothesis, which further experiment may put in the place of (1), need fear nothing from that quarter.[28]

In order to proceed from proposition (1) to tenet (A*), the thesis that 'everything was in everything', we need a further premiss. The premiss is suggested by the following passage:

> For in the same seed he says there is hair and nails and veins and arteries and muscles and bones, and they are invisible because of the smallness of their parts but as they grow they are gradually separated out. 'For how', he says, 'might hair come to be from what is not hair and flesh from what is not flesh?' (**212**: Scholiast on Gregory, **B 10**).

The passage comes from a late scholiast; but the scholiast seems to be

30

familiar with the doxographical tradition, and I assume that the substance of the passage is Anaxagorean, even if the final question is not (as many scholars think) an original quotation.[29]

'Hair cannot come from what is not hair.' The principle suggested by that thought is:

(2) For any pair of stuffs, S, S': if S' comes from S, then $S = S'$.

But (2) is absurd; and Anaxagoras surely has in mind a less extravagant principle, namely:

(3) For any stuff S' and object x: if S' comes from x, then S' was in x.

Hair cannot come from 'what is not hair', i.e. from what does not *contain* hair.

Is principle (3) borrowed from Elea? or is it an empirical observation? or is it, in intention at least, a truism? If I take an egg out of the egg-box, the egg was in the box; if I draw milk from a cow, the cow contained the milk; and in general, if Y comes *out* of X, then Y was *in* X. The sentiment is prehistoric: 'deriving his fire . . . commonly from the friction of wood or bamboo, primitive man naturally concluded that fire is somehow stored up in all trees, or at all events in those trees from the wood of which he usually extracted it.'[30] When the iron-master extracts metal from ore, he does not need Parmenides to tell him that the metal does not spring into being; he knows that it was there all along. When the milk-maid extracts butter from her milk, she has not previously *observed* the butter in the unchurned milk. Principle (3), I suggest, was not forced upon Anaxagoras by Elea; nor did he propose it on the basis of empirical research: rather, it seemed to him to be a self-evident truth.

Principle (3) needs careful statement. It is easy to read it as:

(4) For any stuff S' and object x: if a piece of S' is extracted from x, then x contained a piece of S'.

But Anaxagoras does not want to hold that x contained a *piece* of S'; for that wrongly suggests that extraction is a matter of isolating some part of x; and if x is a piece of S, every part of x is a piece of S and no part a piece of S'. We need to hold clearly in mind a distinction which has underlain most of this chapter: the distinction between pieces and portions.[31] x contains a *piece* of S' only if some physical part of x is a piece of S'; but x may contain a *portion* of S' even if no part of x is a piece of S'. The *pointilliste*'s green patch contains blue pieces and yellow pieces; the orthodox or Anaxagorean green patch contains blue portions and yellow portions, but no blue or yellow pieces.

The principle Anaxagoras needs is this:

31

(5) For any stuff S' and object x: if a piece of S' is extracted from x, then x contained a portion of S'.

And (5) can be defended in the same way as (3): if I extract a pound of salt from a tub of brine, then the brine contained salt; if I get a thimble of water from a cactus plant, the cactus contained water. And if you can't get blood from a stone, that is because (in un-Anaxagorean physics) stones do not contain blood. I propose that we grant Anaxagoras (5), and that we take it not as a piece of Eleatic metaphysics, nor as an inductive generalization, but as a safe truism.

We must make (5) a little more precise by introducing a reference to time, thus:

(5*) For any stuff S', object x, and time t: if a piece of S' is extracted from x at t, then prior to t x contains a portion of S'.

From (5*) it is reasonable to infer:

(6*) For any stuff S', object x, and time t: if it is possible to extract a piece of S' from x at t, then x contains a portion of S' at t.

The principle behind the inference is this: if, given that X is extracted from Y, Y contained X, then if X is extractable from Y, Y contains X; if what is extracted from Y was contained in Y, then what is extractable from Y is contained in Y.

Sentence (1), like sentence (5), requires to be made more precise, thus:

(1*) For any stuffs S and S', object x, and time t: if x is a piece of S, then it is possible to extract a piece of S' from x at t.

Now (1*) and (6*) entail:

(7) For any stuffs S and S', object x, and time t: if x is a piece of S, then x contains a portion of S' at t.

Finally, we make two trivial deductions from (7), viz:

(8) For any stuffs S and S', and object x: if x is a piece of S, then x contained a portion of S' at the time when the cosmogony began.

(9) For any stuffs S and S', and object x: if x is a piece of S, then x now contains a portion of S'.

Now (8) is, of course, nothing more than tenet (A*); and (9) is tenet (C*). Thus from the two Anaxagorean principles, (1) and (5), we have successfully inferred two of the basic tenets of Anaxagorean physics. If 'everything comes from everything', and if 'what comes from a thing must have been in it', then 'everything was originally in everything', and 'everything is now in everything'.

So far so good. But the two formulations of (A) and (C), viz. (8) and (9), immediately suggest a potentially embarrassing question: (8) seems to ascribe to the original mass exactly the same constitution that (9) ascribes to the present world. Does not that lead at once to an

Eleatic universe, stable and changeless? How is any sort of 'extraction' possible, given the fundamental similarity holding between the world past and the world present? How can Anaxagoras allow a cosmogony? How can change and variation take place in the world we know?

I shall return to these questions. First, however, I want to look at the second of Anaxagoras' three tenets: what does (B) amount to? and how is it related to (A) and to (C)?

(f) *Anaxagoras and infinity*

That second tenet has it that 'there is no smallest portion of anything'. The tenet is advanced in **198** and **202**. I begin with **198**:

> [i] For neither of the small is there the least, but there is always a less (for [ii] what is cannot not be)—but [iii] of the great too there is always a greater, and [iv] it is equal in quantity to the small. And [v] in relation to itself each is both great and small.

Sentence [i] states tenet (B); I paraphrase this (for reasons which will become clearer later) as follows: 'However small an object may be, there is no smallest portion of S contained in it.' The reference to the object's smallness is, I take it, a literary rather than a logical device; thus the tenet reads, formally:

(B*) For any stuff S and object x: if x contains a portion of S, S^b, then there is a portion S^c contained in x such that $S^c < S^b$.

It is easy to see that (B*) entails that if there are any portions of S in an object, there are infinitely many such portions. And there is every reason to think that Anaxagoras saw the implication: when **197** asserts that 'all things were together, unlimited both in quantity and in smallness', we may suppose (as I have already suggested) that the unlimited quantity of portions of stuffs as well as their unlimited smallness is inferred from thesis (B*). Anaxagoras, I think, 'shows an understanding of the meaning of infinity which no Greek before him had attained'—not even Zeno, if Zeno indeed came before him.[32]

But how did Anaxagoras acquire that understanding? And why did he adhere to thesis (B*)? A tempting suggestion has him derive (B*) directly from (C*). Take any piece of S, say a. By (C*), a contains a portion of S'. Extract that portion, or part of it, and call the resulting piece of S' b. By (C*) b contains a portion of S: extract that, too, and call the new piece of S c. Plainly, $c < a$; equally plainly, successive applications of (C*) will yield an infinite sequence of pieces of S, each smaller than its predecessor. Since the extracted pieces of S all come from a, we may safely conclude that a contained no smallest portion of S.

198 does not contain that argument; instead, it offers the parenthetical reflexion, [ii]: 'what is cannot not be'. That has foxed the commentators. Some refer, loosely and unconvincingly, to Zeno's argument in **175 = 29 B 3**.[33] Others offer Anaxagoras arguments of ludicrous implausibility: 'If one presupposes that there is a smallest, one must assume that that which is less than the smallest does not exist, and consequently that there is a void.' Others again have Anaxagoras equivocate: 'If the division of something into smaller and smaller pieces could ever come to an end, this would mean that there was nothing further to divide; i.e., by cutting up an existing thing one would have reduced it to non-existence.'[34] (After such a division there is 'nothing further to divide', i.e. no magnitudes left which are divisible; it does not, of course, follow that the only thing left to divide is nothing—so that the dividing has somehow produced nothing or a nonentity.)

Can anything better be done for sentence [ii]? Suppose that a contains c; then, plainly, c exists. Now let a be the smallest portion of S. Then by the argument I have already rehearsed, c is smaller than a; but if a is the smallest portion of S, c cannot exist. Hence c exists and c does not exist—but 'what is cannot not be'. On that view, sentence [ii] does not introduce the notion of division: it does not say 'what is cannot *become* non-existent'. It is not making an Eleatic point at all, but stating the simple truism that what exists cannot also not exist.[35] The parenthesis, in short, is a reminder that a *reductio* argument is readily constructed for (B*).

I continue the discussion of **198**. Sentence [iii] is usually taken to state either that there is an infinitely large amount of every stuff in the world (which is absurd and contradicts **197**), or that the total world stuff is infinite in extent (which is implied by **197** but is wholly irrelevant to **198** and thesis (B*)). Comparison with (B*) suggests rather the following interpretation:[36]

(1) For any stuff S and object x: if x contains a portion of S, S^b, then there is a portion S^c contained in a such that $S^c > S^b$,

In short: there is no largest portion of S in any given piece of stuff.

How might Anaxagoras have argued for (1)? Let S^b be the largest portion of S in a. Extract S^b from a, and call the remainder of a c. By (C*), c contains a portion of S, S^c. Now the compound portion $S^c + S^b$ was contained in a and is greater than S^b. Hence S^b is not the largest portion of S in a. We can, of course, say that a contains no portion of S of magnitude greater than n (if n is the magnitude of a itself); but then there is no portion of S equal to n. However much S

you extract from a, there is always a little left; however large a portion of S you have discovered in a, it is possible to enlarge it.

The argument for (1) is parallel to my argument for (B*), just as (1) itself is parallel to (B*). And the language of **198** leads us to expect such a parallelism. Moreover, we can now ascribe an easy sense to sentence [iv], '. . . it is equal in quantity to the small'. Of the many interpretations of that phrase,[37] one has all the advantages: 'there are as many large portions of S in a as there are small portions'. Let X count as a 'large' portion if $X \geqslant 3/4a$; and let X count as a 'small' portion if $X \leqslant 1/4a$. Then, as Anaxagoras has in effect already shown, a contains infinitely many large and infinitely many small portions of S. The large and the small portions can be matched one to one: they are, as Anaxagoras says, 'equal in quantity'. Here again, Anaxagoras shows a sophisticated grasp of the method of 'counting' infinite sets.[38]

The final sentence of **198** is no less vexing than its predecessors. A popular reading of [v] again connexts **198** with Zeno. Anaxagoras is alleged to mean something like this: 'Considered in itself, a is great—for it contains infinitely many parts or ingredients, each of them having some finite size; but, again, a is small—for each of its component parts is infinitesimally small.' That is a very silly argument; and it hardly 'answers Zeno': it is silly in that neither leg contains a decent inference; and to think that 'a is great and small' is an *answer* to Zeno is grotesque—it is a mere parroting of Zeno. We do better to follow Simplicius and read 'each (*hekaston*)' not as 'each piece of stuff' but as 'each stuff'. The sentence then merely says that there are both large and small portions of any stuff; and that unexciting fact follows from what has gone before.

202 is closely related to **198**:

> And [i] since too there are equal portions of the great and the small in quantity, for this reason too [ii] everything is in everything; [iii] nor can they exist separately (*chôris*), but [iv] everything shares a portion of everything. [v] Since the least cannot be, [vi] things cannot[39] be separated (*chôristhênai*) [vii] nor come to be by themselves (*eph'heautou*); but [viii] as in the beginning [ix] so too now everything is together. [x] And in all things there are many even[40] of the things that are separating off, equal in quantity in the greater and the smaller.

The burden of **202** is the proof of [ix]; and [ix] states the third thesis, (C*), of Anaxagorean physics. The argument proceeds from (A*) via (B*) to (C*): the word 'too' in [i] marks the argument as a secondary proof; and (C*) has, of course, already been argued for.

The further proof is offered, I suggest, in order to make it quite certain that you cannot have (A*) and reject (C*); you cannot suppose that an originally commingled world is now entirely separated out. Such an argument, from past commingling to present commingling, is adverted to again in **201**; and it lies behind the statement in **203** that stuffs today 'have not been separated from one another, nor have they been cut off by an axe'.

How, in detail, does the argument run? I assume that [ii], [iii], [iv] and [ix] express, in different words, the same proposition: thesis (C*); and I assume that [vi] and [vii] are equivalent to one another. Thus **202** in effect consists of three implications: the first infers [ii] from [i]; the second infers [vi] from [v]; the third infers [ii] from [viii]. (Sentence [x], as I understand it, simply presents a special case of [ii]: 'even if S is separating off from other stuffs, still some portion of S will remain in every piece of every other stuff'.) The three implications can be moulded into a single argument: 'Given [viii], i.e. (A*), we can infer [v] and hence [i], by the argument of **198**. But from [v] or [i] it follows that [vi]; and [viii] and [vi] yield [ii].' In words: 'Since everything was originally mixed, there are no smallest portions of any stuff. Hence, no stuff can become entirely separate from all other stuffs; hence no stuff can—now or ever—be separate from all other stuffs.'

That interpretation makes a number of disputable assumptions; and it is by no means wholly satisfactory: in particular, it leaves sentence [i] with no serious work to do; for [v] is all that Anaxagoras needs. But it does have two advantages: it gives Anaxagoras a coherent-looking argument; and it ties **202** closely to **198**.

Of the three constituent implications of the argument, the first has already been discussed in connexion with **198**; and the third is an evident truth: if things *were* once F, and if nothing can *become* non-F, then things still *are* F. What, then, of the second implication? Why, if there is no smallest portion of S, should it be thought to follow that no object can consist of nothing but S? Anaxagoras implies that 'the very act of separation presupposes a smallest that can be separated'[41]; but why does he think that? Perhaps he imagines that the only way to assemble a piece of pure S would be to conglomerate a number of microscopical pieces of pure S; and those microscopical pieces could only have their purity guaranteed if they were minimal *quanta* of stuff, if they were simply too small to contain any impurities. That is a feeble argument; but I can find no better way of understanding Anaxagoras here.

My suggestions about how the main principles of Anaxagorean physics interlock have been a trifle complicated; and I shall end this section with a brief summary. Thus: amazed at the variety of material interchanges. Anaxagoras posits the hypothesis that any stuff can be extracted (by some method and through some intermediaries) from any other. The hypothesis leads to the conclusion that every stuff contains every other; and that, in turn, yields tenet (A), that 'originally all things were together', and tenet (C), that even now all things are together. Further reflexion shows, first, that matter cannot be particulate in structure; and, second, that there can be no smallest portion of any stuff, (B). Finally, the structure of the proof is strengthened by a cross-argument deriving (C) from (A) and (B).

(g) *The vortex*

At the beginning of the world, everything was in everything; now, everything is still in everything. How, then, have things changed? In what does cosmogony consist? How, indeed, can cosmogony, or any other less massive process, take place at all? If a is a piece of S, then a and every part of a is predominantly composed of S; no clipping or cutting, however ingenious, can scissor off a bit of S' from a. And if originally the world-mass, and all its parts, are pieces of air, how can it be that the world-mass now presents so various an appearance?

Anaxagorean cosmogony cannot consist of an *apokrisis*, or separating off, in the crude and simple sense of a cutting or chopping off of parts of the *Urstoff*: such operations will produce no differentiation. But Anaxagorean 'extraction' is not (despite the contrary hint in **203**) a 'chopping off'. Miners may hack coal or gold from the rock-face; but in Anaxagorean physics extraction is a different operation: earth 'separates off' from the *Ur*-mass of air and aether as cheese separates off from milk, or butter from cream. The churn produces cheese or butter; but it does not do so by picking bits of cheese and butter from the milky liquid. Extraction is, to put it roughly and anachronistically, a chemical and not a mechanical operation: just as every piece of stuff is a chemical union and not a mechanical juxtaposition, so every change in stuffs is a chemical reaction and not a mechanical locomotion.

What is extraction? And how can it occur? No *general* account of extraction can be offered: different stuffs are extracted by different operations, and the discovery and description of such operations is an empirical, not a philosophical, chore. Thus straining will produce salt from brine; squeezing will produce water from cheese; boiling will produce jam from raspberries; and the technical sciences of biology and chemistry will gradually uncover a host of further and subtler extractive operations by which blood is produced from bread, hair from beer, nitrogen from air, copper from copper sulphate, and so on. The details are unimportant; it is the general point that matters: the general way to get a piece of S' is to start from a piece of S and extract the portion of S' which it contains. Philosophically, that is all that happens: we do not generate a new stuff, but only bring into perceptible form some portion of a pre-existent stuff; and how that operation is to be performed is not to be determined by *a priori* argument.

Yet Anaxagoras was a scientist as well as a philosopher; and he did offer some explication of extraction, though his explication remains, necessarily and properly, at a high level of generality. Part of Anaxagoras' vocabulary for 'extraction' I have already mentioned: *apokrinesthai, diakrinesthai, summignusthai*, etc. Here I stress the locomotive element in such terms, and set them alongside three other overtly locomotive words which Anaxagoras uses in a cosmogonical context: cosmogony begins when the *Ur*-mass is 'moved' (*kinein*: **B 13**); its characteristic form of locomotion is 'revolution' (*perichôrêsis*: **B 12**, etc.); and as a result of the revolution or vortex certain stuffs 'come together' (*sunchôrein*: **B 15**).[42] Science, Anaxagoras implies, can be saved if locomotion is possible: give the scientist a set of stuffs and the power to move their masses, and he will build on these slight foundations the mass of the physical world. It is worth underlining the economy, the power, the sophistication, and the relative coherence of Anaxagoras' position. As an answer to Elea, it is far from despicable: how successful it is will be discussed in a later chapter; I end this chapter with two minor questions.

First, is Anaxagoras' account of 'extraction' scientifically adequate? Can Anaxagoras really explain the phenomena of change in terms of the impoverished vocabulary and the non-particulate physics he allows himself? I suppose that the answer is: No. Certainly, Anaxagoras' Abderite successors gave a firmly negative answer to it. But the question is surely an empirical one: the world might, logically, be as Anaxagoras describes it.

The second question is this: why does Anaxagoras suppose that the primordial *Ur*-mass was an undifferentiated mixture of stuffs, wearing the external appearance of 'air and aether'? Nothing in the fragments suggests any answer to that question; and it cannot have been motivated by Eleatic worries. Here, I think, Anaxagoras is most clearly connected with his Milesian ancestry: those old Milesians offered as the simplest cosmogonical hypothesis a material monism and a uniform *Ur*-state. Anaxagoras abandons material monism; but he holds onto the second limb of the hypothesis: present differences are best explained by way of a primordial uniformity. Assume that there was a cosmogony; and that cosmogonical change had a clear point of origin. What, then, is the simplest assumption about the state of the world-stuffs at that original point? Surely, uniformity. In making these assumptions Anaxagoras proves himself a follower of the Milesians: he was attempting to salvage as many planks as possible of the old Ionian galleon from the wreck it suffered in the Eleatic tempest.[43]

III

The Corpuscularian Hypothesis

(a) *The origins of atomism*

'Leucippus of Abdera, a pupil of Zeno, first excogitated the discovery of the atoms' (pseudo-Galen, **67 A 5**). The attribution seems to be correct: Anaxagoras and Empedocles did not have particulate theories of matter; and Democritus, the great name in ancient atomism, was Leucippus' pupil. Leucippus is naturally praised: we are all atomists now; and we are both obliged and delighted to pay homage to the first inventor of that subtle truth.

A famous paragraph in Newton's *Opticks* states succinctly enough the elements of modern atomism: 'All these things being consider'd, it seems probable to me, that God in the Beginning form'd Matter in solid, massy, hard, impenetrable, movable Particles, of such Sizes and Figures, and in such Proportion to Space, as most conduced to the End for which he form'd them; and that these primitive Particles being Solids, are incomparably harder than any porous Bodies compounded of them; even so very hard, as never to wear or break in pieces; no ordinary Power being able to divide what God himself made one in the first Creation. While the Particles continue entire, they may compose bodies of one and the same Nature and Texture in all Ages; But should they wear away, or break in pieces, the Nature of Things depending on them, would be changed.' Those minute rondures, swimming in space, form the stuff of the world: the solid, coloured table I write on, no less than the thin invisible air I breathe, is constructed out of small and colourless corpuscles; the world at close quarters looks like the night sky—a few dots of stuff, scattered sporadically through an empty vastness. Such is modern corpuscularianism.

Against that Newtonian paragraph let us set Aristotle's description of ancient atomism. The account comes from his lost monograph on Democritus, a fragment of which Simplicius preserves:

> Democritus holds that the nature of what is eternal consists of little substances, unlimited in quantity; and to these he subjoins something else—space, unlimited in magnitude. He calls space by the names 'the void', 'nothing', 'the unlimited'; and he calls each of the substances 'things', 'massy' and 'being'. He thinks that the substances are so small that they escape our perception. There belong to them every kind of shape and every kind of form and differences in magnitude. Now from these, as from elements, he generates and combines the visible and perceptible masses. And they battle and are carried about in the void on account of their dissimilarity and the other differences aforesaid, and in their courses they hit upon one another and bind together with a binding that makes them touch and be next to one another but does not generate any genuinely single nature whatever out of them; for it is absolutely silly to think that two or more things could ever become one. The reason why the substances stay together with one another up to a point, he finds in the overlappings and interlockings of the bodies; for some of them are scalene, some hooked, some hollow, some convex—and they have innumerable other differences. Thus he thinks that they hold on to one another and stay together for a time, until some stronger necessity comes upon them from their surrounding, shakes them about, and scatters them apart (213: fr. 208 = **68 A 37**).

The connexions between Democritus and Newton are evident; and it would be absurd to deny the link between ancient and modern atomism: conceptually, there are narrow ties; historically, an unbroken (if curiously circuitous) line reaches from Leucippus to Rutherford.

Modern atomism is a scientific theory, based upon and confirmed by a mass of experimental data: if the layman does not have those data at his fingertips, the textbooks will refer him to such things as chemical isomerism and Brownian motion. We are tempted, therefore, to welcome Leucippus and Democritus as the founders of modern science.

But there is, alas, no such thing as 'modern science', and the theory I have called 'modern atomism' is a myth: Newton states only one of several very different theories which have been propounded in the last four centuries and which have claimed the name of atomism. There is no unitary atomic theory, invented by Leucippus and successively refined by later scientists; rather, there is a group of theories, loosely connected, all owing something to Leucippus but each differing in vital ways from its companions. Moreover, Newtonian atomism, if I understand aright, is *passé*; and according to the physicist Heisenberg, 'concerning the structure of matter, Plato has come much nearer to the truth than Leucippus or Democritus, in spite of the enormous success of the concept of the atom in modern science'; for 'these smallest units of matter are not physical objects in the ordinary sense; they are forms, ideas which can be expressed unambiguously only in mathematical language'.[1]

Second, by stressing the scientific and empirical aspect of modern atomic theories, we give a false show of virtue to their ancient ancestors: Leucippus and Democritus had not observed Brownian motion; they were largely ignorant of chemistry; they did not rest their atomism on a host of special observations. Their theory was indeed a scientific one, in the old Ionian fashion; it was not a myth, nor an abstract philosophy. But its foundations, unlike the foundations of modern atomisms, were solidly philosophical: if we treat Leucippus as a Presocratic Dalton we shall miss the characteristic touches to his theory.

In short, a naively panegyrical attitude to ancient atomism distorts both the subject and its history. In this chapter I shall gaze at Leucippus and Democritus through antique blinkers: if they restrict the scope of my vision, they may enhance its accuracy.

The first thing to do is to forget the word 'atomism': the Abderite theory[2] was undeniably atomistic; but to label it atomism gives, I think, a misleading prominence to the notion of atomicity or indivisibility. The fragments of Democritus do indeed use the adjective '*atomos* (uncuttable)', in the neuter phrase '*ta atoma* (sc. *sômata*)', 'the uncuttable [bodies]' (**68 B 9**; **B 125**); and the doxography uses '*hê atomos* (sc. *ousia*)', 'the uncuttable [being]' (**68 B 141**; cf. **B 167**; Plutarch, **A 57**). But alongside that overtly atomic vocabulary stand other terms: Democritus is said to have referred to the atoms by the word '*phusis*' (**68 B 168**)[3]; Aristotle, an opponent of atomism who devoted much attention to the views of Leucippus and Democritus, regularly uses the words '*to plêres* (the full)' and '*to stereon* (the solid)' to designate the Atomists' material principle (cf. especially *Met* 985b4–22 = **67 A 6**); and in his monograph on Democritus, he says that Democritus calls each of the substances [*ousiai*, i.e. the atoms] 'thing (*den*)', and 'massy (*naston*)' and 'being (*on*)' (**213**).

That last report implies that *den*, *naston* and *on* were Democritus' preferred ways of referring to his substances; and I see no reason to doubt the implication. Indeed, it is tempting to suppose that the term *on* ('being') gives the starting point of Abderite theorizing: the fundamental designation of the Atomists' substances was, trivially enough, *onta*. Abdera, like Elea, embarked upon an inquiry into *onta* and their attributes: the discipline at Abdera was the study of *onta*, of beings *qua* being. Atomism, in its ancient form, begins with metaphysics.

And Abdera follows Elea in thesis as well as in discipline. The first property of Abderite *onta* is solidity: whatever is is *naston, stereon, plêres*. The thesis is starkly Melissan (vol. 1, pp. 223–8). The Abderites may indeed have adopted a Melissan style of argumentation for the principle that *onta* are solid; but our sources ascribe neither that argument nor any other to the Atomists, and it may be that they took solidity as a self-evident property of substances: beings, in the primary sense, are plainly bodies;[4] and bodies are plainly solid.

Solid, the Abderites' substances are also eternal, *aïdion* (213); they are ungenerable (cf. Plutarch, **68 A 57**) and indestructible (Dionysius, **A 43**). The thesis is Eleatic, and the doxographers duly offer Democritus the old Eleatic argument, 'nothing comes into being from what is not or is destroyed into what is not' (Diogenes Laertius, IX. 44 = **68 A 1**); Plutarch indeed ascribes the pseudo-Parmenidean dilemma to him (**68 A 57**). But that argument is not easily embraced by a man who happily concedes the being of 'what is not';[5] and 'Leucippus thought he had arguments which, by stating what was in agreement with the senses, would not do away with generation or destruction' (Aristotle, *GC* 325a23–5 = **67 A 7**). Leucippus wanted to preserve generation and destruction, in some cases at least; he cannot therefore have indulged in the Eleatic argument, and he must have found an argument against the generation and destruction of atoms which would not do away with generation and destruction as such.

Aristotle presents a different argument:

As for time, with one exception [i.e. Plato] everyone is clearly in agreement; for they say that it is ungenerated. And in this way Democritus proves that it is impossible for everything to have been generated—for time is ungenerated (**214**: *Phys* 251b14–17 = **68 A 71**).

Simplicius says that Democritus took the ungenerability of time as self-evident (**68 A 71**); but what did that self-evident axiom prove? Did Democritus merely and trivially urge that since time is ungenerated, then at least one thing, viz. time, is ungenerated? or did he, more interestingly, urge that some substances at least must be ungenerated, since at any moment in time there must exist some substances, 'empty' time being an absurdity? The interesting argument is, alas, invalid; and in any case, neither the trivial nor the interesting version will show that all substances are ungenerated.

In the absence of a satisfying tradition we are tempted to invent; and an argument for substantial eternity can be cooked up: I shall postpone the concoction for a few pages.

Solid and eternal, Abderite substances are also immutable:

> The atoms do not suffer (*paschein*) or change, by reason of their solidity (**215**: Plutarch, **68 A 57**);

they are 'impassive (*apathês*) because of their being massy and having no share in the void (**217**: Simplicius, **67 A 14**).[6] 'Impassivity' is unalterability: a body is *apathês* if any features it ever has it always has. Impassivity, again, is an Eleatic property; but the Abderites did not use an Eleatic argument to establish it. Instead they argued that solidity rules out mutability. Why should that be so? Why may a solid body not change its colour or its temperature? Why cannot an atom grow wet or become smooth? The questions require a detour.

(b) *Atoms characterized*

I turn now to the property *par excellence*, the eponymous property, of Abderite substances: atomicity. Atoms are indivisible, uncuttable, unsplittable; they are the ultimate and unanalysable bits out of which the material world is constructed. That Abderite property is no more an Abderite invention than solidity, ungenerability or immutability: Eleatic entities, whether Parmenidean or Melissan, do not divide. It is not easy to disentangle what the Eleatics said about division; but it is clear enough that the first atoms came from Elea.[7]

If the atomic thesis is Eleatic, the arguments by which Leucippus and Democritus supported it were fresh. I begin with a perforated quotation from Simplicius; the holes will be made good later:

> Those who rejected unlimited cutting, on the grounds that we cannot cut without limit and thus gain evidence for the incompletability of the cutting, said that bodies consist of indivisibles and are divided into indivisibles—except that Leucippus and Democritus think that not only their impassivity, but also their smallness . . . explains why the primary bodies are not divided, whereas Epicurus . . . says that they are atoms because of their impassivity (**216**: **67 A 13**).

44

In another passage Simplicius says of Leucippus, Democritus and Epicurus that

> they thought that [the principles] are atomic and indivisible and impassive because of their being massy and having no share in the void; for they said that division comes about by virtue of the void in bodies (217: 67 A 14).

In the same mood, Dionysius says of Epicurus and Democritus that 'both say they are atoms, and are called so, because of their indissoluble solidity' (68 A 43).

These passages appear to contain four distinct arguments: (A) We cannot cut bodies infinitely often (216); (B) the primary bodies are impassive (216); (C) the primary bodies are solid (217; 68 A 43); (D) the primary bodies are small (216). All four arguments are explicitly ascribed both to Leucippus and to Democritus;[8] and there is no reason why they should not have advanced more than one argument in favour of indivisibility.

I begin with argument (D), which according to Simplicius was not adopted by Epicurus. Epicurean atoms were all very small—indeed imperceptibly so (*ad Hdt* §§55–6), and the same is regularly said of Democritus' substances: according to Aristotle, 'he thinks that the substances are so small that they escape our perception' (213); But there are three curious passages to the contrary: according to Diogenes,

> the atoms are unlimited in magnitude and quantity (218: IX. 44 = 68 A 1):

and the most plausible gloss of that text gives Democritus atoms of every size. Again, Dionysius contrasts Epicurus with Democritus on precisely this issue:

> They differ to the extent that the one [sc. Epicurus] thought that they are all very small and for that reason imperceptible, while Democritus held that some atoms were actually very large (219: 68 A 43).

Finally, Aëtius avers that in Democritus' view

> it is possible for there to be an atom the size of the universe (220: 68 A 47).

Epicurus attacks the view that 'every size exists among the atoms';

for were it true, then 'some atoms would be bound to reach us and be visible—but that is not seen to happen, nor can we conceive how an atom might become visible' (ad Hdt §§55–6). It is natural to suppose that Epicurus is attacking a live target; and Democritus is the obvious candidate.[9] On that assumption Epicurus' text yields a nicer message: if Democritus both allowed that some atoms could be visible and also denied that we ever perceive any, that would account for Epicurus' two objections: that visible atoms are simply inconceivable, and that if there could be such things they would be sure to have come to our notice.

Suppose, then, that Democritus said something like this: 'The primary bodies are not essentially small: as far as logic goes, there may be atoms of a cosmic size. As far as science goes, there must be a variety of atomic sizes. As far as experience goes, it seems that all the primary bodies in our part of the universe are too small to be perceived.' That view is self-consistent; and it accommodates, more or less, all the superficially irreconcilable evidence we possess. It carries an important consequence: smallness is at best a contingent property of the primary bodies; it is not a feature of *onta qua onta* that they are imperceptible. Simple observation suggests that all macroscopic objects, even the most durable, can be smashed, split, broken, crushed or whittled away in the course of all-devouring time. Since the primary bodies are unsplittable, and macroscopic things split and dissolve, the primary bodies are microscopic. The argument is healthy; and it is *a posteriori*.

What of argument (D)? Democritus may have said something like this: 'The primary bodies are in fact very small; so small, indeed, that they defeat the finest blade of the sharpest knife; and hence they are indivisible.' The argument is naive: we are not impressed by the hypothetical suggestion that if Democritus cannot get his pocket-knife into an atom, atoms cannot be split. And if, as I imagined, Democritus argued that atoms must be small because they are unsplittable, he can hardly also urge their atomicity on the grounds of their minuscule size.

Argument (B) is curious. It occurs only in **216**, where Simplicius ascribes it to Epicurus, as well as to the Abderites. Now Epicurus' surviving argument for indivisibility goes thus: 'These are atomic and changeless . . . being full in their nature, not having any way or means by which they will be dissolved' (ad Hdt §§41). The passage presents argument (C); and it explains the reports of Dionysius in **68 A 43** and of Simplicius in **217**. It puts impassivity on a par with indivisibility; and that seems to be its proper place: how then, can impassivity ground indivisibility? Argument (B) is found only in **216**

46

and it is intrinsically implausible: I wonder if Simplicius is not using '*apatheia*' loosely here; perhaps it denotes solidity and 'argument (B)' is merely a ghost of argument (C). At all events, if that suggestion is rejected, then in 216 Simplicius ascribes to Epicurus as his sole argument for indivisibility a train of reasoning found nowhere else; and he ignores a genuinely Epicurean argument which elsewhere he shows himself perfectly familiar with.

Argument (C) rests on the firm Abderite thesis of solidity: atoms are indivisible because they are solid, i.e. because they contain no void; and solidity precludes division because division must occur 'in virtue of the void'. I take it that we have here a physical, not a metaphysical, hypothesis: in order to split an object we must be able to get a knife between its parts and prise them away from one another; but in a solid body there is no vacant gap, however narrow, into which the knife-blade might be inserted. We can only cut along the dotted line; and solid bodies offer no vacancies or dots. Solidity does not logically imply indivisibility; but the physical process of division requires a porous body to work upon.

An objection arises: take two atoms and juxtapose them so that there is no void in the interstices between them; then by the argument I have just offered they cannot be parted; yet on atomist principles any two atoms may be conjoined and parted. I guess that Leucippus anticipated that reflexion: Aristotle says that Leucippan atoms may 'touch', *haptesthai* (*GC* 325a33 = **67 A 7**); Philoponus offers the following gloss:

> Democritus does not use the word 'touch' strictly when he says
> that atoms touch one another; . . . but he talked of touch when
> the atoms are near one another and not far away—for they are in
> any event separated by void (**221: 67 A 7**—the same view is
> ascribed to Leucippus, ibid.)

Between any two atoms there is always a void; hence they can never conjointly form a solid molecule, and they can always be separated (cf. Alexander, **68 A 64**).

In the same passage of the *GC* Aristotle reports that:

> from what is truly one, a plurality (*plêthos*) could never come
> about, nor one from what are truly plural; but that is impossible
> (**222**: 325a35–6 = **67 A 7**; cf. **213**; *Cael* 303a6).

The second part of the doctrine will prove important later; here my concern is with its first part: 'no plurality from a unity'.

It is possible that Aristotle is merely elaborating upon argument

47

(C): units are solid; hence they cannot be split; hence they cannot yield a plurality. But the *Metaphysics* suggests a more sophisticated view:

> If a substance is a unit, it cannot consist of inherent substances in this way, as[10] Democritus rightly says; for he says that it is impossible for one thing to come from two or two from one (for he makes the atomic magnitudes his substances) (**223**: 1039a7–11 = **68 A 42**).

The argument is this: 'Democritus' bodies are substances; substances are units, i.e. not aggregates; hence no substance can split into two or more substances; hence no Democritean body can split'. That genuine substances cannot be aggregates is a Democritean view, and it has had many adherents (see below, p. 143). Yet if a substance cannot *be* an aggregate, may it not *become* one? why cannot a unit split up and become a plurality? Aristotle's text suggests that if *b* and *c* 'come from' *a* at *t*, then prior to *t* they must have conjointly constituted *a*, so that *a* consisted of 'inherent substances' and was an aggregate. Why should that be so? Well, neither *b* nor *c* can be identical with *a*; since each is, by hypothesis, a part of *a*. But in that case either *a* ceases to exist at *t* (which is impossible, since substances are eternal), or else *a* was all along the aggregate of *b* and *c* (and hence not a primary substance). In short, substances are unitary and eternal; hence they cannot split.

That account provides a philosophical argument for indivisibility; and one of some power. If I hesitate to put it alongside (A)—(D) and ascribe it to Democritus himself, that is because no source outside the *Metaphysics* knows it. Probably, it is a genial Aristotelian development of Democritean views; but it is, at worst, a development fully in the spirit of atomism.

I have left argument (A) to last; it too appears only once in our sources, and perhaps it is an invention by Simplicius. It is, however, worth a brief exposition. If I read it aright, it goes thus: 'We cannot actually divide any body into infinitely many parts; hence we can never have reason to believe that bodies are infinitely divisible; hence we should believe that bodies are not infinitely divisible.' We cannot have evidence for the falsity of atomism: we therefore have reason to believe it true.

The principle behind the argument is this: if we cannot have evidence that not-*P*, we should believe that *P*. In a weaker form (if we do not have evidence that not-*P*, we should believe that *P*) the principle has supported any number of bad arguments. Why the principle is popular I do not care to guess; that it is false is evident: if I have no evidence for not-*P*, I may also have no evidence for *P*; and in most cases it is irrational to believe that P without having evidence for P. Moreover, the application of the bad principle to atomism requires the use of a second bad principle. For in asserting that because we can never actually cut up a body infinitely often, we can have no evidence for infinite divisibility, the Atomists appear to assume that we have no evidence that P is true unless we possess knowledge that entails P. And that is absurd.

Thus argument (A) is both ill-attested and disreputable. Yet it has two points of mild interest. First, it is the earliest example of a perennially seductive mode of argumentation. Second, it introduces a different problem from those dealt with by arguments (C)—(D): they argue that substances are indivisible; it argues that there are indivisible substances. It is one thing to show that no substance can be divided, another to prove that there exist indivisible substances. The former task is futile unless the latter has been successfully undertaken (what scientist cares for a proof that unicorns have only one horn?); and, if we disregard argument (A), the Atomists have not yet attempted the latter task. The question will arise again.

It is fair to say, I think, that solidity supplies the chief argument for the eponymous atomicity of Abderite substances. Atomicity is not inferred *a priori* from solidity: the inference rests upon a physical thesis about the nature of splitting. Impassivity or immutability also depend on solidity. I suggest that here again we must supply a physical hypothesis as the link in the logical chain: alteration was deemed by the atomists to involve either the splitting or the combining of atoms; a cubic atom, say, could only become spherical if bits were chipped off or added to it (or both); an atom could only grow or diminish by the addition or the loss of bits of stuff. (And those, as we shall see, are the only intrinsic changes an atom could possibly undergo.) But a solid atom cannot have bits chipped from it; and an atom with bits conjoined to it will never constitute a solid body. That may, I suppose, be Aristotle's meaning when he says:

> It is necessary to say that each of the indivisibles is impassive, for it cannot 'suffer' except through the void (**224**: *GC* 326a1–3).

It is tempting to find a similar connexion between solidity and ungenerability (cf. Plutarch, **68 A 57**). The generation of macroscopic objects, according to the Atomists, consists merely in the rearrangement of particles at the microscopic level. Did they reject microscopic or atomic generation on the basis of a similar thesis? An atom *a* could only be generated in virtue of some rearrangement of sub-atomic particles; but such a mode of generation is impossible: were *a* compounded from sub-atomic fragments, it would not be solid; and were there sub-atomic parts, they could only have been produced by the shattering of an atom. Since atoms are solid, they cannot have been put together; and such a putting together is the only sort of generation not evidently outlawed by Eleatic logic.

My discussion has rambled; and it may be convenient to provide a summary before advancing any further. The Atomists asked themselves what were the properties of *onta qua onta*; and (as I have surreptitiously presupposed) they were concerned with *onta* of the primary sort, with *ousiai* or substances.

Every substance, they argued, was *unitary* (not an aggregate) and *solid*. What is solid is, by a physical necessity, *indivisible* or atomic; and what is unitary is indivisible by logical necessity. What is solid is, again by physical necessity, *eternal* (or ungenerable and indestructible); and also *immutable* or impassive. Primary substances are bodies, solid and unitary; they are physically indivisible, they endure for ever; and they are subject to no change. That, I think, constitutes the basic account of the Abderite theory. We may now proceed to its further elaboration.

(c) *Fractured atoms?*

Atoms, though indivisible, may have parts: we may not be able, physically, to split an atom; but we can, theoretically, divide it into notional parts: 'the half nearer to *b*', 'the part with the point on', and so on. And if we take a large Democritean atom we may even be able to measure it, to mark it into parts, to draw a design upon it; the only thing we cannot do is cut it along our marks or carve it to the drawn design. The doxographers say nothing about the notional parts of Abderite atoms; but both Alexander (*in Met* 36. 25–7) and Simplicius (*in Phys* 82. 1–3) mention them casually.

Epicurus said more about sub-atomic particles (*ad Hdt* §§58–9). His views are controversial;[11] but an orthodox interpretation runs thus: every atom is theoretically, but not of course physically, divisible; but just as physical splitting eventually reaches atoms or physical indivisibles, so too theoretical division ultimately reaches *minima* or theoretical indivisibles; and an atom is thus composed of a finite set of theoretically indivisible *minima*, conjoined by a physically indissoluble bond. Epicurus is a second-hand thinker; and it is proper to wonder if his theory was not taken from Democritus, along with the other trappings of atomism. Alexander implies that it was:

[Leucippus and Democritus] do not say whence the weight in the atoms comes; for the partless items (*ta amerê*) conceptually present in (*epinooumena*) the atoms and parts of them are, they say, weightless: but how could weight come about from weightless components? (**225**: *in Met* 36.25–7).

I shall return to the issue of weight in a later section. Here I am concerned only with Alexander's assertion that the Abderite atoms have conceptually distinguishable parts which are themselves conceptually partless. That is precisely Epicurus' view.

Few scholars believe Alexander, imagining that he is, carelessly or deliberately, projecting back onto the Abderites a theory he found in Epicurus. And it is observed that Aristotle nowhere distinguishes between atomic and sub-atomic indivisibles in his many discussions of Abdera, even though in one or two passages (e.g., *Cael* 303a21) he could hardly have failed to mention the distinction had he known it. Arguments *e silentio Aristotelis* are not conclusive; and Democritus may, I suppose, have advanced the Epicurean theory in an inconspicuous or informal fashion; but I doubt it, and I shall proceed on the assumption that Alexander's report is in error.[12]

A somewhat subtler suggestion now presents itself. Suppose that Democritus had held his substances to be both physically and theoretically indivisible; then Epicurus is still a follower, but not a slavish adherent: he retains both varieties of indivisibility in his theory, but attaches them to different objects. Where Democritus asserted that atoms were both physically and theoretically indivisible, Epicurus maintained that atoms were physically indivisible, their minimal parts theoretically indivisible. Democritus does not allow sub-atomic particles, notionally distinguishable within the atom: his atoms have no parts at all—neither by the axe nor by the mind can you splinter them.

Are Democritean atoms theoretically indivisible? Some scholars think that they are, arguing thus: 'The Abderites were concerned, *inter alia*, to answer Zeno's dichotomy arguments; only theoretically indivisible atoms will give them an answer. Hence they ought to have embraced theoretical indivisibility. Moreover, several ancient texts in fact support the attribution of theoretical indivisibility to the Abderite atoms.' I shall first set this argument out in more detail, exhibiting the texts on which it is based, and then offer some critical comments.

At *Physics* 187a1 Aristotle reports thus:

Some surrendered to both arguments—to the one concluding that everything is one (if being signifies one thing) by saying that what

is not is; to the one from the dichotomy, by positing indivisible
magnitudes (226).

Plainly 'some' refers to the Atomists;[13] for only the Atomists *both*
said that 'what is not is' *and* posited 'indivisible magnitudes'. It is
the second move that we are concerned with here: Aristotle represents
atomism as an answer to Zeno's dichotomy argument.

The brief notice in the *Physics* is expanded in the *de Generatione*:

> One can see from this too the great difference between those who
> study scientifically (*phusikôs*) and those who study dialectically
> (*logikôs*). For on the question of atomic magnitudes, some [i.e.
> the Platonists] say that the triangle itself will be many [sc. if there
> are no atomic magnitudes], but Democritus would seem to have
> been persuaded by appropriate and scientific arguments. What we
> mean will become clear as we proceed (227: *GC* 316a10–14).

There follows an involved argument, of Zenonian flavour, which I
have already mentioned (vol. 1, p. 247). I summarize it as follows:
'Suppose a magnitude is infinitely divisible, and that such a division
is possible. Carry it out: what are you left with? Not a magnitude; for
then you have not carried out the division. Not nothing; for bodies
are not compounded of nothing. Not points; for points cannot
constitute a magnitude. It won't do to suppose that the process of
dividing produced some quantity of sawdust; for the same questions
apply to that. Nor can you say that the division separates qualities
from underlying points or contacts' (*GC* 316a15–b19 = **68 A 48b**).
Aristotle then offers to 'restate' the puzzles (316b20–8), and
concludes with the following paragraph:

> But that it divides into magnitudes that are separable and always
> smaller and apart and separated, is evident. Now if you divide part
> by part the breaking will not be unlimited, nor can it be divided at
> every point at the same time (for that is not possible), but only to a
> certain point. Necessarily, then, invisible atomic magnitudes
> inhere in it, particularly if generation and destruction is to come
> about by dissociation and association. This, then, is the argument
> that seems to necessitate the existence of atomic magnitudes (228:
> *GC* 316b28–317a2).

The *GC* expands the brief aside of the *Physics*: Zenonian anxiety
causes the spots of atomism.

Four passages, or groups of passages, support the inference drawn
from the *GC*. First, in a passage I mangled earlier, Simplicius says:

. . . except that Leucippus and Democritus think that not only their impassivity but also their smallness and their partlessness explains why the primary bodies are not divided, whereas Epicurus later does not regard them as partless but says that they are atoms because of their impassivity (**229: 67 A 13**—cf. **216**).

By 'partlessness (*to ameres*)' Simplicius clearly intends theoretical indivisibility;[14] otherwise the contrast with Epicurus is nonsensical. Second, a scholiast on Euclid X.1 reports:

That there is no smallest magnitude, as the Democriteans say, is proved by this theorem, that it is possible to take a magnitude less than any given magnitude (**230: 68 A 48a**).

The report is iterated by Simplicius (*in Cael* 202.27–31).

Third, the passage in the *de Caelo* on which Simplicius thus comments illustrates the catastrophic results of a small initial error:

E.g. if someone were to say that there is a smallest magnitude; for he, by introducing a smallest, overthrows the greatest part of mathematics (**231: 271a9–11**).

The same accusation is levelled later against Leucippus and Democritus:

Again, it is necessary that those who talk of atomic bodies clash with the mathematical sciences, and do away with many reputable opinions and data of perception, about which we have spoken in our remarks on time and motion (**232: 303a20–4**).[15]

Atomism clashes with mathematics only if atoms are theoretically or mathematically indivisible.

Finally, there is a strange passage in Plutarch usually supposed to quote Democritus' own words:

If a cone is cut by its base in a plane, what should one think of the surfaces of the segments—are they equal or unequal? For if they are unequal, they will make the cone uneven, with a lot of step-like corrugations and roughnesses; and if they are equal, the segments will be equal and the cone will evidently have suffered the fate of a cylinder, being constructed from equal and not unequal circles—which is utterly absurd (**233: B 155**).

The fragment connects with a further passage in the *de Caelo* (307a17 = B 155a) which appears to ascribe to Democritus the view that a sphere has angles, i.e. is a polyhedron. Why should a cone be corrugated and a sphere polyhedral? The only explanation is that geometrical solids are composed of theoretically indivisible parts.

So much for the texts on which theoretical indivisibility is founded. Before examining them it will be prudent to ask just what thesis they are supposed to maintain: what does it mean to say that atoms are 'theoretically' indivisible?

First, the thesis might be that atoms are *conceptually* indivisible: we cannot conceive or think of anything smaller than an atom. Conception is treated as a form of imagining; and the thesis amounts to saying that there is a lower limit to our powers of imagination: just as there is a threshold to our physical eye, so there is a threshold to our inner eye. Some things are too small to be seen; others would be too small to be imagined or conceived. That, if I understand him, is Epicurus' notion of theoretical indivisibility (*ad Hdt* §§58–9); and it was revived by Hume. It is a wretched muddle; for it confounds thinking or conceiving with the forming of mental images; and it supposes that to imagine a small object is a form of small image. But I shall not attempt to tease out all the horrible confusions it contains.

Second, the thesis might mean that atoms are *geometrically* indivisible: the volume occupied by an atom has no mathematically distinguishable parts; there is no quantity designated by such phrases as 'half the volume of an atom', 'two thirds the volume of an atom', and so on. 'But surely,' it is said, 'Democritean atoms are magnitudes, *megethê*, and not points (like the atoms of Boscovich); but all magnitudes (in Euclidean geometry at least) are divisible: hence those atoms are not geometrically indivisible— Democritus was "too good a mathematician" to main any such view.'[16] But we know that Plato and Xenocrates both entertained a theory of geometrically indivisible magnitudes (vol. 1, p. 245), and we may not deny on *a priori* grounds that Democritus anticipated them. There is no *geometrical* error in abandoning the continuous space of Euclidean thought and substituting a granular space; and the theory that atoms are geometrically indivisible is the theory that the geometry of space is granular, that space is made up of minimal volumes.

Finally, the thesis of theoretical indivisibility might mean that atoms are *logically* indivisible: the notion of a sub-atomic body is self-contradictory. There is a trivial sense in which atoms are logically indivisible; for 'atomic' *means* 'indivisible', so that '*a* is an atom and *a* is divisible' is a simple contradiction. But that trivial thesis is not what the supporters of 'theoretical' indivisibility have in mind; for it states only that, as a matter of logic, physically atomic bodies are physically indivisible. Rather, supporters of 'theoretical' indivisibility maintain, on this interpretation, that if *a* is an atom, then it is logically impossible to divide *a*. And that thesis is not a trivial truth: it asserts that atomicity is an essential trait of atoms, much as being even (say) is an essential trait of the number 2.

Theoretical indivisibility is not a unitary thing: which sort of indivisibility, if any, is suggested by the texts I have referred to?

233 is, I think, entirely inconclusive. It presents a dilemma, and the dilemma is based on the supposition of an atomist geometry. 'Take a cone of *n* atomic lengths from base to apex, and divide it into *n* segments. Consider the top surface of segment *i*, and the bottom surface of segment *i* + 1: if the former is greater than the latter, the cone will be corrugated or stepped, like a ziggurat; if the two surfaces are of the same area, the solid will be cylindrical.' Such a reconstruction makes sense of **233** and provides a genuine dilemma. And we may safely infer that Democritus had envisaged the possibility of a non-continuous geometry. Some scholars think that Democritus accepted the first horn of the dilemma: cones are indeed ziggurats; and they infer that Democritus embraced geometrical *minima*. Others think that the dilemma was intended rather as a *reductio ad absurdum* of the notion of such *minima*. We cannot tell: each interpretation is plausible, neither can be favoured.[17]

B 155a is more to the point: if a sphere has angles, then surely that can only be because its surface is composed of minimal planes. But apparently Democritus said not that a sphere 'has angles' but that it 'is an angle (*gônia*)'; and Simplicius offers the following explanation:

> The spherical whole is an angle (*gônia*); for if what is bent (*sunkekammenon*) is an angle, and a sphere is bent at every point on its surface (*kath' holên heautên*), then it is reasonably called a whole angle (*holê gônia*) (**234: B 155a**).

Geometers who talk of 'straight angles'—angles of 180°—do not suppose that straight lines are really bent: Democritus' phrase 'whole angle' need not imply that spheres are really polyhedrons.[18]

Next I turn to *de Caelo* 303a21 and the clash between atomism and mathematics. Surely, the physical indivisibility of atoms cannot pose any problems for mathematics; if there is a clash, it can only be caused by a mathematical indivisibility? The answer is not as simple as it seems; for the question at issue is not whether physical indivisibility conflicts with mathematics, but rather whether Aristotle would have deemed such a conflict to exist. And I think that he would have done: in the *Physics* he argues that since the universe is finite in extent, there are no infinite magnitudes for the geometers to reason about (207b15–21); and he excuses himself by saying that the geometers can get by if they are allowed to divide an object at any point (207b27–34). Geometry, for Aristotle, is essentially an applied science: it talks about lines and planes in the physical world, idealizing them, but for all that treating of them and not of objects of a more aetherial nature. Geometers assume that their subject matter is continuous or divisible at any point; but their subject matter, in Aristotle's view, is the physical world; consequently, the geometers will be at odds with any theory of *physical* indivisibles. If that is so, the *de Caelo* does not provide evidence that Democritean atoms are theoretically indivisible: Aristotle's criticism of atomism, given his own views on the nature of geometry, is compatible with the assumption that he ascribed only physical indivisibility to the Atomists.[19]

Simplicius, *in Cael* 202.27–31, and the scholiast on Euclid depend on the *de Caelo*; and their statements give no independent evidence for mathematical atomism. In **229**, on the other hand, Simplicius is not simply drawing on Aristotle; and there he must be using 'partless (*amerês*)' in the sense of 'theoretically indivisible'. Now Simplicius' ascription of 'partlessness' to the atoms is singular; and I am inclined to think that it is an inference of Simplicius' own.[20] '*Amerês*', I suggest, is Simplicius' gloss on '*smikros* (small)': wanting to explain the inference from smallness to indivisibility; believing (on the basis of the *de Caelo*) that the Atomists' corpuscles were geometrical *minima*; and observing that, unlike Epicurus, the two founders of atomism did not say anything about the 'parts' of their atoms, he understandably inferred that '*smikros*' in their argument connoted theoretical indivisibility. We need not accept Simplicius' inference; and **229** drops from the controversy.

All depends, then, on the Aristotelian view that Atomism grew from a reflexion upon, or a surrender to, Zeno's dichotomy argument. How much of the long argument, or set of arguments, in the *GC* we can safely ascribe to Democritus I do not know: Aristotle speaks tentatively—'Democritus would appear to have been persuaded'—and the passage which I summarized is certainly Aristotle's in form even if it is not so in substance.[21] In any case, I do not see that the argument says anything about 'theoretical' divisibility: Aristotle praises Democritus for arguing *phusikôs*, and that should mean something like 'with a close eye on the relevant scientific facts'—facts, presumably, about physical division. The argument is expressly designed to refute the hypothesis that 'a body is divisible throughout, and that is possible' (316a16): I take that to mean 'bodies are physically divisible through and through, and you can actually effect the division'; for the curious *addendum* 'and that is possible' is otiose unless we read it as meaning 'and you can actually effect the division'. Moreover, the argument speaks of actually dividing a 'body or magnitude', and it refers, only half-jestingly, to the possibility that the process of division may generate a sort of sawdust. All that, and the very language of the argument, suggest a physical and not a notional division. In sum, as I read the passage from the *GC*, it has Democritus reply to the Zenonian argument by positing physically indivisible atoms.

We are left with *Physics* 187a1. Can a physical atomism be represented as a surrender to Zeno's dichotomy? Plainly, if we develop the argument of **29 B 1-2**, we can produce a position which cannot be answered or evaded by positing a physical atomism; certainly, no one who is gripped by the hideous claws of Zeno's logic will think highly of a scientist who simply shrugs his shoulders and says, 'Well, then, I suppose matter is composed of physically indivisible atoms'. But for all that, we can, I think, make sense of Democritus' 'surrender to the dichotomy' without introducing notionally indivisible particles—and that in either of two ways. First we might suppose that Democritus read Zeno's Dichotomy and took it at its face value, as an argument about physical division; had he done so, he would have been justified, if intellectually unadventurous, in asserting physical atomism and getting on with his scientific work. For as Zeno states it, the paradox is adequately solved by physical atomism (see vol. 1, p. 245). It is only when we reflect upon that solution, and attempt to reconstruct the paradox in its face, that we develop an argument impervious to physical atomism. And there is no reason to ascribe such reflexion to Democritus. Second, and more easily, we may construe *Physics* 187a1 in the light of the argument in the *GC*: when Aristotle says that Democritus gave in to 'the argument from the dichotomy' he need not have any precise Zenonian argument in mind; the term 'dichotomy' was certainly used later to refer to any argument of that Zenonian type—any argument turning on considerations of infinite divisibility —and it seems to me most probable that the argument to which, in Aristotle's opinion, Democritus 'surrendered' was none other than the quasi-Zenonian concoction in the *GC*. Thus if the *GC* does not drive us to mathematical atomism neither does the *Physics*.

I conclude that the evidence does not oblige us to make the Atomists' corpuscles theoretically indivisible; the verdict must be *non liquet*. But the investigation of theoretical indivisibility is not wholly negative in its results: I do not want to claim that Aristotle's account in the *GC* has no historical value; on the contrary, I suppose that it gives us the answer to the outstanding question of atomism: Why imagine that there are any physical *minima* in the material world?

Leucippus and Democritus, reflecting in a vaguely Zenonian fashion on physical division, urged that unless macroscopic bodies were ultimately composed of indivisible corpuscles, the material world would fall apart into insubstantial points or bare nothings. When asked to explain what feature of these hypothetical corpuscles could account for their indivisibility and prevent their dissolution, they produced a plausible physical answer: substances are solid, and what is solid cannot be divided. The dichotomy argument assures us that there *are* indivisible corpuscles; further considerations, which I have already rehearsed, explain *why* those corpuscles are indivisible.

Unfortunately, the Atomists mishandle the dichotomy argument. I shall not expose their errors; for my remarks on Zeno have implicitly indicated them. But it is worth noting one fallacy in their reasoning: consideration of what would happen if everything were actually divided through and through leads them to infer that:

(1) It cannot be the case that everything has been divided.

From (1) they conclude to atomism, or:

(2) There are some things which cannot be divided.

From a proposition of the form ' $\sim \Diamond (\forall x) \phi x$' they infer the corresponding proposition of the form '$(\exists x) \sim \Diamond \phi x$'. The invalidity of the inference, which is hidden in the dowdy garb of ordinary language, shows up clearly when it is more formally dressed. Zenonian considerations will only lead to atomism by way of a fallacy.

(d) *Bodies without number*

There are infinitely many atoms. Simplicius has an interesting report:

> Thus they reasonably promised that, if their principles were unlimited, they would account for all affections and substances and explain under what agency and how anything comes into being; and for that reason they say that only for those who make the elements unlimited does everything turn out in accordance with reason (235: 68 A 38).

Observe the character of that argument: only if the atoms are infinite can the phenomena be explained; only an infinity of principles can account for the variety and vacillations we observe among macroscopic substances and their affections. The attitude evinced in such an argument is resolutely un-Eleatic; to Melissus, the phenomena required no explanation: reason, by dictating a rigid monism, revealed the plural world of sense-perception as a false imagining of the jaded mind. In the north of Greece they had a robuster sense of reality: the things we see and touch cannot be mere fictions; monism must be mistaken, and the plural phenomena require an explanation.

Yet Simplicius' argument will not do as it stands: perhaps an infinity of atoms is sufficient to explain the diversity of phenomena. But is it necessary? Or can any other arguments lead us to postulate an infinity? In fact three further lines of thought have been discerned. First, the Atomists believed that there was an infinite variety of atomic shapes; and that belief immediately entails an infinity of atoms. I shall return shortly to the question of atomic shapes: here I note only that the easy inference from shape to quantity is nowhere ascribed to the Atomists in our sources.

Second, Simplicius says that

> [Leucippus] hypothesized unlimitedly many eternally moving elements—the atoms—and the unlimited quantity of the shapes among them because nothing is rather such that such, and as he observed unremitting generation and change in existent things (235: 67 A 8).

Did the observation of 'unremitting generation and change' ground the numerical infinity of the atoms? and does Simplicius ascribe to Leucippus the argument elsewhere ascribed to Anaximander (see vol. 1, p. 30) that eternal generation requires an infinite fund of matter or material particles? I do not think so: as I read Simplicius' text, the observation of 'unremitting generation and change' was adduced to establish the eternal motion of the atoms rather than their numerical infinity.

The third argument infers the infinity of the atoms from the infinity of the space in which they swim. Before examining it, therefore, we might well ask why space should be deemed infinite. Our texts contain no direct answer to that question; but a celebrated argument has been adduced to fill the evidential gap.

> Archytas, according to Eudemus, put the argument thus: 'Standing at the edge (e.g. at the heaven of the fixed stars), could I extend my hand or my cane outside it or not?' That I could not extend it is absurd; but if I do extend it, then what is outside will be either body or space (163: Eudemus, fr. 65 W = 47 A 24).

Lucretius took over Archytas' argument (I. 968–983); hence Epicurus used it: and if Epicurus, why not Democritus?[22]

The Archytan dilemma presupposes that every finite extension has edges; for Archytas imagines himself at the edge of the universe. That presupposition links the dilemma to an argument which Aristotle cities as the fourth of five alleged proofs of the existence of the infinite:

> Again, what is finite is always bounded by something; so that necessarily there is no boundary, if it is always necessary for one thing to be bounded against another (**237**: *Phys* 203b20–2).

That argument too was accepted by Epicurus (*ad Hdt* §41); and it too may have originated with Democritus.[23]

Aristotle answers the argument by distinguishing between 'being bounded (*peperanthai*)' and 'touching (*haptesthai*)': what touches, he asserts, must indeed touch something else; but what is bounded need not be bounded by anything else (*Phys* 208a11–14). The answer is perplexing, and Epicurus was rightly unimpressed by it; yet for all that, Aristotle was unwittingly correct. We are all familiar with two-dimensional extensions that are finite and yet have no edges—'finite and unbounded', in the jargon of the geometers. The surface of a football is a mundane example of such an apparently paradoxical thing. Why, then, should there not be three-dimensional extensions that are finite and unbounded? finite, in that they contain no straight lines of infinite length; unbounded, in that they have no edges. If I understand the doctrine that space-time is 'curved', it implies that our familiar space has precisely those properties.

The Epicurean argument fails; and with it goes Archytas' dilemma; for the presupposition of that dilemma proves unsatisfactory: it is not true that every finite extension has edges. Yet would the dilemma work if its presupposition were true? I do not think so; for I do not see why it is 'absurd' to suppose that I simply could not extend my hand were I in Archytas' situation. Lucretius suggests that if I cannot extend my hand, then there must be something in the way, preventing the extension; but there may be something behind me (a gravitational field, say), holding me back. 'But even if you cannot, physically, extend your hand, still it is logically possible to do so.' Perhaps; but to say that it is logically possible for me to extend my hand two feet in front of me is not to say that there is a *place* two feet in front of me. And Archytas' argument is designed to show that there must be a space (occupied or unoccupied) in front of me.

So much for infinite space. How is it connected with the infinity of the atoms? Plainly, if there are infinitely many atoms, each of a minimum size, space must be infinite if it is to contain them; but if space is infinite, why must it have infinite denizens? Epicurus argued that 'if the void were infinite and the bodies finite, the bodies would not stay anywhere but would be carried about, scattered through the infinite void' (*ad Hdt* §42).[24] In short, a finite number of atoms would be dotted about in an infinite space, and no cosmogonical collisions would ever occur. But why should a finite number of atoms not simply chance to congregate in one corner of infinite space? The answer is, I think, implicit in Aristotle's *Physics*:

> If the region outside the heavens is unlimited, so too, it seems, are body and the worlds; for why should it be here rather than here in the void? Hence mass is, if anywhere, everywhere (**238**: *Phys* 203b25–8).

Aristotle's ancient commentators ascribed this argument to Democritus, and modern scholars accept their judgment;[25] for the argument relies on the *Ou Mallon* Principle, and the principle is known to be Democritean. 'There is no reason for there to be atoms in one place rather than in another; but there are atoms in certain parts of the universe. Hence atoms are scattered throughout the universe.' And we may, if we please, concoct a similar piece of reasoning for Epicurus: 'There would be no reason for a finite group of atoms to congregate in one place rather than in another. But they could not congregate everywhere; hence they would not congregate at all.'

That Democritus did hope to establish the infinity of atoms from the infinity of space by way of the *Ou Mallon* Principle is, I suppose, undeniable. I shall examine the Principle in a later chapter: here it is only necessary to say that the Democritean argument does not succeed.

(e) *Infinite variety*

There are infinitely many atoms, each solid, indivisible, immutable, eternal. How, then, does one atom differ from another? What further characteristics, by which they might be differentiated, do atoms possess? I have already mentioned size: atoms, being bodies, have a magnitude or size; and they differ in size from one another. Perhaps they exhibit an infinite variety of size; perhaps some are gigantic. At any event, even those authors who hold that all atoms are small, allow that they come in different sizes (e.g., **213**).

Having magnitude, the atoms also have shape, or (in the technical terminology of Abdera) *rhusmos* (e.g., *Met* 985b16 = **67 A 6**); and atomic shapes differ: 'There belong to them every kind of shape and every kind of form . . . some are scalene, some hooked, some hollow, some convex—and they have innumerable other differences' (**213**: cf., e.g., Cicero, **67 A 11**). The differences are numberless: atomic shapes are infinitely varied.

61

Two arguments for the infinity of atomic shapes have survived. The first is transmitted by Aristotle:

> Since they [sc. Leucippus and Democritus] thought that the truth was in appearances, and the appearances were contrary and unlimited, they made the [atomic] shapes unlimited (**239**: *GC* 315b8 = **67 A 9**).

The argument is echoed, with an important nuance, by Epicurus: 'It is not possible that so many varieties should come about from the same comprehended (*perieilêmmenôn*) [atomic] shapes. And in each shaping, the similar atoms are unlimited without qualification; but in their differences they are not unlimited without qualification but only incomprehensible (*aperilêptoi*)' (*ad Hdt* §42). To explain the varied phenomena you require a multiplicity of atomic shapes, but not an infinity. The shapes are incomprehensibly, but finitely, many; they have a determinate number, even though we shall never determine it.

It is tempting to read Epicurus' view back into Leucippus: a literal infinity of atomic shapes is theoretically overgenerous; and our texts perhaps allow us to take the terms 'numberless' and 'unlimited' in a relaxed sense. But the Epicurean argument for the finitude of shapes may not have been available to the Atomists: 'the principles of things vary in a finite number of shapes. If that were not so, some seeds would thereby have to be of infinite bodily magnitude' (Lucretius, II. 479–82). This, presumably, was the argument which Epicurus used to show that atomic shapes were finite; and, as Lucretius explicitly recognizes (II. 485), it hangs on the assumption of 'minimal parts': only if there are theoretically indivisible magnitudes will infinite shapes imply infinite sizes.[26] That assumption (as I have argued) cannot be shown to have been Abderite; nor, therefore, can we ascribe Lucretius' argument to the early Atomists.

Let us allow, then, that the Atomists posited an infinite variety of atomic shapes. The argument given in **239** for that hypothesis is a thunderingly bad one: if there are, literally, infinitely many differences in the phenomena, that at most requires that there are infinitely many different atomic structures underlying the phenomena. It does not require that the atomic *shapes* be infinitely various; indeed, it does not require that there be more than one atomic shape. How could the Atomists have failed to see that?

Now Simplicius offers a different reflexion: Leucippus 'hypothesized unlimitedly many eternally moving elements—the atoms—and the unlimited quantity of the shapes among them, because nothing is rather such than such . . .' (**236: 67 A 8**). The *Ou Mallon*

Principle is here applied to atomic shapes: there are, mathematically speaking, infinitely many possible shapes; there is no reason why there should be atoms of shape S rather than atoms of shape S'; hence there are atoms of every shape. I shall look at the argument again when I discuss the Principle it incorporates. The argument is, I suspect, the official Abderite argument for an infinity of atomic shapes; and I am tempted to suppose that 239 does not contain an Abderite *argument* at all: having argued for infinity by the *Ou Mallon* Principle, the Atomists observed that an infinity of atomic shapes would amply explain the phenomenal infinity of the macroscopic world. Their observation was later misconstrued as an independent argument for infinity of shapes.

(f) *Atomic weight and motion*

Solid magnitudes will have a mass or weight (*baros*); and since the atoms differ in size, they will vary in mass. There is ample evidence that this was explicitly stated by the Atomists:

> Democritus says that each of the indivisibles is heavier in accordance with its excess [in size] (**240**: *GC* 326a9 = **68 A 60**).

> The Democriteans, and later Epicurus, say that the atoms . . . have weight (**241**: Simplicius, **68 A 61**).

> Democritus distinguishes heavy and light by magnitude (**242**: Theophrastus, *Sens* §61 = **68 A 135**).

Other equally grave witnesses can be called. Against them there is a single voice: Aëtius twice reports that

> Democritus says that the primary bodies . . . have no weight (**243**: **68 A 47**).

These testimonies have aroused great controversy; orthodoxy now lies with Aëtius—the atoms do not have weight, at least not 'absolute' weight.[27] But I think it is evident that Aristotle and Theophrastus are preferable to Aëtius, who is confused by the whole question; and the thesis that atoms have weight or mass is an obvious corollary of the central tenets of atomism.

Mass goes with motion; and

> Leucippus says that . . . [the atoms] are infinite and always moving and that generation and change are continuous (**244**: Hippolytus, **67 A 10**);

according to Democritus, the atoms 'battle and are carried about in the void on account of their dissimilarity and the other differences aforesaid' (Aristotle, 213). Aristotle once compares the atoms to the motes we see in a sunbeam (*An* 404a3 = **67 A 28**); the image is developed at length by Lucretius in his account of the precosmic motion of the Epicurean atoms:

For observe closely when the light of the sun
is poured by the intruding rays through the darkness of the house:
you will see many tiny bodies mingling in many ways through the empty space
in the very light of the rays,
and as though in eternal combat waging wars and battles,
striving in companies and never giving pause,
harried by constant meetings and partings.
So you can guess from this what it is like when the principles of things
are tossed about for ever in the vast void (**245**: II. 114–22).

Lactantius (*de ira* X. 9) ascribes the image to Leucippus: it was plainly a commonplace in atomist thought, and it is reasonably ascribed to the founder of the school. The atoms are shapes as gay and numberless as the motes that people the sunbeams.

If Leucippus gave an image, Democritus perhaps contributed a technical term:

They . . . said that, moving by virtue of the weight in them, they move through the void which yields and does not resist them;[28] for they say that they *peripalaisesthai* (**246**: Simplicius, **68 A 58**).

Editors emend *peripalaisesthai* to *peripalassesthai*; they then restore the verb, or the noun *peripalaxis*, in other Democritean contexts; and they proclaim that *peripalaxis* is the technical term for atomic motions. Alas, most of the restorations are probably unjustified; and the meaning of *peripalaxis* is itself a matter of dispute (the standard translation is 'vibration'). The whole issue is unenlightening.[29]

However that may be, we have a moderately clear picture of atomic movement: in any area of space, numerous particles are dancing aimlessly, in various directions and at various speeds, sometimes colliding, sometimes moving unimpeded. What determines their different motions? Our sources give three answers: first, the atoms move 'by virtue of the weight in them' (Simplicius, **246**). That is repeated by several authorities (e.g., Hermias, **67 A 17**; Simplicius, **68 A 61**); and it appears to have roused objections from Epicurus (*ad Hdt* § 61 = **68 A 61**). Aristotle, on the other hand, refers to 'dissimilarity and the other differences' in order to explain atomic motion (**213**), and he marks shape as an important determinant of motion (*An* 404a4 = **67 A 28**). Third, the doxographers speak of 'blows':

Democritus says that by nature the atoms are motionless, and that they move by blows (**247**: Simplicius, **68 A 47**).

Democritus says that the primary bodies have no weight but move in the unlimited [void] by counter-striking (*allêlotupian*) (**248**: Aëtius, **68 A 47**).

[Leucippus and Democritus] say that the atoms move by counter-striking, i.e. by hitting one another (**249**: Alexander, **67 A 6**; cf. Aëtius, **68 A 66**).

The commentators find difficulty here. Some distinguish two phases in atomic movement: the first occurs *before* the atoms have struck one another, and is free motion through space; the second occurs *after* a 'counter-striking' and is compelled motion. But there is no textual evidence for a period in which the atoms roamed freely, untouched by their fellow occupants of space; and if the atoms have been moving for all eternity, it is hard to imagine why there should ever have been such a period.

Nor do our sources provide any genuine difficulty. Aëtius' denial of weight to the atoms may be dismissed (above, p. 63); the remaining testimony gives a coherent picture: in themselves, atoms are indeed motionless; that is to say, they would not be moving had they not collided with other atoms and so been jolted into motion. ('How, then, did the atomic motion ever *begin?*' That is a tale for a later chapter.) But if collision is the propellant cause of motion, the speed and direction of an atom's travel is determined by its weight and its shape—more precisely, by the weight, shape, and anterior motions of the colliding bodies. Throw a stone at a cat, and its rebounding path will be determined by its own weight, shape, and anterior motion, and by the corresponding properties of the cat: the stone rebounds because of its 'counter-striking' the cat; the trajectory of its rebound is determined by weight and shape. No doubt it is wrong to construct the dynamics of atomic motion from observations of macroscopic motion through air; and Epicurus' account of atomic motion differs radically from the account I have ascribed to Democritus. For all that, the early atomist account is rational, coherent, and sane: if it is wrong in fact, at least it was intelligently constructed.

(g) *Atomic indifference*

They say that there are these three differences: shape, order and position. For they assert that existents [*to on*, i.e. the atoms] differ only in *rhusmos* and *diathigê* and *tropê*; of these, *rhusmos* is shape, *diathigê* order, and *tropê* position. For *A* differs from *N* in shape; *AN* differs from *NA* in order; and *N* differs from *Z* in position (250: Aristotle, *Met* 985b13–19 = 67 A 6).[30]

Elsewhere Aristotle uses a similar analogy: in explanation of how the rearrangement of a group of atoms can produce radically different macroscopic results, he says that 'tragedy and comedy are put together from the same letters' (*GC* 315b15 = 67 A 9). Scholars infer, with some plausibility, that the alphabetical analogy was employed by the Atomists themselves (cf. 68 B 18b–20).

Aristotle's three differences make a clumsy triad. First, they are not the only, nor even the only important, differences between atoms: atoms also differ in size, in weight, and in velocity. Second, difference in *diathigê* and *tropê* is a relation among groups of atoms and not among individual bodies; that is evident in the case of *diathigê* and only slightly less so for *tropê*—the letter *N* has, in itself, no *tropê* in space. I suspect that Leucippus or Democritus saw that the letter analogy would neatly illustrate *rhusmos, diathigê* and *tropê*, and, pleased by the discovery, overlooked its minor awkwardnesses. However that may be, it is plain that *diathigê* and *tropê* are characteristics of groups of atoms and not of individual corpuscles.

The doxographers several times say that atoms are *apoioi* (Plutarch, 68 A 57; Aëtius, 68 A 124; 125). *Apoios* usually means 'qualityless' (*a* + *poiotês*), but it can mean 'inactive', 'inert' (*a* + *poiein*). Most of the ancient sources take it in its former sense: Galen says that the atoms are all 'small bodies, without qualities' (68 A 49); Plutarch gives as an illustration of *apoios* 'colourless' (68 A 57). Then, uneasy with the bland assertion that atoms are unqualified, our sources explain that this means 'without *sensible* qualities' (cf. Aëtius, 68 A 124; Sextus, 68 A 59; *Pyrr Hyp* III. 33; and see Epicurus, *ad Hdt* §54).

A passage from Aristotle seems to take the other road, implying that atoms are *apoioi* in the sense of impotent:

It is necessary to say that each of the indivisibles is both impassive (*apathes*) . . . and productive of no affection (*pathos*)—for it can be neither hard nor cold (251: *GC* 326a1–3).

Atoms are impassive and inactive, equally incapable of receiving and of giving affection. Some scholars construe inactivity here as the inability to affect other atoms: inactivity then follows immediately from impassivity; for if atoms cannot be changed, then no atom can change any atom. That is a part of the story (cf. 326a11); but Aristotle means to assert not merely that atoms cannot affect other atoms, but that they cannot be 'hard or cold' or anything else—in short, he wants to assert that they are *apoia* in the sense of 'lacking (sensible) qualities'. And his argument is not hard to distil. It relies upon the Principle of Synonymy (vol. 1, pp. 88, 119); if *a* is active, *a* can bring it about that *b* is *F*; but if *a* can bring it about that *b* is *F* (where *F* is a sensible quality), then *a* is *F*. In short, Aristotle means to say, in the concise and somewhat ill-humoured passage at 326a1–24, that atoms lack sensible qualities and, consequently, active powers.

If atoms lack sensible qualities, they cannot differ one from another in respect of sensible qualities. Aristotle takes the point in the same crotchety passage of the *GC*: he asks: 'again, do all those solids [i.e. the atoms] have one nature, or do they differ one from another—as it might be, some being fiery, others earthen in mass?' (326a29–31). And he answers:

> They say that they have a single nature—as it might be, each being a separate bit of gold (**252**: *Cael* 275b31 = **67 A 19**; cf. *GC* 326a17).[31]

Dalton, who is often hailed as the founder of modern atomism, disagreed: his atoms are diverse; they are indivisible particles of different chemical stuffs. Daltonian atomism is familiar from schoolboy chemistry, where we may incautiously take such a formula as 'H_2O' to indicate the amalgam of two atoms of hydrogen with one of oxygen. Atoms of hydrogen have those powers or sensible qualities which characterize the gas hydrogen; and that fact distinguishes them from atoms of oxygen, of chlorine, of iron, and of all the other chemical elements. This chemical atomism, as I may call it, may be contrasted with a physical atomism, according to which the chemical differences between oxygen and hydrogen do not exist at the corpuscular level: there are not atoms of oxygen and atoms of hydrogen, any more than there are atoms of sugar or atoms of soap. Atoms are bits of stuff, having all the characteristics of matter and none of the characteristics specific to any particular type of matter. 'Body, common to everything, is the principle of everything, differing in its parts by size and shape' (*Phys* 203a34–b2 = **68 A 41**). Davy championed physical atomism and the unity of matter; Dalton, chemical atomism and the irreducible diversity of matter: the unitarian view, which had served in an Aristotelian guise as the foundation of alchemical hopes, in the end triumphed.

Democritus is no Daltonian; but his atoms are not, strictly speaking, 'indifferent' or *adiaphoroi*: they differ intrinsically in shape and size, and as a consequence in weight and motion. In a pure physical atomism, each atom would be precisely similar to every other; there would be one atomic shape and one atomic size; macroscopic diversities would be explained solely in terms of differences in atomic structures and not in terms of differences among the components of those structures.

(h) *The status of sensible qualities*

Atoms are not coloured; they have no taste and no smell. Did the Atomists simply deny the reality of sensible qualities? Did they offer any account of the qualities of macroscopic bodies? Did they really mean to assert that atoms lack *all* sensible qualities?

It is clear that the doxographers are speaking loosely when they say that the atoms have no sensible qualities: shape, size and motion are, after all, sensible qualities; and if the atoms are too small for their qualities to be discerned, that does not deprive those qualities of their sensible nature. Moreover, it appears that the atoms had a further and indubitably sensible property: temperature. Aristotle is scathing here: 'Yet it is absurd just to ascribe heat to round shapes' (326a3–5); 'No atoms have any sensible qualities—except that round atoms are hot' (cf. *Cael* 303a12–14 = **67 A 15**). Theophrastus expands the point: it is absurd, he says, for Democritus

> to make intrinsic natures of heavy and light and hard and soft . . .
> but to make hot and cold and the rest relative to sensation—and
> that though he says frequently that the shape of the hot is spherical
> (**253**: *Sens* §68 = **68 A 135**).

On the one hand, heat is treated alongside other sensible qualities and so should not belong to the individual atoms (cf. **B 9**; **B 117**); on the other hand, heat is associated with spherical atoms, because spherical atoms move most easily (Aristotle, *An* 404a7 = **67 A 28**), and easy movers cut and burn (*Cael* 303b32).

The criticism does not apply to Leucippus, who offered a different account of heat (Simplicius, **67 A 14**). Perhaps the criticism is in any case inapposite; perhaps the Atomists never intended to distinguish between sensible and non-sensible qualities and to deny their atoms the former; perhaps they had some other criterion for determining whether or not a quality was of a type to be possessed by an atom.

Here I introduce one of the most celebrated of Democritean sayings. It is transmitted to us in several forms; and indeed it may have been stated in different forms by Democritus himself. I quote Plutarch's version; for although his text is corrupt, his version is the fullest and the best:

> By convention (*nomôi*) is colour, and by convention sweet, and by convention [every] combination (*sunkrisin*), [but in reality (*eteêi*) the void and atoms] (**254**: *adv Col* 1110 E).[32]

Democritus means to draw an ontological distinction between 'atoms and void' on the one hand, and certain other things on the other; and he intends to assign 'atoms and void' a superior ontological rank to those other things. So much is clear: the rest, I think, is more puzzling than is usually allowed.

In all our sources other than Plutarch, the list of 'conventional' items is a list of qualities (hot, cold, bitter, sweet, colour); and Diogenes Laertius says simply that 'qualities (*poiotêtes*) are by convention' (IX.45 = **A 1**). Diogenes is speaking loosely: I assume that we may add to the *eteêi* side of the great divide a list of atomic qualities: shape, size, weight, motion. And I assume too that the distinction between 'conventional' and 'real' qualities gives the criterion for atomic qualities: a quality is non-atomic if it is 'conventional', if it exists *nomôi*. There is no explicit suggestion that *nomôi* qualities are sensible qualities; and the thesis that atoms lack sensible qualities has already been judged erroneous. What, then, is it for a quality to be 'conventional'? (A 'combination' (*sunkrisis*) is not a quality: I return to that word in a later context, below, pp. 141–5.)

The seventeenth-century corpuscularians made much of a distinction between 'primary' and 'secondary' qualities. The classic exposition of the distinction is found in Locke's *Essay*, in a chapter where Locke, as he admits, is more than usually indebted to the scientists, and in particular to Boyle. Locke introduces the distinction as follows: 'Qualities thus considered in Bodies are, First such as are utterly inseparable from the Body, in what estate soever it be; such as in all the alterations and changes it suffers, all the force can be used upon it, it constantly keeps; and such as Sense constantly finds in every particle of Matter, which has bulk enough to be perceived, and the Mind finds inseparable from every particle of Matter, though less than to make itself singly be perceived by our Senses. . . . These I call *original* or *primary Qualities* of Body' (*Essay* II. viii. 9).

Notice first, that Locke does not talk of primary qualities *simpliciter*, but of primary qualities of body (elsewhere he mentions the primary qualities of spiritual substances (II. xxi. 73; xxii. 17–18)—and he might consistently have singled out primary qualities of any kind of thing); second, that the distinction between primary and secondary qualities is not logically tied to a particulate or atomist theory of matter; and third, that primary qualities 'of body' are properties of pieces of stuff and not of stuff *simpliciter*.

Thus we may say, generally:

(D1) Q is a primary quality of F's if and only if necessarily any F has Q; and, particularly:

(D2) Q is a primary quality of bodies if and only if necessarily every body has Q.

Primary qualities, in short, are essential properties (cf. II. iv. 1).

Secondary qualities are introduced as follows: '2*dly*, Such *Qualities*, which in truth are nothing in the Objects themselves, but Powers to produce various Sensations in us by their *primary Qualities*, *i.e.* by the Bulk, Figure, Texture and Motion of their insensible parts, as Colours, Sounds, Tastes, *etc.* These I call *secondary Qualities*' (*Essay* II. viii. 10). Locke is trying to say too much at once; let me be rudely dogmatic and say what I think Locke should have said. First, he wants a definition of 'secondary quality'; and he needs:

(D1*) Q^* is a secondary quality of Fs if and only if some Fs have Q^* and Q^* is not a primary quality of Fs.

Second, he wants to advance a number of theses about the secondary qualities of bodies; these include the following: secondary qualities are not 'real'; they are powers; they are relational; they are mind-dependent; and their presence in objects is explicable in terms of the primary qualities of their component corpuscles.

The last point requires a little elaboration. Consider, first, the property of being cubic. That, clearly, is a secondary quality of bodies; but it stands in a special relationship to the primary quality of figure or shape: *being cubic* is, in a convenient jargon, a determinate of the determinable property *being shaped*. Call qualities which are thus determinates of primary qualities 'proper' qualities. Then Locke's thesis is this: corpuscles, or atoms, have no properties apart from primary qualities and proper qualities of body; macroscopic bodies have secondary qualities, but those qualities are all explicable by way of the primary and proper qualities of the corpuscles which constitute the macroscopic bodies.

It is often suggested that Democritus' distinction between *nomôi* and *eteêi* qualities is the first version of the distinction between primary and secondary qualities: *eteêi* means 'real' or 'primary'; and if *nomôi* does not exactly mean 'secondary', nevertheless *nomôi* qualities are secondary qualities. That view is clearly mistaken (sphericality, say, is a secondary quality, but it is not *nomôi*); but it is on the right road. In its place I suggest the following thesis:

(D3) *Q* is *eteêi* if and only if *Q* is either a primary or a proper quality of bodies.

I do not mean that the Atomists explicitly embraced (D3)—there is no trace of any such defintion in the doxography; but I think that (D3) is the thesis which best explains the atomist attitude to atoms and qualities.

The list of atomic properties—duration, solidity, mobility, mass, shape, size—is close enough to the Lockean list of primary qualities. And it is not implausible to imagine that Democritus ascribed these' qualities to atoms just because he thought them essential to bodies.

Moreover, the Atomists thought that the secondary qualities of macroscopic objects are explicable in terms of the properties of their atomic constituents.

> The elements are qualityless, . . . and the compounds from them are coloured by the order and shape and position [of the atoms] (**255**: Aëtius, **68 A 125**).

> White and black, he says, are rough and smooth; and he reduces the savours to the [atomic] shapes (**256**: Aristotle, *Sens* 442b11 = **68 A 126**).

A long passage in Theophrastus' *de Sensu* is devoted to Democritus and it contains numerous Democritean accounts of the sensible qualities; I quote a short (and controversial) passage:

> Sour taste comes from shapes that are large and multi-angular and have very little roundness; for these, when they enter the body, clog and blind the veins and prevent their flowing—that is why the bowels too come to a stand. Bitter taste comes from small, smooth, rounded shapes whose periphery does have joints; that it why it is viscous and adhesive. Saline taste comes from large shapes which are not rounded or scalene but angular and many-jointed (he means by scalene those which interlock and combine with one another)—large, because the saltiness stays on the surface (for if they were small and struck by those surrounding them they would mingle with the universe); not rounded, because what is saline is rough and what is rounded is smooth; not scalene, because it does not interlock—that is why it is friable (**257**: §66 = **68 A 135**).[33]

In that account of gustatory qualities, and throughout Theophrastus' report, it is the shapes of individual atoms which account for macroscopic qualities. Shape is far more important in the atomism of Democritus (who significantly called his corpuscles *ideai* or 'shapes') than in modern atomism, where it is the interrelations and relative locomotions of the constituent atoms which are primarily responsible for macroscopic phenomena. But fundamentally Democritus and Locke are at one: atomic qualities underlie and explain macroscopic qualities.

Why suppose that atoms have no secondary qualities? First, the atoms, being physical bodies, are logically bound to possess a certain set of properties: solidity, size, shape, etc. Then let us hypothesize that those are *all* the properties they possess, and attempt to explain the phenomena in terms of them. The hypothesis is maximally economical: if it is successful in explaining the phenomena, then we shall certainly have no reason to ascribe any secondary qualities to atoms, and hence should not do so. Moreover, it may well be that an analysis of secondary qualities will show that some or all of them could not in fact belong to atoms. Suppose that elasticity is explained in terms of density, i.e. in terms of a certain distribution of atoms and void in an atomic conglomerate; then clearly no single atom can be elastic. Suppose that sourness is explained in terms of the effect of a mass of corpuscles on the gustatory organs; then clearly no single corpuscle can be sour.

The most perplexing part of Locke's account of secondary qualities is his assertion that they are not real: did the Atomists adumbrate that part of the account too? and can we make any sense of it? 'Improper secondary qualities are not *eteêi*: they are therefore unreal.' An easy gloss suggests itself: if improper secondary qualities can be accounted for by way of primary and proper qualities, then a complete account of the real world need mention no improper secondary qualities at all; for every fact expressible by a sentence of the form 'Macroscopic object M has Q^*' is equally, and more fundamentally, expressible by a sentence of the form 'Atoms A_1, A_2, . . ., having Q_1, Q_2 . . ., are arranged in pattern P'.

But *eteêi* contrasts with *nomôi*; and the contrast suggests a further, and equally Lockean, sort of 'unreality'. The classical contrast with *nomôi* is *phusei*, 'by nature'; and the doxographers deploy the contrast:

The others say that perceptible things are by nature, but Leucippus and Democritus . . . [say that they are] *nomôi* (**258**: Aëtius, **67 A 32**).

By nature nothing is white or black or yellow or red or bitter or sweet (**259**: Galen, **68 A 49**).

72

This, however, does not take us far: we have still to interpret *nomôi*. It is doubtless 'conventional' in some sense that we call sweet things 'sweet' and that the Greeks called them *glukea*; but it is no 'convention' that ripe plums taste sweet and green plums taste sour, nor can Democritus have thought that it was.

Sextus offers a more appealing gloss:

> I.e., perceptible things are thought (*nomizetai*) and believed to exist, but they do not exist in truth (**260**: *adv Math* VII.135 = **68 B 9**).

Galen hints at the same thought:

> Things are thought (*nomizetai*) by men to be white and black and sweet and bitter and all the rest, but in truth there is nothing but [atoms and void] (**261: 68 A 49**).

Let Q^* be an improper secondary quality of body: then Q^* exists *nomôi*, i.e., people think that some things have Q^* but in truth none do. We might compare Democritus' view on 'mixture' or *krasis*:

> He says that in truth things simply are not mixed, but that what is thought (*dokousan*) to be a mixture is a close juxtaposition of bodies which each preserve its own appropriate nature (**262:** Alexander, **68 A 64**).

Things seem to be mixed; they are not—and a microscopic inspection would reveal the fact. Similarly, things seem to be red or warm or bitter or soft; they are not—and a microscopic inspection would reveal the fact.

But that will not do. It is simply absurd to say that fire is only *thought* to be hot, grass only *thought* to be green, sugar only *thought* to be sweet. And what are we to make of Democritus' laborious and detailed accounts of such qualities as heat, greenness and wetness if those qualities are never actually instantiated? Aristotle unwittingly brings home the absurdity:

> That is why he [sc. Democritus] says that colour does not exist—for things are coloured by position (*tropêi*) (**263:** *GC* 316a1 = **68 A 123**).

'Grass is green in virtue of such and such an atomic structure; *ergo* grass is not green.' Could there be a crasser inference than that?

A better gloss on *nomôi* is to hand: improper secondary qualities are not 'natural' because they are mind-dependent:

73

[They are] *nomôi*, i.e., they are in belief and by virtue of our affections (**264**: Aëtius, **67 A 32**).

For '*nomôi*' means the same as 'in thought (*nomisti*)' or 'relative to us', not in virtue of the nature of the objects (**265**: Galen **68 A 49**).

The view is found in Theophrastus: Democritus says that

Of none of the other sensible objects is there a nature (*phusis*), but they are all affections of perception, as it alters and imagination comes from it; for there is no nature of the hot and the cold, but the shape (*schêma*) alters and works the change in us (**266**: *Sens* §63 = **68 A 135**).

'Sweetness and Whiteness', as Locke puts it, 'are not really in Manna' (II.viii.18); they are not *in* manna, because they are relations between manna and the mind of some sentient creature. Thus 'there would . . . be no more Light, or Heat in the World, than there would be Pain if there were no sensible Creature to feel it, though the Sun should continue just as it is now, and Mount *Ætna* flame higher than ever it did' (*Essay*, II.xxxi.2).

Qualities divide into two groups: those which are *eteêi* or real, and those which are *nomôi* or mind-dependent: 'square', 'heavy', 'at rest' name intrinsic properties of objects; 'smooth', 'red', 'sweet' are, as Sextus put it 'names of our own feelings' (*adv Math* VIII.184). Atoms, the fundamental items of the world, possess only real qualities; and those qualities are either primary qualities, qualities which every body as a matter of necessity possesses, or else proper qualities, determinate forms of primary qualities. All improper secondary qualities are explicable by way of *eteêi* qualities; and the explication reveals that they are all mind-dependent.

I shall not attempt to assess the merits of that complex thesis; but it is perhaps worth indicating what any assessment must look to. First, there is the distinction between *eteêi* and non-*eteêi* qualities itself. It is, I think, plausible to believe that the class of *eteêi* qualities can be accurately defined by way of the notion of a primary quality; and it is plausible to believe that the *eteêi* properties of body will constitute a scientifically important sub-class of the class of bodily qualities.

Second, there is the Abderite list of *eteêi* qualities: it needs to be asked just what qualities satisfy the definition of *eteêi*. And it may well be that this question proves unexpectedly difficult; at any event, philosophers have not agreed on any list of primary qualities of body.

Third, there is the status of non-*eteêi* qualities. Are all these qualities in fact explicable by way of *eteêi* qualities? And would such an explication yield a logical or a causal dependence between *eteêi* and non-*eteêi* qualities? (It is often noticed that Locke fails to distinguish clearly between a causal thesis, that secondary qualities are *produced* by primary qualities, and a logical thesis, that secondary qualities are *analysed* into primary qualities; the observation, which I have stated crudely, leads to some difficult and intriguing questions.) And, finally, are non-*eteêi* qualities really mind-dependent? And is that dependency logical or causal?

(i) *The philosophy of Abdera*

The Abderite philosophy of matter began from the notion of *being*, of primary beings, substances or *ousiai*. Substances, they held, are solid and unitary bodies, ungenerable, indestructible, immutable, indivisible, everlasting. These basic items of the physical world are infinitely numerous and exhibit an infinite variety of shape and size; they are in constant motion, and their collisions and colligations form the macroscopic and changing world of phenomenal reality. The qualities they possess are those qualities which every body logically must possess, or at least determinate forms of those qualities.

The phenomenal world reveals a vast range of qualities not included in the list of atomic characteristics. But those qualities exist only 'by convention': they are mind-dependent, and their existence is to be explained in terms of the properties of the fundamental atomic traits. That assertion raises various difficult questions; and the value of the Abderite theory remains uncertain until they are answered. But it is, I hope, very plain that the theory began a line of thought whose influence upon philosophy and upon science was of unparalleled consequence.

IV

Philolaus and the
Formal Cause

(a) *Pythagorean numerology*

The Pythagoreans sailed their intellectual boats on the ocean of anonymity. One name stands out: Philolaus, according to a reliable tradition, was the first Pythagorean philosopher to publish his views; and his book *Concerning Nature* for the first time congealed the fluid oral tradition of the school (Demetrius, *apud* Diogenes Laertius, VIII.85 = 44 A 1).[1] A malicious and silly rumour insinuated that Plato in his *Timaeus* plagiarized the work of Philolaus (Timon, fr. 54 = A 8; Hermippus, *apud* Diogenes Laertius, VIII.84 = A 1); if the gossip has a basis in truth, and Plato was influenced by Philolaus, then that adds an extrinsic interest to the book.[2]

Several fragments of Philolaus' book have been preserved. A majority of scholars has found them spurious, adding them to the vast library of pseudo-Pythagorean literature; but the arguments for scepticism are not very solid, and I am persuaded by those scholars who think that some at least of the texts are genuine productions of Philolaus' pen. It would be pointless to rehearse the published arguments, and I have no new thoughts to contribute to the debate: I shall proceed on the assumption of authenticity, and let the interested or sceptical reader prove the assumption himself.[3]

Philolaus is sometimes taken as a mere mouthpiece: the views he expounds are not his own inventions; they are the common wisdom of his fellow Pythagoreans. And it has been judged that Philolaus' book was 'unscientific and without real understanding of the doctrines it reports'; it reveals 'a thinker of no great stature, whose interest is peripheral'.[4] The later part of this chapter will, I hope, show that Philolaus is a philosopher of some merit; but before turning to that task I shall spend a few pages on Philolaus' anonymous colleagues whose views he allegedly parroted.

If Philolaus was an inaccurate parrot for Pythagorean views, then we need an accurate account of those views against which to measure his mouthings.[5] Such an account is to be found in Aristotle's *Metaphysics*. Aristotle's remarks on the Pythagoreans in *Met* A 5 are intricate and obscure; but three generalities can be essayed with some confidence. First, the Pythagorean views that Aristotle reports belong as a whole to the fifth century.[6] Second, Aristotle is not reporting a single philosophy, but several variations on the broad Pythagorean theme. Third, some of Aristotle's account bears a resemblance to the views expressed in the Philolaic texts.

Aristotle does not name Philolaus in *Met* A 5. Sceptical scholars think that the fragments are part of a post-Aristotelian production designed to repair and defend the Pythagorean philosophy which Aristotle has mauled; others think that the fragments are the wreckage of Aristotle's main source for Pythagorean doctrine.[7] I do not accept the former view, and I think that there are sufficient differences between the fragments and Aristotle's account to rule the latter out of court. For what it is worth, I imagine that Aristotle is reporting the major orthodoxies of Pythagorean thought, and that Philolaus represents a heterodoxy: his heresy was, I suppose, deemed too slight by Aristotle to warrant special treatment. The matter lies beyond our knowledge; but it seems clear that we cannot justly interpret Philolaus' texts by way of Aristotle's reports. (And I shall spare the reader the profound *ennui* which an extended treatment of those reports would surely induce.)

The foundation and the distinguishing mark of the Pythagorean philosophy is number: according to Sextus

> The Pythagoreans say that reasoning [is the criterion of truth]—not reasoning in general but that which comes about from mathematics, as Philolaus said (**267: A 29**).

Plutarch says that in Philolaus' view

> Geometry is the principle and mother-state (*mêtropolis*) of the other disciplines (*mathêmatôn*) (**268: A 7a**).[8]

An old *acousma* runs: 'What is wisest?—Number'; and the primacy of number is a striking feature of Aristotle's account of Pythagorean-ism (e.g. *Met* 985b23 = **58 B 4**; 986a15 = **58 B 5**). In the case of Philolaus himself, **B 4** (= **280**) illustrates the same thesis; and Archytas, the leading Pythagorean of the generation after Philolaus, wrote this:

The mathematicians seem to me to have attained a fine knowledge, and it is not absurd that they should think aright about each of the things that are; for, having a fine knowledge about the nature of everything, they were likely to have a fine discernment too about the particular things that there are (**269: 47 B 1**).

The question of Pythagorean mathematics is a notorious thing. Once upon a time, scholars gave the Pythagoreans most of the credit for the astonishing advances in mathematics made in Greece during the fifth century. Now a contrary scepticism is fashionable; and most, I guess, will assent to the judgment that 'in its essence, mathematics is not Pythagorean but Greek'.[9] Hippasus of Metapontum did not discover the irrationals; Pythagoras' theorem is not Pythagorean; and there was no great Pythagorean mathematician before Archytas of Tarentum.[10]

It is hard to dissent from that negative opinion; but it would be an error to infer from it that the Pythagoreans were not mathematically inclined. Aristotle's testimony is explicit:

At the same time as these men [sc. the Atomists] and before them, those called the Pythagoreans touched on mathematics and were the first to bring them forward; and being brought up in them, they thought that their principles were the principles of everything (**270**: *Met* 985b23–5 = **58 B 4**).

The Pythagoreans, having devoted themselves to mathematics, and admiring the rigour of its arguments, because it alone of the studies men undertake contains proofs, and seeing it agreed that the facts of harmonics are due to numbers, thought that these and their principles were in general the causes of existent things (**271**).[11]

Aristotle's testimony is backed by Eudemus, who ascribes a few of the theorems contained in our Euclid to the Pythagoreans (cf. **58 B 18, 20, 21**). In the case of Philolaus we have a general notice that he was well-versed in the mathematical sciences (Vitruvius, **44 A 6**), and detailed evidence of his work in harmonics (**B 6**; Boëthius, **A 26**). Philolaus' mathematical abilities were not, perhaps, great: a recent scholar accuses him of 'mathematical inconsistencies' and 'gross errors';[12] and we may well imagine that the Pythagoreans, as a group, were students rather than professors of the mathematical arts.

In any case, it is not for their technical but for their philosophical contribution to mathematics that the Pythagoreans win our interest.

Aristotle (270) puts it very clearly: the Pythagoreans only 'touched on (*hapsamenoi*)' mathematics, in the technical sense; but they 'were the first to bring them forward (*proêgagon*)' in a philosophical context.[13]

What philosophical use did the Pythagoreans make of mathematics? The cynical will speak dismissively of number mysticism, arithmology, and other puerilities. And it is undeniable that a great quantity of Pythagorean 'number philosophy' is a 'number symbolism' of the most jejune and inane kind. According to Aristotle, the Pythagoreans 'say that things themselves are numbers' (*Met* 987b28 = **58 B 13**), or that 'existent things are by imitation of numbers' (*Met* 987b11 = **58 B 12**);[14] elsewhere he particularizes:

> The Pythagoreans, because they saw many of the attributes of numbers belonging to sensible things, assumed existing things to be numbers (**272**: *Met* 1090a20–22);

thus:

> Such and such an attribute of numbers is justice, such and such soul and mind, another opportunity, and so on for everything else (**273**: *Met* 985b29–31 = **58 B 4**).

Alexander says that justice was 4, marriage 5, opportunity 7 (*in Met* 38.8–20); comparable assertions are attested for Philolaus;[15] and his younger contemporaries, Lysis and Opsimus, are said to have proclaimed that God is an irrational number (Athenagoras, **46 A 4**).[16]

The Pythagoreans swore by the *tetraktus*. This was a graphic representation of the number 10:

```
        ●
      ●   ●
    ●   ●   ●
  ●   ●   ●   ●
```

And it exhibited in a vivid fashion some of the qualities of that number; for 'the number 10 seems to be perfect and to embrace the whole nature of number' (*Met* 986a8 = **58 B 4**).[17] 'Touching on' arithmetic, the Pythagoreans were impressed by certain properties of the number 10; alas, their impression degenerated into a sort of mysticism: amazement, the nurse of philosophy, soon has her milk soured and turns into silly reverence and superstition. Those with a taste for intellectual folly will have their appetite sated if they go through the *Theologoumena Arithmeticae*. That Pythagorean work is a late compilation; the earliest examples of such symbolism are found in the *acousmata* and probably date from the time of Pythagoras himself from first to last the Pythagoreans engaged in arithmology.

The mumbo-jumbo would not bear exposition but for the fact that certain Pythagoreans attempted to place a rational foundation beneath it.

They believed that the elements of numbers are the elements of everything that exists (**274**: *Met* 986a1–2 = **58 B 4**).

Aristotle's short statement can be illustrated from the *Pythagorean Memoirs* preserved by Alexander Polyhistor:

> The principle of all things is a monad, and from the monad comes an indefinite dyad, to play matter to the monad's cause; and from the monad and the indefinite dyad come the numbers; and from the numbers the points; and from these the lines, from which come the plane figures; and from the planes come the solid figures, and from these the perceptible bodies. (**275**: Diogenes Laertius, VIII.25 = **58 B 1a**).

Alexander's account is influenced by Plato; but it is reasonable to believe that the Platonizing version is based on an earlier theory. Aristotle points to some such theory, and I assume that the fifth-century Pythagoreans did, in some sense, 'generate' the sensible world from the principles of number.[18] And that 'generation' would license or explain the crude assertions of arithmology: if horses, say, are ultimately 'generated' from the principles of numbers, then in an intelligible sense horses *are* numbers.

The 'generation' of things from the principles of numbers may, I fear, seem no less absurd than the primitive number symbolism I have just dismissed: how can men 'come from' numbers? How can abstract principles give birth to solid stuffs? If the 'generation' is construed literally, as a sort of cosmogony, then it surely is absurd; yet cosmogony is easily confused with analysis (witness Plato's *Timaeus*); and if we listen to the 'generation' system as a faltering attempt to play an analytical tune, unhappily transposed into the cosmogonical key, then we may hear something of modest interest.

The generation system becomes an abstract ontology. The thesis of this ontology is simple: the only ultimate entities in the world are the 'principles of number'. The ontology relies on three reductive analyses. First, the numbers can be reduced to a few basic principles. This rudely anticipates the insights of Leibniz and Peano: the number system can be built up from the unit (or monad) and the successor-operator (or 'indefinite dyad'). The ontology of arithmetic is reduced to a minimum. Second, geometry is arithmetized: the truths of geometry can be expressed in purely arithmetical terms; and geometrical objects can be constructed from numbers. That claim, I suppose, adumbrates the Cartesian discovery of analytic geometry. Finally, physical objects are reduced to geometry. There are two ways of effecting the reduction: first, each object has a characteristic shape; it is determined by, and can thus be identified with, some three-dimensional solid; second, the elemental stuffs which constitute the physical world are atomically structured, and their atoms have a characteristic stereometrical configuration. The former reduction will occupy us again; the latter is familiar from the *Timaeus*.

All truths of science are ultimately truths of arithmetic; all scientific entities are ultimately arithmetical. The generation system points to an ontological desert that is clean and arid even by the obsessively puritanical standards of American pragmatism; and at the same time it holds out the heady prospect of a rigorously mathematical approach to every branch of science. Yet if the Pythagorean ontology is stimulating, it is also wholly vague and programmatic; and I sympathize with the reader who remains unimpressed.

(b) *The philosophy of Philolaus*

Philolaus' book came to possess the traditional Ionian title *Concerning Nature*. And it seems probable that its contents followed the old Ionian models: we know that it elaborated an astronomy, a biology and an embryology (Menon, **44 A 28**; cf. **B 13**), and a psychology; and it is a plausible guess that it covered most of the traditional topics of the *phusiologoi*.

In a later chapter, I shall say something of Philolaus' psychology; here I may briefly describe his revolutionary astronomy. For Philolaus was the first thinker who dared displace the earth from its central position in the universe, and to suggest that, contrary to appearances, the earth was not stationary (Aëtius, **A 21**). In the Philolaic system, the centre of the cosmos was occupied by a mass of fire; around the fire circled the sun, the spherical earth, the moon, the planets, and that celebrated invention of Pythagorean astronomy, the *antichthôn* or counter-earth (cf. Aristotle, *Cael*, 293a17–27 = **58 B 37**; Aëtius, **44 A 16**). The system contained a few grotesqueries. (The moon is inhabited, like the earth; and lunar creatures 'are fifteen times as powerful [as their terrestrial counterparts], and do not excrete' (Aëtius, **A 20**).[19]) Some judge it harshly: it was not 'a scientific astronomy' but 'a *mélange* of myth and *phusiologia*'; it was 'a superficial conglomeration of heterogeneous elements and naive speculation, not an attempt to find a deeper penetrating explanation of the phenomena'.[20] Those judgments are unfair: the fact is that we do not know what considerations led Philolaus to propound his startling innovations; and without such knowledge we cannot pass judgment. Astronomically, of course, the Philolaic system is inadequate; but so are all the admirable astronomical systems of antiquity.

However that may be, Philolaus' views did not catch on. In the fourth century, Hicetas of Syracuse allowed the earth to move (Theophrastus, *apud* Cicero, **50 A 1**); but Hicetas' system was geocentric.[21] It was not till Aristarchus that the earth was again pushed from the centre of things; and since Aristarchus customarily wins credit for his heliocentric innovation, it is only decent to remember that the innovation was not an entirely unprecedented intellectual accomplishment.

If the superstructure of Philolaus' account of the world was Ionian in tenor, its foundations were characteristically Pythagorean.[22] The marriage of these two traditions (if I may change metaphors) was bound to produce curious offspring: how the consummation was effected must be discovered from the first six fragments of Philolaus' work.

Like the other neo-Ionians, Philolaus began by confronting the Eleatic challenge; and his starting point was, in one respect, even closer to Elea than theirs. For, like Parmenides, Philolaus approached metaphysics from epistemology: Parmenides' initial question was: What conditions must any object of scientific inquiry satisfy? Philolaus began by asking what things must be like if they are to be known; and the connexion between being and knowledge remains prominent in the development of his ideas.

According to Diogenes, Philolaus' treatise opened thus:

Nature in the universe[23] was harmonized from both unlimited and limiting things—both the universe as a whole and everything in it (**276: B 1**).

That initial statement was backed up by argument. It will be convenient to begin with **B 6**, which reads thus:

And about nature and harmony things stand thus:—[i] The being (*estô*) of the objects, being eternal, and nature itself, admit divine and not human knowledge—[ii] except that none of the things that exist and are known by us could have come into being if there did not subsist (*huparchousas*) the being of the objects out of

82

which the universe is compounded, both of the limiting things and of the unlimited. [iii] And since the principles subsisted being neither similar nor of the same tribe, it would have been thereby impossible for them to be arranged into a universe (*kosmêthênai*) if a harmony had not supervened, in whatever fashion it did come about. [iv] Now things that were similar and of the same tribe had no need of harmony; but those that were dissimilar and not of the same tribe and not of the same order (?)—it was necessary for such things to have been locked together by harmony if they were to be held together in a universe (277).[24]

The text of 277 is in several places uncertain; and interpretation is always hard. I shall deal with sentences [iii] and [iv] later on; sentence [i] is a conventionally sceptical or pious exordium (see vol. 1, p. 137): it is sentence [ii] which engages immediate attention.

The curious phrase 'the being of the objects (*ha estô tôn pragmatôn*)' must, I suppose, mean something like 'the existents *par excellence*'; at all events the phrase clearly denotes the same thing as 'the principles (*hai archai*)' of sentence [iii]. Of these principles we can know very little: first, that they are 'eternal'; second, that they consist of limiters and unlimiteds; third, that they require, in some cases at least, a harmonizing force. Why our knowledge is thus restricted Philolaus does not say: he implicitly rejects all Presocratic attempts to say what stuff or stuffs are primary, but he does so without argument. Perhaps he means only that a complete, and hence humanly impossible, knowledge of the present world would be required if we were to grasp just what types of principle were needed to generate it.

The eternity of the principles is presumably the *probandum* of sentence [ii]: 'the being of the objects subsists (*huparchein*)' means 'the principles are eternal'. The nerve of Philolaus' argument is constituted by two propositions:

(1) If a exists and is known to us, then a came into being.

(2) If a came into being, then the principles of a are eternal.

That (1) and (2) have an Eleatic background is plain enough; how precisely they relate to that background is a harder question to answer.

I take it that (1) is meant as an empirical observation: entities in the familiar world about us do, as a matter of fact, all have origins, near or remote. The epistemological *motif* which some have seen in (1) is only apparent: Philolaus does not mean that our knowing something requires that it be generated; he means only that the ordinary things that we do know are in fact generated.[25]

Epistemology proper does not enter until **B 2** and **B 3**.

Premiss (2), on the other hand, fits easily into the box of neo-Ionian answers to Elea: things cannot come into being *simpliciter*, Philolaus avers, but they may spring from eternal, ungenerable and incorruptible, principles. The roots of Empedocles, the 'things' of Anaxagoras, and the atoms of Leucippus and Democritus are all eternal; and their eternity is generally regarded as a concession to Elea. Philolaus, in (2), makes an analogous concession; how useful these concessions are will be discussed in a later chapter.

Thus far nothing of a peculiarly Pythagorean character has emerged from **277**: it is the reference to 'limiters' and 'unlimited' things that gives the fragment its characteristic flavour; I shall approach this by way of **B 3** and **B 2**:

> For there will not even be anything that will be known if all things are unlimited (**278: B 3**).

> [v] It is necessary for the things that exist to be all either limiting or unlimited or both limiting and unlimited. [vi] But they could not be only unlimited [or only limiting]. [vii] Since, then, the things that exist are evidently neither from things all of which are limiting nor from things all of which are unlimited, it is clear then that both the universe and the things in it were harmonized from both limiting and unlimited things. [viii] And the facts too make this clear; for some of them, coming from limiting things, limit; and others, coming from both limiting and unlimited things, both limit and do not limit; and others, coming from unlimited things, are evidently unlimited (**279: B 2**).

The logical form of Philolaus' argument is fairly clear. Let P abbreviate 'All existing things are limiting', Q 'All existing things are unlimited', R 'All existing things are both limiting and unlimited'. Then [v] asserts:

(3) P or Q or R.

[vi] asserts:

(4) not-P and not-Q.

and [vii], inferring R, makes the further deduction that:

(5) Existing things were harmonized from both limiting and unlimited things.

Why does Philolaus expect us to assent to this curious argument? Premiss (3) is, I suppose, meant as an exhaustive disjunction, a logical truth. It is natural to read R as 'everything is both limiting and unlimited'; but that is ruled out by sentence [viii], which plainly places among 'the facts' the existence of some unlimited limiters and of some unlimiting unlimiteds. Hence if 279 is to be consistent, *R* must be read as: 'Some things are limiting and others are unlimited'. The reading is confirmed by the fact that it makes (3) a logical truth: the disjuncts are indeed logically exhaustive.

278, I take it, argues for not-*Q*: if we know anything, then not-*Q*; and we do have knowledge. The truth of 278 cannot be assessed until we have come closer to grips with the notion of a 'limit'. The first conjunct of (4), not-*P*, is a conjectural addition to the text; but not-*P* is plainly necessary to Philolaus' argument. No argument for not-*P* survives, but one is readily invented: surely if *a* is limiting, then *a* limits something; limiters logically require limitees. And again surely limitees are themselves intrinsically unlimited; if *a* limits *b*, then *b* is *per se* unlimited. But in that case the argument in 278 only needs a slight prolongment to prove not-*P* as well as not-*Q*.

The conclusion (5) is familiar from 276 and 277; and it is the kernel of Philolaus' ontology. The thought that carries Philolaus from *R* to (5) is simple: what is itself a limiter cannot be compounded purely from unlimited things; no conjunction of unlimiteds will produce a limit. And conversely, what is unlimited requires unlimited constituents: a set of limiters will never give the unlimited its constitutional freedom. Thus (3) is a turth of logic; epistemology guarantees (4); (3) and (4) yield *R* by elementary logic; and *R* produces (5).[26]

(c) *Shape and number*

The 'facts'[27] alluded to in sentence [viii] are intended to convince us of the truth of (5): their form is logically appropriate but their content is obscure. Indeed, I fear that the fastidious reader will long ago have given up Philolaus in distaste: perhaps 279 contains a formally clear argument; but its substance is certainly misty and probably mystical. If that natural and entirely commendable feeling is to be dispelled we must discover what Philolaus has in mind when he talks of 'limiters' and 'unlimiteds'.

The fragments give no elucidation and no concrete illustration of 'limiters' and 'unlimiteds'; and the slim doxography is helplessly silent. Some scholars point to a notorious passage in Plato's *Philebus* which speaks of limits and the unlimited;[28] but that dialogue's gross obscurities give no help to a mind puzzling over Philolaus. Others read infinite divisibility into the 'unlimited' and speak of limiting atoms; but that will hardly fit the text. We are reduced to conjecture; but conjecture is not difficult, for an obvious interpretation is to hand: to apply a limiter to an unlimited is to give specific shape or form to a mass of unformed stuff. The 'facts' appealed to in [viii] will then consist of elementary examples of that type of operation: a potter moulds a wedge of clay into a pot; a sculptor casts a mass of bronze into a statue; a baker pats his dough into a loaf; a carpenter shapes a table from rough timber: all these artists apply a shape to a stuff, a limiter to an unlimited. Shapes are essentially limiting: anything shaped in such and such a way has, *eo ipso*, limits beyond which it does not extend; it is determined and circumscribed by its shapely boundaries. Stuffs, on the contrary, are essentially unlimited; clay and bronze, dough and wood, have no shapes. Any particular parcel of clay does, of course, possess some shape, however irregular or unaesthetic; but clay as such has no shape: 'What shape is clay?' is a nonsense question.

If we look at 'the facts', we find an abundance of cases in which things 'come from both limiting and unlimited things'; and they 'both limit and do not limit', i.e., they are compounds of a limiting shape and an unlimited stuff. But the 'facts' are also supposed to give us examples of compounds made exclusively from limiters, and of compounds made exclusively from unlimiteds. The former set of examples must, I imagine, be geometrical: a geometer may construct a square by conjoining two triangles, or a cube by adding two pyramids. Here two limiters are put together, and the result is a limiter; two shapes, conjoined, yield a third shape. Unlimiteds, too, are compounded: a metalworker may pour copper and tin together to make bronze; a cook mixes oil and vinegar; a painter blends one pigment with another. Such familiar operations are compoundings of one stuff from other stuffs, of one unlimited from other unlimiteds.

That interpretation seems to me to fit the Philolaic texts better than any other; and it gives Philolaus an original and important role in the development of philosophy.[29] The early Ionians, as Aristotle rightly insists, concentrated their attention on 'the material cause'; they inquired into the stuff of the universe, and supposed that one or two fairly simple operations on that *Ur*-stuff would suffice to generate our well-formed world. Empedocles and Anaxagoras also focussed their minds on matter: it was the diversity of stuffs rather than the diversity of substances which drew their attention and which they aspired to vindicate in the face of Eleatic objections. Atomism, it is true, pays some attention to form: the atoms have shapes, and are indeed referred to as *schemata* or *ideai*; but there is no evidence that the Atomists placed any particular stress on the diversity of forms in the world, or that they went out of their way to account for the shape as well as the stuff of things.

Philolaus stands in strong contrast to that long tradition: he recognizes stuffs, but he insists equally on shapes. His fundamental tenet, expressed at the outset of his book in 276, is that both matter and form are required in any analysis or explanation of the phenomena; we have to account not only for the diverse materials present in the mundane world, but also for the diverse ways in which those materials present themselves to us: we live in a material world, but the material is informed. And that, after all, is the essence of Aristotle's judgment on the Pythagorean contribution to natural philosophy: they 'began to talk about what a thing is, and to make definitions' (*Met* 987a20 = **58 B 8**); in other words, they began to investigate form as well as matter.

'But', Aristotle continues, 'they treated the issue too simply.' To see how Philolaus treated the issue we must look at two further fragments:

> And indeed all the things that are known have a number; for it is not possible for anything to be thought of or to be known without this (**280: B 4**).[30]

> Number indeed has two proper kinds, odd and even [and a third from both mixed together, even-odd];[31] and of each kind there are many forms (*morphai*) which each thing in itself signifies (**281: B 5**).

These two fragments stand in an intelligible relationship to **279**. The two 'kinds' of number are the odd and the even; and a strong tradition connects limit with odd numbers and unlimitedness with even numbers: in the *Metaphysics* Aristotle briefly delineates two Pythagorean views:

> These evidently believe that number is a principle . . . and that the elements of number are the even and the odd, and of these one is unlimited, the other limited; and the unit is from both these (for it is both even and odd). . . . Others of the same group say that there are ten principles, set out in a column:
> limit and unlimited
> odd and even
> one and plurality
> right and left
> male and female
> resting and moving
> straight and bent
> light and darkness

good and bad
square and oblong
(**282**: 986a15–26 = **58 B 5**; cf. Aristotle, fr. 203).

There is much in that column of 'principles' to excite the curiosity. Here I observe simply that odd associates with limit, even with lack of limit. (And there are explanations, of a vaguely arithmetical sort, for those associations.[32])

It is easy to suppose that Philolaus, who has limiting and unlimited principles, and who refers to the two 'kinds' of number, made the same association between the members of these two pairs: Philolaic limiters are odd numbers; Philolaic unlimiteds are even numbers. I do not believe the interpretation. The main argument against it is that it does not, as far as I can see, lead to any clear overall understanding of Philolaus' theory of principles, whereas the alternative interpretation which I shall shortly offer gives Philolaus a fairly coherent philosophy. Two small points tell in the same direction: first, **280** suggests that 'having a number' is a sufficient condition for knowability; but if even numbers characterize the unlimiteds, then the unlimiteds too will be knowable—*contra* **278**. Second, the numbers, both odd and even, are said to be 'forms (*morphai*)'; that surely connects having a number with having a shape; but 'the unlimiteds' have no shape. I conclude that Philolaus differs from those Pythagoreans who assimilated odd and even to limited and unlimited. (That, indeed, is my chief reason for doubting that Philolaus was a main source for Aristotle's account of fifth-century Pythagoreanism.)

The 'forms' of **281** are presumably the natural numbers themselves: 2,4,6 . . . are the forms of the kind *even*; 1,3,5 . . . are the forms of the kind *odd*. 'Each thing in itself signifies' one of the natural numbers in that each thing is essentially determined by a natural number: what is known must have or be a limit or form; forms are expressed by numbers; hence whatever is known 'has a number'.

An explicit account of this sort of thing is ascribed to Eurytus, a pupil of Philolaus (cf. Iamblichus, **45 A 1**). Archytas told how Eurytus 'used to set out some pebbles, and say that *this* is the number of man, *this* of horse, *this* of something else' (Theophrastus, *Metaphysics* 6a19 = **45 A 2**). Aristotle refers to the same practice (*Met* 1092b8 = **45 A 3**), and a commentator explains it at length:

Suppose for the sake of argument that the number 250 is the definition of man, and 360 of plant. Positing this, he used to take

250 pebbles—some green, some black, some red, and in general coloured in all sorts of hues; then, smearing the wall with plaster and sketching a man and a plant, he would stick these pebbles on the drawing of the face, these on that of the hands, others elsewhere, and he would complete the drawing of the pictured man by means of pebbles equal in number to the units which he said defined man (**283**: pseudo-Alexander, **45 A 3**).[33]

That sounds intolerably puerile; and puerile it doubtless was. Yet it is not quite as frivolous as it is sometimes imagined to be: Eurytus was not just 'drawing pictures with pebbles'; nor did his pebbles represent physical—or atomic—constituents of man.

Rather, he must have started from a geometrical observation: three points, however disposed, determine a triangle; and any triangle is determined by three points; four points determine a quadrilateral, and any quadrilateral is determined by four points. In general, then, geometrical and stereometrical figures will be determined by natural numbers; and since men and plants are stereometrical figures, they too will have their defining numbers. Eurytus' task was to work out 'the minimum number of points necessary to ensure that the surfaces formed by joining them would represent a man and nothing else';[34] and his pebble-dashing provided a striking if crude analogy to that grand scientific task. Philolaus, I assume, anticipated Eurytus; and in **278** and **279** we have the theoretical statement of the view which Eurytus' pebbles illustrate.

Is all this mere comical arithmology? or is it the first scrabbling essay towards a quantitative and mathematically-based science? Surely it is both of those things. Scientific theorems must be mathematical in their expression if they are to have the precision and utility we require of scientific knowledge: the early Milesian theories were largely unquantitative (vol. 1, p. 48), and their neo-Ionian successors seem to have done little better in that respect; even the Atomists made no attempt to apply arithmetic or geometry to scientific knowledge. Philolaus and Eurytus saw their failing, and attempted to meet it: the shapes of things are essential to them (we recognize things by virtue of their shapes); shapes can be expressed arithmetically; and the consequent arithmetical definitions of substances may be expected to function as the foundations of a mathematical physics.

In aim and scope the Philolaic project is admirable; in practice it is, inevitably, jejune. Shapes are not determined by natural numbers in the way Philolaus apparently imagined: does 4 determine a quadrilateral or a tetrahedron? does 8 determine an octagon or a hexahedron? Natural numbers alone will not do: if geometry is to be 'reduced' to arithmetic, the reduction must be carried out by more sophisticated means. Again, however important shapes may be in our recognition of substances, it is plain that they do not constitute the essence of substances. A poodle is not simply a mass of stuff formed in such and such a shape; it is a thing with certain powers and dispositions; decoy ducks and waxwork men, however cleverly modelled, are not ducks and men. Conversely, it is hard to imagine that there is *a* shape of man, let alone of dog or of plant: men come in different shapes and sizes; species of dog differ considerably in outline; and any attempt to distinguish the shape of a plant would be laughable.

Finally, stuffs have no shape—they are essentially unlimited; yet we surely do have knowledge of stuffs. Philolaus' fundamental assumption that 'there is no knowledge of the unlimited' seems to be a baseless prejudice; and it is implicitly contradicted by the third type of 'fact' to which the end of 277 appeals. No doubt genuine knowledge of stuffs must be in some sense quantitative: we do not have genuine knowledge if we only 'know' that tin and copper alloy to bronze; we need to know that a mixture of n per cent tin and m per cent copper yields bronze. But even if knowledge is thus connected with quantity and number, there is no connexion with shape or form, and we are left, it seems, with knowledge of 'the unlimited'. Some may feel that this point is at once so evident and so strong that it rules out my whole interpretation of Philolaus' philosophy. That feeling engages my sympathy; yet I still incline to accept the interpretation, and its consequent inconcinnity: no alternative fares any better, and Philolaus, I fear, is not wholly consistent or clear-minded.

(d) *The harmony of things*

Limiters and unlimiteds do not exhaust Philolaus' conceptual resources: these principles, by themselves, would not have sufficed for a universe 'if a harmony had not supervened, in whatever fashion it did come about' (277); and the 'harmonizing' of the principles is adverted to again in 276, 279 and B 7.

'Harmony' translates—or rather transliterates—'*harmonia*'; and the word, familiar to us from Heraclitus (vol. 1, p. 318, n. 13), may mean no more than a conjoining or fitting together. It is thus tempting to read no more than a tautology into sentence [iii] of 277: if there were no *harmonia*, then, quite trivially, limiters and unlimiteds could not have been fitted together. But sentence [iv] makes it plain that Philolaus meant more than that: *harmonia* is required not for any compounding, but for the compounding of things that are dissimilar or 'not of the same tribe'.

The dissimilar things are limiters and unlimiteds: why should conjunctions of limiter and unlimited require a *harmonia* when conjunctions of limiter and limiter, or of unlimited and unlimited, do not? Any two limiters may be fitted together: limiters are shapes, shapes are numbers, and any two numbers can be added together. What is more, their compound is eternally stable: the truths of arithmetic are indestructible. Again, most stuffs can be mixed or amalgamated into a moderately stable compound; such, at least, was the implicit assumption of all the Presocratic cosmogonies, and if a few trite examples tell against it (oil and vinegar proverbially separate), then either Philolaus ignored them or he supposed that they are not 'of the same tribe' even though they are 'similar': similar *qua* unlimited, they do not belong to the same kind of unlimiteds.

On the other hand, it is a clear empirical fact that not every shape can be fitted to every stuff: you may fashion a sphere of wood or metal, but you will not impose a spherical form on water or fire; the characteristic form of flames cannot, or cannot easily, be matched in wood; sand will form dunes but not pinnacles; mercury, globules but not cubes. Of the innumerable matchings of form and stuff that are possible, few are actual; and therefore some explanation is required for those matchings that do occur. In short, there must be a harmony between certain shapes and certain stuffs which accounts for their felicitous association. To say that there is a harmony is not to offer an explanation; it is to point out the need for an explanation. Just as the terms 'limiter' and 'unlimited' are schematic designations of types of principle, so the term 'harmony' is a schematic designation for a type of explanation: we cannot know what the essential nature of limiters and unlimiteds is; nor can we know how, in concrete terms, shape and matter cohere. What we do know is, first, that there must be both shape and matter; and second, that there must be an explanatory harmony of their conjunction.

Harmonia is not a static thing: it is introduced in a dynamic cosmogonical context. Nature 'was harmonized (*harmochthê*)' (276); the universe 'was compounded (*sunesta*)' (277); things were 'arranged into a universe (*kosmêthênai*)' (277); 'everything comes about (*gignesthai*) by necessity and harmony' (Diogenes Laertius, VIII.84 = **A 1**). Two fragments of the cosmogony survive. One says merely that:

The first thing to be harmonized in the middle of the sphere is called the hearth (**284: B 7**).[35]

The other is longer; I quote it for its interesting attempt to deal with the notions of 'up' and 'down':

> The universe is one, and it began to come into being at the middle, and from the middle upwards in the same way as downwards. And what is upward is over against the middle from the point of view of those below; for to those below the lowest part is like the uppermost part, and similarly for the rest. For both have the same relationship to the middle except that their positions are reversed (**285: B 17**).[36]

This fragment coheres well enough with the Philolaic astronomy, and it might easily come from a cosmogony in the traditional Ionian style; but the fact is that we know almost nothing of Philolaus' cosmogonical speculations.

A naive interpretation of Philolaus would imagine a pre-cosmic state of things in which on the one side there rose a vast mass of completely shapeless stuffs, and on the other side there stood a tailor's shop of forms: at the cosmogonic moment, something caused a suit to be taken from the shop and fitted harmoniously to the first fortunate lump of clay; and cosmogony proceeded, in orderly fashion, in the same general way, pre-existing forms being successively wrapped around suitable lumps of pre-existing stuff.

Aristotle makes two criticisms of the Pythagoreans which seem to tell against Philolaus even if they were not expressly aimed at him. First, he says that:

> They did not think that the limited and the unlimited and the one are different natures—e.g., fire or earth or something else of that sort, but that the unlimited itself and the one itself are the substance (*ousia*) of the things they are predicated of; and for that reason number is the substance of everything (**286:** *Met* 987a15–9 = **58 B 8**).

Second, he says that:

> These men evidently think that number is the principle for existing things both as matter and as affections and properties (**287:** *Met* 986a15–17 = **58 B 5**).

Does not Philolaus in his cosmogony treat limiters, and hence numbers, as physical components of things? And does he not also treat the unlimiteds and the limiters as substances rather than attributes?

One part at least of the Aristotelian criticism does not touch Philolaus: he does not deny that the limiters and the unlimiteds are 'different natures'; that is to say, he does not assert that there are things which are *simply* unlimited and not unlimited fire or water or whatever. He does not imagine that the phrase 'the unlimited' picks out some peculiarly abstract kind of stuff; rather, he means that the original principles, whatever they are, are some of them limiters and some of them unlimited.[37]

The core of Aristotle's criticism, however, remains. Philolaus plainly holds, first, that limiters and unlimiteds are eternal, and second, that their cosmogonic harmonizing was an historical, or pre-historical, event. It follows that at some time there existed limiters or shapes that limited nothing or were shapes of nothing; and also that there existed shapeless, unlimited, masses of stuff. Moreover, the claim that the universe was 'compounded' from limiters and unlimiteds does powerfully suggest a picture in which the formal element in the compound is treated 'as matter'.

Some sort of a defence can be found for Philolaus: his shapes or limiters are, after all, essentially numbers; and the 'Platonist' view that numbers are eternal substances is not to be abandoned merely on Aristotle's ukase. There are deep waters here on which Philolaus may, for a time at least, contrive to float. Again, Philolaus' pre-cosmic masses need not, perhaps, be literally devoid of form: Philolaus might have contented himself with the suggestion that the pre-cosmic form of stuffs was 'form' only in an etiolated sense—shape, but not intelligible shape, not mathematically determinable shape. Cosmogony, thus conceived, is the imposition of intelligible form on unintelligible matter. And finally, the crude conception of form as a quasi-constituent, and of information as a quasi-material colligation, can be purified or replaced by an unobjectionable notion.

I do not intend to follow up those vague suggestions: to do so would impose an anachronistic syncretism on Philolaus, uniting a Platonic account of mathematics with an Aristotelian position on form and matter. I prefer to end by underlining Philolaus' essential mistake. Rightly observing that a bronze sphere could be analysed into form (sphericity) and matter (bronze), Philolaus wrongly conflated that sort of analysis with the analysis of bronze into copper and tin. Bronze is compounded or put together from copper and tin; in much the same way, he supposed, a bronze sphere is compounded or put together from bronze and sphericity. In the latter case, to be sure, the components are 'dissimilar and not of the same tribe'; but the notion of compounding is the same in the two cases.

But the analyses and the compoundings are quite different: a chemical or physical analysis shows that bronze is made of tin and

93

copper; a logical or conceptual analysis shows that a bronze sphere is made of sphericity and bronze. The former analysis, in Aristotelian jargon, breaks a thing down into its real parts, the latter into its logical parts: no physical process will separate the bronze from sphericity, and no logical penetration will reveal the chemical components of bronze. The distinction is not easy to articulate or expound; and the difficulties are increased by the fact that the same language is customarily used for both notions. Aristotle's commentators regularly fell into the confusion I am ascribing to Philolaus; and Aristotle himself only avoided it by the skin of his logical teeth.

Was Philolaus a great wit, or a ninny? We do not possess a vast amount of evidence, and the evidence we do have is of contested value. Certainly there are naive elements in Philolaus' thought; but equally certainly there are elements of bold originality, both in speculative science and in philosophy. I for one am prepared to credit Philolaus with the discovery of Aristotelian 'form'; and to claim that such a discovery was no insignificant achievement.

V

The Logic of Locomotion

(a) *Empedocles and antiperistasis*

The neo-Ionian defence of science against Eleatic metaphysics rests at bottom on their vindication of locomotion: if things can move, science is possible; if locomotion is impossible, science falls with it. All three Eleatics argued against locomotion: Parmenides in **156. 26–33**, Melissus in **168**, Zeno by way of his four or five paradoxes. The neo-Ionian defence takes on only Melissus: Parmenides' obscure lines are justifiably ignored; and nothing is said against Zeno. I have no explanation of the latter omission: perhaps the paradoxes were unknown to the neo-Ionians; perhaps they were despised as sophisms or set aside as insoluble problems. With an adequate chronology some of that puzzlement might evaporate; but we have no adequate chronology (above, pp. 3–5). At best, then, the neo-Ionians will achieve a partial success: however powerful their arguments in Melissan country, they have still to fight on Zeno's territory.

We have considerable evidence for the Atomists' attitude to locomotion; we possess a few straws pointing to the position of Empedocles and of Anaxagoras; we know nothing of Philolaus. In this section I deal with Empedocles and Anaxagoras.

Empedocles 'says in general that there is no void' (Theophrastus, *Sens* §13 = **31 A 86**). Aristotle gives the same report (*Cael* 309a19 = **59 A 68**); and we have Empedocles' own word for it:

Nor is any part of the universe (*tou pantos*) empty, nor yet overfull (**288: B 13**).

It . . . is not empty, nor yet overfull (**289**).[1]

95

The clause 'nor yet overfull (*perisson*)' is not casual: an empty space would contain no body; an overfull space would contain more than one body. Melissus' argument against motion needs to deny both emptiness and overcrowding (vol. 1, p. 226); and Empedocles is perfectly aware of the fact.

According to Anaxagoras, too, 'nothing is empty' (Aristotle, *Resp* 471a2 = **59 A 115**); Aristotle repeats the assertion (*Cael* 309a19 = **A 68**), and it reappears in the *MXG* (976b20), in Lucretius (I.843 = **A 44**), and in Hippolytus (**A 42**). We have no first-hand evidence for the ascription, but the doxographical tradition is unanimous and indisputable. Anaxagoras, it is true, held that 'the dense and the rare' could be found in the world (**B 15**); and 'there are some who think it evident from the rare and the dense that there is void' (Aristotle, *Phys* 216b22). But the examples of Descartes and of Aristotle himself (*Phys* Δ 9) show that a philosopher may deny the existence of void and still assign different degrees of density to different stuffs; and that position is, I judge, logically consistent.

It is regularly supposed that both Empedocles and Anaxagoras offered empirical arguments to show that 'nothing is empty'. The source of the supposition is Aristotle:

> Those who attempt to prove that it [sc. the void] does not exist do not refute what men mean by void but only what they erroneously say; e.g., Anaxagoras and those who refute it in that fashion. For they show that the air is something, by twisting wineskins and proving that the air is strong, and by capturing it in clepsydras (**290**: *Phys* 213a22–7 = **59 A 68**).

We know that Anaxagoras talked about the clepsydra (pseudo-Aristotle, *Prob* 914b9 = **59 A 69**), and Aristotle (despite his plural 'they') may have Anaxagoras alone in mind in this passage. It is, however, regularly connected with a celebrated fragment of Empedocles (**31 B 100**). That fragment attempts to explain the phenomena of respiration by means of an elaborate analogy with the clepsydra, an ancient device for transmitting liquids from one vessel to another, similar in function and action to the modern chemist's pipette.[2] It is often alleged that the fragment describes an experiment, and that the experiment was designed to disprove the existence of empty space. I shall not try to elucidate **B 100**, which has aroused a busy hum of commentary. But it is, I think, perfectly plain that no 'experiment' is described in the fragment;[3] that if the fragment incidentally implies the corporeality of the air, it was certainly not meant to demonstrate it; and that the whole piece says nothing whatever about the void. Empedocles' clepsydra is a red herring: let us return to the *Physics*.

Air pressure forces liquid out of the pipette and holds liquid in it; the force or 'strength' of the air is tangible in an inflated balloon or a twisted wineskin. There is no reason to doubt that Anaxagoras made these observations, and that he used them to confirm the long familiar fact that air is corporeal. Quite evidently, such observations do not prove the non-existence of the void: some scholars infer that in the *Physics* Aristotle merely misrepresents the purpose of Anaxagoras' remarks.[4] But Aristotle cannot be dismissed so lightly; and we may readily connect Anaxagoras' observations to the void without ascribing any childish error to him. Partisans of the void will have tried to establish their case simply by pointing to the air; 'for the air seems to be empty' (Aristotle, *An* 419b34). Against such people, Anaxagoras' observations are pertinent: they do not show that there is no void, nor were they meant to; but they do refute a simple-minded argument for the existence of empty space.

Why, then, did Empedocles and Anaxagoras reject the void? I suppose that they adopted a Melissan argument.

There is no void. Melissus inferred the impossibility of motion; Empedocles and Anaxagoras believed in locomotion: how did they justify their defiant opinion?[5] Of Anaxagoras we know nothing. He allows that the world contains 'the dense' and 'the rare' (**59 B 15**); and he presumably had some answer to Melissus' assertion that 'the rare is thereby more empty than the dense' (**168**). But what answer he might have given I do not know; nor can I invent any connexion between degrees of density and locomotion.

Empedocles' fragments are equally silent; but in his case the doxography comes to our aid:

> Similarly Empedocles too says that the compounds are always moving continually for all time, but that nothing is empty; saying that 'of the whole nothing is empty: whence, then, might anything come?'; and when they are compounded into one form so as to be one, 'it', he says 'is not empty in any respect nor overfull'. For what prevents them from travelling and circulating (*peristasthai*) into one another, if at the same time one always changes into another and that into another and another into the first? (**291**: *MXG* 976b22–9 = **30 A 5**).

The doctrine ascribed to Empedocles in this passage is that of counter-circulation or *antiperistasis*:

Nature that hateth emptiness,
Allows of penetration less:
And therefore must make Room
Where greater Spirits come.

Abhorring emptiness and penetration alike (288), Empedoclean nature must 'make room' if it is to encompass locomotion. The *MXG*'s mode of expression implies, perhaps, that Empedocles did not make his doctrine fully explicit; but he did, I think, come fairly close to it:

Empedocles said . . . that all [the elements] take one another's places (*metalambanein*) (292: Aëtius, 31 A 35);

He says that they give way to each other (*antiparachôrein*) (293: Achilles, 31 A 35).

The doxographers rely ultimately on the Empedoclean phrase that occurs more than once in the fragments: the elements, he says, 'run through one another (*di' allêlôn . . . theonta*)' (B 17.34 = B 21.13 = B 26.3). In the context, it is entirely reasonable to take the repeated phrase as a first, imprecise, formulation of the theory of *antiperistasis*.[6]

What exactly was the theory? And how does it answer the Eleatic challenge? Melissus' argument against motion relied on the following principle (vol. 1, p. 219):

(1) If a moves to p at t, then immediately prior to t p is empty.

A mobile opponent will not grant (1). First, he might suggest that prior to t p is occupied by a body, b, which is compressible: at t a compresses b by the force of its trajectory and thus comes to occupy a region formerly occupied by a part of b. But that will not trouble Melissus, who has argued that no bodies are compressible: being 'full', bodies are not 'dense and rare'. The opponent turns to a second suggestion: up to t p is occupied by b, but at t, just as a enters p, b moves to a new position p_1.

Melissus will still remain unshaken: instead of (1) he will offer:

(2) If a moves to p at t, then immediately prior to t some place or other must be empty.

Admittedly, p may be occupied up to t; but its occupant, b, must move at t; and there must be some empty place or other for b to move into. Proposition (2) will do all the work Melissus required of (1); and it turns the opponent's second suggestion.

Yet why should a proponent of locomotion accept (2)? Motion, he will say, does not require *any* vacancies. Let b occupy p up to t: then a

may move to p at t provided that there are two series of bodies, c_1 . . . c_n and d_1 . . . d_m such that, first, the places occupied by a, b, each c_i and each d_i are all identical in shape and size, and, second, a is contiguous with c_1, c_1 with c_2, . . . c_{n-1} with c_n, c_n with b, b with d_1, d_1 with d_2, . . . d_{m-1} with d_m, and d_m with a. Then a may move to p at t, provided that each of the contiguous bodies moves, at the same time and the same speed, to fill its neighbour's position. Imagine a card circle, divided by two diameters into quarters labelled a, c, b, d. At t revolve the cricle through 180°; then a comes to occupy the place of b; and at no time is any part of the circle empty.

That is the theory of *antiperistasis*; and it is that by which Empedocles hoped to vindicate locomotion. The theory had an illustrious life: Plato formulated it clearly (*Timaeus* 80C); and Aristotle produces it as his own answer to the Melissan challenge: 'For it is possible for things to yield place to one another at the same time, even though there is no separable interval [i.e. no empty space] apart from the moving bodies. And this is clear in the case of whirls of continuous things, just as it is in the case of those of liquids' (*Phys* 214a29–32).[7] Aristotle illustrates *antiperistasis* by pointing to children's tops and water eddies; the best known illustration was first produced by Straton of Lampsacus, head of the Peripatetic school in the third century BC: 'Straton's example offers a more suitable escape from these difficulties; for if you put a pebble into a jar full of water and turn the jar upside down while holding the stopper over the mouth, the pebble will move to the mouth of the jar as the water moves around (*antimethistamenon*) into the place of the pebble' (fr. 63 W = Simplicius, *in Phys* 659.22–6).

Those modern thinkers who held that the universe is a *plenum* accepted the ancient theory of *antiperistasis*. Thus Descartes: 'The only possible movement of bodies is in a circle; a body pushes another out of the place it enters, and that another, till at last we come to a body that enters the place left by the first body at the very moment when the first body leaves it'.[8] I see no logical objection to *antiperistasis*. Russell once observed that 'it should . . . be obvious, even to the non-mathematical, that motion in a closed circuit is possible for a fluid. It is a pity that philosophers have allowed themselves to repeat [the argument that motion presupposes a vacuum], which a week's study of hydrodynamics would suffice to dispel'. It has been asserted that 'the plenum theory inevitably implies the existence of instantaneous physical actions, that is, of actions spreading in space with infinite velocity';[9] for the force transmitted, in my schematic example, from a to c_1 must pass in an instant about the 'circle' of bodies to b. But that is not so, as the case of the spinning top demonstrates; moreover, it does not seem to me to constitute a logical objection to *antiperistasis*. Melissus' principle (2) is not a logical truth; and locomotion within a *plenum* is a logical possibility.

(b) *The Atomists and the void*

The Atomists did not move by counter-circulation: motion, they held, took place through a void; and there *is* a void.

> Leucippus and Democritus . . . [said] that there is void not only in the universe but also outside the universe (**294**: Simplicius, **67 A 20**).

The world contains interstitial void between its component atoms; and the world itself is separated from other atomic conglomerates by acres of extra-mundane vacuity. 'In truth, there are atoms and void' (**68 B 125**): in that famous fragment, and in countless doxographical reports, void has a place alongside the atoms as one of the twin pillars of the Abderite universe.[10]

Melissus' rejection of vacancy depended on the premiss that what is empty is non-existent, or nothing (vol. 1, p. 218). The Atomists boldly accepted his premiss:

> Leucippus and his associate Democritus say that the full and the empty are elements, calling one existent and the other non-existent; the full and solid is the existent, the empty and rare the non-existent. That is why they also say that what exists exists no more than what does not exist—because the empty [exists no less than] body (**295**: Aristotle, *Met* 985b4–9 = **67 A 6**).

> What exists subsists no more than what does not exist; and both alike are explanations for what comes into being (**296**: Simplicius, **67 A 8**).

The void is non-existent; the void exists: hence the non-existent exists.

The void is also nothing. And Plutarch quotes a passage from Democritus

> in which he asserts that 'the thing exists no more than the nothing'—calling body thing and the void nothing—on the assumption that this latter too possesses a certain nature and substance of its own (**297**: **68 B 156**).

We need not delay over the order of the phrases in this quotation: '*a* exists no more than *b*' and '*b* exists no more than *a*' both mean no more than '*a* and *b* alike exist'; the relative order of *a* and *b* has at most astylistic point. Nor need the phrase 'the thing' detain us: 'nothing' in **297** translates '*mêden*'; *mê* means 'not'; subtract *mê* from *mêden* and you get *den*, and that is the word I translate 'thing'. Subtract 'not' from 'nothing' and you get 'hing'; and some scholars proudly offer 'hing' as their translation of *den*. But 'hing' is a nonsense word, *den* is not: it occurs once elsewhere, in a fragment of Alcaeus (fr. 130 LP), and was, it seems, a rare word meaning '*chrêma*' or '*pragma*'—'thing'.[11] Clearly, *den* in **297** is present only for its rhetorical effect: the fragment says no more than that nothing, no less than existent things, exists.

Melissus, in **168** uses 'nothing (*mêden*)' to mean 'non-existent (*mê on*)'; and Democritus in **297** is, I suppose, simply following Melissus, Even so, 'the non-existent exists' does not seem much more promising as an axiom of science than '(the) nothing exists': the axiom looks flatly self-contradictory. It is tempting to dismiss the remark as a piece of *ad hominem* abuse: 'The void exists, and if Melissus chooses, absurdly, to call the void non-existent, why then, the non-existent exists. But we Atomists will not be outfaced by such a trivially verbal manoeuvre.' Yet Melissus, I have argued, did not simply mishandle the notion of non-existence; and our texts give no hint that, in asserting the existence of the non-existent, the Atomists were merely indulging in raillery.

If we are to take seriously the assertion that 'the non-existent exists', we must make it something more than a simple self-contradiction; and the only way of doing that is to posit two different senses for 'exist'. Democritus, we know, was alive to the possibility of ambiguity (cf. **B 26**); but there is no evidence that he saw an ambiguity in '*einai*'. Nonetheless, I am inclined to think that the Atomists were feeling towards such an insight: at all events, without that supposition we must leave them in the gloomy depths of blank contradiction.

Frege has familiarized us with the distinction between *Esgibtexist-enz* and *Wirklichkeit*. In English, the normal phrase for expressing *Esgibtexistenz* is 'there is (are)', and a standard way of expressing *Wirklichkeit* is by means of the predicate 'real'. But both notions can be put across by the verb 'exist'; and similarly in Greek both notions are customarily expressed by the one verb '*einai*'. There are horses, and horses are real (they exist, whereas unicorns do not exist—they are fictional, not real); there are numbers, but numbers (in my book at least) are not real—they do not exist. When 'exist' signifies reality it is a predicate, and the formula '*a* exists' is well-formed; when 'exist' signifies *Esgibtexistenz* then it is not a (first-order) predicate and '*a* exists' is not well-formed.

Let us distinguish the reality sense of 'exist' as 'exist₁' and the *Esgibtexistenz* sense as 'exist₂'. Then I suggest that the proper sense of 'the non-existent exists' is given by 'the non-existent₁ exists₂'; i.e., by 'There are things which are not real'. Atoms and void exist; i.e., atoms and void exist₂, there are atoms and empty spaces. The void does not exist; i.e., the void does not exist₁, the void is unreal.

Now to exist₁ or to be real is to be a space-filler; and it is therefore a necessary truth that atoms exist₁: atoms are bodies, and bodies exist₁. On the other hand, 'void exists₁' is necessarily false; for only bodiless places are void. Thus 'the void is non-existent₁' is necessarily true, even though it is an axiom of physics that there are empty spaces or that the void exists₂. The Atomists can be given a consistent thesis; moreover, their thesis has, to my mind, a considerable plausibility: if we agree with Locke, and several of the ancients, that 'to be (i.e. to exist₁) is to be somewhere (i.e. to occupy a space)', then bodies and atoms do necessarily possess a being that empty space necessarily lacks. To pursue that hare further would lead to some of the more horrid thickets of philosophical logic: I shall assume that I have given the Atomists' slogan at least a *prima facie* plausibility, and proceed to the existence₂ of the void.

In the *Physics* Aristotle offers a list of arguments which had been used to show the existence of the void: local motion requires void, and so do rarefaction and condensation; growth presupposes a void; a jar full of ashes will hold as much water as the same jar when empty of ashes (213b2–29 = **67 A 19**). Some scholars ascribe those arguments to the Atomists;[12] and the argument from locomotion was canonical in Epicureanism: 'If there were not that which we call void and place and intangible nature, bodies would not have anywhere in which to be or through which to move—and they evidently do move' (*ad Hdt* §40; cf. §67; fr. 272 Us.). Evidently, bodies move; locomotion demands void: *ergo* there is void. Yet no ancient source attributes any of the arguments of the *Physics* to the Atomists; and the arguments are dialectically inapposite: Melissus rejects the void, and therefore motion; the Atomists, seeking to rehabilitate motion, restore the void. If they do so merely because motion requires it, their argument falls shamefully flat.

Metrodorus of Chios, a pupil of Democritus, said that:

Everything that anyone thinks of (*noêsai*) exists (**298: 70 B 2**).

The sentiment is Eleatic in substance and form; and an easy

conjecture has Metrodorus attacking Elea with its own weapons: we can think of the void (for we can readily imagine vast oceans of empty space); thus, by the Eleatic principle that thinkability implies being, the void exists. I like to think that Metrodorus used that argument; but no text explicitly mentions it, nor is the Eleatic principle ascribed to Metrodorus' master.

To establish the void, the Atomists used, I believe, their own *Ou Mallon* Principle: Democritus said that 'the thing exists no more (*ou mallon*) than the nothing' (297); and *ou mallon* is used in the same context by Aristotle (*Met* 985b8 = 67 A 6) and by Simplicius (67 A 8). The phrase *ou mallon* does not in itself prove the presence of the *Ou Mallon* Principle: '*a* is *ou mallon F* than *b*' may simply mean '*b* is just as *F* as *a* is'. And in 297 it is possible to take *ou mallon* in that way: 'the void is just as existent as the atoms are'. But I dislike that interpretation: the phrase 'more existent' grates on the logical ear; and if Democritus thinks that atoms exist$_1$ and exist$_2$ whereas the void exists$_2$ but does not exist$_1$, then it is false to say that void exists just as much as atoms. Thus I read the *Ou Mallon* Principle into 297, and thereby discover the Atomists' argument for introducing the void: 'there is no more reason for there to be occupied than for there to be unoccupied areas of space'; 'there is no more reason for the existence$_2$ of atoms than for the existence$_2$ of void'. And since atoms exist$_2$, so too does void.

The argument rests on two premisses. First, it assumes that Melissus' argument *against* the void has no power; for otherwise there would be 'more reason' for the existence$_2$ of atoms than for the existence$_2$ of void. Second, it assumes the truth of the *Ou Mallon* Principle itself. I shall discuss those two premisses at a later stage of my argument: for the nonce, I leave the Atomists in possession of the field.

(c) *Anaxagoras and mind*

If the neo-Ionians are to succeed in their endeavours, motion must be more than a logical possibility: it must be an actual feature of the world. Parmenides objected to generation by asking, rhetorically, 'what *need* would have aroused it to come into being later or sooner?' (156. 9–10); and the same question can be applied to motion: nothing will move unless there is some explanation of its movement; yet what *need* impels things to move? *Aitiologia* or the giving of explanations, is in any case a part of the scientist's art: even without the prick of Parmenides' spur the neo-Ionians would have searched for explanations; goaded by it they only galloped faster. In the remaining sections of this chapter I shall look at some of the results of their search for explanation; and I begin with the most celebrated of them.

[Anaxagoras] was the first to add mind to matter, beginning his book, which is pleasantly and grandly written, thus: 'All things were together; then mind came and arranged them' (299: Diogenes Laertius, II. 6 = 59 A 1).[13]

Anaxagoras' invention earned him the nickname of 'Mind' (Timon, fr. 24 = A 1) and it won him rare praise from Aristotle:

Someone said that mind is present as in animals, so in nature as the explanation of the universe (*kosmos*) and of the whole order of things; he appeared as a sober man compared to his predecessors who spoke at random (300: *Met* 984b15–18 = A 58).

What was Anaxagoras' mind? How was it related to the ordinary stuffs of his world? And how did it operate in and on the world?

Mind (*nous*) is a stuff, or at least stuff-like. The term 'mind' generally functions in Anaxagoras' fragments as a mass-noun, like 'gold' or 'flesh', and not as a count-noun, like 'ingot' or 'arm'. Moreover, mind 'is the finest of all things and the purest' (B 12): the reference to the rareness or 'fineness' of mind is often thought to represent an attempt, only partially successful, to express the thin notion of incorporeality. But mind is certainly extended in space (B 14), and I am inclined to think that Anaxagoras, far from hinting at mental incorporeality, was bent on the opposite tack: 'mind' is not, after all, a very stuff-like term in its ordinary behaviour; Anaxagoras, given to an ontology of stuffs, was determined to ascribe to mind a material existence and nature which by no means evidently belongs to it.

Since mind is a stuff we might expect it to act like other Anaxagorean stuffs, to have a share of everything and to be in everything; that is, we should expect the following two propositions to hold:

(1) If a is a piece of mind, then for any stuff, S, a contains a portion of S.

(2) For any stuff S, if a is a piece of S, then a contains a portion of mind.

But mind is no ordinary stuff: its peculiar features are expressed in four fragments:

In everything there is present a portion of everything, except mind; and in some things mind too is present (204: B 11).

104

The other things share a portion of everything; but [i] mind is unlimited[14] and independent (*autokratês*) and has been mixed with no thing but alone is itself by itself. For [ii] if it were not by itself but had been mixed with something else, it would share in all things if it had been mixed with anything (for [iii] in everything there is a portion of everything, as I have said earlier); and [iv] the things commingled with it would obstruct it so that it would not control (*kratein*) any thing in the same way as it does when being actually alone by itself. For [v] it is the finest of all things and the purest; and [vi] it has every knowledge about everything, and greatest power; and [vii] mind controls all the things that have soul (*psuchê*), both the greater and the smaller. [viii] And mind controlled the whole revolution (*perichôrêsis*), so that it revolved at the beginning. And [ix] first it began to revolve in a small way, but it revolves more, and it will revolve more. And [x] the things that commingle and those that separate off and those that separate out: mind knew them all. And [xi] what was to be and what was and is not now and what is now and what will be—all these mind ordered, and this revolution in which now revolve the stars and the sun and the moon and the air and the aether that are separating off. But the revolution itself made them separate off. And the thick is separating off from the thin, and the hot from the cold, and the bright from the dark, and the dry from the wet. And [xii] there are many portions of many things; but nothing is altogether separating off or separating out one from another, except mind. And [xiii] all mind is homogeneous, both the greater and the smaller. And nothing else is homogeneous; but each single thing is and was most clearly those things of which most are present in it (**301: B 12**).

And when mind began to move things, it separated off from everything that was moved; and whatever mind moved, all that was separated out. And as things were moving and separating out, the revolution made them separate out much more (**302: B 13**).

Mind . . .[15] is now where all other things are: in the surrounding multiplicity and in what are conjoined and in what are separated off (**303: B 14**).

At first blush, **204** seems to deny proposition (2), and sentences [i] and [xii] of **301** seem to deny proposition (1). I begin with (2).

'In some things mind too is present': Anaxagoras is simply stating the common-sense fact that some things have minds and others do not; the things that do are presumably those creatures with a soul or *psuchê* which mind 'controls' (**301**, [vii]); the things that do not are stocks and stones.[16] Can we infer from that common-sense proposition to the metaphysical thesis that some stuffs contain no portion of mind? and hence that (2) is false? It would be a rash inference: Anaxagoras might consistently maintain both (2) and the thesis of **204**; after all, when I drink a glass of gin, a 'mindless' stuff, my spirits revive—perhaps I extract a little mind from my drink.[17] And **303** does appear to imply (2): if mind is 'in the surrounding multiplicity' and in everything else, then surely every piece of stuff must contain a portion of mind? That easy interpretation is not inevitable; but as far as I can see it is both intelligible in itself and consistent with everything else that Anaxagoras has to say. And I conclude that Anaxagoras in fact assents to (2).

Mind, of course, is pure, unmixed, and by itself; but to say that is to deny (1), not to deny (2); more precisely, it is to assert the contrary of (1):

(3) If a is a piece of mind, then for no stuff S does a contain a portion of S.

Why does Anaxagoras maintain (3)? Some see it as an inference from the negation of (2); but Anaxagoras does not deny (2); the inference is plainly invalid; and Anaxagoras himself tells a different tale. In sentences [ii]—[iii], **301** explicitly infers (3) from the negation of (1); and the inference, given Anaxagorean physics, is correct. Given that every stuff contains a portion of every stuff, it follows that if mind does not contain every stuff, it does not contain any stuff.

Why, then, does Anaxagoras reject (1)? Why cannot pieces of mind, like any other bits of stuff, be omnivorous in their appetites? If they were, the characteristic powers of mind would be 'obstructed' according to sentence [iv], and it would lose 'control'. Sentence [v] explains sentence [iv] by reference to the 'fineness' of mind. Perhaps mind's fineness explains why mixture would obstruct its powers: mind is, as it were, a fine penetrating oil; and its penetrative powers, to which it owes its ability to control and know all things, would be inhibited by any commingling with grosser matter. But there is no reason to suppose that commingling would inhibit mind's penetrative capacities: in Anaxagorean physics, 'everything is in everything' and even the grossest body may penetrate the finest of stuffs. Fineness will not explain why mind should be obstructed; and I suppose that sentence [v] justifies the last part of [iv]: fineness explains mind's control 'when being actually alone by itself'. (Thus Diogenes of Apollonia held that *psuchê* was air, the 'most fine-bodied of all things', and that *psuchê* is 'mobile *qua* finest': Aristotle, *An* 405a21–5 = **64 A 20**.)

106

A different argument has been offered against (1): mind, alone of stuffs, has motive powers; hence mind must be distinguished from other inert stuffs; and the only mode of distinction is the denial of commixture to mind. But that argument has no textual basis. In any case, every other stuff has powers or properties of its own, yet those stuffs contain portions of everything else: why should mind alone lose its characteristic powers if it were not pure?

A man is made of flesh and blood and bone and mind; the universe contains earth and air and fire and water and mind. Those are platitudes. But, as Aristotle stressed, mind is not on a par with the other stuffs of the world: when we talk of a man's mind we are not speaking of any physical constituent, nor even of a quasi-physical constituent; we are referring, in a collective way, to his powers and his dispositions. If mind is treated as a constituent, physical or non-physical, of a man, confusion is likely to follow. I guess that Anaxagoras half saw that: mind is not like the other things of the world; its defining functions, knowledge and control (cognition and volition in a later argot), reveal the fact. Yet Anaxagoras could not grasp the full implications of his insight: he made mind pure, unmixed, and so on; but he deliberately construed it as a stuff. By accepting (2), he strongly affirmed its stuff-like nature; by denying (1), he hoped, vainly, to preserve its special status as a cognitive and active force.

What, then, are the powers of mind? and how does it operate in the world? The second half of **301** answers those questions. The details of mind's cosmic activity are of no philosophical interest; and I shall note only the main heads under which that activity can be subsumed: they are four.

First, mind knows everything. Perhaps, like the Homeric Muses, Anaxagorean mind knows everything because it is everywhere (**303**); or perhaps mind knows everything because it ordered everything and thus foresees all events in the world's history. (In the same way, some Christian theologians connect God's omniscience with his creativity.) Second, mind ordered or arranged everything: it planned the blueprint for cosmogony and determined how the primordial mass should be articulated into a world. Third, mind controls some things: some of the events in the present world are brought about by thought or ratiocination; and these, trivially, are the work of mind. Fourth, mind moved the *Ur*-mass; it set the stuffs into a whirl and thus began assembling a cosmos according to its blueprint.

That summary of mind's functions raises several questions. In this section I consider only the most obvious feature of mind: it is, above all, a 'moving cause', a source of locomotion and of change: 'he makes it a principle of motion' (Aristotle, *Phys* 256b25 = **A 56**); 'he linked the artist to the matter' (Aëtius, **A 46**); 'he filled out the missing explanation' (Simplicius, **A 41**).[18] Why did the mass of homoiomeries ever begin to whirl and form a cosmos? Because of mind. Why do the heavenly bodies now pursue their ordered courses? Because of mind. The general formula of explanation is this: 'Mind brought it about that P'. What is this 'mind'? Some think of a cosmic mind, a vast mass of pure mind which dreamed up and executed the cosmic plan.[19] But **302** implies that there was, at the cosmogonic starting point, no large central mass of mind; and no other text implies that such a mass ever existed. Nor are the ordinary events which mind controls plausibly assigned to any cosmic mind. Perhaps, then, 'mind' refers to the totality of mind stuff, the whole collection of mind portions; and to say that 'mind brought it about that P and mind brought it about that Q' is not to ascribe two acts to a single subject: water surrounds New Zealand and water flows from Oxford to London, but no one bit of stuff does both these things. For 'Mind brought it about that P' we should read: 'Some piece of mind brought it about that P'.

'Some', said Berkeley, 'have pretended to account for appearance by *occult qualities*, but of late they are mostly resolved into *mechanical causes*, to wit, the figure, *motion, weight*, and such like qualities of insensible particles: whereas in truth there is no other agent or efficient cause than *spirit*' (*Principles*, CII). If a facile comparison sets Anaxagoras on Berkeley's side in this dispute, conjecture readily suggests Democritus as the ancient representative of the proponents of mechanical causes; and there is, I think, a distinction here that is worth bringing out.

Some philosophers, concerned to understand the notion of causation, take the performances of rational agents (in particular, of themselves) as paradigms of causal activity: when I observe myself or another man striking a billiard ball or driving a motor-car, then I am attending to a plain piece of causation. This attitude suggests that causes are *agents*, and that the causal structure of the world is tied together by powers and capacities to act and be acted upon. The canonical formula for causal propositions is: 'Agent a brings it about that P'.

Other philosophers look outward: causation is the cement of the universe, the adhesive which binds event to event; and we should seek it in the external universe and not in ourselves. When I observe one billiard ball strike and move another, or when I study the intricate mechanism of an internal combustion engine, then I am in the presence of causality. This attitude suggests that causes are antecedent *events*, and that the causal structure of the world is primarily a matter of regularity. The canonical formula for causal propositions is: 'Event E_2 occurs because event E_1 occurs'.

I shall call the first of those approaches to causation Berkeleian, the second (with some historical impropriety) Humean; and I suggest that Anaxagoras adopted a Berkeleian approach to causation, and the Atomists a Humean approach.

I have talked, somewhat feebly, of different approaches: do the approaches point to different theories of causation, or offer rival accounts of the notion of causation, or show that we have at least two distinct concepts of what it is to cause something to happen? Let us start by expanding the Humean approach: as well as events, we sometimes cite states of affairs as causes (the glass broke because it was brittle, and the man died because he was old). Since every true proposition describes either an event or a state of affairs, the canonical formula for the expanded Humean notion is simply: 'P_1 because P_2'.

The Berkeleian approach admits of a similar expansion: objects as well as agents are designated as causes (Pompeii was destroyed because of Vesuvius, the cricket ball brought about the death of the sparrow). Thus the canonical formula of Berkeleianism is: 'a brings it about that P_1' (where a names any object or agent).

, It seems plausible to suppose that 'a brings it about that P_1' is true if and only if some proposition of the form 'P_1 because a is ϕ' is true: Pompeii was destroyed because of Vesuvius, i.e. because Vesuvius erupted; the sparrow was killed by the cricket ball, i.e. because the cricket ball struck it. In general, Berkeleian causation is explicable in terms of Humean causation; for Berkeleian formulae are merely abbreviations of Humean formulae. 'a brings it about that P_1' is equivalent to a special type of the formula 'P_1 because P_2', viz. 'P_1 because a is ϕ'.

Now even if that unpolished account has some truth at its foundation, there remains an important way in which Berkeleian causation differs from Humean. For in cases where a is an agent, the translation of 'a brings it about that P_1' into Humean language will always include a reference to a's mind—to his intentions, his desires, his beliefs. 'Brutus', we say, 'killed Caesar.' And that causal hypothesis may be put into canonical Berkeleian form: 'Brutus brought it about that Caesar died.' That sentence is expandable to a Humean sentence of the form: 'Caesar died because Brutus ϕed'; and that in turn must expand into something like: 'Caesar died because Brutus stabbed him and wanted him to die and believed that if he stabbed him he would die.' Thus even if Berkeleian causes in some sense reduce to Humean causes, they still mark an important sub-class of Humean formulae, viz. those in which P_2 is a complex proposition including a reference to intentions, desires or beliefs. Let us call that sub-class of formulae the Berkeleian formula: then Anaxagoras, I suggest, held that science required Berkeleian formulae; the Atomists that it did not.

(d) *Causas cognoscere rerum*

[Democritus said that] he would rather find a single causal explanation (*aitiologia*) than gain the kingdom of Persia (**304: 68 B 118**).[20]

We possess a quantity of Democritean explanations; many of them are preserved by Theophrastus (**A 135**), from whom I have already quoted (above, p. 71). If we ask, on a more abstract level, how Democritus conceived of causation, we have less information; but a clear and consistent picture emerges.

Epicurus says of the Abderites that:

Though they were the first to give adequate explanations, and far surpassed not only their predecessors but also their successors many times over, yet here, as in many other places, they did not realize that they were making light of grave matters in ascribing everything to necessity and the spontaneous (**305: 68 A 69**).[21]

For the moment let us ignore 'the spontaneous'; then Epicurus charges that all phenomena in the Atomists' world are necessitated.

Refusing to mention the final cause (*to hou heneka*), Democritus reduces everything that nature handles to necessity (**306**: Aristotle, *GA* 789b2 = **68 A 66**).

Everything happens by fate, in the sense that fate applies the force of necessity (**307**: Cicero, **68 A 66**).

Everything comes about by necessity, since the whirl, which he calls necessity, is the cause of the generation of everything (**308**: Diogenes Laertius, IX.45 = **68 A 1**).

These reports bear on Democritus; but Leucippus held the same view. Only one Leucippan fragment survives. It reads thus:

Leucippus says that everything occurs by necessity and that that is the same as fate; for he says in *On Mind*: No thing comes about in vain (*matên*); but everything for a reason and by necessity (*ek logou kai hup' anankês*) (**309**: Aëtius 67 B 2).

Leucippus appears to be stating some version of a principle which we have already met, the Principle of Causality (vol. 1, pp. 24–6).[22] He talks of things 'coming about (*ginetai*)', but he presumably means to encompass all events in that term and not merely generations; and it will not be absurd to allow that states as well as events were probably in his mind. Thus **309** asserts that all states and events are explicable by reason and necessity; and I gloss that by:
(1) For any proposition *P*, if *P* is the case, then there is some *Q* such that the fact that *P* is necessitated by the fact that *Q*.
In (1) *Q* is the *logos* or reason for *P*; and the 'necessity' of **309** is expressed by the link of necessitation between *Q* and *P*.
It is, of course, in atomic nature that we must seek the proper explanations of things:

The reason why the substances [i.e. the atoms] stay together with one another up to a point, he finds in the overlappings and interlockings (*epallagai kai antilêpseis*) of the bodies. . . . Thus he thinks that they hold on to one another and stay together for a time, until some stronger necessity comes upon them from their surrounding, shakes them about, and scatters them apart (**213**, Aristotle).

The 'stronger necessity' is created by atomic clashings; and thus it is the atomic 'whirl' which ultimately causes all change, and which can therefore be called 'necessity' (**308**). We are, I think, entitled to particularize proposition (1), and say that: every macroscopic state is explicable by way of some atomic state; every macroscopic event by way of some atomic event. Every atomic state is determined by the properties of its atomic constituents; every atomic event is explained by the locomotion of its atomic constituents. Every atomic locomotion is explained by way of atomic collisions; and atomic collisions depend on the velocity, size and shape of the colliding corpuscles. In that way, the world is explained; and if a complete aetiology of the universe is for ever beyond our powers, at least it is in principle possible.
The Atomists are Humean, in the loose sense in which I use that adjective: they do not talk of agents; and the formula '*a* brings it about that *P*' does not figure in their aetiologies. Were the Atomists

111

Humean in a more historical sense of the term? Humean causes are prior and contiguous to their effects; and they adhere to their effects with a necessity which Hume explains (or explains away) in terms of regularity. The Atomists are concerned with two different kinds of explanatory hypothesis. First, a macroscopic state or event, M_1, is explained by way of a microscopic state or event, M_2. ('The kettle of water is cold, because its constituent atoms have such and such a structure'; 'The kettle is coming to the boil, because its constituent atoms are moving in such and such a way.') Here M_2 is not prior to M_1, but simultaneous with it; M_2 is not contiguous to M_1, but identical with it; and M_1 and M_2 do not illustrate a merely Humean regularity: rather, M_2 necessitates M_1 (in a somewhat Pickwickian sense); for, being identical with M_2, M_1 cannot but occur when M_2 occurs.

Second, a microscopic state or event, M_2, is explained by reference to an atomic collision, C. Here C is presumably prior to M_2. In a loose sense we can say that C is contiguous to M_2, if we suppose that only collisions involving the constituent atoms of M_2 can result in M_2. And C necessitates M_2. Is that necessitation to be explained à la Hume, by way of regularity? Do the Atomists think that states or events like M_2 come about whenever collisions like C occur? and that such regularity is all that there is to C's necessitating M_2? Our evidence is silent. That the Atomists believed in causal regularity is not implausible in itself, and it is perhaps implicit in Leucippus' use of the word *logos*. But nothing suggests that the Abderites took a Humean view of necessity.

(e) *Agents and purposes*

'No thing comes about in vain (*matên*)' (309): the sentiment is Aristotelian in expression; and when Aristotle asserts that 'God and nature do nothing in vain (*matên*)' (*Cael* 271a33), he means to subscribe to a teleological theory of nature. That cannot, however, be Leucippus' meaning; and we must take *matên* in 309 to mean 'without cause', not 'without purpose'. For the Atomists rejected all teleological or purposive explanation:

Leucippus and Democritus and Epicurus [say that the universe is]neither animate nor governed by purpose (*pronoia*), but by a sort of irrational nature (*phusis alogos*) (310: Aëtius, 67 A 22).

Is there a providence which looks after all things, or is everything created and governed by chance? The latter opinion was propounded by Democritus and corroborated by Epicurus (311: Lactantius, 68 A 70; cf. Aëtius, 67 A 24).

112

Humean explanations do not rule out purposive or teleological explanation; but they do not require it. Berkeleian explanations do not entail purposive explanation; but they suggest it. And Anaxagoras for one is generally thought to have fallen in with the suggestion: the issue is celebrated, and it warrants rehearsal at some length.

Socrates bought a second-hand copy of Anaxagoras' book in high hopes; here was a thinker who, unlike his materialistic predecessors, was wise and bold enough to give intelligence a part in the formation of the world. But:

> Proceeding and reading on, I see the man making no use of mind, nor indicating any explanations for the ordering of things, but making explanations of airs and aethers and waters and many other such absurdities (**312**: *Phaedo* 98 B = **59 A 47**).

Aristotle makes the same point more pregnantly:

> Anaxagoras uses mind as a theatrical device (*mêchanê*) for his cosmogony; and whenever he is puzzled over the explanation of why something is from necessity, he wheels it in; but in the case of other happenings he makes anything the explanation rather than mind (**313**: *Met* 985a18–21 = **A 47**).

And the point is constantly repeated (e.g., Eudemus, fr. 53W = **A 47**; Clement, **A 57**). 'Mind,' the objection runs, 'is not systematically applied: it is used to explain the initial cosmic whirl; and it is later used to account for one or two otherwise inexplicable interactions in the course of nature; but apart from that, it has no function: mind is not invoked to account for the circulation of the blood or the shape of an oak tree, for the functioning of the nitrogen cycle or the design of a spider's web.'

The point, we might hastily judge, is right in substance but wrong in evaluation. On the one hand, **301** says that mind moves and controls some but not all things: it sets the whirl in motion; but after that, the revolution itself, by its own unmeasurable speed and force (**B 9**), suffices to bring things about. Mind is the cosmic starter, initiating action by its own intrinsic powers; but once it has imparted motion to the cosmic masses, natural events proceed in a purely mechanical way. That is Anaxagoras' view; and Socrates and the rest represent him correctly. On the other hand, the Socratic criticism is misplaced: the vast majority of cosmic happenings do not require an explanation in terms of mind; most natural events are in fact explicable in a mechanical fashion, and a reference to mind would be an absurd solecism in a treatise on chemistry or meteorology.

Anaxagoras was right, Socrates and Aristotle wrong; for Anaxagoras wished to banish teleology from science, and they desired to recall it from its exile. As Simplicius saw, Anaxagoras advocates 'the method proper to natural science' (*in Phys* 177.9).

That flattering portrait of Anaxagoras may be embellished. According to Aristotle,

> Anaxagoras says that man is the cleverest of animals because he has hands; but it is reasonable to hold that he required hands because he is the cleverest; for hands are a tool, and nature (like a clever man) always distributes each thing to those who are capable of using it (**314**: *PA* 687a7–12 = **A 102**).

How pleasantly Anaxagoras' assertion contrasts with Aristotle's superstitious speculation. An anecdote in Plutarch presses the point home:

> It is said that the head of a single-horned ram was once brought from the fields to Pericles, and that Lampon the seer, when he saw that the horn grew strong and firm from the middle of the forehead, said that of the two power groups in the state—that of Thucydides and that of Pericles—control would come to the one to whom the sign was brought. But Anaxagoras had the skull split open and showed that the brain had not filled out its position, but had drawn together to a point, like an egg, at the very place in the cavity where the root of the horn began (**315: A 16**).

Anaxagoras' explanation is wholly naturalistic; Lampon indulges in a childish superstition. And our admiration for Anaxagoras is scarcely tempered by the fact that Lampon's prediction turned out true.

But that admiration is perhaps hasty: after all, Anaxagoras does not 'banish teleology from science', he merely limits its scope. And those who dislike teleology will be distressed by a cosmogony which rests firmly on teleological principles. Yet perhaps we can alleviate their pain? At all events, several scholars have heroically urged that Anaxagoras gave no teleological explanations at all.[23]

Aristotle's teleology is, in a sense, impersonal: he explains the form and operation of an animal's organs in terms of the function of those organs, not in terms of the purposes of an Author of Nature. Why do cows have a fourth stomach? In order to digest their cud. Why do men blink? In order to moisten their eyes and sharpen their vision. Good digestion is not the purposed end of the cow; for cows do not deliberate. Moist eyes are not my purpose in blinking; for my blinking is a reflex act. Nor is bovine digestion or human sharp-sightedness the goal of some superhuman or superbovine

114

artificer. Teleology, thus construed, posits a *telos* or end; but it does not imply that the *telos* is the goal of any purposive act.

If we look for Aristotelian teleology in Anaxagoras we shall not find it: as far as we know, Anaxagoras did not attempt to explain anything by way of impersonal ends. (For my part, I put that down to Anaxagoras' credit; but the question is controversial, and I have no space to broach it.) Yet there are personal as well as impersonal ends, and a reference to purpose, aim or design will often figure in our explanations: why do men take exercise? In order to keep fit. Why do men learn Greek? In order to raise themselves above the vulgar herd and reach positions of considerable emolument.

Roughly speaking, an impersonal teleological explanation will be expressed in the form:

(1) *a* is *F* because being *F* leads to being *G* and it is in *a*'s interest to be *G*.

A personal teleological explanation will be expressed by:

(2) *a* is *F* because *b* wants *a* to be *G* and believes that being *F* leads to being *G*.

Now proposition (2) is a Berkeleian explanation; and since Anaxagoras was a Berkeleian, he was thereby given to personal teleological explanation.

Personal teleology is not normally a feature of natural science; yet it will enter the world of nature if natural phenomena are viewed as the operations of an intelligent artificer. Anaxagoras took just such a view; and it is merely perverse to deny that he was a teleologist in that perfectly intelligible sense. Simplicius puts it clearly:

> He seemed to say that all things were together and at rest for an unlimited time, and that the cosmogonical mind, wanting to separate out the kinds which he calls homoiomeries, created motion in them (**316: A 45**).

Mind 'wanted (*boulêtheis*)' to make a world: the existence of the cosmos is explicable as the aim of an intelligent actor. If the word 'want' does not occur in Anaxagoras' fragments, the verbs 'know' and 'order' do: mind ordered or arranged things, and it knew what was to be. There is, surely, no doubt about the teleological import of all this; and indeed, the very enterprise of setting up mind as a cosmic force is hardly to be detached from a teleological view of cosmic history.

'And what was to be, and what was and is not now, and what is now and what will be—all these mind ordered' (**301**, [xi]). The difficulty with Anaxagoras' view is now the very opposite of the difficulty Socrates discovered: Socrates objected that mind did too little work—the danger is rather that mind does too much. What room is there in Anaxagorean physics for natural causes? If mind arranges everything, what can the 'revolution' do?

Anaxagoras distinguishes between ordering (*diakosmein*) and controlling (*kratein*): mind orders everything but controls only some things. The following explanation suggests itself. Take any causal chain, $E_1, E_2, \ldots, E_n$, in which each E_i accounts for its immediate successor. We may say, using a convenient Aristotelian distinction, that E_i is the *proximate* cause of $E_i + 1$, and that E_1 is the *ultimate* cause of each subsequent E_i. According to Anaxagoras, E_1 will always be an act of mind, and it will be expressible by the formula 'Mind arranges that E_2 shall occur'. Now since all events hinge on an initial arrangement by mind, we may say that mind arranges everything; for E_1 is the ultimate cause of each E_i. But only E_2 is immediately linked to E_1; only for E_2 is an act of mind a proximate cause. And if we say that mind controls E_i only if mind is a proximate cause of E_i, then mind will not control everything. Anaxagoras' teleology is now reconciled with the possibility of naturalistic explanations: by attending to Anaxagoras' distinct terms, 'order' and 'control', we can give mind overall responsibility for the world while leaving room for natural necessity.

There is a vulgar objection to that sort of theory: 'The *real* cause of E_n is E_1; E_{n-1} is only a seeming or spurious cause. For if E_1 causes E_2, E_2 $E_3, \ldots$ and $E_{n-1} E_n$, then it is E_1 which is the true cause of E_n. Thus if E_1 is an act of mind, then naturalistic explanation has no room; for the real cause of *everything* is E_1, and E_1 is supernaturalistic.' That strangely persuasive line of argument involves an inconsistency and a false presupposition. The inconsistency is palpable; for the argument asserts both that E_{n-1} causes E_n and also that E_{n-1} does not cause E_n. The false presupposition is that in any causal chain there is some one item which is 'the' cause (or the 'real' cause) of any E_i. In fact, as the distinction between ultimate and proximate causes shows, every E_i (for $i > 2$) will have several causes; for each E_j (for $j < i$) is a cause of E_i. The noun 'cause' is the evil genius here: instead of talking of causes, we might well stick to the connective 'because': E_n occurs because E_{n-1} occurs; E_{n-1} occurs because E_{n-2} occurs; hence E_n occurs because E_{n-2} occurs. There is no temptation to make the absurd inference that, since E_n occurs because E_{n-2} occurs, E_n does not occur because E_{n-1} occurs.

(f) *Chance and necessity*

According to the Atomists, necessity governs the world; yet I have already quoted two passages which ascribe great influence to chance. Chance and necessity are surely polar opposites: is not the atomist account of explanation simply contradictory? A similar question arises over Empedocles; and I shall return to the Atomists after running quickly through the Empedoclean material.

At first glance, Empedocles' explanatory mechanism seems simple enough: in addition to the four 'roots' or elements that constitute the world, there are two forces which control their congresses and separations. These forces are denominated Love (*Philia*) and Strife (*Neikos*):

> And dread Strife apart from them [sc. the roots], balanced in all directions,
> and Love amongst them, equal in length and breadth (**317: 31 B 17.19–20**).

Love accounts for elemental conjunction, Strife for elemental separation:

> Now by Love all coming together into one,
> now again each carried apart by the enmity of Strife (**194: B 17, 7–8**).

How are Love and Strife to be conceived? Aristotle, for one, thought that Empedocles' conception of them was hopelessly muddled (e.g., *Met* 1075b2–4; cf. Simplicius, **A 28**).

First, Love is frequently treated as an internal moving cause:

> [Love] is thought innate in human limbs,
> by which men think loving thoughts and accomplish fitting deeds,
> calling her Joy by name and Aphrodite (**318: B 17.22–4**).

Nor in human limbs alone; for the elements

> come together in Love, and desire one another (**319: B 21.8**)

Elements, like animals, unite because they are in love.[24]

Second, Love and Strife are sometimes treated as material constituents of natural bodies. The treatment is implicit in **317**, where Strife is 'apart from' the roots and Love 'amongst' them; and it is plain in **B 109** which enumerates the four roots and the two forces without indicating any ontological distinction between them. Thus:

> [Love] gathers together and sets together and holds together [the elements], thickening them by consortings and friendships
> As when rennet pegs and binds white milk (**320: B 33**).

In its material form, Love functions as a sort of catalyst: earth, air, fire and water, taken together, will not of themselves unite; pour in a little Love and the reaction will take place.

Most frequently Love is an external force, a divine or semi-divine agent.[25] Thus:

The divine Aphrodite fitted together the tireless eyes (321: B 86; cf. B 73, B 87);

and in general:

They first grew together under the hands of Cypris [= Love] (322: B 95).

Strife too is an agent; for at the start of the cosmogony

Strife still held [some things] aloft (323: B 35.9).

As an internal force, Love wears a Newtonian aspect, being the counterpart of attraction or gravitation; as a material constituent, Love appears in a chemical role; and in its third form, Love is an agent, comparable to Anaxagoras' mind. The ancient commentators, having broken Empedocles' single pair of causes into three disparate fragments, do not desist from their attack; for beside Love and Strife they find three more 'causes' in Empedocles' science.

First, the elements themselves are sometimes endowed with powers of their own.

[Plants] root downwards because the earth [in them] naturally moves thus, and they grow upwards because the same goes for the fire [in them] (324: Aristotle, *An* 415b29–30 = A 70).

The same point is made anecdotally:

The natural philosophers actually arrange the whole of nature by taking as a principle the thesis that like goes to like; that is why Empedocles said that the bitch sits on the tiles because she contains a great deal of like matter (325: *EE* 1235a10–12 = A 20a).[26]

And we might cite B 62.6:

Fire sent them up, longing to come to its like (326),

or B 90:

Thus sweet seized on sweet, bitter jumped on bitter, sharp climbed on sharp, and (?) salty rode upon salty (?) (327).

Second, there is necessity: according to Aristotle,

Empedocles would seem to say that the alternate domination and moving of Love and Strife belong to things from necessity (**328**: *Phys* 252a7–9 = **A 38**). ˹

Plutarch reports that Empedocles gives the name of necessity to 'Love and Strife together' (**A 45**); and many more *testimonia* give necessity a niche in the Empedoclean system.[27] From the fragments there is only one reference:

There is an oracle of necessity, an old edict of the gods, eternal, bound by broad oaths (**329: B 115**.1–2).[28]

Third, there is chance. Aristotle complains that his predecessors said nothing about chance:

That is absurd, whether they did not believe it to exist or supposed it to exist and ignored it—and that though they sometimes use it, as Empedocles says that the air is not always separated off upwards, but as it may happen. (At any rate, he says in his cosmogony that: 'running, it met up then in this way, but often in other ways [= **B 53**]'), and he says that the parts of animals mostly come about by chance (**330**: *Phys* 196a19–24).

Commenting on this passage Simplicius quotes six further verses to show the power of chance in Empedoclean physics, and he observes that 'you might find many similar passages from Empedocles' *Physics* to set beside these' (*ad* **B 85**).[29]

We have an *embarras de richesse*. As explanatory powers Empedocles offers us: (a) Love and Strife as physical forces; (b) Love and Strife as catalysts; (c) Love and Strife as semi-divine agents; (d) the natural strivings of stuffs; (e) necessity; and (f) chance. Can we discover a seemly frugality behind this seeming prodigality?

First, (d) and (e) are not in conflict; indeed, it is easy to take (d) as a specification of (e):˙ events occur by natural necessity, and in particular by virtue of the natural powers of the world's constituent stuffs. Nor, second, are (d) and (a) at odds; for, again, (a) is a specification of (d); the natural powers of stuffs are attractions and repulsions. In a syntactically difficult couplet Empedocles observes, it seems, that:

The things that are more suitable for mixture are likened to and loved by one another by Aphrodite (**331: B 22**.4–5).

The lines suggest that the natural striving of like for like is explicable by the action of Love. Again **327** employs sexual metaphors to account for the conjunction of like stuffs: like goes to like because like loves like. Thus (d) does indeed reduce to (a).

Third, we may ask how (a) is to be explained: what is it to act 'from Love'? An answer is given by (c): Love is one of the material constituents of any substance, *a*; and for *a* to move 'from Love' is simply for *a*'s motion to be caused by the catalytic action of its connate portion of Love. Moreover, once Love is thus materialized, it is readily deified: before cosmogony has intermingled the roots, Love was present in a great and separate mass; it will not then have worked as a catalyst, but rather as an agent or an artificer goddess. Thus (a), (c), (d) and (e) are reconciled; and (b) is given a natural and reasonable explanation.

The possibility of such a reconciliation explains how Empedocles could offer so many different explanatory notions without blush or apology: the notions are, to a large degree, different ways of expressing one idea. But the reconciliation will not quite do: there is potential conflict between (b) and (e). It is indicated in **B 116**, which says that *Charis* (Grace or Love) 'hates unbearable necessity'; and Aristotle finds it in a second fragment:

> And at the same time he gives no explanation of the change itself [i.e. of the change from the period of Love to the period of Strife] except to say that it occurs thus by nature:
>> But when Strife grew great in the limbs,
>> and rose to office as the time was accomplished
>> which had been fixed in alternation for them by a broad oath
>> [B 30]
> —that it is necessary for the change to occur; but he gives no explanation for the necessity (**332**: *Met* 1000b12–17).

The operative times of Love and Strife are determined by a broad oath, and hence (cf. **329**) by necessity: that explains why Love hates unbearable necessity; for necessity fixes the range of Love's affairs. The doxographers, for what it is worth, imply that necessity has a status superordinate to Love and Strife (cf. Aëtius, **A 32**, **A 45**).[30]

Anaxagoras gives a controlling position in the universe to agent-like causation, and he subordinates natural necessity to the arrangements of mind; the Atomists give universal power to natural necessity and profess to find no domain of agency in the world. Empedocles, it seems, was not so clear: on the one hand, Love and Strife are the supreme causes, and they work as agents; on the other hand, some bond of necessity controls everything, even the workings of Love and Strife.

I have not yet mentioned (f), chance; and some will find in (f) the deepest flaw in Empedocles' explanatory system. The same flaw, as I said at the beginning of this section, is found in the Atomists.

First, let us consider more closely the evidence that chance played a part in Empedoclean and Abderite physics. Of the passages which Simplicius assembles to prove the prevalence of Chance in Empedocles, four contain the verb '*sunkurein*' and two '*tunchanein*': Simplicius evidently interpreted the words as 'chance across' and 'happen to occur'; but both verbs are standardly used in the sense of 'come about', 'actually happen', and they do not by themselves point to chance. But chance cannot be eliminated from Empedocles' system by cunning translation. **B 53**, which Aristotle quotes in **330**, countenances infrequent conjunction, or coincidence.[31] And one fragment appeals explicitly to Dame Fortune:[32]

Thus by the will of chance everything possesses thought
(**333: B 103**).

For the Atomists we possess no first-hand texts; but the doxography is rich and unanimous:

From them [sc. the atoms] the earth and the universe are made
. . . by a certain chance concurrence (**334:** Cicero, **67 A 11**).[33]

He sets up chance as mistress and queen of universal and divine things and says that everything happens in accordance with it (**335:** Dionysius, *ad* **68 B 118**).

Democritus too, in the passage where he says that a whirl of every sort of form was separated off from the whole [cf. **B 167**] (he does not say how or by what cause), seems to generate it spontaneously and by chance (**336:** Simplicius, **68 A 67**).

In his discussion of chance in the *Physics* Aristotle reports the following theories:

Some . . . say that nothing comes about by chance, but that there is some determinate explanation for everything which we say comes about spontaneously or by chance (**337:** 195b36–196a3 = **68 A 68**).

There are some who make the spontaneous the cause both of this world and of all the universes; for they say that it is spontaneously that the whirl comes about, i.e. the dissociative motion which sets everything into its present order . . . saying that animals and plants neither exist nor come to be by chance, but that either nature or mind or something else of that sort is their cause . . . but that the heavens and the most divine of visible things come to be spontaneously and that there is no cause for them of the sort there is for animals and plants (338: 196a24-35 = **68 A 69**).

Simplicius identifies the second group of men as the Atomists (**68 A 69**); and on the authority of Eudemus he connects the first view too with Democritus:

> For even if in his cosmogony he seems to have used chance, yet in particulars he says that chance is the cause of nothing, and refers them to other causes (**339: 68 A 68**).

The identification in the second passage is certain (though the reference to 'mind or something else of that sort' indicates that Aristotle does not have the Atomists uniquely in his thoughts); and the identification in the first passage is corroborated by Diogenes of Oenoanda, who criticizes Democritus for 'saying that the atoms have no free (*eleuthera*) motion' but that 'everything moves necessarily (*katênankasmenôs*)' (**68 A 50**).

At first sight those passages seem to import a horrible muddle. As we have already seen, Democritus is committed to:

(1) Everything happens by necessity.

Eudemus and Diogenes now give him:

(2) Nothing happens by chance.

But the doxography offers:

(3) Everything happens by chance.

and Simplicius produces:

(4) Some things happen by chance and others are caused.

Surely (1)–(4) are flatly inconsistent, and the Atomists foolishly confused?

The confusion is, I think, purely verbal.[34] Plato helps to clear it up:

> They say that fire and water, and earth and air, all exist by nature and chance, and none of them by art (*technêi*), and that as to the bodies that come next in order—earth, and sun, and moon, and stars—they have been created by means of these absolutely inanimate (*apsucha*) existences. The elements are severally moved by chance and some inherent force according to certain affinities among them: of hot with cold, or of dry with moist, or of soft with hard, and according to all the other things which are mixed by the mixture of opposites in accordance with chance from necessity (*kata tuchên ex anankês*). In this way and in this manner the whole universe was created, and everything in the universe, and animals too and all plants; and all the seasons come from these elements,

not because of a mind, they say, nor because of some god or by art, but, as we said, by nature and chance only (**340**: *Laws* 889 BC trans. Jowett = **31 A 48**).[35]

There are obscurities of detail in this paragraph; but one moral emerges quite plainly from it: '*E* happens by chance (*tuchêi*)' and '*E* happens of necessity (*ex anankês*)' are not, as we might incautiously think, incompatible. Plato plainly ascribes to his opponents the view that everything happens *both* by nature or necessity *and* by chance; and the sense he gives to 'by chance' indicates how he can do so. '*E* happens by chance' means '*E* happens and *E* was not brought about by design'; no mind, no god, no art planned or executed the event. That is a normal sense of 'chance' in English, and evidently it was a normal sense of '*tuchê*' in Greek: in that sense, every event in a wholly deterministic world might occur by chance.

Empedocles' bow to Dame Fortune in **333** is thus perfectly compatible with his reverence for stern necessity (though it is not compatible with a strictly agent-like interpretation of Love and Strife); and the Atomists' proposition (3), which simply reflects their denial of *pronoia* (Aëtius, **67 A 22**), sits in happy concord with (1).

But 'by chance' does not only denote the absence of purpose: it may also denote the absence of causality or natural necessity. '*E* happened by chance' may mean not only '*E* happened and was not purposed' but also '*E* happened and was not necessitated'. And in that sense, (2) follows at once from (1), and is perfectly compatible with (3). Aristotle knows that in this sense chance and necessity are oppugnant; and that is why he objects to Empedocles' use of chance. His own analysis of chance in *Physics* II 5–7 is intricate; but it is worth pulling out one relevant strand of it here. Chance is standardly construed by Aristotle as coincidence: if *E* occurs by chance, then *E* is a conjunctive event, described by a formula of the form '*Fa* and *Ga*'; and *E* occurs by chance if and only if neither all nor most *F*s are *G*. Chance contrasts with regularity: a chance event is a rare event, a freak or extraordinary occurrence. Whether or not that is a decent account of chance I do not ask; I mention it only to draw attention to one obvious feature: a fully deterministic world may, on this analysis, be riddled with chance events. If E_1 is necessitated and E_2 is necessitated, then the conjunctive event $E_1 + E_2$ is necessitated; yet that event may be a coincidence. *a*'s being *F* and *a*'s being *G* may be necessary, even if few *F*s are *G*.

Thesis (4) remains to be accounted for. According to Aristotle, 'some think that chance is a cause, but one unclear to human intelligence, being something divine and somewhat demonic' (*Phys* 196b5 = **68 A 70**): when we say '*E* occurs by chance' we may mean only 'We cannot tell why *E* occurs'. That use is, I think, found in English; and I assume that Aristotle speaks with authority for Greek. If we apply it to (4), then (4) is rendered consistent both with (2) and with (3); and it becomes an honest confession of the weakness of the human mind—a weakness which, as we shall see, Democritus was quick to notice and to emphasize.

For the sake of clarity, then, we may rewrite (1)–(4) as follows:

(1*) All states and events are causally determined.

(2*) No states or events lack a necessitating cause.

(3*) No states or events are the results of purposive agency.

(4*) Of some states and events the causes are accessible, of others they are not.

Together, (1*)–(4*) form a consistent theory of the possibility of explaining natural phenomena. And they form a popular and a plausible theory: here, too, the Abderites prove themselves hard-headed and influential philosophers of science.

VI

The Neo-Ionian World Picture

(a) *Scientific explanation*

The Eleatic philosophers had argued that nothing can ever be generated or destroyed, that nothing can ever alter, that nothing can ever move—and that, were change possible, there would be no reason why it should ever occur. In this chapter I shall discuss the neo-Ionian response to those perturbing conclusions; and I begin with the last: could the neo-Ionians explain change, if change should prove to be possible?

The Peripatetics gave the verdict to Elea. Of Empedocles Aristotle writes:

> And at the same time he gives no explanation of the change itself [i.e. of the change from the rule of Love to that of Strife], except to say that it occurs thus by nature (*houtôs pephuke*):
>
>> But when Strife grew great in the limbs,
>> and rose to office as the time was accomplished
>> which had been fixed in alternation for them by a broad oath
>> [B 30]
>
> —that it is necessary for the change to occur; but he gives no explanation for the necessity (332: *Met* 1000b12–17).[1]

Eudemus faults Anaxagoras not only because he says that motion which did not before exist begins at a certain time, but also because he omits to say anything about its continuing or future cessation, though the matter is not evident. 'For,' he says, 'what prevents mind from determining at some time to stop all things,

125

just as, according to him, it determined to move them?' (341: Eudemus, fr. 111 W = 59 A 59).

And of the Atomists:

About motion—whence or how it belongs to existent things—these men too, like the others, lazily shelved the question (342: *Met* 985b19 = 67 A 6).

Whence the principle of natural motion comes, they do not say (343: Alexander, 67 A 6).

In detail these criticisms presuppose Peripatetic doctrine, but behind them there lies a simple question: *Why* does Strife give way to Love and vice versa? *Why* does mind start the cosmogony rolling? *Why* do the atoms move?

The case of Empedocles is complicated, and it raises no issue which does not arise in the other two cases; hence I shall consider only the criticisms of Anaxagoras and of the Atomists. According to Anaxagoras, all things were motionless up to the cosmogonical instant t; then, at t, mind began to move stuffs and to create the cosmos. Eudemus' question, which has evident Eleatic ancestry, is just this: Why t? The question is ambiguous: it may mean either 'What feature of the world before t brought it about that mind acted at t?' or else 'What feature of the world at t gave mind its reason for creating at t?' But on both interpretations the question seems fatal: before t, there was no change and there were no events; any two times, t_1 and t_2, prior to t were quite indistinguishable. Suppose, then, Anaxagoras suggests that the state S, holding at $t-n$, caused mind's creation at t, or was mind's reason for creating at t; then, by way of an argument already familiar, we can infer the absurdity that for any t_i prior to t, mind created at t_i. For S obtains at every instant up to t; hence it obtains at t_i-n; and if S's obtaining at $t-n$ brings it about that mind creates at t, then S's obtaining at t_i-n brings it about that mind creates at t_i.

The argument is not, in fact, lethal. Anaxagoras has more than one answer.[2] First, he may deny that there is any time earlier than t at which mind could have created things: take a Peripatetic leaf from your opponents' book, and hold that time implies change; infer that before t, the first instant of change, there was no time: how, then, could mind have created the world before t? The state S at t itself caused mind to embark on its cosmogonical operation; and since there was no t_i prior to t, the *reductio* argument does not begin. Was there a time before the creation? The question was hotly debated by later philosophers, and it is too deep and difficult to be discussed here. It is worth saying, however, that many philosophers have taken the view I have offered to Anaxagoras, and that it is not simply silly.

Second, Anaxagoras may reject the Universalizability of Explanation. Suppose that S at t-n explains creation at t; why infer that S at t_i-n requires creation at t_i-n? Why not take it as a brute fact that S is effective at t-n but not at t_i-n? A cigarette lighter sometimes flames when the cap is flicked, and when it does, the flicking causes the flaming. But not every flicking, as ordinary experience confirms, causes a flaming. This second answer of Anaxagoras' has also had adherents: it, too, raises difficult questions; and it, too, is far from being captious or silly.

Third, Anaxagoras may reject the Principle of Causality: that 'every event has a cause' is an unargued dogma; it has no basis in experience where, for all that we know, countless events and states are uncaused; and it is not an *a priori* truth, for we can easily conceive of an undetermined event. (Physicists who believe in sub-atomic indeterminacy conceive of such events daily; and if their belief is true then a myriad of events do really lack causes.) Elea asks: Why does cosmogony start at t? Anaxagoras answers: Mind moves things at t. The Peripatetics come to the defence of Elea: 'You explain why cosmogony *starts*, but not why it starts *at t*; for why does mind begin its operations at t?' And Anaxagoras in effect, says: For no reason. I can see nothing philosophically disreputable in his retort.

The Atomists are committed to the Principle of Causality and cannot countenance uncaused events. How, then, can they explain 'whence and how motion belongs to the things that exist'?

Their explanation is simple: atom a moves because it was struck by moving atom b. An infinite regress opens up; for if there were a first moment of motion, then the first atomic motion would be inexplicable, since it could not have been occasioned by collision with a moving atom.[3] But the regress is not vicious; and it was explicitly embraced by the Atomists:

Leucippus and Democritus say that the primary bodies [i.e. the atoms] are always moving in the unlimited void (**344**: Aristotle, *Cael* 300b8 = **67 A 16**);

and in the doxography eternal motion is a standing characteristic of the atoms (see above, p. 63). Since the atoms are always in motion, each atomic trajectory was preceded by, and may be explained in terms of, an atomic collision: a moves because b hit it; b moved because c hit it; and so on. And that is all there is to say; every atomic

127

locomotion, and hence every natural change, is equipped with an explanation.

Aristotle was not satisfied.

> They should say what motion it is and what is their natural motion (345),

he grumbles in the *de Caelo* (300b9–10 = **67 A 16**). But the Atomists do say a fair amount about the nature of atomic motion; and they implicitly deny that atoms have any 'natural' motion: all atomic motion is, in Aristotelian jargon, violent, *biaios*. The *Metaphysics* adds another criticism:

> Some—e.g., Leucippus and Plato—suppose an eternal activity; for they say that motion always exists. But they do not say why or what, nor the explanation of why it is thus or thus (**346**: 1071b31–3 = **67 A 18**).

It is the first 'why' that bears the weight; it is repeated in the *Physics*:

> In general, to think that it is a sufficient principle to say that it always is or comes about thus, is to hold a mistaken belief; Democritus reduces the causes of nature to this state, saying that earlier things also happened thus, but he does not think to look for a cause of the 'always' (**347**: 252a32–b1 = **68 A 65**; cf *GA* 742b17–29).

There are, I think two ways of construing Aristotle's criticism. The first fits **346** better: 'Any individual atomic motion can perhaps be explained; but the explanation implies eternal atomic motion: and why do atoms move eternally?' To that question Democritus has an entirely adequate answer, and his answer has an important generalization. All atoms move eternally provided that every sentence of the form '*a* moves eternally' is true; and '*a* moves eternally' is true provided that every sentence of the form '*a* moves at *t*' is true. Now every sentence of this last form is, by hypothesis, true; and the fact it expresses is in every case explicable by way of some sentence of the form '*b* struck *a* in fashion ϕ at *t-n*'. In this way the eternity of atomic motion is explained; for every fact necessary for the occurrence of eternal motion has been explained.

It is worth looking at the argument schematically. The *explanandum* is:

(1) For every object, *x*, and time, *t*, *x* is moving at *t*.

For every case of (1), there is available, in theory, a truth of the form:

(2) *a* moves at t_n because Q.

Hence (1) itself is explained. In general, we explain why everything is

ϕ if we explain, in the case of every individual, why it is ϕ: All the people I invited to the party stayed away. Why? One was ill, one forgot, one couldn't stand the thought of another party, and so on; once individual explanations for each invited friend are given, the complete vacuity of my party is explained. It is absurd for me to accept all these individual excuses and still ask why *everyone* stayed away, as though that were a further question. The case is analogous to the explanation of conjunctive facts: Why is the grass so long and wet that the mower won't cut it?—It is long because it hasn't been cut for two weeks; it is wet because last night's dew has not had time to evaporate. There is no room for the further question: Why is it long *and* wet?

The second interpretation of Aristotle's criticism seems to fit the *Physics* passage quite neatly. Suppose that atom *a* moves with velocity *v* at *t*. Why so? Because, Democritus answers, *b* collided with it at *t-n*, and the velocities of *a* and *b* at *t-n* were v^a and v^b. But what makes that an *explanation* of *a*'s velocity at *t*? Well, 'it always . . . comes about thus'; i.e., whenever an atom of the same type as *b* moving at v^b strikes an atom of the same type as *a* moving at v^a, *a*'s subsequent velocity is *v*. But why is *that* the case? Democritus offers no answer: 'he does not think to look for a cause of the "always"'.

That is an entirely different criticism from the former one. In effect, Aristotle ascribes to Democritus a regularity theory of explanation; and he rejects it as inadequate. Democritus explains individual causal links in terms of universal regularities; but he does not think to explain those regularities. *E* occurs because *C* occurs. Behind this there lies a regularity: every *C*-type event is followed by an *E*-type event. That regularity may, in a sense, be explained; for it may be subsumable under a higher regularity: every *C*-type event is a C_1-type event; and every C_1-type event is followed by an *E*-type event. And C_1 may give place to C_2, and so on. But the regress cannot be infinite; for the ways of specifying atomic events are finite. Thus there will be some ultimate regularity which evades explanation.

Aristotle may mean no more than that Democritus did not push his explanations far enough: he was satisfied with low-level regularities and did not attempt to construct high-level laws. And that criticism was doubtless justified. But I suspect that Aristotle intends a more profound criticism: regularity as such, he thinks, requires explanation; and Democritus cannot satisfy that requirement, since he has nothing but regularities to appeal to. No doubt Aristotle requires a teleological account of natural regularities: things regularly happen thus because it is good that they should so happen. But here again, the Atomists are right: even if teleological explanation has a place in natural science, it is far from clear that every natural regularity is teleologically grounded; and I see no reason for believing that there is anything ultimately unsatisfying about the notion of an inexplicable regularity.

The first round goes to the neo-Ionians: even with Aristotle on their side, the Eleatics lose the fight.

(b) *Locomotion*

Empedocles and Anaxagoras accepted the Eleatic *plenum* and attempted to insinuate locomotion into it; the Atomists boldly defended a universe riddled with vacancies, and thereby dulled the edge of Melissus' logical razor: has Melissus any reply to either of their suggestions?

Antiperistasis does, I believe, show that locomotion in a *plenum* is possible; and to that extent Melissus' arguments fail. And if the Atomists are successful in their defence of the void, then the arguments are inapplicable. But Melissus, I think, should not have been unduly dismayed by either of these facts; for his arguments constitute what is, logically speaking, an unnecessarily devious manoeuvre. Consider any volume of space, V, whether full or pitted with void; and suppose that some of the occupants of this space move between t_1 and t_2. Suppose that, at t_1, the occupants are arranged in a pattern P_1, and that at t_2 they are arranged in P_2. Now it may be that $P_1 = P_2$; and indeed, it may be that at every instant t_i between t_1 and t_2, $P_i = P_1$: locomotion does not strictly imply any change in pattern, as Aristotle's spinning tops indicate. But such a changeless locomotion is no good to the neo-Ionians: if the only locomotion the universe may undergo is of that sort, then plainly locomotion cannot lead to the minglings and collisions which in neo-Ionian physics explain the diverse appearances of the world. Moreover, if V is the whole of space, and if at any t_i $P_i = P_1$, then it is plausible to infer that the occupants of V do not move at all; for none of them ever changes its position relative to anything else.

If locomotion entails change of relative position, Melissus is home. Formally, his argument runs like this: 'Suppose, as before, that there is locomotion in V between t_1 and t_2. Then there must be some volume V^1, whose inhabitants are rearranged between t_1 and t_2; i.e., there must be some t_i between t_1 and t_2 such that $P_i^1 \neq P_1^1$. But rearrangement, or *metakosmêsis*, is a kind of alteration; and the general argument against alteration shows, as Melissus explicitly points out, that *metakosmêsis* is impossible. Therefore locomotion is impossible. Void or no void, motion involves rearrangement; void or no void, motion is logically absurd.'

I do not know whether Melissus saw that point: he does not make it expressly, though his particular attention to *metakosmêsis* leads me to suppose that it was not far from the surface of his mind. I do not think that any neo-Ionian got a glimpse of the danger, or took any evasive action. And evasive action is necessary: if the neo-Ionians hope to do away with alteration and retain locomotion, then Melissus has thwarted their hope before it was expressed; and if they intend to admit alteration by grounding it on locomotion, then Melissus has proved their intention topsy-turvy—before they can vindicate locomotion they must defend alteration. In either case, victory goes to Melissus: only if the neo-Ionians can defeat him on alteration will they obtain their mobile world.

What of the void? The Atomists argued that there is empty space, on the grounds that there is no more reason for there to be body than for there to be space. Melissus will hardly accept that: after all, he has provided a reason against the existence of the void, and the Atomists have done nothing to discountenance it. The Atomists agree with Melissus that no substance has vacuous parts: Abderite bodies, like Melissan bodies, are full, massy or solid. But Melissus has argued that any existent body is spatially infinite; hence there is no empty space outside his body. And if vacancy can be found neither within nor without body, vacancy cannot be found at all. Melissus may accept the distinction between existence$_1$ and existence$_2$ (above, p. 102); but he has no reason to accept the existence$_2$ of void.

Here, too, Melissus wins the fight. But here his victory is only a technical one: the Atomists should have attacked his argument for the spatial infinity of body; they did not do so, but they could have done so with little difficulty. For that argument is perhaps the weakest link in Melissus' deductive chain.

(c) *Alteration*

Alteration, it might appear, is the key to the neo-Ionian treasure chest: give them that, and they will show us again the familiar world of changing phenomena; withhold it, and they cannot even describe a mobile world. Alas, the neo-Ionian attitude to alteration yields no satisfaction at all: either they were discreetly taciturn, or fate has chosen to hide their wisdom from us; at all events, we can learn remarkably little about this crucial issue. I shall briefly survey the few facts that do present themselves.

First, Anaxagoras. According to Aristotle,

131

He states that coming to be and being destroyed are the same as alteration (**348**: *GC* 314a13 = **59 A 52**).

Some scholars find an original fragment lurking in this sentence; but that is improbable.[4] In any case, the purport of the sentence is quite obscure: does it mean that Anaxagoras held on to alteration and explained generation in terms of it? Or does it rather imply that, in conflating generation and alteration, he abandoned the latter along with the former? Some look to **B 10** for a general rejection of alteration; but the fragment cannot be taken in that way (below, p. 135). Nor will general considerations of Anaxagorean physics help us. Take a pint of water and freeze it: has it, according to Anaxagoras, lost one set of qualities and acquired a new set? Is there something which was fluid and is now solid? which was transparent and is now opaque? Or is it rather the case that the stuff has had all its qualities all along, now manifesting one set, now another? And if that is so, is not its coming to manifest a different set of qualities in itself an alteration in the stuff? There is no advantage in pursuing these questions: as far as we know, they were never posed by Anaxagoras.

The Abderites fare a little better: atoms are unequivocally immutable (above, p. 44); so that if there is any alteration in the Abderite world, it can only occur at the macroscopic level. And atomic motions are said to account for macroscopic changes:

> Democritus and Leucippus, having made their shapes, make
> alteration and generation from them: generation and destruction
> by association and dissociation, alteration by order and position
> (**349**: Aristotle, *GC* 315b6–9 = **67 A 9**).

The Atomists ascribe locomotion to their atoms:

> and this is the only *kinesis* they give to the elements, reserving the
> others for the compounds; for they say that things grow and
> diminish and change and come into being and perish as the
> primary bodies congregate and separate (**350**: Simplicius,
> **68 A 58**).

But what exactly are these macroscopic changes? Does freezing water change from being transparent to being opaque? Does grass in high summer change from green to brown? Transparency and opacity, green and brown are not 'real' qualities; they exist only 'by convention' (above, pp. 68–75). Then perhaps the changes are similarly unreal, occurring only 'by convention'. Does the world contain *apparent* changes from green to brown, or *genuine* changes from apparent green to apparent brown? As far as I can see, the

Abderites did not pose these questions; nor did they grasp the importance of alteration in the neo-Ionian answer to Elea.

Of Empedocles we hear a little more; but that little is hardly satisfying. Once, Empedocles seems to allow that his 'roots' may alter:

> . . . running through one another,
> they become different-looking (*alloiôpa*): such is the change that
> mixture makes (**351: 31 B 21**.13–14).

But the corresponding lines in **B 17** are significantly different:

> . . . running through one another,
> they become different things (*alla*) at different times and are
> always absolutely homogeneous (**352: B 17**.34–5).

Aristotle perhaps has this last phrase in mind when he argues that, according to Empedocles, the elements are 'preserved (*sôzomena*)' when they mingle to form compounds (*GC* 337a29 = **A 43**). And Philoponus expands the point critically:

> He contradicts the phenomena when he does away with alteration
> which evidently occurs, and himself when he says on the one hand
> that the elements are immutable and that they do not come from
> one another but the other things come from them [= **B 17**.35],
> and on the other hand he says that when Love is in power they all
> become one and form the Sphere which is qualityless [cf., e.g., **B
> 35**.5], since in it is preserved the characteristic property (*idiotês*)
> neither of fire nor of any of the other [elements], each of the
> elements losing its own form (**353: A 41**).

There are thus two related criticisms of Empedocles: he expressly makes his elements 'always absolutely homogeneous' or immutable; yet first he holds that at the time of the cosmic Sphere there is just *one* mixed stuff in the universe; and, second, he says that during the periods of cosmic growth and decay the elements 'become different-looking'. I think that Empedocles is undeniably confused on both these counts; and I see no plausible answer to the first charge of inconsistency. But it is the second charge that is more interesting here: what should Empedocles have said about the status of macroscopic alteration?

First, he might have said that his elements, like Abderite atoms, never alter: no quantity of fire ever loses any of its characteristic qualities or ever gains any extra properties; masses of fire may split or coagulate, mix, mingle and associate with other elements; but no bit of fire ever alters. When Empedocles says that fire 'becomes different-looking' or 'different things', he is speaking with the vulgar, not with the learned (cf. **B 9**.5), and we should not charge him with strict inconsistency.

Yet that defence leaves us uneasy: what, after all, happens when we vulgar speakers say that Socrates grows pale? Not, admittedly, an alteration in any constituent element of Socrates; but surely the mixed mass of elements which we vulgarly call a man alters? Surely that particular volume of stuff, considered as a whole, changes in colour? Does Empedocles mean to deny this? Would he say that Socrates does not really change at all? and would he explain this by a theory of sensible qualities Abderite in tone? Again, we simply do not know.

These animadversions on the neo-Ionian attitude to alteration may seem a trifle crotchety or at least ungenerous. Yet it does appear to be the case that the neo-Ionians were careless and cavalier in their account of alteration: locomotion and generation engaged their close attention; but they failed to see the strength and cohesion of the Eleatic position—of the Melissan version in particular—and they made no attempt to come to grips with the neat argument by which 'change in bright colour' was allegedly abolished.

But after all, the Eleatic rejection of alteration is firmly based on their rejection of generation; and it will be said, reasonably enough, that if the neo-Ionians saw a route to the defence of generation they may properly have taken the defence of alteration for granted. I turn, therefore, to generation.

(d) *Generation*

Empedocles is forthright and plain:

[Mortal men are] fools; for their thoughts are not deep,
since they think that what before did not exist comes into being,
or that something dies and is completely destroyed (**354: 31 B 11**).

That Eleatic conclusion was based on Eleatic reasoning; for **354** must originally have been followed by **B 12**:

It is impossible for anything to come into being from what is not;
and it is unattainable and unaccomplished for what exists to perish;
for wherever anyone ever takes a stand, there it will always
be (**355**).[5]

The argument is cribbed from Parmenides, **156**.7–9. (Empedocles' argument against destruction is presented in a corrupt text: no emendation I know of gives a sense which is both clear and interesting.)

Anaxagoras holds the same Eleatic view: 'No thing comes into being or is destroyed' (**59 B 17**). And he too probably adopted the Parmenidean argument; for

> He held the common opinion of the natural scientists to be
> true—that nothing comes into being from what is not (**356**:
> Aristotle, *Phys* 187a27–9 = **A 52**; cf. Aëtius, **A 46**).

Some scholars catch the Eleatic scent in **B 10** which asks, rhetorically, 'How could hair come into being from non-hair, or flesh from non-flesh?' (**212**). Aristotle appears to connect the view implicit in **B 10** with 'the common opinion of the natural scientists'; and we can make sense of the connexion. Suppose that the general principle lying behind **B 10** is:

(1) If something F comes into being from a, then a is F.

Evidently, (1) is closely related to the Principle of Synonymy which I have already discussed (vol. 1, pp. 88, 118). A special case of (1) is:

(2) If something existent comes into being from a, then a is existent.

And (2) can be read as bearing on the Parmenidean problem of 'absolute' generation; for it effectively denies the possibility of generation 'from what is not'.

Unfortunately the application is un-Eleatic and pointless. It is un-Eleatic because in (1) the phrase 'from a' marks a as the *source* of the F product; and in the Eleatic argument 'from a' is taken in a different sense. It is pointless because there is no way of moving from (2) to a rejection of generation; indeed, (2) comes uncomfortably close to rehabilitating generation. The purpose of (1) is to indicate that Fs are produced from other Fs; why, then, cannot (2) be taken to indicate that generation is possible, provided that existents are produced from other existents? At the very least Anaxagoras needs to argue that generation 'from what is' is impossible; and there is no hint in our texts that he ever did that. Thus I do not believe that **B 10** has any bearing on generation (for my reading of it see above, p. 31); and I suspect that Anaxagoras, like Empedocles, simply adopted the orthodox Parmenidean argument for his own.

In two respects, however, the accounts of generation in Anaxagoras and Empedocles do go beyond anything in Parmenides. First, they both reject 'epigenesis', the theory that there might come into being new things in addition to the present ungenerated furniture of the world. Here is Anaxagoras' argument:

And when these things are separated out in this way, you must
know that all of them are in no respect less nor more (for it is not
possible to have more than all), but all are always equal (357: B 5).

Thus: 'There can never be more than all the things there are; so
things will always be equal in number.' Both the premiss and the
conclusion of this argument are 'untruisms' (vol. 1, p. 167). The
premiss may be glossed by either of:

(3a) For any time t, if there are exactly n things at t, then there are no
more than n things at t.
(3b) For any times t and t', if there are exactly n things at t, then
there are no more than n things at t'.

And the conclusion may be glossed by either of:

(4a) For any time t, the number of things existing at t = the number
of things existing at t.
(4b) For any times t and t', the number of things existing at t = the
number of things existing at t'.

Anaxagoras is certainly not entitled to (3b), so it is natural to take his
parenthetical premiss as (3a); he is hardly interested in the trivial
conclusion (4a), so it is natural to take his conclusion to be (4b). Now
(3a) does not entail (4b); but (3b) does: Anaxagoras surreptitiously
mates the truth of (3a) with the powers of (3b), and produces a logical
monster.

Empedocles' argument against epigenesis goes like this:

And in addition to these [sc. the four roots, (?) and Love and
Hate], nothing comes into being or declines.
For if they perished outright they would no longer exist.
And what could increase this totality? And whence could it come?
And where could it be destroyed, since nothing is empty of these?
(358: B 17.30–3).

The argument is not pellucid;[6] but the following gloss seems
possible. 'Suppose that at t some new root R comes into existence,
and suppose that there is an empty space for R to occupy at t. Since at
present the four roots occupy all the space there is, some of them
would have to have perished before t to make room for R; and it is
impossible for the roots to perish. Hence there is no empty space at t
for R to occupy; thus R cannot be added to the universe at t; nor, for
that matter, can it come *from* anywhere or pass away *to* anywhere.'

The argument presupposes Empedocles' rejection of 'the void' or
empty space (287); and its last two clauses are jejune, reminiscent of
Epicharmus' satire rather than of Parmenides' philosophy. But those
points apart, the argument is sound; and it makes a mildly

interesting addition to the Eleatic armoury. What is its purpose? Why argue specifically against epigenesis when you have a general argument against generation as such? Perhaps Empedocles indulged in the following train of thought: 'Parmenides' argument shows that if *a* exists, then *a* was not generated, and hence that none of the present furniture of the world can have come into being; but he has omitted to show that the present furniture cannot be augmented; and I shall repair the omission.' But that is a poor line of thought: Parmenides' argument does not apply simply to present existents.

The second respect in which Empedocles and Anaxagoras went beyond Parmenides reflects their greater consideration for the common man and his common language.[7] I have already quoted a sentence from **59 B 17**; here is the whole fragment:

> The Greeks do not think correctly[8] of coming into being and being destroyed; for no thing comes into being or is destroyed, but it is from existing things that things are commingled and separated out. And in this way they would correctly call coming into being commingling and being destroyed separating out (359).

In place of the generation of new items Anaxagoras offers us the rearrangement of old items; instead of the destruction of existent items Anaxagoras offers us the rearrangement of their parts.

There is a similar passage in Empedocles:

> I will tell you another thing: there is birth (*phusis*) for none of all mortal things, nor is there an end in doleful death;
> but there is only mixing and interchange of what is mixed
> —and the name of birth is applied by men to this (**360: 31 B 8**).[9]

Again:

> And when they [sc. the four roots] are mixed in the shape of a man† and come into the light,†
> or in the shape of a kind of wild beast or of plants
> or of birds, then (?) they say that this comes into being (?);
> and when they [sc. the roots] are separated apart, this again [they call] wretched fate:
> (?) they do not name them as is right (?) but I too myself comply with the custom (**361: B 9**; cf. **B 10, 15, 35**).

The text of **361** is desperately corrupt;[10] but its general drift is clear enough: like Anaxagoras, Empedocles is offering us comminglings and separations in place of generations and destructions.

Men talk of 'generation' and 'destruction': according to

Parmenides, such talk is mere verbiage (**156**. 40); Anaxagoras and Empedocles agree that the talk is necessarily false, but they assert that it is readily translated into an unobjectionable idiom: replace '*a* is generated' and '*a* is destroyed' by 'comminglings and separations of such and such a sort occur'. And Empedocles at least is prepared to 'comply with the custom' and speak with the vulgar: 'It is impossible, even in the most rigid of philosophic reasonings, so far to alter the bent and genius of the tongue we speak, as never to give a handle for cavillers to pretend difficulties and inconsistencies. But a fair and ingenuous reader will collect the sense from the scope and tenor and connexion of a discourse, making allowance for those inaccurate modes of speech which use has made inevitable' (Berkeley, *Principles* §LII).[11]

Philolaus and the Atomists differ from Empedocles and Anaxagoras in the matter of generation. In **277**, Philolaus asserts that 'the things that exist . . . have come into being'; and nothing forbids us to take this text at its face value. Leucippus set up his system precisely in order to defend generation and destruction; for:

> He thought he had arguments which, by saying what agreed with perception, would not do away with either generation or
> destruction or motion and the plurality of existent things (**362**: *GC* 325a33–5 = **67 A 7**).

Philolaus' principles, and the Abderites' corpuscles, are ungenerated and indestructible; but the macroscopic objects of the world which come from the principles and are constituted by the corpuscles can and do come into existence and cease to exist. .

In Philolaus' system, macroscopic entities are generated by a harmonizing (*harmozein*) or arranging (*kosmein*) of the elements; and it is reasonable to suppose that he hoped to immunize generation against the Eleatic disease by explaining it in terms of the interconnecting of the ungenerated elements. Thus '*a* is generated' may be true; but its truth conditions are given by some proposition of the form 'b_1 and b_2 are harmonized'. The same account is explicitly ascribed to the Atomists:

> If generation is the association of atoms and destruction their dissociation, then generation will be alteration (**363**: Simplicius, **68 A 37**).

> These atoms, separated from one another in the unlimited void and differing in shapes and sizes and position and order, travel in the void and overtake and strike one another; and some rebound

138

wherever it chances, but others catch onto (*periplekesthai*) one
another by virtue of the symmetry of their shapes and sizes and
positions and orders, and stay together (*summenein*), and in this
way the generation of composites is achieved (364: Simplicius,
67 A 14).

Empedocles and Anaxagoras deny that anything is ever generated:
the process we habitually call generation is, they say, in fact a
commingling of ungenerated stuffs. Philolaus, Leucippus and
Democritus, on the other hand, hope to save generation: things, they
say, certainly are generated and destroyed; but generations and
destructions are in fact comminglings and dissolutions of one sort or
another. Consider the two sentences: P—'an F is generated'; Q—'a,
b, c, ... commingle in such a way as to take on an F-like
appearance'. According to Anaxagoras and Empedocles, P is always
false, Q sometimes true; and Q in fact describes the type of event
men typically mean to refer to when they use P. According to
Philolaus and the Atomists, Q is sometimes true; and P is equivalent
to Q; so that P, too, is sometimes true.

That distinction may seem fairly trifling: after all, both parties
'reduce' generation to comminglings (and hence to locomotion); for
both claim to account for the phenomena we usually refer to as
generations by way of comminglings.[12] Yet there are at least two
significant differences between the parties: one will emerge in the
next section; the other I state briefly now. The Atomists' analysis of
generation has certain formal similarities to Aristotle's; in particular,
they, like Aristotle (vol. 1, p. 197), make generation *ex nihilo*, or
creation, a self-contradictory notion. For a to be generated is for
pre-existent entities to rearrange themselves: the sentence form 'a was
generated at t and nothing existed before t' is inconsistent. Now
Empedocles and Anaxagoras are equally opposed to generation; and
they too think that creation is logically impossible. But the
impossibility in their case has Parmenidean roots: sever the stem of
the Eleatic argument, show the objections to 'not-being' misguided,
and creation becomes possible. If Elea were refuted, Empedocles and
Anaxagoras might countenance creation: the refutation would have
no such liberating consequence for the Atomists.

What, finally, would Melissus have said to all this? He would not
have been impressed: 'Empedocles and Anaxagoras deny generation
but accept locomotion; they thereby commit themselves, whether
they like it or not, to alteration; and alteration entails generation.
Their position is tediously inconsistent. Philolaus and the Atomists
accept generation for non-elementary objects, and defend it by

analysis in terms of commingling. They do not explain how their analysis constitutes a defence; and they do not indicate where they think the Eleatic arguments against generation fail. Their position may not be internally contradictory; but it amounts to no more than an unargued rejection of Eleatic metaphysics.'

I have sympathy with Melissus' hypothetical retort; and I believe that the neo-Ionians never apprehended the power of the Eleatic deduction. Empedocles and Anaxagoras must drive a wedge between 'a becomes F' and 'a's Fness comes into being'. I do not see how they can do that. Philolaus and the Atomists must point to the flaws in Parmenides' argument: flaws there certainly are; but no Presocratic put his finger upon them. The neo-Ionians threw off the intellectual paralysis with which Parmenides had threatened Greek thought: they manfully attempted to tread again the scientific road, and they took many progressive steps even if their feet remained shackled by Elea. And of course the neo-Ionians are more right than the Eleatics: things do move, they do alter, they are generated. For all that, the neo-Ionian revival is fundamentally a flop: it does not answer Elea.

(e) Ontology

Generation and existence are connected by the tightest of conceptual bonds: to be generated is to come into existence; if a is generated at t, then a exists immediately after t. Thus anyone who holds that 'a is generated' is always false must maintain that 'a exists' is true only if a is eternal—ungenerated and indestructible. Now philosophers, evidently, are not eternal; nor can they be generated, according to Empedocles and Anaxagoras: hence no philosophers exist. Do men, horses, trees, clouds, chairs, books exist? Empedocles and Anaxagoras must answer: No.

As far as we know, Anaxagoras did not recognize this consequence of his views; Empedocles perhaps did. At **31 B 17**.34 (= **B 26**.3) he says of the four roots:

> But these themselves exist; and running through one another
> they become different things at different times and are always
> absolutely homogenous (**365**; cf. **352**).

The words 'these themselves exist' translate '*aut' estin tauta*': one permissible paraphrase of the Greek is: 'these alone exist'.[13] If that paraphrase is right, Empedocles assigns existence to his roots and to nothing else. At least one ancient critic seems so to have understood Empedocles: Colotes, Plutarch's Epicurean opponent, asserted that in Empedocles' view men do not exist (Plutarch, *adv Col* 1113 AB).

And it is worth quoting a fragment of Empedocles' younger contemporary, Ion of Chios. His philosophical work, the *Triagmos*, began as follows:

> The beginning of my account is this: all things are three, and there is nothing more or less than these three things (366: 36 B 1).[14]

We know almost nothing of Ion's philosophical stance; and it would be rash to put much weight on these words. Yet the obvious interpretation is this: apart from the basic, primordial, entities, nothing at all exists.

But can we really believe that Empedocles or Ion meant to deny the existence of chalk and cheese? Of course not: Empedocles means that there are no *elemental* stuffs other than the four roots; and Ion means that everything is made from just the three things that constitute his elements. Empedocles surely did not see what he was committing himself to in denying generation.

Philolaus and the Atomists have not the same need for a parsimonious ontology: macroscopic objects are generated; they may be ephemeral and yet existent. Philolaus explicitly asserts that macroscopic objects do exist; indeed, they are paradigmatically *ta eonta* (cf. 277). Yet Philolaus distinguishes, I think, between the ontological status of his elements and that of their compounds. At all events, he uses, in 277, the ordinary verb '*einai*' for the existence of ordinary things, but applies '*huparchein* (subsist)' to the elements; and while ordinary objects are designated *ta eonta*, the elements are *ta pragmata*. The difference in terminology may, I suppose, be merely an accident of style; yet I am inclined to think that it is deliberate: the difference in language is employed to signal a difference in fact. To see the point of this we may turn to the Atomists.

In discussing the Abderite divide between what exists *nomôi* and what exists *eteêi* I considered only the status of qualities on the *nomôi* side of the fence (above, pp. 68–75). And indeed all our authorities, with the exception of Plutarch, make *nomôi* entities exclusively qualities. Plutarch adds *sunkrisis*, 'combination', to the *nomôi* list. A *sunkrisis* is a macroscopic body, or atomic conglomeration: '*sunkrinein* (to combine)' is regularly used for the formation of complex bodies from the elementary corpuscles (e.g., 213, Aristotle; Sextus, 68 A 59); and elsewhere those bodies are called *sunkrimata* (e.g., Diogenes Laertius, IX.44 = 68 A 1; Galen, A 49) or *sunkriseis* (e.g., Aëtius, A 105). Plutarch's gloss on *sunkrisis* is thus correct:

> And when [the atoms] come close to one another or fall together or
> intertwine, of the conglomerated masses one seems to be water,
> one fire, one a plant, one a man; and the atoms, which he calls
> *ideai*, are all that exist; nothing else does (**367: 68 A 57**).

Stuffs and macroscopic substances only *seem* to be (*phainesthai*);
atoms alone really exist: water and men, fire and plants, stand on the
nomôi side of the great divide.

The obscure philosopher Cleidemus gave the following account of
lightning:

> There are some who, like Cleidemus, say that lightning does not
> exist but is an appearance (*phainesthai*), suggesting that the
> occurrence is similar to what happens when one strikes the sea with
> a stick; for the water appears (*phainetai*) as flashing in the night.
> In this way when the moisture in the clouds is struck, the
> appearance (*phantasia*) of brightness is the lightning (**368**:
> Aristotle, *Meteor* 370a10–15 = **62 A 1**).

Cleidemus' point is this: when water is struck with an oarblade, it
cannot be supposed to undergo a genuine change of colour, or to
emit a tongue of flame or the like; all that happens is that the water
appears differently to the striker. Similarly, the lightning flash is not
a substance in its own right, nor yet a coloration of the clouds: what
happens is simply that the cloud *appears* differently.

Why Cleidemus advanced this view we do not know; nor am I
interested here in Cleidemus' meteorology. I cite the passage because
it is echoed in the doxography on Leucippus:

> All things happen in accordance with *phantasia* and *dokêsis* and
> none in accordance with truth; but they seem (*phainesthai*) in the
> way of the oar in the water (**369**: Epiphanius, **67 A 33**).

The report is not clear, and the reporter is not worth much; yet
behind his words there may lie an account of macroscopic items
similar to the one which Plutarch ascribes to Democritus—they do
not really exist.

At all events, the Atomists have a good argument for denying
reality to macroscopic ephemera—not the Eleatic argument, which
they cannot employ, but a reasoning of their own.

> Democritus says . . . that it is impossible for one thing to come
> from two or two from one (**223**: Aristotle, *Met* 1039a9 = **68 A 42**).

Thus the interweaving (*periplokê*) of the atoms

makes them touch, and be next to one another but does not generate any genuinely single nature whatever out of them; for it is absolutely silly to think that two or more things could ever become one (213, Aristotle).

Anything that truly exists is *one* thing, a unity; macroscopic objects are conglomerations of atoms; no conglomeration of objects can ever constitute *one* thing, a unity; hence macroscopic objects do not truly exist. That, I suppose, is the metaphysical foundation of the Atomists' view that macroscopic objects are unreal.

But why suppose that 'two or more things cannot become one'? As it stands, that proposition seems to be a trivial falsehood. Two or more things do frequently make one: a nib and a penholder make a pen; four limbs, a head and a torso make a body; engine and bodywork make a motor-car; and—in just the same way—many million corpuscles make a desk or a tree or a cloud. Most of the things we see are compounds in an evident way. That does not derogate from their unity: my pen is *one* thing, viz. one pen; it is a cohesive item with a unifying function; it shows no tendency to fall apart, atomize, or disintegrate. What could be more unitary than that?

Yet it would be wrong to dismiss the Atomist principle out of hand. Let us approach it obliquely. There is a classical conception of substance, originating with Aristotle, according to which substances are ultimate subjects of predication: things are said of them, they are not said of anything else. Substances are ontologically indispensable objects. In a more up-to-date jargon: 'If a complete account of what there is would need some substantival expression referring to the *F*s, then the *F*s are substances; but not otherwise'.[15] Non-substances may be said to exist or to 'have being'; but their existence is essentially parasitic upon the existence of substances. Pride, doubtless, exists: there is such a thing as pride. But all talk about pride can be analysed, one would imagine, into talk about proud men; and for pride to exist is simply for there to exist men who are proud. Prejudice exists; but truths about prejudice are presentable as truths about men who prejudge matters; for prejudice to exist is simply for there to be men who are thus given to prejudging.

Pride and prejudice are non-substances. A further type of non-substance is an aggregate: aggregates are the sums of their parts; any truths about aggregates can be expressed as truths about those parts, and all facts about aggregates are no more than facts about their parts. The meteorological truths about clouds dissolve into truths about their constituent water-particles; anatomical facts are facts about the constituent cells of the body; and, in general, macroscopic facts are facts about the constituent atoms of macroscopic bodies. Clouds exist just in so far as water droplets congregate; there are bodies only if cells are suitably harmonized; and, in general, for macroscopic bodies to exist is for atoms to be collected together.

We can now give a more plausible sense to Democritus' assertion that two things cannot be one: no aggregate of two or more real things or substances is itself a real thing or substance. Aggregates are not substances; hence aggregates of substances are not substances. Since all macroscopic objects are atomic conglomerates, no macroscopic object is a substance: no such object exists *eteêi*.

Anaxagoras and Empedocles, it might be thought, are not far from the Atomists here: they make certain stuffs eternal and substantial, and they are committed to denying real existence to everything else. They differ from the Atomists only in a certain conceptual poverty: denying existence to men and clouds, they were obliged to say that, in strictness of speech, there are no men and there are no clouds; the Atomists, availing themselves of a distinction between two senses of 'exist' (above, p. 102), can say that men and clouds do exist$_2$ but do not exist$_1$. There are men and clouds; but men and clouds are not real. In Philolaic terminology, men and clouds exist (*einai*), they do not subsist (*huparchein*).

However that may be, it is only the Atomists from among the neo-Ionians whose ontology and philosophy have had any influence on later scientific ages. That philosophy can be briefly stated as follows: 'The proper language of science is thin and meagre: the only objects it names are atoms; the only predicates it contains are those denoting primary or proper qualities of bodies, and those denoting certain elementary spatio-temporal relations between objects. All facts can be expressed in this language; for any sentence in our ordinary language can be uniquely paired with a scientific sentence which has the same truth conditions as it has: ''grass is green'', ''bread is nutritious'', ''ink dries quickly'', can each be paired with a sentence mentioning only atomic structures and atomic predicates. Ordinary language is, ordinarily, indispensable; but for the purposes of science—that is to say, with regard to the pursuit of truth—it is grotesquely ornate, and a plain, severe style is preferable.'

Scientifically, Atomism is ancient history. No scientist believes anything that Democritus said; and the modern successors to atomism have long ago repudiated the primitive image of a world of billiard balls rolling about on a vacant three-dimensional cloth. Philosophically, on the other hand, the Atomist system remains an interest and a challenge: as the first exercise in reductive ontology, it is the ultimate source of a popular pastime of modern philosophical logicians. The questions 'What *really* is there?' and 'What *must* there be?' still trouble and perplex; and some at least of the modern answers to them have a complexion curiously reminiscent of Abdera. Again, as the first fully conscious attempt to provide a thorough-going materialist account of the world, Atomism remains alive: to that issue I shall turn in a later chapter.

VII

The Sophists

(a) *Anthropology*

Gorgias of Leontini has already made an appearance on the Presocratic stage. Gorgias was a Sophist; and his fellow Sophists will have a larger part to play in this and the following chapters. Who, then, were these Sophists? They do not constitute a school, like the Milesians and the Eleatics, bound together by a common philosophy; rather, they are a group of outstanding individuals—Protagoras, Gorgias, Hippias, Prodicus, Antiphon, Thrasymachus—who are associated not by any common doctrines but by a common outlook on life and learning. The term 'sophist (*sophistês*)' was not originally a term of abuse: when Herodotus calls Solon and Pythagoras sophists (I.29; IV.95) he is praising them as sages and men of wisdom (*sophia*) (cf. Aristides, 79 A 1). But '*sophistês*' became connected not with '*sophia*' but with '*to sophon* (cleverness)'; and *to sophon ou sophia*. Thus Plato offers us six uncomplimentary 'definitions' of the sophist as a tradesman in cleverness (*Sophist* 231 D = 79 A 2); and Aristotle defines the sophist as 'a man who makes money from apparent but unreal wisdom' (*Top* 165a 22 = 79 A 3). Xenophon, that stuffy old prig, put the classical view clearly:

> The sophists speak to deceive and they write for their own gain, and they give no benefit to anyone; for not one of them became or is wise, but each is actually content to be called a sophist—which is a term of reproach in the eyes of those who think properly. So I urge you to guard against the professions of the sophists, but not to dishonour the thoughts of the philosophers (370: 79 A 2a).[1]

The sophist sells his cleverness: he is an intellectual harlot; and, not inappropriately, he adopts a meretricious intellectual pose (Xenophon, *Mem*. I.vi.13).

A Protagorean anecdote is apposite. Protagoras taught rhetoric for cash; and, confident of his tutorial abilities, he stipulated that his legal pupils need not pay him until they had won their first lawsuit. A pupil, Euathlus, had not paid his fees, and Protagoras took him to court. Euathlus argued that he had not yet won a case: Pythagoras retorted that if he, Protagoras, won the present case, then clearly Euathlus must pay the tutorial fee; and if Euathlus won, then by the terms of the tutorial, he must equally pay the fee (Diogenes Laertius, IX.56 = **80 A 1**).

A spurious cleverness, and a love of cash: those are the marks of the sophist in the unflattering portrait painted by Xenophon and Plato. I shall not trace out the somewhat tedious dispute among modern scholars over the reasons for Plato's judgment and its fairness. Certainly, the Sophists taught for money; but no modern scholar will dare to hold that against them (cf. Philostratus, **80 A 2**). Certainly, they were clever; but cleverness is not an intellectual vice. In some cases their seriousness is in doubt; but only the solemn will find fault with that. And it is an indisputable fact that many of the Sophists were men of wide interests and vast knowledge; the most cursory perusal of their remains will convince any reader of that.[2] I shall not attempt a rounded picture of the contribution to philosophy of the Sophists, nor even a portrayal of any individual Sophist: to do so would require a volume in itself. But in this and the following two chapters I shall discuss several of the larger and more interesting theses ascribed to one or another of those men; and some rough idea of the nature and value of the sophistic movement will, I hope, emerge.

> About gods I cannot know either that they are or that they are not.
> For many things prevent one from knowing—the obscurity, and
> the life of man, which is short (**371: 80 B 4**).

Later generations reported those resounding words with a frisson of pious horror, and alleged that they caused the Abderite Protagoras to be expelled from Athens, that bastion of liberty, and his books to be publicly burned (e.g., Diogenes Laertius, IX.52 = **A 1**).[3] Protagoras was listed among the ancient *atheoi* (e.g., Eusebius, *ad* **B 4**); but **371** is not atheistical: as Philostratus (**A 2**) correctly observes, it indicates *aporia* or agnosticism (cf. Cicero, *de natura deorum* I.42.117). Diogenes of Oenoanda, it is true, offers an atheistical interpretation:

> He said he did not know if there are any gods, and that is the same
> as to say he knew that there are no gods (**372:** fr. 11 Ch = **A 23**).[4]

But Diogenes crassly conflates a profession of knowledge, ('I know that not-*P*') with a confession of ignorance ('I do not know that *P*'). To the believer, agnostics may be as bad as atheists; but to the atheist agnostics are not much better than believers.

Agnosticism is an interesting stance; but Protagoras' reasons for adopting it are disappointing. The term 'obscurity (*adêlotês*)' recalls Xenophanes; and we wonder if Protagoras developed arguments of the sort he found in Xenophanes' poem. But the second of the 'many things [that] prevent one from knowing' suggests that Protagoras offered no such support for his agnosticism: *vita brevis*—theology is dismissed with a shrug.

The significant part of 371 is the part we do not possess: the fragment begins '*peri men theôn* . . . (About gods on the one hand . . .)'; the word *men*, we may guess, had its answering *de*: 'On the other hand'. A further guess has it that the *de* sentence asserted the possibility of knowledge about men: 'Of the gods I know nothing; about men I speak thus'.[5] If we presume to scan god we shall observe nothing; theology is to be adjured, and replaced by anthropology.

And anthropology, in a broad sense of the term, was, as we know from Plato, an interest of Protagoras: the origins of man, and more particularly, the origins of human skills, of human customs, and of human social and moral conventions, were for him an object of speculative study. The long story put into his mouth in Plato's *Protagoras* (320C–322E = **C 1**) is doubtless Plato's own production; but it was produced on the basis of a Protagorean original.[6] The subject was popular in Abdera; for Democritus also offered an anthropology. A few fragments survive:

> Democritus says that music is a younger art, and he gives the reason, asserting that necessity did not separate it off but it came about from superfluity (**373: 68 B 144**),

and thus anticipating the familiar Aristotelian account of the origin of the arts and sciences (*Met* 981b13–25). Again:

> In the most important things we became learners: of the spider in weaving and healing, of the swallow in building, of the songbirds—swan and nightingale—in imitative song (**374: B 154**; cf. Aelian, **A 151**).

These are pitiful remnants of a grand work. In a passage of Diodorus (**B 5**) many scholars see a comprehensive epitome of that original; but their view is on the whole unlikely to be true.

In scope and in emphasis Democritus' work and its Protagorean offspring represent a new departure; but behind them lies the old

Ionian ideal: a complete and systematic account of the generation, growth and present state of the universe. Democritus' anthropology was probably set within a cosmogony (cf. Censorinus, etc. **A 139**): the universe began; life was formed; man, and human institutions, were founded. Anaximander or Xenophanes might have written the work; all that is new in Democritus is the anthropological slant: instead of the natural world it is the human world which absorbs his interest; instead of a history of the stars a history of human culture fires his intellectual imagination. (Or so at least it seems: we are dealing with fragmentary reports, and inference to the emphasis and focus of a work from a few fragments is a chancy thing.)

I shall not attempt to outline the speculations of Democritus or of Protagoras, nor yet to fit them into their historical contexts: both tasks are exceedingly intricate, and in any case I find anthropology— especially armchair anthropology—a fearful bore.[7] Instead, I shall expand a little upon two topics included in the Democritean anthropology which do possess some philosophical interest. And the first of these, paradoxically, is theology.

(b) *The origins of atheism*

I begin, not with Democritus, but with Critias, a man of black fame: 'he seems to me the worst of all men who have a name for evil' (Philostratus, **88 A 1**). He was one of the Thirty who overthrew the Athenian democracy in the last desperate years of the Peloponnesian War, and who in turn received a swift and fatal overthrow. By all accounts he was an unlovely character, cruel, cynical, overbearing. He was also the scion of a noble house, and a literary dilettante: we possess fragments of occasional poems, of verse comedies, and of prose 'constitutions' full of recondite trifles. Critias was no philosopher; nor was he a sophist in the Protagorean or Gorgian mould; indeed, his nearest connexion to philosophy was by blood, for Plato was his nephew. He might well be left for the historians and literary scholars to write upon; but one long fragment has won him, by accident, a place in the history of thought, and the fragment is amusing enough to bear transcription. It comes from a satyr play, *Sisyphus*:

There was a time when the life of men was unorganized,
and brutish, and the servant of force;
when there was no reward for the good,
nor again any punishment came to the bad.
And then I think men set up laws   5

as punishers, in order that justice might be ruler
[of all alike], and hold violence a slave.
And anyone who might transgress was penalized.
Then, since the laws prevented them
from performing overt acts by force,   10
but they performed them secretly, then it seems to me
[for the first time] some man, acute and wise in mind,
invented the fear of the gods for mortals, so that
there might be some terror for the bad even if in secret
they do or say or think anything.   15
Hence, then, he introduced divinity,
saying that 'There is a spirit enjoying undying life,
hearing and seeing by its mind, thinking and
attending to everything, carrying a divine nature;
and he will hear everything said among men   20
and will be able to see everything done.
And if in silence you plan some evil,
that will not escape the gods; for thinking
belongs to the gods.' Saying these words
he introduced the pleasantest of teachings,   25
hiding truth with a false account.
And he said that the gods dwell there, where
he might most confound men by naming,
whence he knew fears came to men
and toils in their wretched life   30
—from the celestial orbit where he saw
the lightnings were, and the terrible crashings
of thunder, and the starry shape of heaven,
fine embroidery of the wise craftsman Time,
and whence the bright mass of the star steps
and the damp rain travels to earth.   35
Such fears he set about men,
because of which in his account he fairly housed
the spirit in a fitting place—
and extinguished unlawfulness by fears.

Thus first I think someone persuaded
mortals to believe that a tribe of spirits exists (**375: B 25**).

This is a speech from a play, and a semi-comedy at that: it is not a
theological tract; nor need the view it expresses coincide with the
sentiments of its author. For all that, its content is worth taking
seriously, even if it was designed only to outrage or to entertain.

'Some clever man, dismayed at the inability of human laws to curb human evil, invented the gods: by persuading them of the existence of a divine law and divine judges, he succeeded, to some extent, in making social life less nasty and less brutish.' Such is the message of the *Sisyphus* speech. I shall use it, in this and the following section, to introduce two issues in philosophical theology. The first issue concerns divine justice.

In the *Sisyphus*, the *raison d'être* of the gods is a moral, or at least a social, matter: the gods are invented to supplement the laws; and by their invention the god-giver 'extinguished unlawfulness by fears'. The notion that the gods punish malefactors is ancient and ubiquitous; in Greek literature its *locus classicus* is an elegy by the Athenian statesman Solon: Zeus, he proclaims, punishes all transgressors; and if justice sometimes proceeds at a limping pace, it is for all that unrelenting and inevitable (fr. 1. 25–32 D).[8]

Not all Greeks were equally convinced of the efficacy of divine justice. Against Solon's solid affirmation we may set a poem in the collection ascribed to Theognis: the gods, he says, ought indeed to love the just and to hate and punish the unjust; but alas, they do not; for the unjust evidently prosper (Theognis, 731–52).[9] Thrasymachus drew an unpalatable moral:

> The gods do not observe human affairs; for they would not pass over the greatest of human goods, justice; for we see that men do not use justice (376: 85 B 8).

'O Zeus, what shall I say? That you do not observe mankind?' (Euripides, *Hecuba* 488).[10] The gods, lovers of justice, could not overlook the myriad unjust successes which Theognis laments; hence they cannot observe them—the gods are not omniscient.

Later, from a different perspective, Epicurus drew a different conclusion: 'The statements of most men about the gods are not cognition but false suppositions, according to which the greatest harms befall the bad from the gods, and the greatest benefits the good' (*ad Men* §124). Unlike the Thraymachean divinities, Epicurus' gods do observe our miserable lives; but they do not care: omniscient, they are not practically benevolent.

The prevalence of successful malefaction provoked a third reaction. The ancient doxographers possessed a traditional catalogue of *atheoi*, godless men or atheists.[11] The *atheos par excellence* was Diagoras of Melos who 'made the downright assertion that god does not exist at all' (Athenagoras, III, 9 J).[12] We know little about Diagoras, and that little is confused. He lived in the second half of the fifth century; 'he committed verbal impieties about foreign rites and festivals [i.e. the

Eleusinian mysteries]' (pseudo-Lysias, VI. 17 = I. 5 J); and as a result he was prosecuted in Athens and forced to flee the country. Some scholars judge that the offending work—if indeed Diagoras really put his offensive thoughts to paper—was only 'a sensational pamphlet published by an otherwise insignificant man'; and that 'nowhere do we find evidence of an intellectual defence of atheism'. Perhaps, indeed, Diagoras was an *atheos* only in the old sense of an 'ungodly' man; he was not, properly speaking, an atheist. To other more generous scholars Diagoras appears as one of 'the leaders of progressive thought' in Athens.[13]

We lack the evidence to determine this dispute; but a few straws indicate a mildly philosophical breeze. If we find no 'intellectual defence' of atheism ascribed to Diagoras, we do find two or three rationalistic anecdotes. Cicero reports that Diagoras' friends, attempting to convince him of the existence of the gods, pointed to the numerous votive tablets set up by mariners saved from the storms of the sea; Diagoras replied that there would be many more tablets had the drowned sailors survived to make their dedications (*de natura deorum* III. 89 = III. 12 J). Sextus reports that Diagoras became an atheist when an opponent of his perjured himself and got away with his perjury (*adv Math* IX. 52 = V. 5 J): the Suda makes the opponent a rival poet who had plagiarized Diagoras' work (s.v. Diagoras = III. 3 J), and a scholiast on Aristophanes' *Clouds* has the opponent refuse to return a deposit entrusted to him by Diagoras (III. 4 J). The anecdotes bring out, in a personal form, the same point which Theognis and Thrasymachus expressed more generally: injustice thrives. And it is suggested that Diagoras used that truism as a basis for atheism.[14]

That very inference was made in Euripides' *Bellerophon*. One of the fragments of this lost drama reads thus:

Does someone then say that there are gods in heaven?
There are not, there are not, if a man will
not in folly rely on the old argument.
Consider it yourselves; do not build your opinion
on my words. I say that a tyranny
kills many men and deprives them of their possessions,
and breaking oaths destroys cities;
and doing this they are more happy
than those who live each day in pious peace.
And I know of small cities that honour the gods
which obey greater and more impious ones,
overcome by the greater number of spears. (377: fr. 286 N)

Euripides' fragment, the anecdotes of Diagoras' conversion to atheism, and the judgments of Thrasymachus and of Epicurus, all converge on an issue which Christian theology knows as the Problem of Evil.

The Problem concerns an apparent incompatibility between the existence of an omniscient, omnipotent and benevolent god, and the prevalence of badness in the world. There is no unique statement of the Problem, and therefore no single answer to it. One version of it runs like this: Assume:

(1) Unjust actions often go unpunished.
(2) God loves justice.
(3) God observes all human actions.
(4) God can intervene in mortal affairs.

Here (2), (3) and (4) reflect the benevolence, the omniscience, and the omnipotence of God; and (1) is the mournful observation of Theognis. Now it is argued that (1)–(4) are mutually incompatible: suppose, by (1), that an unjust action A goes unpunished. Then, by (3) God observes A; by (2), he dislikes A and wishes it punished; and by (4) he has power to punish A. But if God—or anyone else—wants to ϕ and has the power to ϕ, then he will ϕ. Hence God does punish the perpetrator of A. But, by hypothesis, A is unpunished. An almighty and omniscient god, who loves justice, cannot, logically, allow the unjust to thrive: if injustice is seen to thrive, that fact provides a conclusive disproof of the existence of any such god.

Different thinkers will react to that argument in different ways. Some, following in Solon's footsteps, will deny (1), and take the position pilloried in Voltaire's *Candide*. Heraclitus, in effect, adopts such a view (vol. 1, p. 131); and its most celebrated adherent is Leibniz. Modern philosophers have exercised their imaginations to provide reasons for rejecting (1): I assert, dogmatically, that (1) is a plain and patent truth.

Epicurus in effect denied proposition (2): his gods have no particular concern for justice. And the same denial is implicit in Theognis. Thrasymachus preferred to reject proposition (3). Both (2) and (3) may seem undeniable to those educated in a Christian tradition; and to many Greeks they will have carried the same air of self-evidence. But the Homeric gods were not remarkable for their love of justice, nor were they all omniscient; and a religion can, I suppose, survive the observation that its gods are neither all-knowing nor utterly devoted to the good of mankind.

Diagoras, and the speaker in the *Bellerophon*, take (1) for what it is: a platitude. And they implicitly accept (2)–(4): gods, they suppose, are by definition lovers of justice, possessors of knowledge, and repositories of power. Their conclusion is atheism: there are no gods.

I hold no brief for theism; but Diagoras has too easy a victory here. Doubtless there is a logical connexion between divinity and a love of justice; yet Diagoras requires a remarkably strong connexion: he must take it as a logical truth that gods wish for justice at any price. But a benevolent ruler, ardently desiring the prevalence of justice in his kingdom, may deliberately let some unjust acts go unpunished: the consequences of a constant intervention in the name of justice may be even less desirable than a state wherein injustice occasionally triumphs. It is a platitude of political philosophy that justice and liberty frequently conflict. In theology the same conflict is found; and Christian apologists who explain the existence of 'moral evil' by reference to the free will of man are urging, in effect, that liberty is not always inferior to justice. Nor does that argument seem bad; proposition (2) is true, but in a sense too weak to yield any atheistical conclusion: God loves justice, but he also loves liberty.

I conclude that the Problem of Evil, in its original form, does not lead to atheism. It does not follow that the Problem holds no embarrassment for theists: first, the ascription of liberty to humans is itself hard to reconcile with many popular forms of theism; and second, other versions of the Problem, which refer to natural rather than to 'moral' evil, are not so easily evaded. If Diagoras failed to refute theism, he did at least invent an argument whose more sophisticated and subtle forms still cause the acutest difficulties for many types of contemporary theism.

(c) *The aetiology of religious beliefs*

I turn now to the second issue raised by the fragment of Critias' *Sisyphus*. One of the *atheoi* in the ancient catalogue was Prodicus of Ceos, another sophistical contemporary of Critias. Atheism was ascribed to him on the basis of a fairly innocent assertion:

> The ancients thought that sun and moon and rivers and springs, and in general everything that benefits the life of men were gods, because of the benefit coming from them (378: 84 B 5).

Something very similar was said by Democritus:

> The ancients, seeing what happens in the sky—e.g., thunder and lightning and thunderbolts and conjunctions of stars and eclipses of sun and moon—were afraid, believing gods to be the cause of these (379: Sextus, 68 A 75).

According to Sextus, this passage offers an aetiology of religious belief: fear, inspired by a contemplation of celestial pyrotechnics, led men to postulate a divine pyrotechnician. The interpretation is plausible; and it receives some support from a fragment of Democritus' treatise *On the Things in Hell* (cf. **B O c**):

> Some men, ignorant of the dissolution of mortal nature, but conscious of the miseries of their life, crawl, during their lifetime, in troubles and fears, inventing falsehoods about the time after their death (**380: B 297**).

Men are mortal, but they will not acknowledge their mortality: doomed to a wretched life, they invent stories of *post mortem* bliss. There is an evident parallelism between this account of eschatological belief and the religious aetiology described by Sextus in **379**.[15]

We may possess an actual fragment of Democritus' aetiology:

> Of the sage men, a few raising their hands to what we Greeks now call air, said: 'Zeus is everything; and he knows everything, and gives, and takes away; and he is king of everything' (**381: B 30**).[16]

Some scholars compare these wise men to Critias' god-giver: cleverly and for political ends, they invent a ruler who knows everything and has supreme power of giving and taking. Others, more plausibly, take the reference to 'wise men' ironically, thus: 'some *soi-disant* sage, impressed by the weather, called the common air Zeus, and gave it divine powers'. Either interpretation will offer some sort of illustration of **379**; for each gives an aetiology of religious belief. But scholars dispute over **381**; and against those who find a cynical or contemptuous aetiology in the fragment there are others who find it a beautiful and touching assertion of faith: 'Those old, wise, men piously stretched out their hands; and rightly divinized the air'. In the absence of any context such a reading cannot be excluded: **381** must leave the arena; it cannot help us to understand Democritus' theology.

Critias, Prodicus and Democritus all offer anthropological aetiologies of religious beliefs: Critias and Prodicus are listed as *atheoi*, Democritus is not.[17] Is that fair?

The *Sisyphus* speech implies that all present religious belief can be traced back to the pronouncement of the original god-giver. And that pronouncement was false (**375. 26**); the gods are an invention (**375. 13**).[18] The speech is thus overtly atheistical, but its atheism is so far ungrounded. Xenophanes, I argued (vol. 1, p. 142), held that an inappropriate causal ancestry might deprive a belief of the title to knowledge; in particular, our beliefs about the gods, being causally explicable in terms of our local environment, fall short of knowledge. In effect, then, Xenophanes offered an anthropological aetiology of religious belief, and inferred that religious belief is unrational. Critias, I suggest, did just the same: all religious beliefs, he imagines, are explicable ultimately by reference to the god-giver's pious fraud; that fraud has a purely social explanation—hence the religious beliefs it grounds are unrational.

The same thought occurs more cleanly in Prodicus. In itself, 378 is innocent of sceptical implications;[19] but Prodicus meant more than 378 says:

> [He] attaches all human cults and mysteries and rites to the needs
> of farming, thinking that both the conception of gods and every
> sort of piety came to men from here (382: Themistius, *ad* 84 B 5).

All religious beliefs are explicable in terms of agricultural fears and hopes; those farming feelings are, plainly, irrelevant to the question of whether or not there are any gods: religious beliefs are therefore irrational.

What is irrationally believed is not thereby falsely believed. Why were Critias and Prodicus atheists? or were they called *atheoi* not for rejecting the gods outright but for a gentle Protagorean agnosticism? Suppose (truly) that very many very clever men have for many years searched for reasons for believing in the existence of gods; suppose (again, truly) that all their researches have failed to produce a single argument of any substance. Then, I suggest, we are entitled to lean towards atheism. The common inference from 'There is no reason to believe that P' to 'not-P' is puerile; the less common inference from 'Extensive inquiry has produced no reason to believe that P' to 'Probably not-P' is sound. Atheism is a negative position in two ways: first, it is essentially of the form not-P; and second, the strongest indication of its truth is the failure of all attempts to prove its contradictory. Did Critias or Prodicus glimpse something of that? Did they reflect that long generations of religious believers had produced no rational account of a position which remained causally tied to an old fraud or an ancient superstition? And did they infer that religion was not only groundless but also false? It would be beautiful to think so; but beauty, alas, is not truth.

Democritus remains, and his texts pose far greater problems. Comparison with Prodicus and Critias leads us to expect an atheistical or at least an agnostic stance; but certain fragments and reports appear to make Democritus a theist. First, in several of his ethical fragments Democritus refers, unapologetically, to gods and things divine:

He who chooses the goods of the soul chooses the more divine; he who chooses those of the body, the human (**383: 68 B 37**).

It is best for a man to live his life with the most good cheer and the least grieving; and that will happen if he takes his pleasures not in mortal things (**384: B 189**).

They alone are dear to the gods, to whom injustice is hateful (**385: B 217**).

But popular moralizing may appeal to the divine without committing itself seriously to theism; and we cannot ascribe theism to Democritus on the basis of a few disjointed platitudes.

Second, there is a confusing set of doxographical reports:

Democritus [says that] god is intelligence (*nous*) in spherical fire (**386**: Aëtius, **68 A 74**).

Democritus imagines that the gods arose with the rest of the heavenly fire (**387**: Tertullian, **A 74**).

He thinks that 'our knowledge (? *sententia*) and intelligence', or 'the principles of mind' are divine (Cicero, **A 74**). The reports are uninspiring: Aëtius is corrupt, Cicero uses a hostile source, Tertullian is a Christian. Perhaps Democritus said that the fiery soul-atoms constitute the 'divine spark' in us; more probably, such a view was generously ascribed to him on the basis of his moral fragments. This second group of texts will not make Democritus a godly man.

The third and final set of evidences is of far greater importance.

Democritus says that certain *eidôla* approach men, and that of these some are beneficent, some maleficent—that is why he even prayed (*eucheto*)[20] to attain felicitous *eidôla*. These are great, indeed enormous, and hard to destroy though not indestructible; and they signify the future to men, being seen and uttering sounds. Hence the ancients, getting a presentation of these very things, supposed that there was a god, there being no other god apart from these having an indestructible nature (**388**: Sextus, **B 166**).[21]

The passage has been interpreted in a variety of contradictory ways: does it offer an atomistic aetiology of religious notions? does it reduce gods to mere figments of the common fantasy? Or does it attempt to justify religious belief? and are its *eidôla* genuine divinities?

Cicero poses one of the problems: Democritus, he complains,

'seems to nod over the nature of the gods', treating the *eidôla* sometimes as being themselves divine, sometimes as images produced by the gods (**A 74**). The latter view is taken by Clement, who says that '*eidôla* fall on men and brute animals from the divine substance' (**A 79**); it interprets the term '*eidôla*' in the psychological sense of '*deikela*' or '*aporrhoiai*' 'films' or 'effluences' (see below, p. 175). The former view is taken by Hermippus, who says that Democritus 'naming them [sc. daemons] *eidôla*, says that the air is full of these' (**A 78**). Pliny, who asserts, in evident allusion to **388**, that Democritus only admitted two gods, Penalty and Benefit, probably adhered to this interpretation (**A 76**); and Diogenes of Oenoanda may have accepted it. [22]

Some scholars attempt to conjoin those reports into a unified theology; but I am inclined to think that they all spring from one source, the original of **388** and that that source has an atheistical tendency. **388** is talking about dreams: in praying for 'felicitous *eidôla*' Democritus was praying for happy dreams, in particular, I suppose, for dreams which 'signify the future'. These *eidôla*, then, will be the dream images whose functioning is described by Plutarch in **A 77**; and '*eidôlon*' has its psychological sense. (It will not do to object that images cannot utter sounds, or that they cannot be hard to destroy: to say that some dream images speak and are almost indestructible is simply to say that, in dreams, we imagine speaking and almost indestructible entities.)

Dreaming of huge and indestructible prophets, the ancients believed that they were perceiving gods: they looked behind their dream images for divine originals (cf. Lucretius, V. 1161–93). Democritus will, I suppose, have agreed that every *eidôlon* has an original; but he will not have allowed that divine-seeming *eidôla* require divine originals. Perhaps they are somehow 'compounded' or 'enlarged', by the process which gives us *eidôla* of chimaeras or giants; perhaps they are ordinary human *eidôla* which their observers fail to identify. (They are human in shape: Sextus, *adv Math* IX.42.) How can these *eidôla* 'signify the future'? Plutarch ascribes a sort of telepathic theory to Democritus: human dream *eidôla* will include *eidôla* of the thoughts and plans of their originals; for those thoughts and plans, being physical structures, will emit effluences. Consequently, a dreamer, in grasping an *eidôlon*, may sometimes apprehend the thoughts and plans of its original (cf. **A 77**). It has been suggested that the 'felicitous *eidôla*' of **388** are just such images: the dreamer grasps the intentions of others, and hence gains a knowledge of the future entirely analogous to his knowledge of his own future actions. [23] The suggestion is ingenious, but strained:

dream *eidôla* 'speak'; sometimes it happens that what they 'say' is true—and in that way, unexcitingly, they 'signify the future'. **388** does not imply that certain *eidôla* come overtly branded as truth-tellers, or that an attentive dreamer may distinguish good from bad dream utterances; it says only that some dream utterances will turn out true.

Thus, according to Democritus, religion arose first (as Prodicus suggested) from attention to natural phenomena (**379**), and second (his own contribution) from attention to the contents of the sleeping mind (**388**). **379** and **388** offer two complementary aetiologies of religion; neither is inconsistent with the other, and neither implies any adherence to theism.

388, indeed, seems to commit Democritus to atheism: if 'there is no other god apart from these' dream *eidôla*, then there are no gods at all: evidently, the *eidôla* themselves are not gods; and, so Democritus says, there is in fact no divine source of origin behind or apart from the *eidôla*.

A final fragment stands strongly against that conclusion:

> The gods grant men all good things, both in the past and now. But what is bad and harmful and useless, that neither in the past nor now do the gods donate to men; but they themselves strike against these things from blindness of mind and ignorance (**389: B 175**).

Does **389** make Democritus a theist? If so, we must credit him with an important distinction: **379** and **388** show that the *origins* of our religious beliefs are disreputable; but it does not follow that the beliefs themselves are irrational; a belief may overcome its low breeding. A full-blooded aetiologist will say that anthropology explains the origins of religious thought, and that all present beliefs are exclusively accountable for in terms of those origins; Democritus, we are now imagining, allows that anthropology explains the origination of religion but denies that all our present beliefs are explicable solely by reference to those origins. A rational theism may transcend its irrational childhood.

That is a consistent and an interesting view; and I hesitate to deny it to Democritus. Yet if it was his, it is strange that no explicit trace of it remains, and that no justification of religious belief is ascribed to its author. I incline still to an atheist Abderite. **389**, I guess, came from one of Democritus' literary pieces: it is not a piece of philosophy but an exegesis of a passage in Homer's *Odyssey* (I. 33). But the guess will not be found very appealing; and Democritus' stand on religious belief will remain shrouded in the fogs of the past.[24]

(d) *Poetics*

'First, as Prodicus says, you must learn about the correctness of words' (Plato *Euthydemus* 277E = **84 A 16**). Interest in language and the various disciplines associated with it was a feature of the Sophists. 'I agree'ₓ says Protagoras in Plato's dialogue, 'that I am a sophist, and that I educate men' (317B = **80 A 5**). The primary art by which the Sophists sought to educate, and which they sought to instil in their pupils, was rhetoric, 'the craftsman of persuasion' (*Gorgias* 453A = **82 A 28**).²⁵ Gorgias, 'the first to give the power and art of speaking to the rhetorical form of education' (Suda, **82 A 2**), wrote a treatise on rhetoric (Diogenes Laertius, VIII.58 = **A 3**) of which we possess a scrap or two (**B 12–14**); and in *Helen* he dilates with evident satisfaction upon the persuasive powers of his art (**B 11**, §§8–14; see below, p. 227).

The matter as well as the mode of education led to language: study of language is a part of literary criticism, and literary criticism was a great part of education in a land where 'from the beginning everyone learned from Homer' (Xenophanes, **21 B 10**). There is an example of the Sophist's literary art in the analysis and criticism of the verse of Simonides which Plato's Protagoras conducts (339A = **80 A 25**); and we know that Protagoras was famed for 'interpreting the poems of Simonides and others' (Themistius, *oratio* 23, 350. 20 D). Hippias (**86 B 6**) and Gorgias (**82 B 24–5**) engaged in literary studies; and the practice was no doubt widespread. The Sophists did not originate the studies of rhetoric and of literary criticism; but they were professed masters of those high arts.²⁶

One part of their studies dealt with strictly linguistic matters. Protagoras has some claim to be called the inventor of syntax;²⁷ and Prodicus dabbled in semantics. Prodicus is credited with a 'nicety (*akribologia*) about names' (Marcellinus, **84 A 9**); and Plato's dialogues contain numerous examples of his subtle distinctions in sense: between 'strive' and 'vie' (*Protagoras* 337B = **84 A 13**), between 'enjoy' and 'take pleasure in' (ibid.), between 'wish' and 'desire' (ibid. 340A = **84 A 14**), between 'end' and 'limit' (*Meno* 75E = **84 A 15**). Some of Prodicus' distinctions are significant: Aristotle rightly availed himself of that between 'wish (*boulesthai*)' and 'desire (*epithumein*)', and he would have improved his account of pleasure had he attended to Prodicus' differentiation between 'enjoy (*euphrainesthai*)' and 'take pleasure in (*hêdesthai*)'. But there is no evidence that Prodicus himself saw any philosophical point in his linguistic diversions. If 'the Sophistic explanations of poetry foreshadow the growth of a special field of enquiry, the analysis of language', yet 'the final object is rhetorical or educational, not literary'—and still less philosophical.[28]

In two ways, however, the literary interests of the late fifth century did make a direct contribution to philosophy: the period was exercised by a problem about the nature and origins of language; and it saw the birth of that Cinderella of modern philosophy, aesthetics. Gorgias had an aesthetic theory:

> Tragedy flourished and was famed, an admirable object for those men to hear and to see, and one which gave to stories and passions a deception (*apatê*), as Gorgias says, in which the deceiver is more just than he who does not deceive and the deceived wiser than he who is not deceived (**390**: Plutarch, **82 B 23**).[29]

In his *Helen* (**82 B 11**) Gorgias shows how speech, that 'great potentate', can 'persuade and deceive (*apatân*) the soul' (§8); and he illustrates his thesis from poetry:

> All poetry, as I believe and assert, is measured speech; and upon those who hear it there comes a fearful shuddering (*phrikê periphobos*) and a tearful pity (*eleos poludakrus*) and a mournful yearning; and for the misfortunes and calamities of the affairs and the bodies of other men, the soul, through words, experiences an emotion of its own (**391**: §9).

(I refrain from commenting on the connexion between this passage and Aristotle's account of the effects of tragedy in *Poet* 1449b27.) The *Dissoi Logoi* offers the following consideration in support of the thesis that 'the just and unjust are the same':

> In tragedy and in painting whoever deceives (*exapatai*) most by creating what is similar to the truth is best (**392**: **90 A 3**, §10).

There is nothing original in the view that poets and artists are purveyors of falsehoods: *polla pseudontai aoidoi*. The Muses, according to Hesiod, 'know how to say many false things similar to the true' (*Theogony*, 27); and references to the deceptions of art are not infrequent in Greek literature.[30] Again, the gullibility of the vulgar, which leads them to believe in soap operas as well as soap advertisements, naturally breeds a puerile admiration for *trompe l'oeil* art and 'realistic' drama. Such phenomena were familiar enough in Greece: they are exhibited in the naive wonderment of the Chorus in Euripides' *Ion* (184–219), and in the conversations of Herodas' fourth *Mime*: 'What lovely statues, Cynno dear. . . . Look, dear, at that girl up there, looking at the apple: you'd say she'd pass away if she didn't get the apple' (IV. 20–9).

Gorgias' theory perhaps began from those commonplaces; but it goes far beyond them, and offers a genuine theory of art—or at least of literature and painting; for whether or not Gorgias intended the theory to extend to music and sculpture we do not know. Art essentially strives for illusion: the better the deception, the greater the art; and good artists will always try to deceive their public. As a dramatist, Sophocles is concerned to express, verbally and by action, a set of false propositions. As a good dramatist, Sophocles will regularly convince his audience that those falsehoods are true.

The theory had an enormous attraction; and it became a standard item of Philistine thought; for if Gorgias ironically asserted that a deceived audience would grow wiser by the deception, later men, condemning deceit, condemned art with it. Thus Macaulay: 'Poetry produces an illusion on the eye of the mind, as a magic lantern produces an illusion on the eye of the body. And, as the magic lantern acts best in a dark room, poetry effects its purpose most completely in a dark age. As the light of knowledge breaks in upon its exhibitions, as the outlines of certainty become more and more definite and the shades of probability more and more distinct, the hues and lineaments of the phantoms which the poet calls up grow fainter and fainter. We cannot unite the incompatible advantages of reality and deception, the clear discernment of truth and the exquisite enjoyment of fiction' (*Essays*, 'Milton'). Art, like all fiction, will gradually lose its power and its attraction as knowledge of truth advances.

Some thinkers deny that art is a deceiver on the grounds that art has no connexion with truth or falsity at all. In the arts, according to the *Dissoi Logoi*:

> Justice and injustice have no place; and the poets do not make
> their poems with a view to truth but with a view to giving men
> pleasure (**393: 91 A 3** §17).

Coleridge echoes the point: a notion of Wordsworth's, he maintains, 'seems to destroy the main fundamental distinction, not only between a poem and prose, but even between philosophy and works of fiction, inasmuch as it proposes *truth* for its immediate object, instead of *pleasure*' (*Biographia Literaria*, I. 104). Neither belief nor disbelief is an appropriate attitude to art; rather, we must experience 'that *illusion*, contra-distinguished from *delusion*, that *negative* faith, which simply permits the images presented to work by their own force, without either denial or affirmation of their real existence by the judgment' (ibid., I. 107). Frege assents: 'In hearing an epic poem, for instance, apart from the euphony of the language we are interested only in the sense of the sentences and the images and feelings thereby aroused. The question of truth could cause us to abandon aesthetic delight for an attitude of scientific investigation' (*Philosophical Writings*, 'On Sense and Reference').

That answer to the Gorgian theory has something to be said for it: certainly, it is silly to wonder whether Achilles really dragged Hector's corpse around the walls of Troy, or to ask how the Ancient Mariner really managed to steer his ship with a dead albatross hanging about his neck. Such things are fictions, and they are presented as fictions; they do not deceive or delude us, and the poet does not fail if we remain unconvinced. But it will not do to answer Gorgias by saying, simply, that artists do not aim at truth: first, that answer will not appease the Philistines—if art is no longer a criminal falsehood, it is something just as bad: an empty fantasy; and second, it is simply untrue to say that contemplators of art must refrain from putting 'the question of truth'. Many artists regularly aim at a fairly mundane sort of truth: portraiture is a species of painting; Gibbon's *Decline and Fall* is a work of literature. And many more artists aim, I guess, to convey a higher and less ordinary truth: the *Oedipus Rex* does not tell us a true history of a king of Thebes, but it does tell us some large truths about human destiny; *Pride and Prejudice* is not a journal or diary of events in an English country town, but it does make shrewd and true comments on human nature. Any reader will multiply those examples and give flesh to their skeletal frames: only the most insensitive philosopher will judge that there is no 'question of truth' in the *Iliad* on the grounds that Homer's account of the Trojan War is doubtful history.

Most generalizations about art are false. I do not suggest that all art purports to express truth (unaccompanied music cannot); I do not think that art can only be defended if it aims at truth; nor do I think that Macaulay's condemnation is just even in those few cases (mime, perhaps, is the best example) where deception and falsity are desired and attained. My aim in the last paragraph has merely been to recall the elementary truth that works of art very often do purvey truths, and the slightly less elementary truth that not all the sentences of a work of fiction are intended to be believed.

How, then, did Gorgias arrive at his false and influential theory? I suspect that he was led to it by puzzling over the emotive powers of art. 391 hints at an argument: when I attend to a work of art (Verdi's *Traviata*, say) I am affected by genuine emotions of a fairly strong variety; and my feelings are not capricious but seem an appropriate and rational response to the opera. Now if my feelings are rational, they must be backed by belief; hence if Verdi's aim is to arouse my

163

passions, he must first instil some beliefs in me. And since his plot, like that of most dramatists, is a fiction, he must endeavour to instil false beliefs in me, or to deceive me. If a friend dies, you feel grief because you believe her to be dead; when Violetta dies you feel a grief of the same intensity and variety: that can only be because you believe, falsely, that Violetta is dead. Verdi is a great artist because he can move us; he can move us only if he can deceive us: art, therefore, is essentially deceptive.

I do not endorse that argument; but I do not think it despicable. And it does raise in a clear form the genuinely puzzling question of why Violetta's death infects us with grief: is the grief (and hence the opera) an emotional sham? or does it give us something to weep for? Gorgias saw that there were questions here to be asked.

(e) *Language and nature*

The second contribution of fifth-century linguistic studies to philosophy is due not to sophists but to Democritus. Diogenes' catalogue of Democritus' writings lists eight titles under the heading *Mousika* ('Literary Studies'): 'On rhythm and harmony', 'On poetry', 'On beauty of words', 'On consonant and dissonant letters', etc. (IX.48 = **68 A 33**). But the few fragments of these works that remain (**B 15–26**) are not of great interest. What is of interest, I think, is Democritus' contribution to the Greek debate on the status of human language: is language a natural or a social phenomenon? do words have their meaning by nature or by convention? is *phusis* the subtle *éminence grise* directing our speech, or are we rather governed by *nomos* or *thesis*? The classic text on the subject is Plato's *Cratylus*; and after Plato's time the debate rarely slackened. Aulus Gellius, writing in the second century AD, could say that 'it is ordinarily asked among philosophers whether names are by nature (*phusei*) or by legislation (*thesei*)' (X. iv. 2). The debate began in the fifth century BC.

There are two quite distinct questions involved: much of the literature confuses them. The first question concerns the *origins* of language, or of 'names': was language deliberately created and imposed by a 'name-giving' person of divine, heroic, or human status? or did language gradually evolve from brutish grunts and growls, without the intervention of any conscious agent? The former view is taken by the Book of *Genesis* and by the *Cratylus* (e.g. 388D). It posits a *thesis*, or laying down, of names; and since what is laid down is a *nomos*, the view may be stated by saying that words exist *nomôi*. But that statement is misleading; for the *thesis* theory need not hold that the name-giver set up purely conventional or arbitrary connexions between words and objects. The *thesis* theory was vigorously expressed by saying that 'words are by convention'. The view was vigorously and mockingly attacked by the Epicureans, who advanced the alternative, 'natural', account (Epicurus, *ad Hdt* §§75-6; Diogenes of Oenoanda fr. 10 Ch; Lucretius, V. 1041-90).

The second question concerns the relation between language and the world: does language fit the world naturally, like skin on an animal? or is it an artificial matching, like clothes on an Edwardian *belle*? Are names fixed to what they name by a natural adhesive? or is the glue man-made? Metaphorically stated, the questions are impressive and imprecise; a major part of the interpretation of the ancient answers consists in understanding the ancient questions.

Four texts bear on the two issues. Diodorus' anthropology contains the following passage:

> Their sounds being without significance and confused, they
> gradually articulated their locutions; and by making signs for one
> another for each of the objects, they made their remarks about
> everything intelligible to one another. Such gatherings took place
> all over the inhabited world, and all did not have a
> similar-sounding language but each group ordered their locutions
> as it chanced; that is why there are all types of languages
> (394: I.viii. 3 = **68 B 5**).

Diodorus offers a 'natural' answer to my first question: language originated not with the *fiat* of a name-giver, but from the need, and the gradually increasing competence, of groups of men to communicate with one another.

Once a language has been rudely articulated within a group, some clever men may pose as a primitive *Académie Française*. But the Diodoran account of the first beginnings of language is surely true, and logically so: the existence of a name-giver presupposes the existence of a language; for he himself must have the names already articulated if he is to bestow them on his community. (Those philosophers who think that there can be no 'private languages'— languages intelligible only to one person—will go further and say that a communal dialect, of the sort imagined by Diodorus' source, must have preceded the activity of any name-giver.) Now if language is 'natural' in this way, then it is a product of specifically human nature; for the brutes do not in fact possess any articulated dialect. The mark of humanity is rationality; and rationality, if not thought itself, depends on language; for without language none but the simplest and crudest thoughts are possible. This amounts to a justification of the ancient and vain belief that humans are set apart from the other animals. Only a natural account of the origins of language will lead to that belief: on the *Cratylus* view, the divine name-giver might as well have bestowed his gift on apes or peacocks.

We cannot, however, rely on Diodorus, whose connexions with Democritus are unsure. My next two texts are genuine fragments of Democritus, but they are unreliable for different reasons. **B 145** reads simply:

The word is shadow of the deed (395).

Some have read this as implying that names are naturally attached to the world; for shadows are naturally attached to the objects that throw them. But the fragment is an apophthegm out of context; and a thousand interpretations can be found for it. In **B 142** Democritus says that the names of the gods are their 'speaking images (*agalmata phôneenta*)'. Images are made by an image-maker, and they are usually tied to their originals by the natural relation of resemblance: the one word '*agalmata*' thus suggests both that the origins of language were unnatural and that words are naturally attached to the world. But it is absurd to read so much theory into a single word. A simpler explanation of *agalmata* suggests itself: from Homer onwards the Greeks liked to see significance in the etymologies, or purported etymologies, of proper names. Aeschylus provides the best-known example when he describes Helen as '*helenaus, helandros, heleptolis* (destroyer of ships, destroyer of men, destroyer of cities': *Agamemnon*, 689), and Democritus is known to have indulged in the sport: Tritogeneia is etymologized in **B 1** and '*gunê* (woman)' is repellently connected with '*gonê* (semen)' because a woman is 'a receptacle for semen' (**B 122a**). Some words are 'speaking images' by virtue of this etymological turn: a word may speak volumes.[31]

The fourth and last Democritean text comes from Proclus' commentary on the *Cratylus*. It reads thus:

Democritus, saying that names are by legislation (*thesei*), established this by four arguments. From homonymy: different things are called by the same name; hence their name is not natural (*phusei*). From polyonymy: if different names will fit one and the same thing, [they will fit] one another too—which is impossible. From the changing of names: why did we change Aristocles' name to Plato, and Tyrtamus' to Theophrastus, if their names were natural? From the lack of similar names: why do we say 'think' from 'thought' but do not form a derivative (*paronomazomen*) from 'justice'? Hence names are by chance

(*tuchêi*) and not natural. And he calls the first argument
polysemy, the second equipollence, [the third metonymy], the
fourth anonymy (396: B 26).

Only the last sentence of this extract pretends to quote Democritus'
own words: both form and content of the 'four arguments' are due to
Proclus; and we do not know whether the form of the conclusion is
Democritean or Proclan. What thesis can the arguments have been
designed to establish?

Proclus believes (if I understand him aright) that Democritus is
offering a *thesis* account of the origins of language: no *onomatothetês*
laid down language; names evolved by nature. But on that view the
four arguments are very feeble. Other scholars associate **396** with **B
142**: some, but not all, names are *agalmata phôneenta*: the original
names of Plato and Theophrastus did not reveal the nature of their
bearers; that is why we changed them to the more descriptive terms
Flatfoot and Godspeaker. (The examples are post-Democritean: I do
not know what instances Democritus himself might have cited.) But
neither the second nor the fourth argument of **395** has any tendency
to support that thesis.

A third interpretation of **396** encourages us to attend to a less
trivial aspect of the relation between language and the world. 'Mean'
in English, like '*sêmainein*' in Greek, can be used in at least two
quite different contexts. On the one hand, spots mean measles;
clouds mean rain; and a child's cry means hunger. Meaning, in such
cases, is a matter of pointing to, indicating, being a sign of. On the
other hand, 'measles' means measles; 'rain' means rain; and
'hunger' means hunger. In these cases meaning is the relation which
links language to the world. The question: 'Are words by nature?'
can be interpreted in terms of these two sorts of meaning; for it can
be taken to ask whether or not the relation which links language to
the world is the relation of pointing to, indicating, or being a sign of.
To say that 'words are by nature' is thus to say that the word 'mean'
in ' "Measles" means measles' names the same, natural, relation as
the word 'mean' in 'Spots mean measles'.

The first argument in **396** from homonymy, now works well
enough: if clouds mean rain, then if clouds appear rain will follow;
natural signs are inevitable followed by what they signify. But though
'rain' means rain, not every utterance of 'rain' is followed by rain;
and homonymy provides clear instances: not every utterance of
'mole' signifies the presence of a furry rodent (or of an idea or image
or thought of such a rodent); for 'mole' may mean jetty. The third
argument in **396** is even better: if a child's crying means hunger, no

agreement or compact will make it mean anything else; if spots mean measles, we cannot, by *fiat* or convention, get them to mean intoxication. But the meaning of 'hunger' or 'measles' could be altered by consent: vague words regularly replace standard English; and marriage usually changes a woman's name as well as her nature.

The fourth argument is harder. I suspect that Proclus' 'paronyms' are an anachronistic illustration of his own, and that by 'anonymy' Democritus meant nothing more impressive than the fact that language does not contain a term for every natural object: we may come across a new element, an unknown species of bird, a fresh frisson to titillate our jaded minds. If those new objects are to have signs, we must bestow them; and we can bestow any sign we care to. Natural signs do not work like that: we do not instruct a hungry child to cry, or fix clouds to the heavens as a sign of rain.

Finally, there is the argument from polyonymy or 'equipollence (*isorrhopon*)'. Proclus' remarks here are very obscure. 'If different names will fit (*epharmozein*) one and the same thing, [they will fit] one another too'. Perhaps that means: 'If A means C and B means C, then A means B.' At least, that interpretation yields a truth; and I can find no other that does. For that 'is impossible'; i.e., 'that is impossible if words are natural'. Now if 'mean' is used in the 'natural' sense, then it is indeed false that if A means C and B means C, then A means B; for though a drought means poor crops, and a flood means poor crops, a drought does not mean a flood. If, on the other hand, 'mean' has its linguistic sense, then if A means C and B means C, then A does mean B.

The distinction between 'natural' and 'non-natural' meaning— between the way in which spots mean measles and the way in which 'measles' means measles—is not a trivial one: many classical theories of meaning founder on the failure to draw it, or on the assumption that the relation of a word to what it means is similar to that of a clouds to the rain it portends.[32] **396** is not a simple fragment to interpret; and perhaps no simple thought lies behind it. But I incline to believe that one of the points that Democritus was attempting to make was the one I have briefly mentioned; and if that is so, then Democritus stands at the head of a long line of thinkers who have laboured to uncover the meaning of meaning.

(f) *Gorgias on communication*

The third part of Gorgias' treatise on *What Is Not* (vol. 1, p. 173) attempts to show that even if what exists can be known, our knowledge cannot be communicated. The argument is a curiosity: I present it with no comment beyond the observation that it treats significance as a natural relation. Again, I follow Sextus' text, though here the *MXG* differs from and expands upon Sextus to a considerable degree.

(83) And even if it were grasped, it is incommunicable to anyone else. For if what exists is visible and audible and, in general perceptible (I mean, what lies outside us), and if what is visible is grasped by sight, and what is audible by hearing, and not vice versa, then how can these things be signified to anyone else? (84) For that by which we signify is a formula (*logos*), and what lies outside us and exists is not a formula; therefore we do not signify to our neighbours what exists but a formula which is different from what lies outside us. Thus just as what is visible could not become audible, or the reverse, so, since what exists lies outside us, it cannot become our formula; (85) and if it is not a formula, it will not be signified to anyone else.

And a formula [, he says,] is constructed from the things which hit us from outside, i.e. from the objects of perception; for it is from meeting with a savour that the formula we utter about this quality is produced in us; and from the incidence of a colour comes the formula about a colour. And if this is so, it is not the formula which reveals the external object, but the external object which signifies the formula.

(86) And one cannot say that the formula lies outside us in the same way as the visible and the audible, so that, lying outside us and existing, it can signify what lies outside us and exists. For, [he says,] even if the formula lies outside us, yet it differs from the other things that lie outside us—and visible bodies differ very greatly from the formulae; for what is visible is grasped through one organ, the formula through another. Thus the formula does not reveal most of the external objects, just as they do not show the nature of each other (**397: 82 B 3**).

VIII

De Anima

(a) *Material beginnings*

The *psuchê* or animator is that part or feature of an animate being which endows it with life; and since the primary signs of life are cognition and mobility, the *psuchê* is the source of knowledge and the source of locomotion. That gives a formal or functional account of *psuchê*; but it leaves us to ask what the psychic nature consists in: what sort of thing is it that provides us with life? is it the same sort of thing in men, in animals and in plants? where (if anywhere) is it located in the body? is it separable from the body?

To those questions the early Presocratics had, by and large, no interesting answers. The doxography regularly deals with the question: What is *psuchê* made of?

> Anaximenes and Anaximander and Anaxagoras and Archelaus said that the nature of the *psuchê* is airy (**398**: Aëtius, **12 A 29**; cf. **13 B 2**; Philoponus, **13 A 23**).[1]

> Parmenides and Hippasus and Heraclitus [say that the *psuchê*] is fiery (**399**: Aëtius, **18 A 9**).

And a fragment of Epicharmus indicates that the fiery soul was familiar enough outside professional scientific circles (**23 B 48**). Water and earth, the other two canonical elements, had fewer backers; but Hippo went for water (Hippolytus, **38 A 3**), and late stories give souls of earth and water to Xenophanes (Macrobius, **21 A 50**).[2] In the physics ascribed by Diogenes to Zeno, 'soul is a mixture of [the hot, the cold, the dry and the wet], with none of them having dominance' (IX. 29 = **29 A 1**). The doxographers do not usually expand upon these unilluminating *dicta*.

170

Heraclitus at least had a little more to say. His views, painfully obscure to us, were mildly sceptical and unpretentious:

> You would not find in your journey the limits of soul, even if you travelled the whole road—so deep is its account (133: 22 B 45 = 67 M).

The crude report of Aëtius that Heraclitean souls are fiery appears in Aristotle as the suggestion that the soul is an 'exhalation' (*anathumiasis*: *An* 405a24 = A 15). The suggestion is repeated in the doxography (e.g., Aëtius, A 15; Arius Didymus, *ad* B 12), and it connects readily with B 36 = 66 M:

> For souls it is death to become water, for water it is death to become earth, from earth water comes to be, from water soul (400).

If souls are warm, moist exhalations, it is plausible to think both that they come from water (like steam from a kettle or mist from a morning lake), and also that they perish on becoming water (as the steam disappears when condensed). Three further fragments are enigmatic. Perhaps

> A dry soul is wisest and best (401: B 118 = 68 M)

because it is furthest from watery death. I do not know why

> Souls smell in Hades (402: B 98 = 72 M),[3]

or what Heraclitus meant when he said that the soul was

> a *logos* increasing itself (403: B 115 = 112 M).

A late source contains the following report:

> Thus the vital heat proceeding from the sun gives life to all things that live. Subscribing to that opinion, Heraclitus gives a fine simile comparing the soul to a spider and the body to a spider's web. 'As a spider', he says, 'standing in the middle of its web is aware the instant a fly breaks any one of its threads and runs there swiftly as though lamenting the breaking of the thread; so a man's soul when any part of his body is hurt hastily goes there as though intolerant of the hurt to a body to which it is strongly and harmoniously conjoined' (404: B 67a = 115 M).

The authenticity of this charming report is dubious; but it may contain some genuine echoes of Heraclitean thought. I imagine that the simile is intended to explain a puzzle about pain: pain is a mental affection yet it derives from a bodily harm; how can that be?

Heraclitus answers that the *psuchê* is immediately aware of bodily damage, runs to the scene of the harm, and grieves over it: psychic grief over corporeal damage is pain; and we suffer pain because our souls are immediately sensitive and sympathetic to our bodily condition. Even if **404** is Heraclitean at bottom, it cannot be pressed too hard: it appears to reveal the *psuchê* as a living, sensitive, independent substance, localized in some central part of the body but capable of moving about within its corporeal dwelling. It may be that Heraclitus had just such a picture in mind; but **404** is only a picturesque analogy, designed to explain a single psychic phenomenon.

If the spider is idiosyncratically Heraclitean, the notion of *anathumiasis* suggests a way of finding a common and intelligible element in the early accounts of the *psuchê*. The parallel between a warm, moist 'exhalation' and our warm, moist breath is evident; and it is a commonplace of classical scholarship that the word '*psuchê*' originally denoted a 'breath-soul'. We live just as long as we breathe; and the conjecture that our life-giving part is breath, or a breath-like stuff, is easy. The antiquity of the view is attested by Aristotle, who reports that in 'the so-called Orphic verses' it is said that 'the soul enters from the universe as we breathe, and is carried about by the winds' (*An* 410b29 = **1 B 11**); and it is referred to by Plato in the *Phaedo* (70A, 77D). Diogenes ascribes the view to Xenophanes (IX.19 = **21 A 1**); and Aëtius says, plausibly, that when Anaximenes refers to the *psuchê* as 'our air' he uses 'air' synonymously with 'breath' (**26: 13 B 2**). The *psuchê* is variously specified as air, fire or water; but those rival specifications have a common core: breath is airy, moist fire; or hot, wet air; or warm, airy water.

The 'breath-soul' is doubtless a 'primitive' notion; but it has a grounding in solid scientific fact: we live by breathing; our *psuchai*, therefore, are breathlike. Moreover, the 'breath-soul' seems to explain with admirable neatness the twin functions of any *psuchê*, cognition and locomotion:

> Diogenes [of Apollonia], like certain others too, [said that the *psuchê*] is air, thinking that this is the finest of all things and a principle. And that explains why the *psuchê* knows and moves things: in so far as it is primary, and the rest come from it, it knows; in so far as it is finest, it is motive (**405**: Aristotle, *An* 405a21–5 = **64 A 20**).

The atomist account of the *psuchê* is comparable to earlier doctrines, though it is, of course, expressed within the terms of their new-fangled physics. One quotation will suffice:

Of these [shapes] the spherical form the *psuchê*; for such *rhusmoi* are especially able to pass through everything and to move other things while moving themselves—for they suppose that the *psuchê* is that which provides animals with motion. And that is why breath is the determinant of life; for as the surrounding matter compresses the bodies and squeezes out those shapes which provide animals with life because they themselves are never at rest, help comes from outside when other such [atoms] enter in breathing; for they actually prevent those inhering in the animals from being separated out, by restricting the compressing and fixing body; and animals live as long as they can do this (**406**: Aristotle, *An* 404a5–16 = **67 A 28**).

Since spherical atoms account for the perceptible quality of heat, the Atomists can also say that the *psuchê* is 'a sort of fire, and hot' (*An* 404a1 = **67 A 28**).[4] The atomist soul is hot breath: the thesis is explained in characteristically Abderite terms, but it is essentially traditional.

To the modern ear, attuned to a Christian or Cartesian notion of soul, one feature of these Presocratic accounts is striking: they are all thoroughly and uncompromisingly materialistic. The *psuchê* is made of some ordinary physical stuff: the matter of body is the matter of soul. A *psuchê* may be thin and ethereal; but it is for all that material: its thinness is the thinness of fire or air, not the insubstantiality of an unextended Cartesian spirit.

That conclusion is sometimes resisted: 'The concept of an immaterial being was not invented until the fourth century BC; and the contrast between materialism and dualism, between a physicalist and a Cartesian account of mind or soul, is a creature of modern philosophy. It is an impertinent anachronism to apply those modern categories to Presocratic philosophy: Anaximenes' assertion that the soul is air is not a materialist thesis—nor, of course, is it non-materialist; the terms are simply inapplicable.' It is worth stating what a miserable bit of argumentation that is. If our modern categories of materialism and dualism are well-defined, then *any* intelligible theory of the soul is either materialistic or dualistic, whenever it may have been framed. Of course, Presocratic theories may be too crude, or too vague, or too confused, to be categorized; but in that case they are too crude, or too vague, or too confused, to be understood and interpreted. If intelligible, they fall into one or other of our categories. (The distinction between valid and invalid arguments was discovered by Aristotle; for all that, we do not regard it as anachronistic to judge Presocratic reasoning by modern canons of validity.)

'But at least the Presocratics were only materialists *faute de mieux*: they adopted a materialistic stance because no other occurred to them; had they been offered spiritual substance they would gladly have accepted it.' That is a judgment difficult to assess; yet I am inclined to reject it. The materialism of the early Presocratics was, so far as our evidence goes, implicit: they do not expressly say that the *psuchê* is a body like any other body. But the Atomists made materialism explicit: Democritus' account of thought is, according to Theophrastus, 'reasonable for one who makes the *psuchê* a body' (*Sens.* §58 = **68 A 135**; cf. Aëtius, **A 102**); and if Aristotle can say that fire, the stuff of Democritean souls, is 'the most incorporeal (*asômatos*) of the elements' (*An* 405a6 = **68 A 101**), he means only that the *psuchê* is very fine or rare (cf. Philoponus, **68 A 101**); '*asômatos*' is used loosely, as we might use 'insubstantial'.[5] We possess no original text from Democritus announcing the corporeality of the soul; but the Peripatetic insistence on it indicates some fairly explicit avowal, and it was, after all, no recondite implication of Atomist psychology.

The atomists were self-conscious materialists in psychology; and their thesis was original, if at all, only in the explicitness with which it was held. Perhaps the Atomists insisted on materialism because they had found some immaterialist psychology to object to? did materialism become explicit only because an alternative theory had arisen? Many scholars believe that the Pythagorean doctrines of metempsychosis and immortality require an immaterial soul. Yet if the Pythagoreans were profoundly concerned about the cultivation and fate of their souls, they apparently remained reticent about the nature of *psuchê*. Pythagoras is credited with a lecture *On the Soul* (Diogenes Laertius, VIII.7 = **14 A 19**), and so is Archytas (**47 B 9**); but neither ascription is believed by scholars. A late source ascribes to 'Hippo of Metapontum' (i.e. Hippasus?) the judgment that

> The soul is one thing, the body quite another; when the body is at rest, the soul thrives, when the body is blind, it sees; when the body is dead, it lives (**407**: Claudianus, **18 A 10**).

The same Claudianus ascribes a similar view to Philolaus (**44 B 22**), from whom Clement quotes the following words:

> The old theologians and seers also bear witness that as a punishment the soul is yoked to the body and is buried in it as in a tomb (**408: 44 B 14**).

That evidence will bear little weight. Claudianus is confused, and is probably relying upon some late Pythagorean forgery;[6] and Clement's report is hard to reconcile with the rest of what we learn about Philolaus' psychology.[7] In any case, none of the three reports strictly implies an incorporeal soul: each is concerned to distinguish the *psuchê* from the human body; and such a distinction does not entail that the *psuchê* is not itself bodily. A *psuchê* distinct from the body it inhabits may be corporeal: human prisoners are distinct from their physical jails, but they are physical substances. Moreover, Aristotle says that

> Some of them [sc. the Pythagoreans] said that the motes in the air
> are a soul, or that what moves them are. It was said of them
> because they are seen to be continually moving even in a complete
> absence of wind (**409**: *An* 404a17–9 = **58 B 40**).[8]

That little analogy does not yield a 'theory of the *psuchê*'; but it does suggest a fairly crudely materialistic notion of soul.

There is, however, at least one other Pythagorean theory to be described; and that, in many scholars' opinion, will be a more probable target for Democritean attack than the minor *dicta* that I have just quoted. I hold the target back for a section.

(b) *Empedoclean psychology*

Leucippus and Democritus say that perceptions and thinkings are alterations (*heteroiôseis*) of the body (**410**: Aëtius, **67 A 30**).

Democritus 'places perceiving in changing (*alloiousthai*)' (Theophrastus, *Sens* §49 = **68 A 135**): we perceive a poker or think of a theorem if our bodies, or certain parts of them, alter in certain ways. Alteration is a matter of atomic locomotion, so that mental events will occur when certain types of atoms clash in certain ways; that is how Aristotle can say that

> Democritus and most of the *phusiologoi* who speak of perception
> do something quite absurd; for they make all objects of perception
> objects of touch (**411**: *Sens* 442a29–30 = **68 A 119**).

As an illustration, take the atomist account of seeing. It is founded on the hypothesis of images (*eidôla*) or, in Democritus' language, *deikela*; and a *deikelon* is 'an effluence (*aporrhoia*) similar in kind to the objects [from which it flows]' (**B 123**). The full theory is somewhat complicated; here is Theophrastus' account of it:

He has seeing occur by reflexion, but he gives an idiosyncratic account of this; for the reflexion does not occur immediately in the pupil, but the air between sight and the object of sight is given an impression as it is compressed by the object seen and the seer; for from everything there is always some effluence issuing. Then this [air], being solid and different in colour [from the eyes], is reflected in the moist eyes; and the thick part [of the eye] does not receive it, but the moist part lets it through (**412**: *Sens* §50 = A 135).

Thus an observer, *a*, sees an object, *b*, in the following fashion: 'effluences', or thin atomic films similar in form to their begetter, leave *b* continuously; the passage of the effluences compresses a volume of air against the eye of *a*, and impresses it with the form of *b*. That airy impression then causes a reflection of *b* in certain receptive portions of *a*'s eyes. And thus *a* sees *b*.[9]

The theory of sight was generalized to explain the phenomena of reflexion (Aëtius, **67 A 31**) and of dreaming (Plutarch, **68 A 77**; Aëtius, **68 A 136**). As it stands it contains nothing specifically atomistic; but it is a thoroughly materialist account. It has no room for any dubiously physical operations or entities, like imaging and mental images; there are physical operations of effluxion, compression and reflexion, and physical entities—nothing else. No doubt reflexion and effluxion were ultimately explained in terms of atomic motions; but that apart, the Democritean account of perception is highly unoriginal. Theophrastus explains his views on sight and hearing, and notes the few novelties they include; he adds:

On sight and hearing this is what he says; the other senses he accounts for in a way pretty similar to most people (**413**: *Sens* §57 = **68 A 135**).

The evidence we possess bears out Theophrastus' judgment. Of Democritus' predecessors the most interesting is Empedocles, the earliest (from whom Empedocles probably borrowed) Alcmeon of Croton.

Alcmeon is said to have dissected an eye (**24 A 10**); and he believed, presumably on experimental evidence, that 'all the senses are connected in some way to the brain' (Theophrastus, *Sens* §26 = A 5). He gave a purely physical account of the senses; e.g.:

We hear by our ears because there is a vacuum in them; for this echoes (it makes a sound by being hollow), and the air echoes back (**414**: ibid., §25 = **A 5**; cf. Aëtius, **A 6**).

The text of Theophrastus is corrupt;[10] but the general lines of Alcmeon's account are clear: we hear external sounds by virtue of the physical properties of certain echoing parts of our ear. That account can hardly be complete, though it is all that Theophrastus offers us: it does not mention the brain, but implies, as it stands, that hearing is a function merely of the ear. For a fuller treatment of Alcmeonic psychology we must turn to Empedocles.

Like Alcmeon, Empedocles was a doctor (e.g., Satyrus, *apud* Diogenes Laertius, VIII. 58 = **31 A 1**; Galen, **A 3**); and he is said to have written a medical treatise (Suda, **A 2**). To his pupil Pausanias, the addressee of *Concerning Nature*, he says:

> You will learn what medicines there are for evils, and a remedy against old age (**415: B 111**.1-2);

and in the *Katharmoi* he claims that crowds followed him about,

> . . . some wanting prophecies, some for sicknesses
> of every sort asked to hear a healing word,
> long ravaged by harsh pains (**416: B 112**.10-2).

These boasts were the seeds of the later legend, of which the celebrated story of Empedocles on Etna is only the final dramatic scene.[11] And the medical theories and practices by means of which Empedocles tried, apparently with success, to give substance to his words had a significant influence on later medical men.

From doctors we expect physiology; and Empedocles does not disappoint us. Plato gives a brief account of his general theory of perception:

> Do you agree with Empedocles that existing things give off a sort of effluence (*aporrhoia*)?

> Certainly.

> And that they have pores into which and through which the effluences travel?

> Yes.

> And of the effluences some fit some of the pores while others are too small or too big?

> That is right.

> And there's something you call sight?

> There is.

From this, then, 'grasp what I say to you' as Pindar puts it: colour is an effluence of things which is fitted to (*summetros*) sight and perceptible (417: *Meno* 76C = **A 92**).

Theophrastus continues Plato's dialogue in plain prose:

Empedocles speaks in the same way about all [the senses] and says that we perceive by things fitting (*enharmottein*) into the pores of each [sense]. That is why [the senses] cannot discriminate one another's objects; for the pores of some are too broad and of others too narrow relative to the percept, so that some slip through without touching and others cannot enter at all (418: *Sens* §7 = **A 86**).

The surviving fragments do not mention pores (*poroi*),[12] but they do contain a reference to *aporrhoiai*:

. . . knowing that there are effluences of everything which has come into being (419: **B 89**);

and a corrupt text refers thus to the activities of hounds on the chase:

Searching out with their nostrils the particles (*kermata*) of animal limbs . . . which their feet have left behind in the soft grass (420: **B 101**).

The hounds snuffle up the effluences of their quarry and thus track it down. Empedocles' *aporrhoiai* are plainly the fathers of Democritean *deikela*; but they should not be identified with them: first, *aporrhoiai* come to all the senses, *deikela* only to the eyes; second, nothing indicates that Empedoclean *aporrhoiai* are likenesses of their origins: the *aporrhoia* for sight is light (Philoponus, **A 57**) or perhaps colour (Theophrastus, *Sens* §7 = **A 86**).

The details of Empedocles' theory are uncertain and in some places controversial. A long fragment, **B 84**, describes the eye. Many scholars attempt to extract a theory of vision from it, but in fact the fragment means only to describe the structure of the eye. The doxography on vision is confusing rather than clarifying.[13] Here is Theophrastus' account of the other four senses:

Hearing comes about from internal sounds; for when the air is moved by the noise, it echoes inside. For the ear is like a bell (?) of equal echoes (?)—he calls it a 'fleshy shoot'; and when the air is moved it strikes against the solid parts and makes an echo. Smelling comes about by breathing. That is why those creatures smell best whose breathing motion is most violent. Most smell flows from (*aporrhein*) the finest and lightest things. About taste and touch he says nothing in particular, neither how nor by what means they come about, but only the general thesis that perception occurs by things fitting (*enharmottein*) the pores (**420**: *Sens* §9 = **A 86**).

Streams of effluent flow from all bodies; their waters differ in outline and magnitude, some representing colours, some sounds, some smells, and so forth. When the streams strike against sentient creatures most of them are diverted; but some hit an appropriate sense organ, equipped with *summetroi* pores into which they can fit (*enharmottein*). Colour streams hit the eyes and fit the eye pores; and that is how we can see colours; sound streams fit the ears, and we hear; colour streams are asymmetrical with the ears, sound streams with the eyes—so we neither see sounds nor hear colours.

Perception is thus a purely physical occurrence: Empedocles' theory is expressed, crudely but firmly, in the language of physical science; and to that extent he is at one with the Atomists, and indeed with all Presocratic psychological speculation. Any such materialist theory lays itself open to an obvious objection; Theophrastus brings it against Empedocles, and repeats it for Anaxagoras and Diogenes (whose theories are only uninteresting variants on the Empedoclean tradition). Thus: 'one might wonder . . . first, how inanimate objects differ from the rest with regard to perception; for things fit into the pores of inanimate objects too' (*Sens* §12 = **A 86**; cf. §36 = **59 A 92**; §46 = **64 A 19**). If perception is just a matter of effluences fitting pores, why is the phenomenon so rare? In general, if perception is a purely physical interaction, why is it that only select physical objects perceive?

Some scholars reply boldly: perception, on Empedocles' theory, is widespread, if not universal; for he himself says that:

Thus, then, everything has breathing and smellings (**422: B 102**).

And he ascribes understanding, which presupposes perception, to all things:

Thus by the will of chance everything possesses thought (**333: B 103**).

For know that everything possesses sense and a portion of thought (**423: B 110**.10).

But that reply is no good. First, the texts it cites give uncertain support: the word 'everything' in **422** and **333** has no context; and it may well have referred only to animate things (the two fragments probably come from Empedocles' zoogony). **B 110** is a difficult fragment: I shall argue later that line 10, read in its context, does not after all say that 'everything has thought' (below, p. 183).[14]

Second, even if Empedocles did ascribe perception to everything, that will not help him against Theophrastus' criticism. For not every fitting of effluences into pores is a case of perception. No one recognizes that more clearly than Empedocles himself: *aporrhoiai* and *poroi* are not only employed in the elucidation of perception; they account for the phenomena of reflexion (**B 109a**; Aëtius, **A 88**); for some aspects of breathing (Aristotle, *Resp* 473b1; cf. **B 100**); for magnetism (Alexander, **A 89**); for chemical mixture (**B 91, B 92**); and for the way in which certain trees lose their leaves in autumn (Plutarch, *ad* **B 77**).[15] Far from being a distinguishing mark of perception, the fitting of effluences into pores is a common feature of natural phenomena: *aporrhoiai* and *poroi* are general principles of physics, not special principles of psychology.

According to Theophrastus, perception in Empedocles comes about 'by likes' (*Sens* §1 = **A 86**; cf. §10); and Theophrastus asserts that

> He assigns knowledge to these two things, similarity and touch;
> that is why he uses the word 'fit (*harmottein*)'. So that if the less
> should touch the greater, there will be perception (**424**: §15).

The point is supported by a fragment:

> For by earth we see earth, by water water;
> by air bright air, and by fire brilliant fire;
> love by love, and strife by horrid strife (**425: B 109**).

For sight to occur, an *aporrhoia* must enter a *poros* in the eye; and it must 'fit' (*harmottein*): i.e., it must be of the right shape and size to fill the pore (it must 'touch'), and it must also be homogeneous with the walls of the pore (it must be 'like'). Thus I shall see red if a red *aporrhoia* (a ray of red light, perhaps) fits snugly into a red-edged pore in my eye. The lesser red touches the greater; and I perceive.

Will the 'likeness' principle thus eke out the theory of pores and defend Empedocles from Theophrastus? Hardly: how can auditory *aporrhoiai* be 'like' the ears they enter? or why suppose that the iron filings attracted by the magnet are 'unlike' it? Theophrastus reports that

> In general, likeness in his theory is done away with and
> commensurateness alone is enough. For he says that the sense
> organs do not perceive one another's objects because they have

incommensurate pores; and whether the effluent is like or unlike he does not determine (**426**: *Sens* §15 = **A 86**).

The 'like by like' principle is vague; it solves nothing; it was not seriously used by Empedocles. (**425** fits a different context: see below, pp. 182–6.)

But Empedocles' theory is not dead yet: Theophrastus may show that it is not enough to talk of *aporrhoiai* and *poroi*, but he does not show that no modification can defend the theory. Empedocles' *aporrhoia* in the case of vision is light, his *poroi* are rods and cones: modern physiologists can doubtless tell us how the impact of light on rods and cones differs from its impact on the glass of a mirror or from the impact of air on the breathing passages; and they will thereby complete Empedocles' account and establish it as a full theory of visual perception.

'But surely such an account can only aspire to the status of a physiological description: it cannot tell us what perception really is; it cannot touch on the properly psychological side of sight, hearing and the rest. Physiology of perception is interesting enough; but it is no substitute for philosophy of perception.' Empedocles had no means of anticipating that objection; and he might well have been puzzled by it: what facts remain unaccounted for by the physical account? What opening or need is there for philosophy? 'There are illusions, hallucinations, after-images and other paraperceptual occurrences.' But surely the physical theory can be extended to account for them? 'Perception has a subjective or experiential side; and physiological theorizing necessarily ignores the felt qualities of sensation; it accounts only for what happens in our bodies, not for what we experience ourselves.' But *is* there an 'experiential' side to perception, distinct from the 'physical' side? What are its characteristics? and why cannot an Empedoclean account explain experience too?

There are modern materialists, of a sophisticated sort, who are at bottom Empedocleans; and it is by no means evident that their Empedoclean efforts to give a purely physiological account of the subjective elements in perception are unsound. In tacitly rejecting any non-physiological 'philosophy' of perception Empedocles is curiously modern.

If perception is materialistic, what of thought, that supremely Cartesian operation? According to Aristotle,

The old thinkers said that perception and thought were the same; thus Empedocles said:

For men's wit is increased by reference to what is present
[= **B 106**];

and elsewhere:

To the extent that they become different, to that extent always
does thinking present different things to them [= **B 108**].[16]

(**427**: *An* 427a21–5; cf. *Met* 1009b17–20.)

Theophrastus qualifies Aristotle's judgment and offers a new text:

He speaks in the same way about thought and ignorance; for
thought is by likes and ignorance by unlikes, thought being either
the same as or similar to perception. For having enumerated the
way in which we recognize each thing by itself, he adds at the end
that:

From these are all things fitted and formed,
and by these they think and feel pleasure and pain [= **B 107**].

That is why we think especially with the blood; for in this of all
parts are the elements especially mixed (**428**: *Sens* §10 = **A 86**).

Before his quotation of **B 107** Theophrastus summarizes **425**: clearly
425 immediately preceded **B 107** in Empedocles' poem, and 'these'
in **B 107**.1 refers to the four 'roots' (together with Love and Strife)
which are 'enumerated' in **425**.[17] Theophrastus' final sentence is also
a paraphrase of a surviving fragment:

. . . (?) turned (?) in seas of surging blood;
and there especially is what men call thought
—for the blood about the heart is thought for men (**429**: **B 105**).[18]

In **B 105**–**B 109** we have the passages upon which the Peripatetics
based their account of Empedocles' theory of thought. Some modern
scholars think that the Peripatetics should have attended also to
B 110:

For if you establish them (*sphe*) in your stout **mind**
and guard them kindly with pure exercises,
they will indeed all remain with you throughout your **life**,
and you will gain many others from these; for they themselves
increase
each in its kind, as is the nature of each.   5
But if you reach for different things such as among men

there are, innumerable, evil, which blunt the mind,
they will at once abandon you as their time is accomplished,
desiring to come to their own dear kind;
for know that they all have sense and a portion of thought (430;
cf. 423).

The interpretation of the fragment turns on the identity of 'them (*sphe*)' in the first line. Some scholars make 'them' the elements, and are then able to construe 430 as an account of thought.[19] But '*sphe*' in line 1 contrasts with 'many others' in line 4, and with the 'different things, . . . innumerable, evil' of lines 6–7: the elements have nothing to contrast with, for they embrace all the things that there are. Moreover, 'they' may 'abandon' Pausanias (line 8); but the elements could never do that.

Accordingly, we must find a different identity for *sphe*; and the orthodox view is that *sphe* are the axioms of Empedoclean physics. 430 then reads thus: 'Remember my words and keep them fresh in your mind; then you will possess not only them but also the consequences and implications to which they will lead you. But if you attend to other foolish philosophies, my thoughts will leave you; for they have more sense than to dwell in a mind given to un-Empedoclean views.' That construe is not easy: it takes lines 6–10 as a highly coloured statement of a fairly mundane possibility. But it is the best we can do in the absence of a larger context; and it removes 430 from the theory of perception and thought. (It also shows that line 10 does not commit Empedocles to the view that 'everything has thought': '*panta*' means not 'everything' but 'all [my words]'.)

What, then, was Empedocles' analysis of thought? Aristotle's statement that 'thinking and perceiving are the same' should not be taken *au pied de la lettre*: he argues only that thinking, in Empedocles' view, is, like perception, a physical process; he does not mean that thinking is exactly the same process as perception. Similarly, Theophrastus is concerned only to point out that the 'like by like' principle applies, in Empedoclean doctrine, to thought no less than to perception; and there is again no question of a strict identity between the two processes. 'The blood about the heart is thought for men' (429. 3): Empedocles does not say that it is the blood which thinks; nor does he say that the heart, or the heart's blood, is the *sole* organ or instrument of thought; the heart is of pre-eminent importance, but it is only the place where 'especially' we think.[20] Heart's blood is a peculiarly fine mixture of the elements; since, as B 107 implies and 425 makes explicit, each of the elements is an organ or instrument of thought, then heart's blood is a peculiarly fine cognitive medium.

At this point I shall turn to discuss a Parmenidean fragment. The quatrain is of interest in its own right; and it is relevant here as it expresses, in a fuller and reasoned form, the theory of thought that Empedocles hints at. The lines run thus:

> For as on each occasion is the mixture of the much-wandering limbs,
> so does the mind stand in men. For the same
> as what it thinks of is the nature of the limbs for men,
> for each and for all; for what preponderates is thought
> (431: 28 B 16).

The text of lines 1–2,[21] and the syntax of lines 2–4, are highly controversial; and my interpretation will inevitably be uncertain.

Theophrastus quotes the lines to show that 'he treats perceiving and thinking as the same' (*Sens* §3 = 28 A 46; cf. Aristotle, *Met* 1009b12–25, also quoting 431). Again, all that he means is that thinking, like perceiving, is treated as a physical change; and we need make no more of it. Equally, we may put aside a question that has troubled some critics: how, they ask, can Parmenides maintain the theory of 431 and still say what he does about the objects of thought in 148–9? The answer is simple: 431 appears in the Way of Opinion; it represents Mortal Thoughts, not Eleatic doctrine.

What does Parmenides mean by 'limbs (*melea*)'? Some gloss the word by 'sense-organs'. 'Men', as Archilochus had observed, 'think the things they come across':[22] the first couplet of 431 means that we only think of the things we meet with in perception, thus precociously formulating the Aristotelian doctrine, *nil in intellectu nisi prius in sensu*. And since the 'limbs' are 'much-wandering', Parmenides is in effect offering a criticism of any epistemology built upon that doctrine: if the doctrine is correct, all our thoughts are based ultimately on our misleading and mischievous senses.[23] In B 106 Empedocles presents the same Aristotelian theory: 'men's wit is increased by reference to what is present'; i.e., if the senses have presented something to a man, then, and only then, is he capable of thinking of it. But Empedocles drops the Parmenidean criticism.

That may be a correct interpretation of Empedocles, but it will not fit Parmenides. First, it must read into 431 not the Aristotelian doctrine, but the far stronger and wholly absurd thesis that we think only of the things we are actually perceiving ('Our thought *on any occasion* is given by the contents of our sense-organs on that occasion'). Second, it ascribes an impossible sense to '*melea*': 'limbs' is not naturally taken as 'sense-organs'; and the word nowhere else bears anything like that meaning.[24] If *melea* are not sense-organs, then there is no empiricist epistemology glanced at in 431; nor, indeed, is there any theory of perception at all in the fragment: 431 offers an account not of perception but of thought.

The crucial sentence of 431 occupies lines 2b–3; in Greek it runs: *to gar auto estin hoper phroneei meleôn phusis anthrôpoisin*. The sentence is multiply ambiguous. *Melea*, 'limbs', may be glossed either by 'body' or by 'elements': the body is the sum and organization of the limbs; the elemental stuffs are the limbs of the universe.[25] '*To . . . auto*' may mean either 'the same thing' or 'that very thing'. *Hoper* may be either subject or object of *phroneei*. The last sentence of the fragment is also ambiguous: *to gar pleon esti noêma*. The traditional reading (cf. Theophrastus *Sens* §3 = 28 A 46) takes *to . . . pleon* to mean 'the more', i.e. 'that which predominates'. Many modern scholars prefer 'the full'; and it has been proposed, ingeniously, to separate *to* from *pleon*: 'For that is full thought'.[26]

Permutation of those different readings yields a mass of conflicting construes of the fragment. More than one can be given a sort of plausibility; and none has any clear claim to superiority. I shall simply present the view I incline towards, leaving the reader to construct his own reading for himself. Thus I take *melea* to refer to the elements; I read *to . . . auto* as 'the same thing'; I make *hoper* object of *phroneei*; and I construe *to pleon*, with Theophrastus, as 'the preponderating [element]'. Lines 1–2 then paraphrase thus: 'The state of a man's thoughts at any time is determined by the elemental mixture [in his body].' The crucial sentence reads: 'The nature of the elements is the same as what they think of'; and since 'the nature of the elements' is merely a paraphrase for 'the elements', the sentence purveys the same thought as Empedocles, 425: by means of element E_1 you can think only of E_1. Finally, the last sentence means: 'the element predominating in a man's body is what he thinks with'.[27] The three sentences that make up 431 are linked by *gar* ('for'); but it is not easy to give that particle its proper force. Perhaps the argument is this: 'Given, first, that by E_1 a man can think only of E_1, and, second, that if E_1 predominates in a man, then he thinks with it; it follows that what a man thinks of at any time is determined by the elemental predominance, and thus by the elemental mixture, in his body.'

If that interpretation of Parmenides is right, it gives us a little help with Empedocles; for in effect 431 infers Empedocles' B 108 from his 425. We think of elements by elements; hence (since thinking is determined by elemental predominance) as we change physically, so do the objects of our thought change. Moreover, Parmenides confirms the decidedly materialistic aspect of Empedocles' theory of thought: to think of E_1 is simply to have E_1 predominant in your body (or in some selected part of it); and to come to think of E_1 is for your physical constitution to change. Intellectual states are physical states, intellectual processes are physical operations. It is entertaining to find a materialist account of thought so self-consciously paraded by a Presocratic; but the account itself is too crude to contemplate, and I hasten on.

(c) *The soul as harmony*

'The fragments of Empedocles contain only a single occurrence of the word *"psuchê"* (B 138), and then it means "life": the fact is no accident; for, strictly speaking, Empedoclean psychology has no room for a *psuchê*. "Empedocles did not hold that the soul is composed of the elements; but what we call the activity of the soul he explained by the elementary composition of the body; a soul distinct from the body he did not assume".'[28] The view that Empedocles had no soul is now fairly common. It was not held in antiquity: the doxographers are ready enough to use *psuchê* in Empedoclean contexts,[29] and their sunny acceptance of Empedoclean souls suggests that the absence of the term *psuchê* from the fragments should be ascribed to chance. In any case, it seems to me that in B 138 ('drawing off his *psuchê* with bronze'—i.e. 'slitting his throat') the word *psuchê* does mean 'soul'.

What was the Empedoclean *psuchê*? In the *Phaedo* Socrates refers anonymously to those who say that 'blood is that with which we think' (96B = 24 A 11); and he surely has Empedocles' 429 in mind. According to Hippo, 'the fact that the semen is not blood refutes those who say that the *psuchê* is blood' (*An* 405b4 = 31 A 4): Hippo, too, had Empedocles in mind.[30] The doxographers, however, pass on a slightly different interpretation of 429:

> The leading part (*to hêgemonikon*) is neither in the head nor in the chest, but in the blood (432: pseudo-Plutarch, A 30; cf. Aëtius, A 97).

Theophrastus, perhaps, disagreed with Plato. And Theophrastus' master confessed his own puzzlement:

> And it is similarly absurd to say that the *psuchê* is the *logos* of the mixing; for the mixing of the elements which produces flesh and that which produces bone do not have the same *logos*. Hence it

will follow that one has many *psuchai* throughout the whole body, if everything is composed of mixed elements and the *logos* of the mixing is {*harmonia* and}[31] *psuchê*. And one might also put the following problem to Empedocles: he says that each of them exists by some *logos*; then is the *psuchê* the *logos*, or is it rather as something else[32] that it comes about in the limbs? (**433**: *An* 408a13–21 = **A 78**).

Let us forget about the blood and consider the view that the *psuchê* is a *logos* of the mixing: what does that mean? and was Empedocles in fact committed to it? Aristotle compares this Empedoclean doctrine to the celebrated theory that 'the soul is a harmony': I shall look at the latter theory before returning to Empedocles.

There is another opinion handed down about the *psuchê*. . . . For they say that it is a sort of harmony; for a harmony is a mixing and composition (*krasis kai sunthesis*) of opposites, and the body is composed of opposites (**434**: *An* 407b27–32 = **44 A 23**).

Many of the wise men say—some that the soul is a harmony, others that it has a harmony (**435**: *Pol* 1340b18 = **58 B 41**).

Our main source for the view is Plato's *Phaedo*:

For, Socrates, I think you are aware that we believe the soul to be something like this: our bodies are, as it were, tensioned and held together by hot and cold and dry and wet and other things of the same kind; and our souls are the mixture and harmony of these things when they have been well mixed in a correct *logos* (**436**: 86 B).

Aristotle leaves the harmony men in comfortable anonymity. The speech in the *Phaedo* is made by Simmias; and the whole discussion is reported by Echecrates, who explicitly says that the harmony theory was familiar to him (88D = **53 A 4**). Now Echecrates is listed as a Pythagorean (Iamblichus, **53 A 2**); and Simmias studied under Philolaus (*Phaedo* 61D). The obvious inference is that the harmony theory was Pythagorean, and, specifically, a doctrine belonging to Philolaus. The importance of *harmonia* in Philolaus' thought adds credibility to the conclusion; and there is external corroboration; three late sources explicitly ascribe the doctrine to the Pythagoreans;[33] and one asserts that:

Pythagoras and Philolaus [say that the soul is] a harmony (**437**: Macrobius, **44 A 23**).

The 'opposites' do not, it is true, figure in what we know of Philolaus' physics; but we have no reason to deny him the Presocratic commonplace that animal bodies are compounds and that their constituents are in some respects 'opposite'. Again, the only genuine Philolaic fragment that explicitly mentions *psuchê* (**44 B 13**) says nothing of *harmonia*;[34] but that fragment is consistent with the *harmonia* theory, and has no particular reason to advert expressly to it. I conclude that the traditional ascription is correct: Philolaus held that 'the soul is a harmony'.[35]

To say that 'the *psuchê* is a harmony' is to say that a person has a *psuchê* just so long as his physical constituents are harmoniously arranged,[36] thus:

(1) *a* has a *psuchê* if and only if *a*'s physical parts are harmoniously arranged.

The essential point about (1) is this: it makes the *psuchê* non-substantial, a dependent entity, like a mood or a cold, not an independent part of a man, like a brain or a heart. There are filthy moods and bad colds if and only if someone is in a filthy mood or has a bad cold; there are harmonies if and only if something is harmoniously arranged; and there are souls if and only if something has a soul. If I say '*a* has a coat', I assert a two-place relation (the relation of *having*) between a man and his apparel; and the predicate '. . . has a coat' is formed from the relation '. . . has—' and the general term 'coat'. If I say '*a* has a filthy temper' I do not assert a two-place relation between a man and some other item; and the predicate '. . . has a filthy temper' is not compounded from a relation and a general term. According to (1), '*a* has a *psuchê*' is like '*a* has a temper' and unlike '*a* has a coat'.

The thesis that a *psuchê* is 'the *logos* of the mixing' has the same implication; and that is why Aristotle treats the two views together. '*Logos*' in this phrase hovers between 'proportion' or 'ratio' and 'definition'; but the difference is trifling, since a mixing is presumably defined by the ratio of the stuffs it mixes. Thus the thesis says that a person has a *psuchê* just so long as his physical constituents are mixed in the right proportion; or:

(2) *a* has a *psuchê* if and only if *a*'s physical parts are correctly mixed.

Evidently, the *psuchê* of (2) is non-substantial in exactly the same way as the *psuchê* of (1).

Psuchê is essentially defined in functional terms: a *psuchê* is that in virtue of which one lives. Similarly, we might define a temper as that in virtue of which one rants and rages; and a waterproof as that in virtue of which one remains dry in rainstorms. Given these formal definitions, we ask after the nature of the *psuchê*, the temper, the waterproof. Answers of very different types emerge for the two latter questions: a waterproof is a piece of oilskin or canvas or similar material; a temper is a disposition or inclination to act in such and such a way. '*a* has a waterproof' is true if and only if *a* possesses a piece of oilskin or the like: 'has' denotes a two-place relation; and the sentence might be symbolized, to bring that feature out, by the formula: $(\exists x)$ (x is a waterproof and a has x). '*a* has a temper' is true if and only if *a* is disposed to act in such and such a way: 'has' does not denote a two-place relation, and the sentence permits no symbolic formalization that parallels the waterproof formula. The *harmonia* theory and the *logos* theory bring *psuchê* to the side of tempers and separate it from waterproofs. The theories contrast both with run-of-the-mill Presocratic notions, which make the *psuchê* a part of a man's bodily stuff, and also with the Cartesian account, which makes the soul an incorporeal homuncule temporarily resident in the body.

Theories (1) and (2) are close to one another; the *Phaedo* perhaps conflates them. Aristotle, however, rightly distinguishes between them, and rightly points out the absurdity of (2): there is no one ratio which gives the 'correct' elemental mixture for all a man's physical constituents; different parts require different ratios, and there is no such thing as '*the logos* of the mixing'. The objection can be countered by rewriting the *definiens* of (2) as 'each of *a*'s physical constituents is correctly mixed'. The difference between (1) and (2) now diminishes; and both theories face a common question: What is a 'harmonious' arrangement, or a 'correct' mixing? What are the canons of harmony, the criteria of correctness?

A lyre is 'harmoniously' arranged if it is correctly strung and attuned for playing: its harmony or attunement consists in its aptitude for performance. Similarly, then, a body's harmony, or correct mix, is one which conduces to its functioning: the arrangement of the bodily parts is harmonious only if the body is capable of performing certain vital functions; and a mixture of bodily constituents is correct only if it is conducive to such performance. Thus (1) and (2) give place to:

(3) *a* has a *psuchê* if and only if *a*'s body is in a state such that *a* is capable of performing the vital functions.

The vital functions will vary from one species of creature to another; no doubt they will include, in the case of man, nutrition, reproduction, perception, locomotion, and thought.

I have deliberately developed the *harmonia* theory in an Aristotelian direction: indeed (3) constitutes as good an account as I can give of Aristotle's thesis that 'the *psuchê* is an *entelecheia* of a potentially living body' (*An* 412a26). Aristotle vigorously rejects the *harmonia* theory, and gives no hint that it approximated to his own view. His hasty dismissal of the theory is a pity; for if, as I incline to think, Aristotle's own view of mind is substantially correct, then it would be pleasant to know more about its first adumbration in the writings of Philolaus: had Aristotle praised the theory, later writers might have prized and preserved it.

(d) *Metempsychosis and immortality*

Philolaus held both a *harmonia* theory of the *psuchê* and a Pythagorean view on metempsychosis and immortality. Most scholars are worried by the conjunction, and some see a difficulty so great that they dissociate psychic harmony from Philolaus. There is, it is true, no direct evidence for transmigration or psychic immortality in Philolaus: scholars point to his alleged prohibition on suicide (*Phaedo* 61DE = **44 B 15**); and to the *mot* that the body is a tomb of the soul. But the prohibition has no bearing on the question; and the *mot* is ascribed to Philolaus by virtue of a misreading of the *Phaedo* (62B = **44 B 15**).[37] Thus if either *harmonia* or immortality must be denied to Philolaus, I should incline to deny him immortality. Yet such a rejection, in a Pythagorean, would have been remarkable; and since our sources do not remark upon it, we must work on the supposition that both *harmonia* and immortality are Philolaic.

In the *Phaedo* Simmias himself discovers an incongruity between harmony and immortality: 'If, then, the soul really is some kind of harmony, it is clear that when our bodies are unduly relaxed or tensioned by disease or some other evil, the soul must immediately perish' (*Phaedo* 86C). There cannot be separate souls; for it is an immediate consequence of the harmony theory that anyone who has a *psuchê* has a body. And souls cannot survive their owner's body; for any destruction of the arrangement of that body is *eo ipso* an end of the *psuchê*. Aristoxenus, who later developed a version of the *harmonia* theory, was perfectly clear that the *psuchê*, not being substantial, could not have a separate immortal existence (cf. frr. 119–20 W).

There are two distinct arguments to consider here. Before discussing them I have two preliminary points to make. First, even if the argument outlined in the last paragraph is correct, we need not suppose that Philolaus knew it or would have accepted it had he known it. Indeed, 'one has the impression that Plato, in this passage in the *Phaedo*, was the first to point out an embarrassing implication of the idea of the soul as a harmony'.[38] Even if harmony and

190

immortality are inconsistent, Philolaus may well have embraced both doctrines, in blissful ignorance or erroneous belief.

Second, we must distinguish clearly between psychic insubstantiality and psychic incorporeality. To say that the soul is insubstantial, as (1)–(3) implicitly do, is to deny that the soul is an independent substance, or that 'soul' is an indispensable substantive (see above, p. 143). To say that the soul is incorporeal is to deny that souls are physical or that a complete account of psychology can be given in terms of physical theory. The distinction allows four types of view on the soul: (a) the soul is substantial and incorporeal—as Plato and Descartes held; (b) the soul is substantial and corporeal—as Democritus and most of the Presocratics held; (c) the soul is insubstantial and incorporeal ('soul' is not a substance word, but there are irreducibly non-physical predicates)—Aristotle, I think, held this view; (d) the soul is insubstantial and corporeal—as modern behaviourism and modern physicalism hold. Philolaus' harmony theory rejects (a) and (b); it does not, so far as I can see, plump definitely for (d) rather than (c). Thus Philolaus was not necessarily a full-blooded physicalist; and any difficulty there may be in reconciling his psychology with his eschatology is due not to materialism or physicalism, but to 'insubstantialism'.

What, then, of Simmias' difficulty? One argument is plain enough: the harmony theory entails the impossibility of independently existing souls. Aristotle saw the entailment clearly (*An* 413a3), and it is indeed obvious: there exists a *psuchê* only if '*x* has a *psuchê*' is true of something; and '*x* has a *psuchê*' is true of *a* only if *a* has a body. No soul without body. The conclusion is anathema to modern advocates of immortality. It does not, however, imply that the soul is mortal: I ignore the tedious and unreal possibility that *a*'s body may be immortal and point to the particular form of Pythagorean immortality: metempsychosis allows psychic immortality without requiring the existence of separate, disembodied, souls (see vol. 1, p. 111). My body perishes, certainly; and so my *psuchê* cannot achieve immortality by cleaving to this flesh. But other bodies survive, and my soul may fly to a new body on the destruction of mine; and if there is an infinite sequence of bodies, my soul may achieve a transmigratory immortality. Metempsychosis, in short, allows Philolaus to make his *psuchê* immortal, even though it cannot exist apart from a body.

The second argument against Philolaus seems to have failed along with the first: the second urges that if a body, b_1, ceases to be harmoniously arranged, then its harmony and its *psuchê* perish;

Philolaus replies that the harmony and *psuchê* need not perish, they may simply pass on to another body, b_2.

Philolaus' victory, however, is spurious. The suggestion is that two different bodies may have the same soul; and that a suitable succession of mortal bodies may support a single immortal soul. In a way the suggestion is correct: there is a perfectly clear sense in which Philolaus can say that b_1 houses the same soul as b_2. Two different lyres may have the same *harmonia*, for they may be attuned in exactly the same way; two different men may have the same bad temper, for they may be disposed to rage at the same things in the same ways; two different bodies may 'house' the same soul, for they may exhibit exactly the same harmonious arrangement. And it is logically possible (though no doubt physically improbable) that my soul should, in this sense, be immortal: at any time *t*, there exists a body exhibiting exactly the same harmonious arrangement that my body now exhibits.

But an immortality of that sort is eschatologically barren. Psychic immortality so construed does not guarantee personal immortality; psychic 'transmigration' (the word is hardly apposite) does not ensure that *I* survive my body's decay. Two different bodies existing at different times may have the same *psuchê*; but in exactly the same way, two different bodies existing at the same time may have the same *psuchê*. For all I know, my body and the body of the Prime Minister of Australia may be attuned exactly alike; hence, the Prime Minister and I have the same soul. But that does not mean that I am the Prime Minister of Australia. Similarly, it may happen that the Australian Prime Minister in 2075 will have the same soul as I have now; but that fact gives me no reason to expect a future Antipodean existence, or to anticipate a prime-ministerial salary. Psychic identity and personal identity fall apart; psychic immortality has no implications for personal immortality: Philolaus has no call to rejoice in the survival of his soul.

In a monogamous country, if *a* has the same wife as *b*, then *a* is the same person as *b*; in the present state of surgical accomplishment, if *a* has the same brain as *b*, then *a* is the same person as *b*. In general, if *F* is a substance term, and *R* a one-one relation, then if *a* and *b* bear *R* to the same *F*, *a* is identical with *b*. That is an elementary truth of logic. Now on the standard doctrine of metempsychosis, it is my soul that makes me the individual I am; consequently, only I can have my soul. Hence the relationship between myself and my soul is one-one; and if the Australian premier of 2075 has the same soul as I have, then I am he. Philolaus, however, cannot employ that argument: '. . . has a soul' is not a relational predicate in his view; consequently

I do not stand in any relation to my soul, and specifically I do not stand in a one-one relation to it. 'He has his father's soul' is perfectly intelligible; but it is not an assertion of metempsychosis, nor does it imply that he is his father. 'He has his father's soul' is, logically speaking, parallel to 'He has his father's temper': both are comments on the similarity of human nature; neither comments on the identity of human persons.

I conclude that Philolaus is at a loss: *harmonia* and psychic immortality are logically consistent; but together they entail the immortality of the body. If bodies rot, then either *harmonia* or psychic immortality is false. For all that, the harmony theory represents a signal advance in the philosophy of mind; and any discussion of the difficulties into which Philolaus unwittingly drove plunges at once into some of the thickest bush of modern philosophy.

(e) *Was Empedocles a centaur?*

My remarks on Empedocles' psychology have drawn exclusively on fragments traditionally assigned to his poem *Concerning Nature*; my earlier account of Empedocles' theory of metempsychosis drew exclusively on the *Katharmoi*. One of the standing problems in Empedoclean studies concerns the relationship between the two poems, and in particular between the doctrine of metempsychosis and the physiological psychology of *Nature*.[39] *Nature*, it is said, is thoroughly materialistic; the *Katharmoi* treats of the fate of an immortal and incorporeal soul: the two poems are thus in flat contradiction. Empedocles' 'two pictures of rationality remain not only heterogeneous but contradictory at crucial points; they admit of no rational or, for that matter, even imaginative harmony'; 'the Orphic piety of his *Purifications* . . . admits of no rational connexion with the scientific temper and doctrine of his work *On Nature*.' Some scholars generalize from the case of Empedocles: 'all through this period, there seems to have been a gulf between men's religious beliefs, if they had any, and their cosmological views': Empedocles was a 'philosophical centaur', in an age when such monstrosities were regularly spawned.[40]

An essay in intellectual biography may solve the paradox: philosophers change their views; and perhaps Empedocles' equine and his human features were not contemporaneous characteristics— the Ionian doctrines of *Nature* were forgotten or abandoned when the Pythagorean *Purifications* intoxicated Empedocles' mind. We have not an incongruous simultaneity of opinions, but a radical *volte-face*. Such changes are not unknown in the history of philosophy.

The fragments of Empedocles which we possess can be assigned to his different poems with some confidence;[41] moreover, we know the order in which the poems were written. **B 131** comes from the *Katharmoi*:

> If for the sake of any of the mortals, divine Muse,
> it pleased you to let my exercises pass through your mind
> now again stand by me as I pray, Calliope,
> and reveal a good argument about the blessed gods (438).

The earlier aid for which **438** thanks the Muse was surely given for the penning of *Nature*; hence *Nature* was penned before the *Katharmoi*.[42]

The biographical solution will hardly do. The *Katharmoi* gives no hint of a change in doctrine; on the contrary, there are well-marked connexions between the two poems. The *Katharmoi* contains constant linguistic echoes of *Nature*; **438** refers complacently to *Nature* at the opening of the later poem. And there are also close connexions of substance: thus **B 111**, from *Nature*, and **B 112**, from the *Katharmoi*, make very similar proclamations, and Clement intelligibly cites both fragments to prove a single point (cf. **A 14**). Hippolytus, who preserves **B 115** of the *Katharmoi*, intelligibly glosses it in the terms of *Nature*.

If we cannot seriously entertain the theory of a radical change in Empedocles' philosophical outlook, we cannot, by the same token, find a lack of 'imaginative harmony' between the two poems; at any rate, Empedocles' imagination, and that of his ancient critics, was broad and bold enough to encompass both poems. It was not unusual to find prophet and scientist united in one person in old Greece; and the religious physicist is no rarity today. I may be astonished to find that one man both has expertise in nuclear physics and practises as a lay preacher; but I can hardly doubt that there are such men, and that they manage to combine their apparently heterogeneous beliefs into an imaginative unity.[43]

There is just one Empedocles, the scientist of *Nature* and the moralist of the *Katharmoi*: we have no grounds for positing an intellectual revolution in his life, or for accusing him of imaginative schizophrenia. The main charge remains: are not the two poems simply inconsistent with each other? Is not the transmigratory soul of the *Katharmoi* incompatible with the psychology of *Nature*?

I begin with **B 15**, which scholars locate in *Nature*:

> A man wise in such matters would not think in his mind
> that while they live what they call life
> so long do they exist, and bad and good things face them,

but that before they were put together as men and once they are dissolved they do not exist at all (439).

The fragment speaks of immortality; and Plutarch, who quotes it, plausibly takes it to be promising a personal immortality:[44] 'only a fool would think that his existence is limited to that short span which men call life'.

439 is not easy to integrate with the rest of *Nature*: strictly speaking (see above, p. 140), Empedocles cannot admit that men exist at all; for only the elements really exist. But 439 is not ascribing immortality to *men*: the things that are immortal are only men for a brief span in their existence. If 439 does announce a personal immortality, it must distinguish persons from men. Persons, of course, must be parcels of elemental stuff; but they need not always be parcels of human form. Thus 439 brings *Nature* into close doctrinal contact with the eschatological promises of the *Katharmoi*. That, I think, shows that in Empedocles' mind the two poems were consistent; it does not, of course, show that they are consistent in reality. We must now look at the incorporeal objects of the *Katharmoi* whose alleged existence breeds the inconsistency.

Four fragments need to be quoted; the first describes 'the divine (*to theion*)':

We cannot bring it near to be approachable by our eyes,
or grasp it with our hands, which is the greatest
path of persuasion leading into men's minds (440: B 133).

The next fragment may well have been continuous with 440:

For its limbs are not fitted out with a human head,
nor do two branches spring from shoulders,
nor feet, nor swift knees, nor hairy chest;
but it is only a holy and superhuman mind,
darting with swift thoughts over the whole world (441: B 134).

The Byzantine scholar, Tsetzes, ascribes 441 to 'the third book of the *Physics*'; and some moderns accordingly place 441, and with it 440, in *Nature*.[45] From the present point of view the attribution is unimportant: if correct, it only strengthens the connexion between the two poems.

The next long fragment is expressly concerned with transmigration:

There is a pronouncement of Necessity, an old decree of the gods, eternal, sealed with broad oaths:
when anyone in wickedness defiles his dear limbs with bloodshed

—a *daimôn* who has been allotted long life—
thrice ten thousand seasons is he to wander apart from the blessed 5
ones,
being born through that time in every kind of mortal form,
treading in turn the wretched paths of life.
For the force of the air pursues him into the sea
and the sea spits him up onto the threshold of the land, and the
land into the rays   10
of the tireless sun, and that casts him to the whirls of the air:
one receives him from another, and all hate him.
This way I myself am now going, a fugitive and wanderer from the
gods,
who trusted in mad strife (**442: B 115**).[46]

Finally, a single line reads:

. . . clothing it about in an alien cloak of flesh (**443: B 126**).

Plutarch makes the subject 'nature'; Porphyry says that 'nature' or
'*daimôn*' is the tailor, and that her clients are 'souls'.[47]
    These four fragments are together taken to show that the theory of
transmigration uses an incorporeal soul: **442** makes the migrating
soul a *daimôn* or godlike thing; **443** shows that *daimones* find flesh,
and hence the four roots, foreign stuff; and **440** and **441** reveal that,
in general, Empedoclean gods are pure, incorporeal minds.
    That argument is wholly mistaken. First, the gods. **440** is quickly
dismissed: it says that *we* cannot see or touch *to theion*. The point is
epistemological: 'since we cannot have immediate perception of the
divine, we must rely on inference or analogy or the like'. From that it
scarcely follows that the divine is absolutely intangible and invisible;
let alone that the divine is incorporeal. As for **441**, that is pure
Xenophanes: as Ammonius observes, Empedocles' point is to
'castigate the stories told by the poets which treat of the gods as being
anthropomorphic' (*ad* **B 134**). A denial of anthropomorphism does
not entail incorporeality; and if the divinity is 'a sacred mind
(*phrên*)', that will not secure incorporeality, for Empedocles is a
psychological materialist.
    In fact, Empedocles' theology is far denser and more difficult than
the simple argument from **440** and **441** suggests. First, the four roots,
together with Love and Strife, are given divine names (e.g., **B 6**);[48]
those gods are, trivially, corporeal. Second, the cosmic Sphere is given
divine status (e.g., **B 31**); and the Sphere too is a massy god. Third,
there are the traditional gods named in **B 128**:

Nor was there among them any god Ares, nor Kudoimos,
nor King Zeus, nor Cronus, nor Poseidon,
but only queen Cypris . . . (444).

The main purport of these lines is to state that men of the Golden
Age made love, not war; and the gods may be no more than
rhetorical window-dressing. If we take the gods of 444 seriously, then
they are to be placed among the fourth set of divinities, the created
gods of **B 21**:

For from these [sc. the elements] comes everything that was and is
and will be—
trees sprang up, and men and women,
and beasts and birds and water-dwelling fish,
and long-lived gods who are first in honour (195: cf. **B 23**. 5–8).

Like men, these gods are not eternal but at best long-lived
(*dolichaiônes*): being elemental compounds, they cannot survive the
complete elemental dissociation at the time of total Strife, nor the
utter fusion in the years of the Sphere. Finally, and fifth, there are
the *daimones* of 442. They have a divine status; yet they are not
eternal, their lot is 'long-lived life (*makraiôn biotos*)'. The *daimones*
and the long-lived gods of 195 have much in common: parsimony
suggests their identification.

If that identification is correct, it has some importance for 442 and
443, to which I now turn. The orthodoxy sees in those two fragments
a picture of the *daimôn* as a journeying *homunculus*, condemned to
lodge in a succession of dirty doss-houses; the *daimôn* is, as it were,
an incorporeal ghost of a thing, which properly exists untrammelled
by any body, but whose sins condemn it to 30,000 seasons in physical
clink. The picture suggests a Cartesian rather than a Presocratic
artist. I do not think that it is entirely wrong; nor even that the
Cartesian touches are all anachronistic. But in one point it is seriously
unrepresentational: nothing at all in 442 implies that the *daimôn*, in
its blessed state, is incorporeal; fallen, it puts on mortal forms; but
that does not imply that unfallen it was wholly bodiless. Nor does 443
imply daemonic incorporeality: the word '*allognôs*', which I translate
'alien', is unique. If the translation is right, 443 does not show that
the *daimôn* is naturally incorporeal, or even that it is naturally
fleshless; if I put on a strange suit of worsted at the tailor's, that does
not mean that I entered the shop naked, nor even that I did not enter
in my familiar worsted. If '*allognôs*' means rather 'making
unrecognizable',[49] the same holds: men who put on disguises need
not have been naked beforehand, nor even undisguised.

197

In short, we are at liberty to have our *daimôn* corporeal; and that liberty becomes a pleasant necessity if the *daimones* of 442 are identified, as I suggest, with the long-lived gods of 195.

Of what stuffs is the material *daimôn* compounded? The natural answer is: of all stuffs. The response is implicit, I think, in 195; and it is necessary if the *daimones* are going to have a knowledge of the world commensurate with their unfallen status; for 'by earth we see earth'. Some modern scholars give a different answer: first, they distinguish between two types of *psuchê*: the seat of cognition and consciousness, and the 'divine spark' or soul. Second, they connect the former *psuchê* with the materialistic psychology of *Nature* and the latter with the *daimôn* of the *Katharmoi*. Finally, they urge that the *daimôn* is not composed of the four roots, but solely of Love (and, perhaps, Strife); thus the *daimôn* is not exactly material, for Love and Strife are only quasi-matter.[50]

That modern theory is, I fear, a modern fantasy, engendered by the desire to give a transmigratory theorist an incorporeal soul. The desire is unwarranted; for transmigration does not require incorporeality. And the fantasy does not satisfy the desire; for Love and Strife are corporeal. No jot of evidence suggests that the *daimôn* is made of Love (and Strife). If the *daimôn* is separated from the psychology of *Nature*, then it is hard to see how the *daimones* will live their blessed life. And the distinction between two types of *psuchê*, if it is found in other Greek texts, is nowhere hinted at by any Presocratic.

Empedocles can now emerge with a coherent psychology-cum-eschatology. Let us replace the term '*daimôn*' by 'person', its nearest English equivalent. Persons are long-lived: they are created fairly early in the cosmic cycle, and destroyed or decomposed fairly late. They are essentially corporeal, being tightly-knit elemental compounds; and thanks to their elemental constitution, they are capable of cognition and of locomotion. In their original state, persons are not human in form, nor do they rely upon human organs of cognition or locomotion; and to that extent an Empedoclean person is a *res cogitans*, a 'sacred mind'.

In their original state persons have some sort of social life. The punishment for moral transgression in that life is severe: the person is obliged to take on human, animal and vegetable forms—to become a man, a horse, a marrow. Throughout these transmogrifications it remains a person, and the same person. Proteus-like, it changes form frequently and radically; like Proteus, it remains the same divine creature. And at last, its sins expiated, it reverts to its original state, and may again flit knowingly through the universe.

The account is doubtless implausible: Empedocles does not tell us how to identify a *daimôn*, or how to trace a daemonic substance from one mortal form to another; and if it is possible to think of ways in which his hypothesis might become scientifically testable, it is hard to think of a way which would not also lead to speedy refutation. But that is only to say what everyone believes: that transmigration does not happen. Logically, the hypothesis is impeccable: no inconsistency is generated by the supposition that one and the same physical *daimôn* passes through a succession of animal and vegetable phases; and those scholars who state that transmigration requires an incorporeal soul are simply in error.

Pedants will deny Empedocles' theory the name of metempsychosis, since it involves no wanderings of a *psuchê*; but if those ancient commentators who called the *daimôn* a *psuchê* were going beyond their evidence, the appellation was intelligible and harmless. Nor need we be puzzled, as Aristotle was, by Empedocles' failure to give a plain account of *psuchê*: he may, if he pleases, say that the soul is a mass of blood, or of whatever stuff is most appropriate to describe the daemonic composition; he may, that is to say, call the *daimôn* a *psuchê*. Alternatively, he may say that the *psuchê* is a '*logos* of the mixing': the *daimôn* has a *psuchê* inasmuch as its component stuffs are arranged thus and so. The two accounts are only verbally distinct.

Empedocles was no centaur: *Nature* and the *Katharmoi* do not state opposing philosophies uneasily coexisting in a single schizophrenic mind. On the contrary, as Hippolytus obscurely saw (*ad* B 115), *Nature* provides the physical foundation for the eschatology of the *Katharmoi*: a proper natural philosophy shows first, that the events we denominate by 'birth' and 'death' are in actual fact comminglings and separations of our elemental parts; and second, that our vital functions are, scientifically speaking, alterations in our physical constitution. Now 'birth' and 'death' evidently do not start from or end in pure elemental stuffs: the processes of association and dissociation are long drawn out. What, then, is more reasonable than to imagine that our selves have pre-existed and will survive those partial dissolutions and reminglings of our gross constituents which men habitually suppose to mark the terminal points of their lives? Natural philosophy does not imply an Empedoclean eschatology; but in a perfectly clear sense it provides the backcloth against which that drama can be played out.

(f) *The whirligig of time*

The gods of **195** are *dolichaiônes*, not *aidioi*; the *daimones* of **442** enjoy a *makraiôn biotos*; and **439**, strictly construed, promises not immortality but only survival of what is vulgarly called death. Moreover *Nature* is incompatible with an unbroken personal immortality: in the homogeneous Sphere, and again at the time of Utter Strife (and doubtless for some considerable periods at the beginning and at the end of the cosmogonical era) there is no place for persons. Men are shorter lived than *daimones*; but *daimones* are not immortal.

The *Katharmoi*, however, promises immortality: greeting the inhabitants of Acragas, Empedocles announces:

I come to you an immortal god (*theos ambrotos*), no longer mortal (**445: B 112**.4);

and at the end of their punishment the *daimones*

spring up as gods, highest in honours,
sharing a hearth with the other immortals (*athanatois*) (**446: B 146**.3; **B 147**.1).

Do we not, after all, have a basic inconsistency between *Nature* and the *Katharmoi*? It is not that the former poem is materialistic, the latter spiritualistic; but that the former countenances no immortals but the elements, while the latter proclaims personal immortality.

The difficulty here is not serious: 'immortal' is a stock epithet of the Greek gods, and 'the immortals' comes to mean 'the gods', its literal sense ('those who never cease to exist') being at most a faint semantic undercurrent; it would be absurd to press the word '*athanatois*' in **446** and to insist that it ascribes literal deathlessness to the gods. It would be equally silly to make anything of '*ambrotos*' in **445**. At worst, Empedocles is speaking loosely: his thought is consistent, and it consistently yields gods and *daimones* who are long-lived but not immortal. Personal immortality is not, in fact, explicitly promised in Empedoclean eschatology.

Yet an ingenious suggestion seems capable, after all, of investing Empedocles' *daimones* with a sort of eternity. Dicaearchus ascribes to Pythagoras the view that 'at certain periods, what has happened once happens again' (**84: 14 A 8a**). The theory of Eternal Recurrence has had a strange hold on the human mind. In an enervated form it is embraced both by Plato and by Aristotle, and adopted by those who claim to find cyclical patterns in human history; in a strong form it was propounded by the Stoic sages, and raised by Nietzsche as the pinnacle of philosophy, the *Gedanke der Gedanken*. The view is ancient and has Eastern origins. Even if we do not believe Dicaearchus' ascription (though I do not see why we should not),

Eternal Recurrence was surely current in fifth-century Pythagorean circles; and it is clearly present in the cosmic cycle of Empedocles.

For Empedocles' universe, on the orthodox interpretation (above, p. 8), gives a perfect example of Eternal Recurrence: the Sphere yields to a cosmological period which ends in total Strife; after Strife comes a second cosmogony, symmetrical with the first; and then the Sphere returns, only to yield again to a cosmology. The cycles roll on infinitely, without beginning and without end; each cycle follows the pattern of its predecessor.

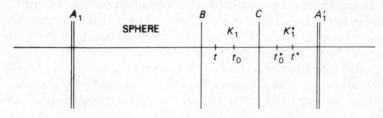

A_1 A_1' represents one cosmic cycle; within it B A_1' is the period of the cosmos, divided at C by the instant of total strife. The state of the world at t in K_1 is exactly repeated at t^* in K^*_1, if $Bt = t^*A'_1$; and the history of K_1 from t to t_0 is exactly repeated, in the opposite direction, from t^*_0 to t^* in K^*_1 (if $t\,t_0 = t^*_0 t^*$). Before and after $A_1 A'_1$ there are infinitely many cycles, $A_i A'_i$; in each cycle there are cosmic periods $K_i + K^*_i$; and in each cosmic period the roll of events exactly mirrors the history of $K_1 + K^*_1$. Empedocles holds a theory of Eternal Recurrence in a remarkably strong form.

Why should anyone have embraced that bizarre theory? Two lines of argument are suggested. The first is scientific: we observe the movements of the heavens; and we see that they are strictly periodical; after a long span or 'Great Year' every heavenly body will be in exactly the same place as it is now. Since the heavens mirror, or even determine, sublunary events, we infer that the world as a whole has its Great Year: 'in the case of the motion of the heavens and of each of the stars, there is a circle: what then prevents the generation and decay of perishable things from being like this, so that these things are generated and decay again?' ([Aristotle], *Probl* 916a25–7). Above, the boarhound and the boar pursue their patterns as before: below, they are faced by the same destiny.[51]

The second line of argument is metaphysical. Crudely stated, it has a certain charm: the universe is finite, and it has finitely many different states; but time flows on infinitely, and every moment in time is the time of some state of the universe. Since the states follow one another in causally ordered succession, they are bound to recur:

the history of the universe is cyclical. More precisely: consider some state of the universe, s_1 (a description of s_1 will specify the total arrangement of the universe at some time). s_1 will cause s_2; s_2, s_3; and so on. Consider the series $s_1, s_2, \ldots, s_n, s_n + 1$. Suppose that there are just n different s_is: then $s_n + 1$ is identical with some s between s_1 and s_n-1. Call it s_j. Then the series from s_j to s_n will repeat itself infinitely in infinite time; and since s_1 was caused by some s_i, s_1 was caused by s_n, so that the cycle s_j—s_n has already been infinitely repeated.[52]

The argument relies on the following large premisses: that time is infinite; that time cannot exist without change; that the universe is deterministic; that there are finitely many distinct states of the universe. None of those premisses is uncontroversially true. For all that, the argument is a rational construction: Nietzsche did not merely adopt, by superhuman intuition, a striking thesis. But alas, I doubt if any such argument ran through Empedocles' head (see above, p. 9).

So far Eternal Recurrence makes no reference to personal immortality. Nietzsche proceeds thus: ' "Now I die and disappear," you would say; "in the totality of things I am nothing. Souls are as mortal as bodies." But the knot of causes in which I am bound up returns—it will create me again. I myself belong to the causes of the eternal recurrence. I come again with this sun, with this earth, with this eagle, with these snakes—*not* to a new life or a better life or a similar life: eternally again to this very same life, the same in largest and in smallest points; and I teach again the eternal recurrence of all things' (*Also Sprach Zarathustra III*, 'Der Genesende'). The Stoics had said the same: 'after our death, when certain periods of time have passed, we shall come to the state in which we are now'; 'this same I will be born again in the renascence'; 'after the conflagration, everything in the universe comes about again, the same in number (*tauta . . . kat' arithmon*)'.[53] And the same point was explicitly made by the Pythagoreans; for, according to Eudemus, they hold that

[Things will occur] again, the same in number (*ta auta arithmôi*), and I shall be holding my stick and lecturing to you sitting like that—and the same will go for everything else (447: fr. 88 W = 58 B 34).

Consider the present stretch of the cosmic cycle, $BC = K_1$. It consists of n successive world states, $S_1^1, S_1^2, \ldots, S_1^n$. Pythagoras' life is included in a subset of those states: it is constituted by the set of states P_1^k—P_1^m where each p_1^i is a part of S_1^i. In the next stage of the cycle, $CA_1^i = K_1$, there is an analogous set of states, P_1^{k*}—P_1^{m*}, and in every one of the infinitely many K_is, there is a set of Pythagorean states, $P_i^k - P_i^m$. Thus Pythagoras lives in each K_i; and since there are infinitely many K_is, he enjoys an immortal existence. His existence is discontinuous; but it never ends. Such an immortality would be tedious if we had perfect memories; and it is, indeed, hard to see why anyone should find comfort in it. Yet Nietzsche certainly did; and so, I suppose, did the Stoa, Empedocles, and perhaps even Pythagoras himself.

The argument I have just presented, simple though it is, is worth setting out more formally. Call the man whose history is constituted by the successive states $P_1^k - P_1^m$ 'Pythagoras₁'. Each K_i will then contain a Pythagoras$_i$. Now every S_1^j is identical with each corresponding S_i^j. Consequently, for any j, $P_1^j = P_2^j$. Hence:

(1) For any property ϕ, Pythagoras₁ has ϕ if and only if Pythagoras₂ has ϕ.

But in general:

(2) If for any property ϕ, a has ϕ if and only if b has ϕ, then $a = b$.

Hence:

(3) Pythagoras₁ = Pythagoras₂.

In general:

(4) For any cycle K_i, Pythagoras₁ = Pythagoras$_i$.

Hence Pythagoras—our familiar Pythagoras—lives in every cosmic cycle; and he is therefore immortal.

The argument is open to objection from two sides. The first objection allows it validity but denies it any immortal significance. Eudemus places his report of the Pythagorean view in a philosophical context: 'If one believes the Pythagoreans, so that [things occur] again, numerically the same . . ., then it is plausible (*eulogon*) that the time too is the same, for it is [the time] of the same motion; and similarly, of many identical things the "earlier and later" are one and the same, and so, then, is their number. All things, then, are the same; so that the time is, too' (fr. 88 W = **58 B 34**). Eudemus expresses himself in terms of Aristotle's philosophy of time; but the main point of his argument stands out independently of that philosophy. Times are necessarily times *of events* (or 'motions'); one time is distinct from another, therefore, only if it is the time of a different event. Now since, by hypothesis, the state of the world S_1^j holding at t_j^1 in K_1 is exactly the same as the corresponding state S_2^j holding at t_j^2 in K_2, the two instants t_j^1 and t_j^2 are identical.

Stated more rigorously, the Eudemian argument runs like this: Take two instants of time, t_1 and t_2. Suppose that every event occurring at t_1 has a counterpart occurring at t_2, and *vice versa*; and suppose further that every event occurring at $t_1 + n$ (for any positive or negative n) has a counterpart at $t_2 + n$, and vice versa: then nothing distinguishes t_1 from t_2, and so $t_1 = t_2$. Now the instant t_j^1 in our period K_1 has, by hypothesis, a counterpart instant t_j^i in every K_i; hence for every i $t_j^1 = t_j^i$. Hence every cosmic period K_i is simultaneous with K_1 ('the time too is the same'). Pythagoras₁ lived from t_x^1 to t_y^1; Pythagoras₂ lived from t_x^2 to t_y^2. But $t_x^1 = t_x^2$; and $t_y^1 = t_y^2$. Pythagoras₁ and Pythagoras₂ are indeed identical; but their lifespan is not infinite, it is simply the three score years and ten between t_x^1 and t_y^1.

Eternal Recurrence not only fails to produce immortality; it appears to produce a cyclical theory of time itself: take any state S_n occurring at t_n, and preceded at t_{n-1} by S_{n-1}. At some point, t_1, S_{n-1} will recur. By the preceding argument, $t_1 = t_{n-1}$. But t_{n-1} is, *ex hypothesi*, *before* t_n; and t_1 is, by construction, *after* t_n. Thus t_1 is both before and after t_n, and time is, as they say, circular. The cyclical theory of time is distinct from the thesis of Eternal Recurrence, though the two things are often confused. Some philosophers, insisting that time has a unique 'direction', would reject circular time out of hand; other philosophers allow that temporal circularity is at least a logical possibility. I cannot decide which view to adopt; and I leave the issue in the air.

For Eudemus, time is the 'measure of change'—not a medium in which events occur but an aspect of the organization of those events. Events necessarily occur in time; but there is no 'absolute' time, independent of events: instants of time are determined by the occurrence of events; periods of time are delimited by ends and beginnings of events. 'Time is a thought or a measure', not a substance (Antiphon, 87 B 9). The Eudemian argument relies on that theory; but the theory does not go uncontested: according to Newton, 'absolute, true and mathematical time, of itself and from its own nature, flows equably without relation to anything external'; and Newton is not without followers. Perhaps Newtonian time can reconcile Recurrence and Immortality, and remove the threat of a circular chronology?

Alas, Newtonian time saves Pythagoras from Eudemus' frying-pan only to deposit him in the fire. The difficulty was adumbrated in antiquity. Pseudo-Aristotle asserts that 'it is silly to aver that those who are born are always the same in number' (*Probl* 916a29); and Simplicius says of the Stoics that 'they inquire, reasonably, whether I am one in number now and then (because I am the same in substance) or rather differ in virtue of my ordering in different cosmogonies' (*in Phys* 886.13 = *SVF* II.627). One salient feature of Pythagoras₁ is not, so far as we can tell, a feature of Pythagoras₂:

Pythagoras₁ taught eternal recurrence in 520 BC; Pythagoras₂ will teach it, but not until AD 29,480. Thus every Pythagoras$_i$ will differ from every other Pythagoras$_i$, at least in his teaching hours. Indeed, every Pythagoras$_i$ will differ from every other Pythagoras$_i$ in respect of countless predicates. For if time 'flows equably' along, independently of events, then t_x^1 is distinct from t_x^2; and '. . . is F at t_x^1' is a distinct predicate from '. . . is F at t_x^2'. Thus the theory of Eternal Recurrence does not lead to (3), nor to immortality.

'Absolute' time does not, of course, entail that Eternal Recurrence does not offer a hope of immortality: we may, I suppose, find some reason for identifying Pythagoras₁ and Pythagoras₂—perhaps Pythagoras₂ experiences a succession of otherwise inexplicable *déjà vu*s;[54] and on the strength of that we might affirm that '. . . teaches at 520 BC' and '. . . teaches at AD 29,480' do in fact apply to the same person. The argument adduced in the last paragraph only exhibits a weakness in the reasoning for immortality; it does not provide an argument against immortality.

IX

Conduct Unbecoming

(a) Antiphon and moral anarchy

According to Aristotle, Socrates invented moral philosophy. Aristotle is hardly fair; for if the moral views associated with the earlier Presocratics are scanty and somewhat unstimulating, the men of the fifth century were much given to ethical speculations. The fragments of the Sophists and of Democritus, and the plays of Euripides, testify to a widespread and excited interest in moral matters; and that interest extended beyond the desire to preach or to enrage, and exhibited an admirable tendency to tunnel and to probe. The testimony is rich and my treatment in this chapter will be partial and selective. I choose two main topics, moral nihilism and systematic ethics—the former associated with the Sophists, the latter with Democritus. And I divide my first topic into three parts: moral anarchism; moral relativism; and moral irresponsibility.

In the nineteenth century the Sophists were generally denounced as immoral charlatans, teaching vice for cash, corrupting the minds and bodies of the young, and leading Athens (or Greece as a whole) into a dank cesspool of iniquity. Against that charge George Grote protested, in a celebrated chapter of his *History of Greece*: 'I know,' he wrote, 'few characters in history who have been so hardly dealt with as these so-called Sophists'; and in twenty brilliant pages he portrayed Protagoras and his crew in the implausible disguise of Victorian moralists, stern and upright men, educators, the ethical leaders of the Greek enlightenment. Grote had some right on his side: the pious homily of Prodicus' *Choice of Heracles* (**84 B 2**) can now be matched by the banalities of the 'Anonymus Iamblichi' (**89 A 1**), of which Grote knew nothing. But Grote overstated his case: the performances of Thrasymachus in the *Republic* and of Callicles in the

Gorgias; the speeches in Thucydides' Mytilenean debate and in his Melian dialogue (III. 37–48; V. 84–111); and the *agôn* between Just and Unjust *Logos* in the *Clouds*, are evidence enough of that.

Yet all that is philosophically uninteresting: the Sophists may have been demon kings or Prince Charmings, they may have preached sobriety or sin; I do not greatly care. This chapter is concerned with questions of a more theoretical nature: did the Sophists propound any general accounts of ethics? and if so, to what extent and in what direction might those accounts have influenced their substantive ethical judgments? If we have no complete theory of ethics from a Sophist's hand, we do possess three substantial pieces, each of which has been supposed to offer some general reflexions on ethics, and each of which has been suspected of immoral tendencies.

The first passage belongs to Antiphon. Of Antiphon's life nothing is known. Indeed, there is a standing dispute, of antique origin (Hermogenes, **87 A 2**), over precisely how many men Antiphon was. We hear of Antiphon the Sophist, who wrote *On Truth*; we possess speeches by the orator, Antiphon of Rhamnous; there is Antiphon the tragedian; and Antiphon the interpreter of dreams. There is no decisive evidence telling for or against the identification of any two, of any three, or of all four of these men; nor is the question of great moment.

The passage in question comes from Antiphon's *On Truth*. Its three parts, preserved on papyrus, were discovered at Oxyrhynchus and published in 1915 and 1922; I translate them in the order in which they are printed in Diels-Kranz, where they figure as **88 B 44**; for convenience I number them separately.[1]

. . . justice . . . consists in not	I
transgressing the regulations (*nomima*) of	
the state in which you are a citizen.	10
Hence a man will deal with justice in the way most	
advantageous to himself if in the	
presence of witnesses he holds the laws	20
high, and when isolated from witnesses the	
dictates of nature (*ta tês phuseôs*). For the dictates of	
the laws are imposed (*epitheta*), those	
of nature necessary; and those of the	
laws are agreed and not grown (*phunta*),	30
those of nature grown not agreed. Hence	II
if in transgressing the regulations you escape	
the notice of those who have made the agreement, you are	
free of shame and of penalty; but	

207

not if you do not escape notice. But if   10
para to dunaton you violate any
of the things which are connate with nature,
then if you escape the notice of all men,
the ill is no less; and if everyone sees, it
is no greater; for you are harmed not   20
in opinion but in truth. The
inquiry is for the sake of all these things,
because most of what is legally just
is inimical to nature: laws   30
have been made for the eyes, telling them
what they must see and what they must not; and   III
for the ears, what they must hear and what they
must not; and for the tongue, what it must
say and what it must not; and for the hands,
what they must do and what they must not; and for   10
the feet, where they must go and where they must
not; and for the mind, what it must
desire and what not. 'On the contrary, by nature the things
these laws turn us from are no dearer or more   20
appropriate than the things they turn
us towards. For living and dying
belong to nature; and living is among
what is advantageous, dying among what   30
is not advantageous.' But of things advantageous   IV
those laid down by the laws are chains,
those laid down by nature are free. Well, it is not true,
by a right account, that what pains   10
benefits nature more than what delights;
nor would what grieves be more
advantageous than what gives pleasure; for
what is truly advantageous cannot   20
harm but must benefit. Thus what is by
nature advantageous. . . . . . . and those   V
who having suffered defend themselves and do not
themselves initiate action; and those who behave
well to their parents even if they are bad
to them; and those who allow others to tender an   10
oath but do not tender an oath themselves. And of the
things I have recounted you will find many
inimical to nature; and in them there
is the suffering of more pain when it is possible
to suffer less, and the getting of less pleasure when   20

it is possible to get more, and being treated
badly when it is possible not to be treated so.
Now if for those who submit to such things there
came any help from the laws, and   30
for those who do not submit but oppose them, some
penalty, then obedience to the laws would not be   VI
unbeneficial; but in fact it seems that
the justice that derives from law is not
adequate to help those who submit to such
things; for, first, it allows the sufferer   10
to suffer and the agent to act, and it does
not there and then prevent the sufferer from
suffering or the agent from acting. (?) And
when it is referred to punishment, it   20
is no more partial to the sufferer than to the
agent(?); (?)for he must persuade those who
will administer punishment that he suffered, and
requires the power to win the case (?). And   30
these same things are left for the agent,
to deny. . . (**448**).

. . . we praise and honour; but those from   II
a family that is not noble we neither
praise nor honour. And in this we
have become barbarians towards one another,
since by nature we are all in all respects similarly   10
adapted to be either barbarians or Greeks.
(?) We may consider this in the case of natural things,
which are necessary to all men (?) . . .   20
. . . and in all these things none
of us is marked off, neither barbarian
nor Greek. For we all breathe into
the air by our mouths and noses . . . (**449**).

. . . since what is just seems to be good,   I
testifying truly concerning one another is
deemed (*nomizetai*) to be just and no less
useful for the practices of men.
Now he who does this is not just, if   10
not wronging anyone unless you have
been wronged yourself is just; for it
is necessary for him who testifies, even if
he testifies truly, nevertheless in a

way to wrong another. And it is
probable that he himself will be wronged later on. For   20
this is possible, in so far as the man he
testified against is condemned
because of the things he testified to,
and loses either his money or
his life because of someone he in no
way wronged. In this way, then, he   30
wrongs the man he testifies
against, because he wrongs someone
who has not wronged him; and he himself
is wronged by the man he testified
against because he is hated by him for
testifying truly—and not only   II
by hatred, but also because for all his
life he must guard against the man he
testified against; for he stands as
an enemy to him, ready to say and do   10
whatever ill he can to him. Now
these wrongs are evidently not inconsiderable,
neither those which he himself suffers nor
those which he commits. For it is not
possible both for these things to be just and for neither
wronging at all nor being wronged oneself to be just.   20
But it is necessary that either
the one set of things is just or both
are unjust. And it seems that to condemn
and to judge and to arbitrate,
however things are settled, are not just;   30
for benefiting some harms others.
And in this those who are benefited are not
wronged, but those who are harmed are
wronged . . . (450).[2]

Modern commentators are distressed by these fragmentary
opinions: on the one hand, they applaud the 'cosmopolitanism' of
449; on the other hand, they are appalled at the 'moral anarchism' in
448 and 450. The two opinions, nice and nasty, are united by a
common prescription: Follow nature, *phusis*; do not follow law or
convention, *nomos*. Social and racial discord is based on conventional
artifice: abandon convention and you enjoy the cosmopolitan
harmony of nature. Ordinary morality is based on law and etiquette:

abandon convention and you may luxuriate in an advantageous immorality.

I have nothing to say about **449**: I suppose that it represents Antiphon's own views; and I suppose that Antiphon means to urge the claims of *phusis* above those of *nomos*. In that case, Antiphon becomes the father of what is surely the silliest of all arguments in political philosophy (a subject where folly spreads like bindweed, choking the few weak shoots of truth): 'By nature all men are equal; hence all men deserve equal treatment.' The evidently false premiss of natural egalitarianism yields, by an evidently invalid inference, the absurdity of moral egalitarianism. But more than one interpretation of **449** is possible; and we are not obliged to file a paternity suit for that argument against Antiphon.

The connexion between **448** and **450**—and between them and **449**—is quite uncertain: the papyrus gives no technical answer; and the content of the fragments does not help.[3] I shall therefore treat **448** and **450** in relative isolation, beginning with **448**.

448 divides into three main sections: first, I.6–II.23 argues that it is in a man's interest to obey the regulations in public and to follow nature when he can do so unobserved; then II.23–V.24 urges that the regulations normally show themselves inimical to nature; and finally V.25–VI.33 remarks that the regulations do not offer the advantages they pretend to. Antiphon uses '*nomima* (regulations)' and '*nomoi* (laws)' interchangeably: both terms, I take it, refer not just to the enactments of the legislature, but generally to the rules and customs, whether legally or socially sanctioned, by which any communal life is ordered. To follow the *nomima* is to conform, to do the done thing. By '*phusis*' Antiphon intends, primarily at least, human nature (cf. II.11). Among the constituents of human nature are certain desires, wants, longings and yearnings: to follow 'nature', or to obey 'the dictates of nature (*ta tês phuseôs*)' is to act on those natural inclinations: crudely, it is to do what you want to do.

Many scholars find in **448** an injunction or recommendation to 'follow nature' and to disregard the regulations, so long as you can do so with impunity: 'Join me, and do what's natural: play, and laugh, and think nothing is wrong' (Aristophanes, *Clouds* 1078). Other scholars, eager to clear Antiphon of so foul a crime, say that the thesis advanced in I.6–II.23 is not advanced *in propria persona*; rather, it represents a view which Antiphon is concerned to refute. That has no foundation in Antiphon's text; and in any case the suggestion that Antiphon is offering an immoral injuction is groundless: there is no word of injunction or recommendation in **448**; Antiphon does not say 'Follow nature when you can get away with it'; he asserts, as a

211

statement of fact and not as a suggestion for action, that if you do follow nature and get away with it you will act in your own interest.[4]

Antiphon offers an argument for his statement: it is advantageous to follow your natural inclinations, because if you ignore them 'you are harmed not in opinion (*dia doxan*) but in truth' (II.21; i.e., 'you will surely be harmed, for the harm does not depend simply upon the beliefs which other men have about your action'). Thus the whole argument of I.23–II.26 runs as follows: 'Suppose ϕing is against the customs or laws; suppose that you want to ϕ; and suppose that you can ϕ unobserved. If you do not ϕ, you violate the dictates of your nature. But those dictates are "necessary (*anankaia*)" (I.26; i.e., it is not up to men to decide what they shall want and when) and they are inborn (*phunta*: I.32); consequently, the penalties attached to their violation are necessary and inborn, and "you are harmed . . . in truth" whether your law-abiding course is overt or covert. If, on the other hand, you do ϕ, you will violate a dictate of custom. Now such dictates are "imposed" and "agreed" (i.e., it is up to men to decide what acts shall be allowed by *nomos* and what forbidden). Hence the penalties they threaten depend on detection; and an undetected piece of ϕing is harmless.' The argument is clear and correct: if I can get away without paying my income tax, it is to my advantage to do so. If I do not pay, I suffer no harm, and gain the advantage of extra cash; if I do pay, I am harmed in truth, for my natural desire not to waste my substance is frustrated.

The second part of 448 runs from II.23 to V.24. Suppose that all *nomima* are in fact in line with nature: then, though it is still in my interest to follow nature when I can, the fact has no bite; for following nature and following *nomima* lead to the same actions. Antiphon shows that the supposition is false by arguing that 'most of what is legally just is inimical to nature' (II.26). 'Law,' as Hippias says in the *Protagoras*, 'is a tyrant of men and violates nature in many ways' (337D = 86 C 1). Again, Antiphon has hold of a sober truth; he is not counselling anarchy but reporting a fact about the relation between law and nature: the purpose of a large part of the law and of many social customs is to curtail the exercise of natural desire; *nomima* would lose their point if they never clashed with *phusis*.

That truth is stated, in roundly rhetorical terms, at II.23–III.17, and repeated, with a different type of example, at IV.30–V.24. The intervening passage, III.17–IV.30, is obscure; I tentatively suggest that it first states and then answers an objection to Antiphon's truth: *me]n oun* at III.17 introduces the objection, and *de* at IV.2 the reply. Objection: '*Nomima* not only discourage, they also promote; and what they promote is just as advantageous to us as what they

212

discourage; e.g., by discouraging murder they promote life.' Reply: '*Nomima*, even where they seem advantageous, are chains on our nature; they therefore involve pain, and things that pain us are not more advantageous than things that give us pleasure.' The reply is feeble; for surely the pain or frustration we suffer by having our liberty chained is outweighted by the advantage we gain from chaining the liberty of other human tigers?

The third part of **448** answers just that point. The tigers pounce with impunity: the law cannot prevent their pouncing; at best it will punish them after they have pounced; and punishment is far from certain if the tigers have honeyed tongues. Is that true? Or rather, was it true in Athens in the last quarter of the fifth century? I do not know; but Antiphon was in a better position to tell than we are.

448 thus argues that *nomima* are not advantageous to those who obey them: almost always, obedience will involve a frustration of natural inclinations; and the bonds of the social contract are not tight enough to constrain the determined criminal. What is the moral? We cannot tell: perhaps, as some believe, Antiphon was out to urge 'natural' behaviour; perhaps, as others assert, he wanted a reform of the laws in order to bring the balance of advantage down on the side of the just.[5] Perhaps he offered his observations with no practical recommendation in mind: his book, after all, is *On Truth*; it was not primarily a practical tract.

450 contains a clear and self-contained argument: men generally think *both* that it is unjust to wrong someone who has not wronged you, *and* that it is just to tell the truth in the witness box. Antiphon correctly points out that those two views will lead to conflict when, as often happens, truthful witnesses who have been unharmed send crooks to jail. And he correctly adds that in such circumstances the just witness may put himself in danger.

The verb 'wrong' translates '*adikein*', which literally means 'treat unjustly'. A defender of the general opinion might say that bearing true witness against a man cannot be a case of *adikein*: a witness may 'wrong' someone in the sense of harming him; but he cannot 'wrong' him in the sense of treating him unjustly. But that defence will not do; for if 'wrong' is construed as 'treat unjustly', then the first of the two general opinions is reduced to a tautology: 'It is unjust to treat a man unjustly unless he has treated you unjustly'. The opinion was plainly meant in a non-tautological sense: 'You should not act against a man's interests unless he has acted against yours'. That, I suppose, sounds like a decent moral principle. And Antiphon proves it untenable.

450 talks a lot about justice; and justice is mentioned in **448**. Many scholars feel that justice is the central concern of the fragments, thus: 'At I.6, **448** defines justice as obedience to the rules of society; at II.20, **450** defines justice as not wronging those who have not wronged you. The function of **448** is to reduce the legalistic account of justice to absurdity; the function of **450** is to substitute a moral account; and the overall aim of the two passages is the establishment of a sound theory of justice.'

I fear that will not wash. There is no definition of justice in **450**: II.20 merely offers the thesis that it is unjust to harm those who have not harmed you; and (if I am right) it implies that we should reject the thesis. There is no suggestion that **450** replaces views dismantled in **448**, and there is no suggestion in **448** that the definition of justice given at I.6 is absurd. **448** does offer a definition of justice; but the definition was a commonplace. It is reflected in Euripides and in Lysias; it was advanced approvingly by Xenophon's Socrates, and Aristotle recognizes it as giving one of the senses of 'just'.[6] In Antiphon's fragment it is neither new nor shocking; and it plays no role in the development of his argument: **448** argues that illegal and irregular conduct may be advantageous, and we may infer that unjust conduct may be advantageous; but Antiphon does not make the inference for us, and he cannot have felt it of great importance.

Fragments **448–50** of Antiphon contain the earliest essay written in the light of the distinction between *nomos* or convention and *phusis* or nature. To accept that distinction does not imply a preference for *phusis* and a leaning to anarchism: Antiphon's *Truth*, so far as I can see, contains no moral or political recommendations at all. It is, in part, a sociological work; but not even a sociologist need preach distasteful doctrines—for he need not preach at all.

(b) *The* Dissoi Logoi *and moral relativism*

The definition of justice, which Antiphon treats so lightly, can be used to promote a view more vigorous than anything he professed. Swiftly and fatally, the argument runs thus: 'What is just is what is *nomimon*; *nomima* are human creations, and vary from one culture and country to another: hence justice—and, in general, morality—is a relative thing.' The first premiss of the argument was a fifth-century commonplace; the second premiss was a familiar truth, classically illustrated by the experiment of Darius (Herodotus, III.38); and the conclusion seems to give the deathblow to morality.

> [Archelaus, Anaxagoras' pupil] composed a *Physiology* and
> believed that the just and ugly are so not by nature (*phusei*) but by
> custom (*nomôi*) (**451**: Suda, **60 A 2**).

Here we have the first appearance of the fatal argument. Aristophanes makes comic use of its elements: Pheidippides is proposing to beat his father, Strepsiades:

STR: But it's nowhere the custom (*nomizetai*) for a father to suffer this.

PH: Wasn't the person who first laid down this custom (*nomos*) a man, like you and me? And didn't he persuade the men of old by making a speech? Then is it any less possible for *me* now to lay down a new custom for sons—to beat their fathers back? (*Clouds* 1420–4).

And Plato spells the argument out: 'And about political things too—things fine and ugly, just and unjust, holy and the reverse—whatever any city thinks to be and lays down as lawful (*nomima*) for itself actually is so in truth for it; and in these matters no individual is any wiser than any other, and no city than any other. But on the question of laying down what is advantageous or not advantageous to it, here if anywhere it will agree that one counsellor is better than another and that the judgment of one city is better with regard to truth than that of another. And it would not dare to say that whatever a city thinks to be and lays down as advantageous to itself will actually be advantageous to it come what may. But in the case I am talking about—the case of the just and unjust, the holy and unholy—they want to insist that none of them has by nature any substance of its own, but that what is communally judged to be the case actually comes to be the case at the time when it is so judged and for as long as it is so judged' (*Theaetetus*, 172AB; cf. *Laws* 889E).

Plato ascribes the argument to Protagoras, and the *Theaetetus* here is sometimes taken to provide genuine Protagorean doctrine.[7] But it occurs at the end of Socrates' long and plainly unhistorical 'defence' of Protagoras; and the doctrine it expounds is not, in fact, very closely connected with Protagoras' epistemological relativism (see below, pp. 243–51). To discover a Sophistic expression of moral relativism we must turn to the *Dissoi Logoi*.

The *Dissoi Logoi* or *Double Accounts* is a strange document. An anonymous piece of some dozen pages, written in an odd dialect by a talentless author, it somehow became attached to the text of Sextus, and so survived along with his works. It is generally dated to about 400 BC;[8] and it is therefore supposed to breathe, in a puerile way, the air of Sophistic Athens. It is a contemporary document on the workings of the Sophistic movement, the more interesting in that it reflects a feeble layman's apprehension of things.

The work is divided into nine sections: 'On Good and Bad'; 'On Fair and Foul'; 'On Just and Unjust'; 'On True and False'; on the thesis that 'things are and are not'; 'On Wisdom and Virtue—whether they can be taught'; on the proper way of choosing state officials; on the relation between speech, knowledge and action; on memory. Some scholars think that the *Dissoi Logoi* is a compilation of two or more originally separate essays, and much effort has been expended in finding traces of the great Sophists in the work. The discussion is sadly inconclusive.[9] No less fruitless are the attempts to categorize the tract: is it a schoolboy's exercise? the notes of a pupil on his master's lectures? the lecture notes, or half-finished lecture, of the master himself? We cannot tell.

Section 1, on Good and Bad, opens thus:

> Double accounts are offered in Greece by those who philosophize about the good and the bad. For some say that the good is one thing, the bad another; others that they are the same—good for some, bad for others; and for the same man now good, now bad (452: **90 A 1 §1**).

First, the relativistic argument, that bad and good are the same, is offered (§§2–10); then the counter-argument, that good and bad are different, is produced (§§11–17). The author concludes:

> I do not say what the good is; but I attempt to teach this: that the bad and the good are not the same, but each is different[10] (453: §17).

The pattern of argument in sections 2, 3, and 4 is precisely analogous. Here are samples of the relativistic arguments:

> Incontinence is bad for the incontinent, good for the sellers and hirers. Illness is bad for the sick, good for the doctors. Death is bad for the dead, good for the undertakers and funeral masons (454: **A 1 §3**).

> For the Lacedaemonians it is fine for girls to exercise(?) without sleeves(?) and to walk about without tunics; for the Ionians it is foul. For the former it is fine for children not to learn music and letters; for the Ionians it is foul not to know all these things (455: **A 2 §§9–10**).

> First I shall say that it is just to lie and to deceive. People would say that to do this to one's enemies [is fine and just], to do it [to one's friends] foul and wrong: [but how to one's enemies] but not to

one's friends? Take your parents: if your father or your mother has
to eat or swallow a medicine and doesn't want to, isn't it just to
give it to them in their food or drink and to say that it is not there?
Then it is [just] to lie to and deceive one's parents (**456: A 3
§§2–3**).

All three ethical sections of the *Dissoi Logoi* begin by advancing a
relativism; yet neither the author nor his modern commentators
realize that three different relativisms are advanced. The relativist of
section 1 in effect argues that '. . . . is good' is an incomplete
predicate, elliptical for the overtly relational predicate '. . . is good
for ——'. Goodness is understood as advantage: '*a* is good' means '*a*
is advantageous'; and if we sometimes omit the *relatum* and say,
simply, '*a* is advantageous', our saying always carries a tacit rider of
the form 'for *b*'. Goodness is advantage; and advantage is relative in
an obvious enough fashion. It follows that items and events cannot be
divided up into the advantageous and the disadvantageous, the good
and the bad: what is good for me is very likely bad for you, and vice
versa. Everything advantageous is also disadvantageous; everything
disadvantageous is also advantageous: in a word, 'the good and the
bad are the same'.

The relativism of section 2 is less clear; but it probably intimates
the thesis that '. . . is fine' is elliptical for '. . . is fine in
culture——'. Sometimes, it is true, the relativist says that things
seem (*dokei*) or are deemed (*nomizonti*) fine in certain cultures; but
he does not distinguish between '*a* seems fine in *K*' and '*a* is fine in
K'.

Section 3 does not imply that '. . . is just' is elliptical; rather, its
message is that '*ϕ*ing is always (un)just' is always false. Lying may be
usually unjust, but it is sometimes just; returning a loan may be
usually just, but it is sometimes unjust. 'The just and the unjust are
the same' in a weaker sense: 'For any *ϕ*, some cases of *ϕ*ing are just if
and only if some cases of *ϕ*ing are unjust.' Nothing is *both* just *and*
unjust in the way in which some things, according to section 1, are
both good *and* bad.

The author of the *Dissoi Logoi* produces a single line of argument
against all his relativists. In the case of 'good' he gets nowhere:

Tell me, have your parents ever done you any good?—Yes, many
great goods.—Then you owe them many great evils, if the good is
the same as the bad (**457: A 1 §12**).

'*a* does *b* good; good and bad are the same: hence *a* does *b* evil.' The
inference sounds right, but it ignores the proper meaning of 'good

and bad are the same'; and it ignores the central fact that the relativist makes 'good' *relative*. The answer is a silly *ignoratio elenchi*.

That 'advantageous' is a relative term is plain; that 'good' means 'advantageous' is less clear. Yet I am inclined to let the relativist win on 'good': sometimes, at least, 'good' does seem to mean 'advantageous' or 'profitable'; when it has a different meaning it is likely to prove a synonym of 'fine (*kalon*)' or 'just (*dikaion*)'; so that the relativist of section 1 wins no significant victory unless he carries the day in sections 2 and 3 as well.

The author of the *Dissoi Logoi* fares no better in section 2: if fine and foul are the same, then

> In Lacedaemon it is fine for the girls to exercise, and in
> Lacedaemon it is foul for the girls to exercise (**458: A 2** §25).

That, again, is a mere *ignoratio elenchi*. But he almost grasps a better retort: answering the relativist claim that 'to wear ornaments and make-up and gold bangles is foul for a man, fine for a woman' (§6), he says that 'if it is fine for a woman to wear ornaments, then it is foul for a woman to wear ornaments, if foul and fine are the same' (§24). A neat point can be extracted from that clumsy remark: the relativist claims that 'ϕing is fine' is elliptical for 'ϕing is fine in K'; his opponent asserts that ϕing is fine in K if and only if ϕing-in-K is fine; and this latter use of 'is fine' is not elliptical. For women to parade naked is fine—'in Lacedaemon'. Then for women in Lacedaemon to parade naked is fine *tout court*. Culture may determine what is fine and what is foul; but the concepts of fineness and foulness are not culture-relative. The difference sounds small but is considerable: it is one thing to say that the *contents* of our value judgments must always refer to some culture, so that 'When in Rome do as the Romans do' becomes the supreme recommendation; it is quite another to claim that our judgments *themselves* are logically culture-bound, that we can no more talk of 'fine *simpliciter*' than we can of 'advantageous *simpliciter*'.

The relativist may fight the equation of 'ϕing is fine in K' with 'ϕing-in-K is fine'. An educated but prudish Athenian will know that naked female sport is fine in Sparta but will deny that naked female sport in Sparta is fine; and the same Athenian may hold that slave revolts in Sparta are fine without holding that such things are fine in Sparta. But in making this case, the relativist destroys himself; for he allows a non-elliptical use of '. . . is fine'. The Athenian does not deny that naked female sport in Sparta is fine *in Sparta*—he knows that to be true; nor does he deny that naked female sport in Sparta is fine *in some other culture*—for no other culture lays down canons for *Spartan* behaviour. What the Athenian denies is that naked female sport is fine, *simpliciter*. And that, I think, crumples the culture relativist: it is simply an error to maintain that 'fine' is an elliptical term, expandable to 'fine in culture *K*'.

The relativist of section 3 is an Aristotelian: 'We shall speak adequately if we are as clear as the subject matter allows; for rigour (*to akribes*) is not to be sought in all accounts alike any more than in all products of craft. And the fine and the just, about which political science inquires, contain great differences and divergences, so that they seem to exist by custom alone and not by nature. And good things too contain such a divergence because harm comes to many people from them (for men have died before now on account of riches, and others on account of bravery). Thus we must be content in arguing about such matters and from such principles to show the truth roughly and in outline—in arguing about what is for the most part and from such principles, to conclude in such a way too' (*EN* 1094b11–22). The details of that celebrated passage remain unclear; but its sophistic background is immediately discernible.

Aristotle seems to mean at least this: every sentence of the form 'ϕing is always wrong (right, just, unjust, fine, foul, good, bad etc.)' is false. We can sometimes say, truly, 'For the most part, ϕing is wrong'; we can never say truly 'In all cases, ϕing is wrong'. And that is precisely the message of the relativist of the *Dissoi Logoi*: lying is not *always* wrong—it is all right to lie to your enemies; lying to your friends is not *always* wrong—it is all right to lie to your parents in order to get them to drink their medicine. No doubt lying is normally wrong; but it is not *always* so. And neither is anything else.

The view can be given a weak or a strong construction. Weakly, it points out that all the customary moral injunctions we daily parrot (Tell the truth, Be kind to your mother, and Brush your teeth after meals) allow exceptions. They are at best rules of thumb, not universally binding laws. That is, I take it, indubitably true; and since people, even philosophers, are sometimes extraordinarily rule-bound, there is something to be said for proclaiming the truth from time to time. From a pedagogic point of view, moral injunctions need to be neat and snappy; and if we issue and accept them with a pinch of salt or a *hôs epi to polu* we shall not do or suffer much harm. But only wretchedness or hypocrisy can result from taking universally and defending rigorously those nursery-room saws which constitute the rough bedrock of our moral beliefs.

A stronger interpretation, however, is surely intended both by Aristotle and by the *Dissoi Logoi* relativist: *every* universal moral judgment—not merely every simple moral saw—is, strictly speaking,

219

false; for *all* ϕ, it is not the case that ϕing is always M (where M is any moral predicate). Moral education, according to some modern philosophers, consists in a progressive refinement and sophistication of our first crude and general moral principles: I reject 'Do not kill' in favour of 'Do not kill except in time of war'; that yields to 'Do not kill except in time of war, and then only kill combatants'; and so on. According to the Aristotelian doctrine, that process of education is incompletable: however complex and refined your moral principles may be, they are (strictly speaking) false; they may be replaced by other principles, yet more complex and yet more refined, but the replacements will still be false.

The *Dissoi Logoi* rejects the view:

> That stealing your enemies' goods is just proves that that very thing is unjust too, if their account is true (**459: A 3 §16**).

That again is an *ignoratio elenchi*; but it hides a clever point: the relativist, attacking the naive thesis that stealing is always wrong, must specify his exceptions to the rule; he must produce a thesis of the form 'Stealing in circumstances C is right'. But such a thesis is, according to the very view he is trying to advance, inevitably false: in arguing for his case, the relativist disproves it. The argument is clever but unsatisfactory: the relativist need only emend his exception clause to read 'Stealing in circumstances C is, at least sometimes, right'. However that may be, the Aristotelian relativist has, so far as I can see, no good argument for his position: in the *Dissoi Logoi* he simply claims to be able to find an exception to any moral generalization; the claim is illustrated by simple cases, and there is no reason at all to believe that every generalization can be so punctured. Aristotelians customarily talk of the 'infinite variety' of human circumstances: circumstances alter cases; and so many and so varied are the circumstances that no universal rule can govern them all. But circumstances, if varied, are not infinitely varied; nor is it clear that all their variations are of moral import. Rules must certainly be complicated; but nothing has yet shown that they are impossible.

These programmatic remarks do not exhaust the question: no doubt more can be said in favour of Aristotelianism. And more should be said; for if the theory is correct, its implications for morals, and for moral reasoning, are serious. The 'relativism' of section 3 of the *Dissoi Logoi* is the most interesting and the most dangerous of the Sophistic relativisms.

(c) *Gorgias and moral irresponsibility*

A certain athlete accidentally struck Epitimos the Pharsalian with a
javelin and killed him; and he [sc. Pericles] spent the whole day
with Protagoras puzzling over whether, in the strictest account,
one should hold responsible (*aitios*) for the accident the javelin or
the thrower rather than the organizers of the games (**460**: Plutarch,
80 A 10).

The story may be apocryphal; but issues of responsibility were
certainly discussed and debated in Athens, a city where litigation was
a popular hobby. Indeed, the second *Tetralogy* of Antiphon contains
four speeches, two prosecuting, two defending, devoted to the very
case that Protagoras allegedly debated with Pericles. A boy was
practising the javelin; as he hurled it, another youth ran across the
stadium, and was transfixed and killed. Who, Antiphon's speeches
ask, was responsible (*aitios*) for the youth's death?

The English word 'responsible' is slippery: '*aitios*' in Greek is
anointed with the same oil. Sometimes in saying of someone that he
is responsible for a certain state of affairs, we mean to hand out
blame: calling someone responsible is calling him guilty. '*Aitia*',
according to Liddell and Scott, means '*responsibility*, mostly in the
bad sense, guilt, blame, or the imputation thereof, i.e. *accusation*'.
('Haig was responsible for the slaughter at Paaschendaele'; 'The
conductor is responsible for the ragged violin entries'.) Sometimes we
use 'responsible' more generously, to saddle someone not with
blame, but with a liability to be blamed: by saying 'he is responsible
for so and so', we mean that any moral, political, aesthetic or other
evaluation of so and so should be laid at his door, whether for good or
for ill. ('Haig was responsible for the strategy on the Western Front';
'The conductor is responsible for the ensemble playing'.)

Again 'responsible' may impute agency: if *a* brought it about that
P, then *a* is responsible for the fact that *P*. ('My cat is responsible for
the holes in the lawn'; 'I am responsible for the broken plate'.) Or
'responsible' may indicate causation: inanimate objects, and events,
may be responsible without being agents; and animate creatures can
sometimes be causally responsible at one or more removes from
agency. ('Bad weather is responsible for the poor batting averages this
season'; 'His great-grandfather is responsible for his Habsburg
profile'.) Thus '*a* is responsible for *X*' may be used to pick out
a as an agent or cause, and it may be used to blame *a* or to mark *a* as
an appropriate object of appraisal: the phrase has a causal and an
evaluative use.

It is easy to think that the evaluative and the causal uses are co-extensive, that I am causally responsible if and only if I am evaluatively responsible; and there is, of course, a close connexion between causal and evaluative responsibility: standardly, 'he is responsible' holds evaluatively only if it holds causally, and vice versa. But that is not always so: vicarious and collective responsibility yield cases in which the evaluatively responsible are not causally responsible (parents must pay their children's debts; the orchestra fails if the horns alone are out of tune); accidents and flukes yield cases in which the causally responsible are not evaluatively responsible (I knocked the jug off the window-sill, but liability for blame attaches to the fool who put it there; I won the rubber by making three no trumps, but the contract was made by way of three inadvertent finesses).

It is easy to confuse the two uses of 'responsible'. Antiphon's defence counsel does so: he wishes to show that his unfortunate client is guiltless and not a suitable subject for blame and punishment, that he is not morally *aitios*. But he argues, bizarrely, that his client did not kill the youth at all (III.10; IV.4; cf. *Tetralogy* 3, II.6), that he is not causally *aitios*. The correct defence, that the boy is causally but not morally *aitios*, was apparently too subtle for Antiphon.

One sophistic document appears to deal *ex professo* and in philosophical depth with the issue of responsibility: Helen left her husband Menelaus and sailed to Troy with Paris, thereby launching a thousand ships and the Trojan War. The Greek poets liked to berate her for her indiscretions. Gorgias in his *Helen* sets out to defend her:

> I wish to give a certain reasoning (*logismos*) in my argument and so to remove responsibility (*aitia*) from her who has a bad repute and to remove stupidity from those who blame her by showing them up as liars and by proving the truth (**461: 82 B 11 §2**).

Gorgias' defence has a lucid structure:

> She did what she did either by the wishes of Luck and the decision of the gods and the decrees of Necessity; or seized by force; or persuaded by arguments; or captured by love (**462: §6**).

Successive paragraphs argue that Helen bears no responsibility if her rape was due to the gods (§6), or to force (§7), or to persuasion (§§8–14), or to love (§§15–19):

> Then how can one think the blame of Helen just, who, if she did what she did either loved or persuaded by argument or seized by force or compelled by divine necessity, in any case escapes responsibility? (**463: §20**).

Gorgias ends his oration on a note of self-deprecation:

I wished to write a speech that would be praise for Helen and a plaything (*paignion*) for myself (464: §21).

Scholars have disputed the seriousness of Gorgias' purpose: is his *paignion* a contribution to moral philosophy, or a rhetorical exercise? the expression of an intellectual position, or a clever speaker's exhibition piece?[11] We can hardly hope to answer the question: Gorgias' psychology is unknown to us, and his use of the term '*paignion*' signifies nothing. In any case, whatever Gorgias may have felt or intended, the *Helen* is the first detailed and challenging contribution to the vexed question of human responsibility; we may take Gorgias seriously whether or not he did so himself.

Nothing ties the argument of the *Helen* to its eponym: if the argument works at all, it lets every adulteress off the moral hook. Indeed, nothing really ties the argument to any particular type of action: if the argument works, it works for all agents and all actions, and no one is ever responsible for anything. I assume that Gorgias was himself aware, and intended his audience to be aware, of the general application of his argument. The speech, after all, is surely meant to shock; and no one is going to be shocked by an argument that applies only to an ancient and fictional delinquency.

Gorgias' argument relies on his fourfold classification of the springs of actions, and it cannot succeed unless that classification is exhaustive. I think that it is: if I ϕ, then either my ϕing was accidental (a fluke or quirk or freak occurrence) in which case it falls under 'divine necessity'; or my ϕing was forced upon me; or my ϕing was the result of thought, in which case I was 'persuaded by argument', my own or someone else's; or, finally, I ϕed impetuously, driven on by my feelings. No doubt many ϕings are complex in their causes, and will fall into more than one of these four categories; but no ϕing, I think, can miss all four pigeon-holes.

First, 'divine necessity': in this case, 'the responsibility must be assigned to Chance and God' (§6). Gorgias is confused: god and divine necessity are irrelevant (their place is in §7 under the heading of Force); and Chance cannot be ascribed responsibility at all. Yet many philosophers will find a serious truth behind Gorgias' confused façade: '. . . if it is a matter of pure chance that a man should act in one way rather than another, he may be free but he can hardly be responsible. And indeed, when a man's actions seem to us quite unpredictable, when, as we say, there is no knowing what he will do, we do not look upon him as a moral agent. We look upon him rather as a lunatic.'[12] Chance, as Gorgias says, removes responsibility.

Now if chance events are simply unintended events, then I may surely be both causally and morally responsible for what happens by chance. If I draw a bow at a venture and the arrow lands in your eye, you will plausibly hold me responsible for the event which I never intended; and if I affix a randomizing device to my bow, so that your transfixion is the immediate result of an uncaused event, you will again take me to task. Chance, *pace* Gorgias, does not in general exonerate. Yet clearly chance does somehow fight against responsibility. I suggest that the connexion is this: if I ϕ by chance, then I am responsible for ϕing only if I am responsible for bringing it about that I ϕ by chance. If I put myself, knowingly, in a position where chance will play a part, I bear responsibility for the effects of chance. Gorgias must, I think, allow that to be true; but he can immunize his position. Let him hold that if chance and chance alone plays a part in my ϕing, then I am in no sense responsible for ϕing.

That force (*bia*) excludes responsibility is a corner-stone of Aristotle's theory of responsibility (*EN* 1109b35–1110b17); and it is taken as axiomatic by modern moralists: what I am forced to do, I cannot help doing; what I cannot help doing, I am not responsible for doing. The argument seems impregnable; but it is ambiguous. One philosopher has argued thus: '. . . if the man points a pistol at my head, I may still choose to disobey him; but this does not prevent its being true that if I do fall in with his wishes he can legitimately be said to have compelled me. And if the circumstances are such that no reasonable person would be expected to choose the other alternative, then the action that I am made to do is not one for which I am held to be morally responsible.'[13] Force or compulsion, on this view, is consistent with choice; so that if I am forced to ϕ, I may still be causally responsible for ϕing. But I am not morally responsible. That seems wrong to me: the bank-clerk who opens the safe at pistol-point acts, I judge, with wisdom and prudence; in ascribing such virtues to him I am praising him (in a fairly mild way); and if I praise him, I deem him liable to praise and hence I deem him morally responsible. Had he refused to give in to the gunman I should have judged him foolhardy; and that judgment again presupposes responsibility. *Bia*, then, does not remove responsibility: it will, no doubt, affect our assessment of the agent, and it may cause us to think pity a more appropriate attitude than disapprobation; but to say that is to say nothing about responsibility.

Aristotle has a different view: 'A forced act (*biaion*) is one of which the principle is external [to the subject], being such that the agent or patient contributes nothing' (*EN* 1110a1–3). That is a contrived reading of '*bia*' or 'force': we *do* say that the bank-clerk was forced to open the safe, even though he did not 'contribute nothing' to the action; and so did the Greeks (e.g. *Odyssey* XXII.351). But the contrivance is intelligible and perhaps intelligent; and we may imagine that Gorgias adopted it. Given the contrivance, *bia* certainly removes causal responsibility. But even so, it does not remove moral responsibility; for the agent may be responsible for putting himself into the situation in which he is forced. (If a captain sails in spite of gale warnings and his ship founders, then he is responsible for the wreck even though it was brought about by *force majeure*.) We can, however, come to Gorgias' aid here in the same way as before: if *bia* and *bia* alone accounts for my ϕing, I am not responsible in either way for what I do.

I turn next to the fourth of Gorgias' arguments, leaving the third and most interesting to last. Gorgias claims that love is either 'a god, having the divine power of gods', or 'a human disease and an ignorance of the soul' (§19): in neither case is the victim of love to blame. He compares the action of love with that of fear:

> Some men on seeing fearful things have actually lost their present mind at the present time: thus fear extinguishes and expels thought (**465**: §17).

And he offers a psychological explanation of the effects of fear:

> We see, having the sight not that we wish but whatever chances; and through the sight the soul is actually moulded in its ways (**466**: §15).[14]

An easy generalization suggests itself: whenever we act from passion, we ourselves are not responsible; the object of passion strikes our senses; our senses directly move the soul; and the soul moves us. Thought (*to noêma*) is by-passed, and we are not involved essentially in the action. Gorgias does not say that the emotions always have this effect: 'many' and 'often', not 'all' and 'always', qualify his remarks in §§15-19; but where love and fear do not have these effects, thought has a place; and thought-induced acts fall to Gorgias' third argument.

Aristotle refers to the view that 'things pleasant and fine are compulsive (for they necessitate, being external)' (*EN* 1110b9-10). The view is found in Euripides: according to Jason 'Eros necessitated you [i.e. Medea] to save my body' (*Medea* 530-1); other tragic figures are 'conquered' against their will (fr. 220), for 'Aphrodite cannot be borne if she comes in force' (*Hippolytus* 443) and sometimes 'anger is stronger than my plans' (*Medea* 1079). Aristotle will have none of that. His arguments are on the whole pretty feeble (1110b9-15, 1111a24-b3), but his final comment deserves quotation: 'Irrational passions seem nonetheless to belong to the man, so that the actions done from anger and desire are the man's; hence it is absurd to make them involuntary' (1111b1–3). Euripides, in one passage, concurs:

> We know and recognize the good
> but do not do it—some through indolence,
> some preferring some other pleasure to the fine (*Hippolytus*
> 380–3).

What the *Medea* rhetorically ascribes to anger, the *Hippolytus* honestly attributes to the angry man: the passions through which we act 'belong to the man', they are *our* passions; and if they are ours, it is we who are responsible for actions done through them. Gorgias says that 'it was love which did all these things' (§15); but that is simply to say that it was the infatuated Helen who did them and was responsible for doing them. 'Love did it' is not incompatible with 'The lover did it'; on the contrary, the two sentences mean the same.

Aquinas develops the Aristotelian view. Actions done from fear, he says 'are, if one considers it rightly, rather voluntary than involuntary' (*Summa Theologiae* 1a 2ae 6.6 resp.); and 'we should say that lust does not cause the involuntary but rather makes something voluntary; for something is called voluntary from the fact that the will is carried towards it; and by lust the will inclines to willing that which is lusted after' (ibid. 6.7 resp.). Fear does not remove responsibility; lust only adds to it. But Aquinas allows a relaxation of his hard doctrine: 'if lust totally removes knowledge, as happens in those who become lunatic because of lust, it follows that lust removes the voluntary' (ibid. 6.7 *ad* 3); and the same, surely applies to those paralysed by terror. Love sometimes is 'unbearable'; and the strength of our emotions—or the power of their inevitable physical manifestations—may close to us all paths of action but one. Sometimes emotion overpowers us; and if that is so, and if we are not responsible for getting ourselves into that unfortunate situation, then (I suppose) we are not morally responsible for our passionate actions. Sometimes, at least, lovers and cowards, Casanova and Falstaff, are not to be blamed or praised.

So far I have endeavoured to defend Gorgias: deeds done exclusively by chance, or exclusively by force, or exclusively by passion, are not to be held against their perpetrator. But a vast range of actions remains; and if Gorgias' argument is to succeed, they must all fall under the third of his categories: persuasion. In §8, 'the sophist now enters his temple—we reach the very marrow of the pamphlet';[15] *logos*, the rhetorical sophist's engine and delight, is 'a great potentate (*megas dunastês*)' (§8), and if it 'persuaded and deceived' Helen, then evidently she bears no responsibility for her actions;

> For the *logos* which persuaded, compelled the soul it persuaded both to obey what was spoken and to approve what was done (467: §12).

Logos is comparable to *bia* (§12);[16] it works on the soul as drugs work on the body (§14).

Gorgias refers to deceit, to falsehood, to persuasion; and it is customary to construe his remarks as bearing properly upon his own craft: §§8–14 argue that if Helen was deceived by a lying speech, she was not responsible for her betrayal of Menelaus. That construe gives sense to §§ 8–14, but removes all sense from the *Helen* as a whole; for it leaves open and untouched the evident possibility that Helen thought out and decided upon her betrayal by herself. The 'persuasive *logos*' is not just the wily speech of the professional orator, and the references to deception and falsity are inessential. *Logos* covers any ratiocination; and Gorgias means that if Helen was influenced by argument, then she was not responsible for her acts. Thus rationally explicable actions, the only type of act not embraced by §6, §7, or §§15–19, are stigmatized as irresponsible.

Gorgias is utterly correct in calling *logos* a *megas dunastês*; and his illustrations of the power of *logos* are apt and true. Yet how does the *logos* remove responsibility from the logical agent? To answer that question we must bring out a skeleton which has long been rattling its bones in the cupboard, the skeleton of causal determinism. Suppose that a ϕs, or Helen runs to Troy. Then, Gorgias assumes, there is some true proposition of the form 'b brings it about that a ϕs' or 'b brings it about that Helen runs to Troy'. If b brings it about that a ϕs, then b is causally responsible for a's ϕing; and if a is not causally responsible for his ϕing then he is not morally responsible either. Now a survey of the possible springs of action yields just four types of substituend for x in 'x brings it about that $a\phi$s': chance, a constraining agent, *logos*, passion. In every case, a, the ϕer, and b, the cause of a's ϕing, are distinct: b is causally responsible for a's ϕing; b is distinct from a; hence a is not causally responsible for a's ϕing; hence a is not morally responsible. Suppose that Helen read *Lady Chatterley's Lover* and was impressed by its argument: then the argument was causally responsible for Helen's flight; and Helen was guiltless.

In the cases of chance, force, and emotion it is possible to defend Gorgias' stance; I can find no defence for the case of *logos*. Moreover—and this is the important point—the general line of

227

argument which Gorgias relies on is fatally flawed. Gorgias assumes that we can always find a cause for a's ϕing; he argues that we can always find a cause for a's ϕing distinct from a; he tacitly assumes that if there is a cause of a's ϕing distinct from a, then a did not cause his own ϕing; and he implies that if a is not causally responsible for his ϕing then he is not morally responsible either. The schema is plausible; but we should not succumb to its attractions. I allow that if $a\phi$s then for some x distinct from a x brings it about that $a\phi$s. But I deny, first, that this entails that a does not bring it about that he ϕs: if x is a's lust, say, then if x brings it about that $a\phi$s, a brings it about that a ϕs. And further I deny that causal irresponsibility entails moral irresponsibility.

Gorgias' *paignion* fails. Yet it is a signal piece of philosophy: it introduces the problem of determinism to moral philosophy; and it anticipates, *in nuce*, many of the bad arguments subsequently advanced with such force and at such length by the passionate opponents of human freedom.

(d) *Democritean ethics*

Of the three hundred surviving fragments of Democritus, some 220 are given to ethical matters.[17] Such an unparalleled treasury raises high hopes: we may surely expect to discover a systematic moral philosophy in Democritus; and to discern a close connexion between his moral and his physical philosophies. Both hopes will be dashed; yet it is worth briefly conning the fragments in order to see why and to what extent that is so. I begin with the quest for an ethical system.

> If anyone attends intelligently to these maxims (*gnômai*) of mine, he will do many things worthy of a good man and he will leave undone many bad things (**468: 68 B 35**).

The key word is '*gnômê*': the vast majority of Democritus' ethical fragments are maxims, brief and pithy sayings of an exhortatory and moralistic nature:

> He who chooses the goods of the soul chooses the more divine; he who chooses those of the body, the human (**383: B 37**).

> It is fine to prevent a wrongdoer; if not, not to do wrong with him (**469: B 38**).

> One should either be or imitate a good man (**470: B 39**).

228

Some of the maxims are, as it were, potentially interesting: thus Democritus stresses the moral importance of the will:

It is not refraining from wrong-doing, but not even wishing it that is good (471: **B 62**; cf. **B 68, B 89, B 96**);

and he anticipates a doctrine of the 'mean':

In everything the equal is fine: excess and deficiency do not seem so to me (472: **B 102**; cf. **B 233**).

And he sometimes shows a flash of wit:

To speak sparingly is an adornment for a woman; and sparingness in adornment is a fine thing (473: **B 274**).

Most of the *gnômai* are trite,[18] but some reveal an idiosyncratic judgment: Democritus dislikes sex (**B 32**) and would not indulge in procreation (**B 275**: cf. Antiphon, **87 B 49**). His political pronouncements, whether or not they reveal a democratic inclination,[19] shows him a severe and uncompromising judge; e.g., **B 260**:

Anyone who kills any cutpurse or pirate, whether by his own hand, by ordering it or by voting for it, let him be free of penalty (474).

In his collection of *gnômai* we may perhaps discern a consistent outlook, but we shall look in vain for a systematic ethics.

Many live in accordance with *logos* although they have not learned *logos* (475: **B 53**).

Perhaps the *gnômai* are guides for the many, and a *logos*, or systematic account, was provided for the intellectual few?[20] Democritus did set up a *telos* or 'end' of life, a goal for human striving:

The Abderites too teach that there is an end; Democritus, in his book on the end, makes it *euthumia* which he also called *euestô*. And he often adds: 'For pleasure and lack of pleasure is the boundary' (476: Clement, **B 4**).

The word '*telos*', though the doxographers repeat it (Diogenes Laertius IX.45 = **A 1**; Epiphanius, **A 166**), is probably not Democritean; but the notion is, as **B 189** shows.

Democritus gave his *telos* various names: it is *euthumia* and *euestô*; *athambia* (Cicero, **A 169**; cf. **B 215, B 216**) or *athaumastia* (Strabo, **A 168**) or *ataraxia* (Stobaeus, **A 167**); *harmonia* or *summetria* (Stobaeus, **A 167**); *eudaimonia* (Stobaeus, **A 167**). *Euthumia* ('good heartedness') and *euestô* ('well-being') give nothing away. *Athambia* and *athaumastia* ('lack of wonderment') and *ataraxia* ('tranquillity') indicate an Epicurean penchant for the quiet life, undisturbed either by the startings and starings of superstition or by the jolts and jostlings of practical activity. And *summetria* and *harmonia* point in the same direction:

> [He says that] *euthumia* is the end, not being the same as pleasure (as some wrongly interpret it) but a state in which the soul lives calmly and in a stable fashion, not disturbed by fear or superstition or any other passion (477: Diogenes Laertius, IX.45 = A 1).

The state is achieved by not engaging in much business, either private or public, and by not trying to exceed one's capacities (**B 3**); it depends on one's mental and psychological state and 'does not live in cattle or in gold' (**B 171**; cf. **B 170**); to reach it you 'must not take your pleasures in mortal things' (**B 189**). Above all, you must practise moderation (**B 191**).

All that is very dull and depressing; but we may find a little more joy in the suggestion that 'pleasure and lack of pleasure is the boundary' (**476**); or rather, that

> Pleasure and lack of pleasure is the boundary of the advantageous and the disadvantageous (478: B 188).

For we should

> Deem nothing pleasant unless it is advantageous (479: B 74).[21]

If pleasure as such is advantageous—indeed the only advantageous thing—it does not follow that we should recklessly pursue all pleasures:

> Inopportune pleasures produce displeasures (480: B 71),

and some pleasures produce wretchedness (*kakotês*: **B 178**). Bodily pleasures in particular are followed by 'many pains' (**B 235**), and we should become masters of sexual pleasure and not be slaves to women (**B 214**). Well-being depends on a wise discrimination among pleasures (Stobaeus, **A 167**). Observe moderation in joy (**B 191**), for

> Temperance increases the enjoyable and makes pleasure greater (481: B 211).

> Great joys come from contemplating fine works (482: B 194: noble deeds? or beautiful works of art?),

It follows that:

One should choose not every pleasure but that which has the fine
as its object (**483: B 207**).

And we should find our pleasures not in 'mortal things' (**B 189**) but
rather in the joys of the mind (**B 146**).

A life without festivity is a long road without an inn (**484: B 230**),

but Democritean festivity will be a fairly sober and earnestly
intellectual business, a symposium rather than a pub-crawl.

All that amounts, I suppose, to a moderately coherent plan of life;
and we may, if we wish, call it a practical system. Lovers of
anachronism (among whom I happily enrol myself) may begin to
think of a Benthamite Utilitarianism: if he did not invent and
advocate a felicific calculus, at least Democritus prepared the way for
one, and Bentham's great moral system was adumbrated at Abdera.
But that suggestion is wholly mistaken: Democritus' hedonism has
nothing at all to do with morality; it does not pretend to tell us what,
morally speaking, we ought to do, or how to live the moral life. It is a
recipe for happiness or contentment, not a prescription for goodness:
the system sets up a selfish end for the individual and counsels him
on how to attain it; it does not set up a moral goal and offer advice on
its achievement. If Democritus' *gnômai* offer an unsystematic set of
moral maxims, his reflexions on *euestô* offer no moral speculations at
all; instead, they offer a systematic theory of prudence.

There is nothing particularly objectionable in presenting a recipe
for personal well-being: there is no reason why all practical advice
should be moral advice. Yet I confess that I find Democritus' recipe,
like that of Epicurus after him, peculiarly unappetizing. Calm and
placidity are tedious virtues; moderation in all things leads to a
confoundedly dull life. I do not hate the Persian apparatus; and *nil
admirari* is a prescription for *ennui*. We can hardly take Democritus
seriously.

So much for the homiletic side of Democritean 'ethics'; I do not
care for it. What, next, of the other great question? How does
Democritus the practical philosopher fit with Democritus the
physicist? Scholars are radically divided:[22] some see a coherent and
self-conscious unity in Democritus' work; some discern only a loose
compatibility; others detect downright inconsistencies. A brief and
negative survey must suffice.

Of the systematists, some interpret the practical *telos* of *euestô* in
an Aristotelian vein as the 'theoretical' or philosophical life; they
then pronounce Democritus the natural philosopher to be the living
embodiment of Abderite ethics. At best that is a very weak way of

231

interlocking practical and theoretical philosophy; and in any case the evidence for taking *euestô* to consist in 'theorizing' is tenuous. Others point out that *euestô*, being a state of the soul, must be determined by some arrangement of its atomic constituents. That is no doubt true; but there is no reason to think that Democritus the scientist speculated about the precise nature and cause of *euestô*, nor, again, would such speculations constitute much of a connexion between ethics and physics. Others, finally, turn from atomism to anthropology: Democritus, they say, tried to ground morals on nature or *phusis*; in particular, certain features of animal behaviour, by revealing what *phusis* really is, point a moral for men. (Camels do not copulate in public: neither, then should we.)[23] Again, the evidence that Democritus offered any such view is nugatory; nor would it unite, in any significant way, his natural and his practical philosophy.

A different sort of connexion has been sought between ethics and physics: there seems to be a parallelism, of which Democritus was conscious (cf. **B 69**),[24] between the role of pleasure in ethics and the role of perception in physics. In ethics the unreflecting man goes all out for immediate pleasure; in physics he believes his senses. In ethics, reason replaces pleasure while yet relying indirectly upon it; in physics, reason replaces perception while yet relying indirectly upon it. I find it hard to care much about that: the parallelism between ethics and physics is not as neat as my brief sentences suggest; and in any case the parallelism hardly amounts to a systematic connexion between physics and ethics.

Democritus' practical philosophy has no metaphysical or physical basis. Nor should we really expect it to have one. For what, after all, would a physical basis for ethics look like? Ethics and physics, so far as I can see, have no systematic interconnexion at all; in many boring little ways a man's natural philosophy will rub off on his moralizing, but no general or systematic influence is even conceivable. The long scholarly discussion of the possible 'materialistic foundation' of Democritus' ethics is empty: it follows a will-o'-the-wisp.

Physics and ethics can, however, be inconsistent; and many scholars find an inconsistency at least potentially present in Democritus: physically, Democritus is a thorough-going determinist (above pp. 121–4); yet 'his moral precepts are given on the assumption that man is free to act as he will'.[25] Epicurus was acutely conscious of the dilemma:

If someone makes use of the theory of Democritus, saying that there is no free movement in the atoms because of their collisions with one another, whence it is clear that everything is moved necessarily, we shall say to him: Do you not know, who ever you are, that there *is* a kind of free movement in the atoms which Democritus did not discover but which Epicurus brought to light, being an inherent swerve as he proves from the phenomena? The most important point is this, that if destiny is believed in, all advice and rebuke is done away with (**485**: Diogenes of Oenoanda, fr. 32 Ch. = **68 A 50**).

There is no trace of the scandalous swerve in Democritus: 'by the time of Democritus this great question was apparently not even simmering and he proceeds to lay down his directions for the moral life with a simple *naïveté*, unconscious of the problem which he himself had raised by his insistence on the supremacy of "necessity" in the physical world'.[26]

But by Democritus' time the 'great question' *was* simmering: the briefest reflexion upon Heraclitus' philosophy would suggest it, and we know that Democritus was a student of Heraclitus; Gorgias had raised it explicitly in his *Helen*; and it was implicit in many of the problems canvassed on the Euripidean stage. Yet no fragment and no doxographical report indicates any discussion of the question by Democritus. He may have held that the emission of moral precepts does not require a 'free will'; he may, alternatively, have held that determinism and free will are compatible. Both views have, after all, been defended by eminent thinkers. But had Democritus sketched any such view, we should surely hear of it; and I incline to the sombre conclusion that physics and ethics were so successfully compartmentalized in Democritus' capacious mind that he never attended to the large issues which their cohabitation produces.

X

The Bounds of Knowledge

(a) *Neo-Ionian empiricism*

Eleatic scepticism was philosophically barren; for it was fundamentally a metaphysical rather than an epistemological thesis, resting
wholly upon Eleatic metaphysics and not at all upon any speculation
proper to epistemology. Thus once it was believed that the
foundations of Elea were undermined, there can have seemed no
need to devote critical attention to the superstructure: fragment **191**
of Melissus offers no challenge to the philosopher who believes that
he has vindicated an Ionian world. That fact, I think, explains why it
took a second attack on the possibility of objective knowledge to elicit
a neo-Ionian epistemology: Democritus was spurred to thought by
Protagoras; Empedocles and Anaxagoras had no such sharp incentive.

For all that, I shall devote a few pages to Empedocles and
Anaxagoras. Both men say something of an epistemological nature;
and the former is usually misunderstood, the latter usually
mispraised.

Sextus made Empedocles a sceptic:

He talks about the fact that the judgment of truth does not reside
in the senses in the following way:
For narrow hands are scattered over the limbs;
and many wretched things impede, which blunt the thoughts.
And gathering a poor part of life in their lives,
swift to die, rising like smoke, they fly away,
persuaded only of that which each meets   5
as they drive everywhere. And who boasts that he has found the
whole?

234

In this way these things can neither be seen by men, nor heard,
nor grasped in their mind [31 B 2.1–8].
And as to the fact that the truth is not utterly unattainable, but is
attainable to the extent that human reason reaches, he makes that
clear in the next lines, continuing:
But you, since you have come here
will learn—more, human wit has not achieved [B 2.8–9].[1]
And in the following lines, having attacked those who pretend to
know more, he asserts that what is grasped by each sense is reliable,
if reason oversees it—although earlier he has run down their
reliability. He says:
But, gods, turn away their madness from my tongue,
and channel from me a pure spring of holy words;
and you, much famed white-armed maiden Muse,
I beg—what things it is right for mortals to hear,
send me, driving the well-reined chariot of Piety.   5
Nor will *you* be forced by the flowers of well-reputed honour
at the hands of mortals to pluck them at the cost of saying more
than is holy
in boldness, and then indeed to sit at the heights of wisdom.
But come, gaze with every hand, in the way in which each thing is
clear,
nor hold any sight in greater trust than what comes by hearing,10
or resounding hearing above the clarities of the tongue,
nor in any way from any of the other limbs by which there is a way
for thinking
take away trust, but think in the way in which each thing is clear
[B 3][2] (486).

Empedocles' language is flowery: partly he is indulging in the
poetical vocabulary appropriate to an exordium; partly he is
hampered by *patrii sermonis egestas*; thus the curious reference to
'hands (*palamai*)' shows only that Empedocles possessed no general
term for 'sense-organs'.[3] Amid the luxuriant rhetoric, Sextus
discerned his own dear bloom of scepticism—and then contrary
evidence of a naive trust in the senses.
Yet B 2 is hardly a sceptical fragment: lines 1–7 attack pretensions
to knowledge; but they do not make a general assault on human
cognitive powers. Lines 1–6 observe merely that ordinary men,
flitting from one experience to the next, do not gain the knowledge
that their 'narrow hands' can supply them with: '*in this way*' truth is
not to be apprehended. (Fragment 68 D of Archilochus is plainly
alluded to in line 5.) Sextus' interpretation is doubly false: B 2 is

not sceptical; nor does it attack, specifically, the *senses*; for ordinary men, as line 8 indicates, are no better at using their minds than their perceptive faculties. The contrast in **B 2** is not between sense and reason but between benighted mortals and Pausanias: by following Empedocles' advice, Pausanias will 'find the whole', or achieve a synoptic appreciation of natural phenomena.[4] In short, **B 2** offers a systematic science in place of the partial and disorderly beliefs of unscientific men.

The first eight lines of **B 3** also contain a contrast; and again, the contrast is between types of thinker, not between the senses and reason. Empedocles piously requests a 'holy' knowledge and dissociates himself from the 'madness' of some anonymous students. There is nothing more in these lines than the familiar deprecation of superhumanly ambitious aspirations.

Thus **B 2** and **B 3** show that Empedocles was no sceptic of sense-perception. All the senses, if appropriately used and systematically deployed, yield trustworthy evidence; and the path to scientific knowledge runs through their separate provinces. That, no doubt, is true enough; and it was worth saying to men who had read Melissus or Parmenides and were prepared to reject perception wholesale. Yet it does not amount to anything like an epistemology; it is a statement, not an argued case; and it offers no objection to any critic of perception.

Nor did Anaxagoras pursue those matters. Sextus reports a statement of Diotimus:

> Diotimus said that according to him [sc. Democritus] there are three criteria: for grasping what is unclear (*ta adêla*), the phenomena—for the phenomena are the sight of what is unclear, as Anaxagoras, whom Democritus praises for this, says . . . (**487: 76 A 3 = 59 B 21a**).

Opsis tôn adêlôn ta phainomena, 'the phenomena are the sight of what is unclear'; we can come to know what we cannot perceive (*ta adêla*) by way of the things we do perceive (*ta phainomena*). That celebrated *mot* has seemed to some scholars to contain a significant contribution to epistemology and scientific methodology: in it Anaxagoras explains and justifies the procedure of analogy and induction which his scientific predecessors had been unselfconsciously using. Anaxagoras is not, indeed, the only ancient to have formulated the general principle (it can be found in Herodotus (II.33) and in the Hippocratic corpus (*vet med* 22; *vict* I.12)); but he was probably the first to do so, and his formulation was certainly the most elegant.[5]

The earlier Ionians had used analogy; and their methods had been adopted by Empedocles and the medical writers. Things unclear and unfamiliar—either by reason of their celestial distance from us or by virtue of their microscopical size—could be illuminated and made intelligible by a sort of extrapolation and extension from the middle-sized data that surround us on earth; and the microscopic features thus apprehended could be offered in explanation of the observed phenomena. That methodology was no doubt welcomed and embellished by Anaxagoras; after all, his whole physics, though founded on empirical observations, goes far beyond the limits of perception in its effort to account for the phenomena. The *adêla* are revealed by *ta phainomena*—and then advanced in their explanation.

We can, I suppose, guess at some of the particular applications of his 'method' that Anaxagoras made; but the fragments and the doxography give little or no solid evidence. Here, for what it is worth, is the sole report that has any near connexion with **487**:

> The fine scientist Anaxagoras, attacking the senses for their
> weakness, says: 'by their feebleness we cannot judge the truth'.
> And he gives as evidence of their unreliability the gradual change
> of colours; for if we take two colours, black and white, and then
> pour one into the other, drop by drop, our sight will not be able
> to discriminate the gradual changes, even though they subsist in
> nature (**488**: Sextus, **59 B 21**).

There are some natural distinctions too fine for our gross senses; some things we cannot discriminate. Yet we can, for all that, know that they are distinct: common observation tells us that if we mix a pint of black paint with a gallon of white, the result is grey; and further observations indicate that the darkness of the grey is proportional to the amount of black added to the original white gallon. A gentle generalization, by way of **487**, allows us to infer that each drop of black, when added to the white, changes its hue to a slightly darker grey, even though these little changes are individually unobservable.

The example is not, perhaps, of great importance; nor is it wholly convincing: why, for example, does Anaxagoras suppose that colour is an intrinsic property of things, existing independently of any observer? Does it make sense to talk of real but indiscriminable differences in colour? Again, why suppose that the colours are *continua*? why does every drop of black turn the mixture a shade greyer? why not suppose (as Aristotle did) a finite number of real shades, and chromatic quantum jumps from one shade of grey to the next? But these are niggling objections; and the grand principle of **487** does not suffer by criticism of its minor application in **488**.

The objections to 487 are of a larger and more abstract order: the methodological principle there enunciated is hopelessly vague and entirely unjustified. It is vague in that it offers no criteria for the admissibility of analogical argument: what comparisons are scientifically fruitful and what are not? It is unjustified because it makes no attempt to exhibit itself as a rational principle: why, after all, think that the *phainomena* guide us to the *adêla*? Why not approach the *adêla*, as many Presocratics did, by way of abstract reasoning? Or why embrace, promiscuously, 'the' *phainomena*? Why not single out some senses above others, or some observers over others? I do not deny that from 487 we can construct some theory that is interesting and even true: my point is simply that 487 does not, in itself, contain any such theory. It is a *bon mot*, an aphorism neatly summing up the general spirit and optimistic hope of Ionian science; it is not a piece of serious philosophizing.

Anaxagoras is also said to have been a sceptic; before leaving him for epistemologically more interesting pastures I shall review the evidence for that assertion. There are two fragments and half a dozen bits of doxography to examine. The fragments can be dismissed instantly: 488, to which Sextus characteristically gives a sceptical interpretation, states only that some distinctions in nature are too fine for our unaided senses to perceive; and 208 (see above, p. 28), while excepting one area from the range of our knowledge, does not remotely suggest a general scepticism.

Cicero idiotically enrolls Anaxagoras among those who say that 'nothing can be apprehended, nothing perceived, nothing known' (A 95); and Aëtius echoes him (A 95). Sextus reports that

> We oppose what is grasped by the mind (*ta noumena*) to what is grasped by the senses (*ta phainomena*), as Anaxagoras opposed the fact that snow is white by saying that snow is frozen water, water is black, therefore snow too is black (489: A 97).

The argument, which is referred to more than once (Cicero, A 97; Scholiast to Homer, A 98; Scholiast to Gregory, B 10), seems to Sextus to have a sceptical moral: either mind trumps perception, or each faculty neutralizes the other. But it is more plausible to connect the argument with the Anaxagorean doctrine that 'Everything is in everything': snow seems purely white; yet reason assures us that there is darkness in it; for snow is frozen water, and water is black. The black in the water cannot be destroyed; it must, therefore, reside somehow in the white snow.

Finally, there is an anecdote in the *Metaphysics*:

A remark of Anaxagoras to some of his friends is preserved:
Existent things will be for them such as they take them to be (**490**: 1009b25 = **A 28**).

I leave the reader to make what he will of that.

(b) *Protagoras: man the measure*

Protagoras, the first of the Sophists, hailed from Abdera. Our sources make him a 'hearer' of Democritus, his fellow-citizen (e.g., Diogenes Laertius, IX.50 = **80 A 1**); there is no particular reason to doubt the story and there are visible links between various aspects of Democritean and Protagorean thought. According to Plutarch, Democritus attacked Protagoras' views on knowledge (**68 A 156**); and for that reason I shall consider Protagoras' epistemology before that of Democritus.

Of all things a measure is man—of the things that are, that they are; of the things that are not, that they are not (**491: 80 B 1**).[6]

That notorious statement, which Plato, Sextus, and Diogenes all quote, opened Protagoras' tract on *Truth* or *Knockouts* (*Alêtheia* or *Kataballontes*: Diogenes Laertius, IX.51 = **A 1**; Sextus, *ad* **B 1**). The Germans compendiously refer to the statement as the *Homomensurasatz*; and I shall adopt their convenient and portentous name, sometimes abbreviating it to a humble *H*.

The *Homomensurasatz* has only one uncontroversial feature: opacity. Protagoras' words are surely transmitted; but their sense is a matter of dispute. The *Satz*, as befits an exordium, is grand and allusive rather than clear and prosaic. Fortunately, we possess a detailed ancient interpretation: Plato, in the *Theaetetus*, offers a reading which, though fanciful in detail, is, I think, correct in its central contention. That central contention reads as follows:

Doesn't he mean something like this: 'As each thing seems (*phainetai*) to me, so it is for me; and as to you, so again for you—and you and I are men'? (**492: 152A = *ad* B 1**).

The same gloss is repeated in the *Cratylus* (385E = **A 13**); and its main point is almost universally accepted: in saying that 'of all things (*chrêmatôn*) a measure (*metron*) is man', Protagoras means that what *seems* to be, *is*. Set a man against a thing and he will provide a measure or accurate assessment of it; for it is as he takes it to be. Man is a measure: seeming is being. That is the philosophical core of the *Homomensurasatz*.

239

The core remains vague; and to clarify it we must come more closely to grips with the wording of the fragment. First, 'man': Socrates objects that Protagoras might just as well have said 'pig' or 'jackal' (*Theaetetus* 161C = **A 1**); and that suggests that 'man' here is used generically: whatever seems to mankind, is. The suggestion is apparently supported by Sextus:

> Thus according to him man (*ho anthrôpos*) becomes the criterion of the things that are; for everything that seems to men (*tois anthrôpois*), actually is; and what seems to no man, is not (**493: A 14**).

Mankind, not the individual man, is the measure of things. Plato, however, does not intend that interpretation: his paraphrase of **491** explicitly refers to individual men, to you and me. Sextus in his introduction to **491** takes the same view; and so does Aristotle (*Met* 1062b12–15 = **A 19**). There is, to be sure, no independent check on that interpretation; and it may be that in accepting it we accept a Platonic travesty not a Protagorean original. But almost all the evidence favours individual men, little speaks for mankind; and we should, therefore, interpret 'Man is the measure . . .' by 'Each individual man is the measure. . .'.[7]

After 'man', 'measure'. Following Plato, I have taken '*a* is a measure of *b*' to mean '*b* is as it seems (*phainetai*) to *a* to be'. How are we to understand '*phainetai*' here? *Phainesthai* in Greek, like 'seem' in English, is ambiguous: it has a judgmental and a phenomenological sense. 'It seems to me that . . .' often means, roughly, 'I incline to believe that . . .'; and 'He seems to me to have been misled' means 'I judge that he has been misled'. But '*a* seems *F*' also has a different sort of sense, roughly equivalent to '*a* presents itself as *F* to the senses'; thus 'Your face seems yellow' means 'Your face is yellow to the sight', and 'The trumpet seems flat' means 'The trumpet is flat to my ear'. Judgmental seeming and phenomenological seeming are distinct: your face seems yellow phenomenologically but not judgmentally—I do not judge it to be yellow; he seems guilty judgmentally but not phenomenologically—his boyish face radiates innocence. Is Protagoras' seeming judgmental or phenomenological?

Plato explicitly gives a phenomenological interpretation: 'and "it seems (*phainetai*)" means "he perceives (*aisthanetai*)"?—It does' (*Theaetetus* 152A = *ad* **B 1**). Some of the doxographers follow Plato (cf. Hermias, **A 16**; Eusebius, **70 B 1**); but Sextus talks of 'everything which *phainetai* or *dokei* to anyone' (*ad* **B 1**) and '*dokei*' means 'it seems' in the judgmental sense only. Aristotle, too, uses *dokei* in the

240

same context (*Met* 1007b21 = **A 19**); and there is evidence that the judgmental account is earlier even than Plato.

> No one can say that all *phantasia* is true, because of the *peritropê*, as Democritus and Plato taught us in their attack on Protagoras; for if every *phantasia* is true, then even the proposition that not every *phantasia* is true, being itself subject of *phantasia*, will be true, and thus it will turn out false that every *phantasia* is true (**494**: Sextus, **A 15** = **68 A 114**).

The *peritropê*, or about-turn, is suffered by the *Homomensurasatz* because it is self-refuting. The argument requires that 'every *phantasia* is true' be interpreted by way of the judgmental sense of *phainesthai*; thus, 'If *phainetai* to *x* that *P*, then it is true that *P*' must be written as:

(H1) For any proposition *P*, and any man, *x*, if *x* judges that *P*, then it is true that *P*.

From (H1) it follows at once that:

(1) For any man *x*, if *x* judges that not-*H*, then it is true that not-*H*. But many men reject the *Homomensurasatz*, or judge that not-*H*. It follows that it is true that not-*H*, and hence that *H* itself is false. Thus the *Homomensurasatz* suffers an about-turn: it marches to its own ruin.

I shall return to the *peritropê* in a later section. My reason for quoting it here is to show first that Democritus accepted the orthodox paraphase of *H* in terms of *phainesthai*; and, second, that he interpreted *phainesthai* in its judgmental and not in its phenomenological sense.

According to Sextus, Plato as well as Democritus used the *peritropê* against Protagoras; and Sextus was right (cf. *Theaetetus* 171A). Use of the *peritropê* implies a judgmental *phainetai*; and in his allusions to *H* Plato sometimes explicitly uses the purely judgmental *dokei* (e.g., *Theaetetus* 161C). Moreover, much of the argument against Protagoreanism which Plato develops in the *Theaetetus* implicitly assumes *dokei* rather than *aisthanetai*. The phenomenological interpretation given at *Theaetetus* 152A is thus not consistently adhered to by Plato.

The weight of the evidence tells, I think, for a judgmental interpretation.[8] The contrary evidence probably all derives from *Theaetetus* 152A; and we may guess that Plato's concern there with the thesis that 'knowledge is perception' encouraged him to give a temporary and unhistorical phenomenological interpretation to Protagoras' *Satz*. At all events, I propose to follow the judgmental view.

Many scholars write as though the dispute between phenomeno-logical and judgmental *phainetai* was only one of scope: is *H* restricted to matters of perception, or does it extend to all judgments? That is mistaken: phenomenological or Φ-seeming, and judgmental or J-seeming, differ not in range but in kind. J-seeming turns *H* into a thesis about the judgments, beliefs or opinions of men—all such judgments are true. Φ-seeming turns *H* into a thesis about perceptual seemings: whatever strikes the senses as such and such, is such and such. An example of Aristotle's brings out the difference: a man, looking at the sun, may judge that the sun is several thousand miles across; yet the sun may *look* to him about a foot in diameter (cf. *An* 428b3). If we interpret *H* by way of J-seeming we shall give truth to the man's judgment, not to the content of his sense experience; if we interpret it by Φ-seeming, we shall give truth to the experiential content, not to the judgment.

So much for 'man' and 'measure'. Next, 'of the things that are (*tôn ontôn*), that they are (*hôs estin*)'. What does '*esti*' mean here? Some scholars say 'exist'. The *Homomensurasatz* can then be tied to the coat-tails of Elea: if anyone judges that a thing exists, then it does exist, for judgment involves thought, and thought requires existent objects. The interpretation has a superficial attraction: and it is perhaps supported by Hermias, **A 16**; but I do not see how *einai* can be taken existentially in the second, negative, clause of the *Satz*.

Plato takes *einai* to be predicative: 'of the things that are, that they are' means 'of whatever is (*F*), that it is (*F*)'. And having glossed *H* in terms of 'such' and 'so', Plato illustrates it thus:

> Sometimes when the same wind blows, one of us shivers and the other doesn't; or one of us mildly, the other violently.—Yes indeed—Then shall we say that the wind is in itself cold or not cold? (**495**: *Theaetetus* 152B = **B 1**).

The wind is one of 'the things that are'; and what it 'is' is cold. Plato's predicative interpretation is tacitly adopted by Aristotle (e.g., *Met* 1007b20 = **A 19**) and by Sextus (e.g., **A 14**); and I have no hesitation in following them.

Thus 'man is a measure . . . of the things that are, that they are . . .' means that if a man judges an object to be *F*, then it is *F*. Man is also a measure 'of the things that are not, that they are not': analogy suggests the meaning that if a man judges an object not to be *F*, then it is not *F*. And that interpretation is clearly implied by Aristotle:

> If the man seems to someone not to be a trireme, then he is not a trireme (**496**: *Met* 1007b21 = **A 19**).

Sextus has a different gloss: 'Everything that seems to men, actually is; and what seems to no man, is not' (493: A 14). If no one judges that a thing is F, then it is not F. Protagoras may have embraced that thesis; but he does not state it in H.

Things[9] are F or not F just in so far as some man 'measures' them, or judges them to be so. The *Homomensurasatz*, then, invites the following formulation:

(H2) For any man, x, and object, O, if x judges that O is F, then O is F; and if x judges that O is not F, then O is not F.

The *Homomensurasatz* is outrageous: was Protagoras' *Truth* an exercise in irony? or a virtuoso display of cleverness? Did the *Satz* aspire merely to shock and to excite? Or was *Truth* serious, and the *Satz* an effort to enlighten and instruct, to surmount some philosophical hurdle? I think that the *Satz* is the keystone of a systematic and sophisticated epistemology, and that it represents one part of an original, and not uninteresting, contribution to philosophy. I shall try to make that view plausible by a somewhat circuitous argumentative route.

(c) *Knowledge and relativity*

[Protagoras] was the first to say that there are two *logoi* about everything, opposite to one another (497: Diogenes Laertius, IX.51 = A 1 = B 6a; cf. Clement, A 20).

Logoi here are arguments, or perhaps, more generally, reasons; for Seneca enlarged upon Diogenes' report:

Protagoras says that on every issue it is possible for it to be argued (*disputari*) with equal force (*ex aequo*) on both sides (498: A 20).

For any proposition P there is an argument for P and an argument of equal strength for not-P. If you claim that the argument for P is in fact stronger, Protagoras will fulfil his wicked promise 'to make the weaker argument stronger' (Aristotle, *Rhet* 1402a23 = B 6b). All sticks are straight: show me a warped lath, and I will bend it straight. All arguments are equal: show Protagoras a feeble reason and he will strengthen it to par. In all things there is an intellectual equilibrium; for any thesis there is an equipollence of argument *pro* and *contra*.

Such paired and equipollent arguments were, it seems, a stock-in-trade of Protagoras' sophistry; and his two books of *Antilogies* (cf. Diogenes Laertius, IX. 55 = A 1) doubtless contained a selection of them. Alas, none has survived, and the *agôn* between Just and Unjust Logos in Aristophanes' *Clouds*, which scholars deem a parody of Protagorean sophistry, is too much of a caricature and too unclever to permit any safe inference about the nature or plausibility of its probable patterns.

For all that, it is not difficult to guess at the areas in which Protagoras hunted for his equipollences. First, ethical argument, in which he is known to have had an interest, must have been a rich quarry. By the second half of the fifth century the differences in moral belief from one culture and age to another were familiar enough; and a Protagorean equipollence would be suggested by them, and corroborated by the actual ease with which ethical argumentation reaches an *impasse*. The *Dissoi Logoi* provides copious illustration. Second, there are the deliverances of the senses: the *Theaetetus* illustrates the *Homomensurasatz* by an example which may well have been taken from Protagoras' own treatise. The wind makes me shiver and leaves you unmoved: is it cold?—Yes; it makes me shiver. No: you do not twitch. That is a simple example: the rich treasury of cases illustrating the relativity of sense perception began to be stocked in Protagoras' time; and we need not doubt that he found material there with which to support his equipollence thesis.

Such examples suggest a generalization: any predication can be supported by argument, and attacked by argument of precisely equal weight. Protagoras was a clever man; and a little ingenuity would enable him to give some initial plausibility to his general thesis even in areas where it seemed wholly inapplicable. Surely mathematics provides innumerable examples of sound argumentation for a theorem where no countervailing considerations can be adduced? But Protagoras, we are told, 'refuted the geometers' (Aristotle, *Met* 998a4 = **B** 7). 'The facts are unknowable and the language unpleasing, as Protagoras says of mathematics' (Philodemus, **B** 7a: Diels-Kranz II.425). The details of Protagoras' 'refutation' of the geometers are unknown; but they can be guessed at. 'The circle does not touch the ruler at a point' (*Met* loc. cit.):[10] geometry is about physical objects; if it does not apply to physical objects it is an empty game and not a science; if it does apply, then the geometers' proofs are subject to empirical checks. Take any *a priori* argument, say for the theorem that the angles of a triangle sum to 180°. Draw and measure a triangle: you will get a result differing from 180°. Any *a priori logos* can be matched by an equipollent *logos* based on empirical observation. Thus even among the apparent certainties of mathematics the Principle of Equipollence holds sway.

If the Principle is to fit into Protagoras' epistemology it must be stated in a slightly more restricted form than the one Seneca gives. I take it to assert that for any object O and apparently objective predicate F, any reason for judging that O is F can be matched by an equally strong reason for judging that O is not F. The point of this formulation, and the sense of 'apparently objective predicate', will emerge shortly.

The wind blows cold on the shorn lamb and warm on its woolly brother: 'should we say that the wind is in itself cold or not cold, or shall we be persuaded by Protagoras that it is cold for the shiverer and not for the other?' (*Theaetetus* 152B = **B 1**). If we have equal reason to believe P and Q, we cannot rationally accept P and reject Q, or vice versa. That fundamental axiom of rationality, coupled with the Principle of Equipollence, forbids us to accept 'O is F' and reject 'O is not F', and also to reject 'O is F' and accept 'O is not F'. Equipollence of argument requires equality of assent.

Three courses are open. First, we might reject both 'O is F' and 'O is not F'. But it is paradoxical to *reject* 'O is F' when we have good arguments in its favour. Second, we might retreat to a forlorn scepticism: no doubt just one of 'O is F' and 'O is not F' is true, but we cannot possibly know which. But again, it is paradoxical to withhold assent from propositions for whose truth we have excellent evidence: if the wind feels cold to me, what more could I wish for by way of evidence that it is cold? Third, we can embrace both 'O is F' and 'O is not F'. That is the Protagorean path.

Surely, though, that is a 'path beyond all tidings'? Even if the Principle of Equipollence is true, we can hardly follow Protagoras' argument and deny the Law of Contradiction. Now just such a denial is in any case demanded by the *Homomensurasatz*: nothing prevents men from making opposite judgments; if I judge that the wine is corked and you deem it excellent, you contradict me. But according to (H2) both our judgments are true. Aristotle puts the point clearly enough: 'but if this is the case [i.e. given *H*], it follows that the same thing is and is not—is bad and good, and the rest of the so-called opposing phrases; because often this seems fine to *these* men and the opposite to *those*, and what seems to each is the measure' (*Met* 1062b15–9 = **A 19**). The Principle of Equipollence may have encouraged Protagoras to embrace both 'O is F' and 'O is not F'; but such intellectual troilism is in any case forced upon him by his *Homomensurasatz*.

Did Protagoras, then, knowingly and cheerfully deny the Law of Contradiction? According to Diogenes,

He was the first to advance the thesis (*logos*) of Antisthenes which attempts to prove that it is not possible to contradict (*antilegein*), as Plato says in the *Euthydemus* (**499**: Diogenes Laertius, IX.53 = **A 1**).

Plato says:

> And *this* thesis [sc. that it is not possible to contradict] I have often
> heard from many people, always with astonishment. The
> Protagoreans used it vigorously, and it was used even earlier; but it
> always seems quite astonishing to me and to upturn (*anatrepein*)
> both other theses and also its own self (**500**: 286BC = **A 19**).[11]

Plato takes the thesis that 'it is not possible to contradict' to be a
denial of the Law of Contradiction; and it is therefore liable to
'upturn itself'. This self-*anatropê* is surely equivalent to *peritropê*:
having attacked *H* by *peritropê*, Plato now uses the same manoeuvre
against the further Protagorean thesis, that *antilegein* is impossible.
'Call the thesis *A*. Let Protagoras assert *A*. Then Plato maintains
not-*A*. But according to *A* not-*P* does not contradict *P*; hence not-*A* is
compatible with *A*. Hence, for all Protagoras has said, not-*A* is the
case: hence *A* is not the case.' That, at least, is the best I can do for
Plato; and it is not good enough. The fundamental misapprehension
is, I think, the assumption that Protagoras 'denies the Law of
Contradiction' in rejecting the possibility of contradiction: to say that
contradiction is impossible is not to assert that a proposition and its
contradictory may both be true at the same time; it is to assert the
perfectly distinct thesis that you cannot contradict me.

Suppose I judge that *O* is *F* and you that *O* is not *F*. Then,
according to Protagoras, I have not yet contradicted you; and if we are
not *antilegontes*, the truth of what I say is compatible with the truth
of what you say. Thus the denial of *antilegein*, far from opening
Protagoras to a peculiarly damning charge of inconsistency, is actually
designed to protect him from that charge: the clouds of contradiction
which lour over *H* and over the Principle of Equipollence are
evaporated by the thesis that 'it is not possible to contradict'.

'But that is a hollow victory: Protagoras' thesis is false; for you and
I patently do contradict one another: what more obvious contradiction could one desire than "*O* is *F* and *O* is not *F*"? Mere *fiat*
cannot abolish contradiction: "*O* is not *F*" contradicts "*O* is *F*",
whatever Protagoras may choose to ordain.'

It is an elementary truth that not every pair of sentences of the
form '*O* is *F*' and '*O* is not *F*' express contradictory propositions. Of
the many exceptions one is peculiarly apposite here: I may say 'The
Marx Brothers make me laugh'; you may say, 'The Marx Brothers do
not make me laugh'. In a loose sense you have contradicted me; but
the loose sense of 'contradict' is not the technical logical one: the
truth of what you say is not incompatible with the truth of what I say.
The reason for the compatibility is plain: in my sentence, 'me' refers

to me; in yours, 'me' refers to you; we are talking about different people, not saying opposing things about one man.

Let us call 'subjective' any sentences containing a word which refers to whoever utters the sentence and whose reference therefore varies from one utterance of the sentence to another. ('I', 'me', 'the speaker', etc. will make sentences subjective in this sense.) And let non-subjective sentences be called 'objective'. Consider, now, the sentence: 'The Marx Brothers are funny'. That is an objective sentence, none of its words refers to whoever utters it. (If the Marx Brothers chorus it, 'the Marx Brothers' refers to the sentence's utterers; but 'the Marx Brothers' does not refer to whoever utters the sentence.) But it is not wildly implausible to suggest that '. . . is funny' means '. . . amuses me'; so that 'The Marx Brothers are funny' is synonymous with the subjective sentence: 'The Marx Brothers amuse me'. If an objective sentence has a subjective synonym, I call it crypto-subjective. English contains many crypto-subjective sentences: 'Condor Flake is nauseating' (it makes me sick); 'Aristotle is fascinating' (he interests me); 'Rock-climbing is terrifying' (it frightens me); 'Irish politics are boring' (I find them tedious).

Many philosophers claim that crypto-subjective sentences are more common than we like to believe. Ethics provides the most familiar case: '. . . is good' has been analysed as '. . . is approved of by me', '. . . excites moral feelings in my breast', and so on. Protagoras, I think, was the first philosopher to plough that furrow, and he ploughed it deep. He suggested that *all* objective predications are in fact crypto-subjective: every sentence of the form 'O is F' is synonymous with some relational sentence 'O is R to S', where 'S' refers to whoever utters 'O is R to S'.

That is an ancient interpretation: Sextus says that Protagoras 'introduces the relative (*to pros ti*)' (**A** 14), adding that this is because 'he posits only what seems to each person' (*ibid.*). Again: 'everything which *phainetai* or *dokei* to anyone thereby is so—*relative to him*' (*ad* **B** 1). And the interpretation is Plato's: 'as each thing seems to me, so it is *for me*' (*Theaetetus* 151E = **B** 1).

I suggested that, according to Protagoras, 'O is F' is synonymous with 'O is R to S'. Plato's words suggest a more specific formulation: 'O is F' is synonymous with 'O is F for S': 'the wind is cold' means 'the wind is cold for the speaker'. Plato's formulation has one great advantage: it enables us to provide, in any given case, the overtly subjective counterpart of a crypto-subjective judgment. It has one disadvantage: 'Cold for me', 'funny for me' and the like are artificial and unnatural predicates. The disadvantage is easily overcome: 'The

Marx Brothers amuse me' can be replaced without change of sense by, say, 'The Marx Brothers are funny to my way of thinking' or 'I find the Marx Brothers funny'. We may reasonably take 'the Marx Brothers are funny' to be elliptical for one of those synonyms of 'The Marx Brothers amuse me'; and the artificial sentence 'The Marx Brothers are funny for me' is an intelligible, if inelegant, way of expressing the thought captured by those natural synonyms.

The generalization is plain: every apparently objective predicate 'F' is to be taken as elliptical for 'F to——'s way of thinking' or 'F for——'. Protagoras suggests that 'O is F' always means 'O is F for S'.

How does that suggestion, which I shall call the Relativity Thesis, bear upon the other Protagorean theories I have endeavoured to express? First, Equipollence: that Principle maintains that any apparently objective predication is precisely as well or as badly supported as its negation. Protagoras should, I think, say this: for any sentence 'O is F', there are judges a and b such that a has just as good grounds for judging that O is F as b has for judging that O is not F. Hence we must be prepared to countenance 'O is F and O is not F'. The thesis that Contradiction is Impossible now relieves the discomfort of that conclusion: 'O is F' does not contradict 'O is not F'; for contradiction is impossible. The Relativity Thesis then explains the impossibility of contradiction: 'O is F' expresses the fact that O is F for a, and 'O is not F' expresses the compatible fact that O is not F for b.

Finally, that happy result not only frees the *Homomensurasatz* from the taint of contradiction, but actually provides it with a proof. For suppose that someone judges that O is F; say:

(1) a judges that O is F.

By the Relativity Thesis, that amounts to:

(2) a judges that O is F for S.

Now since in the present case S is a, we may express (2) by:

(3) a judges that O is F for a;

or in other words:

(4) a judges that O is F in a's judgment.

Now from (4) we can surely infer:

(5) O is F in a's judgment,

for how could a possibly misjudge the contents of his own judgments? But (5) expresses the content of the judgment ascribed to a by (1). Hence we infer:

(6) If a judges that O is F, then a judges truly.

Finally, generalizing, we get:

(H3) For any proposition P and man x: if x judges that P, then x judges truly.

And that is a version of the *Homomensurasatz*. (The differences between (H1), (H2), and (H3) are not entirely trivial; but there is not space to explore them adequately.)

Such is Protagoras' epistemology: surprisingly little of it is known to us at first-hand, and the second-hand doxography is thin: *Truth*, despite the extrinsic interest Plato bestowed on it, was destined to almost total oblivion. Yet the few remains allow us, I think, to reconstruct an original concatenation of thoughts. Protagoras was an epistemologist of some ingenuity. Keen to categorize, scholars have assigned to him a variety of modern isms: the ascriptions are not anachronistic in any vicious sense; but neither are they particularly illuminating. Protagoras was certainly a relativist, a subjectivist and an idealist; equally, he was not a sceptic in the philosophical sense, and to that extent can be called an objectivist. But those labels are old, tired, and multivocal; we shall grasp Protagoras' ideas by studying his four central contentions: the Principle of Equipollence, the thesis that Contradiction is Impossible, the Relativity Thesis, the *Homomensurasatz*; labelling those doctrines as isms may be a helpful (or a misleading) mnemonic device—it is nothing more.

Protagoras' epistemology is a *tour de force*: is that all? It seems to me plausible to represent it as an attempt to come to grips with the rigorous requirements of empiricism. From this point of view, the Relativity Thesis is of fundamental importance: if, as common sense seems to suggest, all our concepts are ultimately taken from experience and all our judgments are ultimately based upon experience, then some relativity may seem inevitable; for the experience on which *my* knowledge rests can only be *my* experience. If my cognitive beginnings are tied to my own experiences, how can I ever escape from myself? And if I cannot escape from myself, is not Protagoreanism the only possible epistemology? My complex judgments are only functions of my primitive judgments; and my primitive judgments are reports of my own experiences. If I say, primitively, 'the wind is cold' or 'the grass is green' or 'the tobacco is tart', my sentences have an objective air; but since those primitive reports report my experiences they are crypto-subjective; they say how things are *for me*.

Modern empiricists start from the self-centred position; and a constant item in empiricist thought has been the attempt to found genuinely objective judgments on these subjective foundations. Protagoras did not make the attempt; instead he trod the lonely path of idealism, and it led him to an idiosyncratic epistemology. It would be idle to pretend that his views constitute a full and clear version of extreme empiricism; and inane to urge that they give a competent and satisfactory account of human knowledge. But I am more concerned to applaud Protagoras for trying than to hiss him for his failings; and in any event, a serious assessment of Protagoreanism would require a lengthy study of the foundations of knowledge. In order to compensate a little for my cowardly refusal to offer such an assessment, I shall end by looking again at the Democritean *peritropê*: after all, the *peritropê* is an ingenious objection; and if it works, Protagoras' main thesis is shown up as logically intolerable.

The relevant portion of text 494 reads thus: '. . . if every *phantasia* is true, then even the proposition that not every *phantasia* is true . . . will be true; and thus it will turn out false that every *phantasia* is true.' Assume that (H3) is true. Now it is indisputable that:

(7) Some men have judged that *H* is false.

From (H3) we infer:

(8) If anyone judges that *H* is false, he judges truly.

And from (7) and (8) it surely follows that:

(9) *H* is false.

Thus if (H3) is true, it is false; and therefore—by the Lex Clavia (vol. 1, p. 277)–(H3) is false. The *peritropê* or about-turn is a species of self-refutation.

How does that argument fare? I shall not consider it in any detail; rather, I shall simply list three lines of argument which any defender of Protagoras might expect to develop. I do not know if any of the lines is successful; but I think that each is worth exploration.

First, then, Protagoras might simply deny the applicability of the *peritropê*: its use involves an *ignoratio elenchi*. For (he might say) sentence (H3) is not an adequate representation of the *Homomensurasatz*: it ignores the fact, plainly set down in (H2), that *H* is a thesis about objects and properties, about judgments of the form '*O* is *F*'. Now *H* itself is patently not of the form '*O* is *F*', and neither is the negation of *H*. The sentence '*H* is false', which appears as a component of (7), does indeed appear to be of the required form; but a short course of reading in modern philosophy will convince any Protagorean that that appearance is deceptive. '*H* is false' does not predicate anything of *H*; it is simply a ponderous way of expressing the negation of *H*. And since the negation of *H* is not of the form '*O* is *F*', neither is '*H* is false'. Thus *H* does not refute itself; for it is a thesis about propositions of the type '*O* is *F*', a type to which it does not itself belong.

Second, Protagoras might question the inference from (7) and (8) to (9). The inference certainly seems to be valid; for if *a* judges that *P*, and *a* judges truly, it surely follows that *P*. To say that he judges truly is simply to say that what he judges is true, i.e. that *P* is true; and if we can infer 'P is true', we can surely infer the simpler 'P'? Now all that is, I think, almost indisputable, given our ordinary understanding of true judgment. But it is not clear that Protagoras will, or ought to, grant us that ordinary understanding. (Suppose that a judges truly that O is F: can I infer that O is F? No, given the Relativity Thesis; for if I infer that O is F, I judge that O is F *for me*; and that conclusion cannot be warranted by the premiss that a judges truly that O is F.)

Third, Protagoras might allow that (9) is indeed validly inferred from (H3); but he might question the significance of the inference for H. After all, he will suggest, the predicate '. . . is false', like any other objective predicate, is crypto-subjective; and (9), the conclusion of the *peritropê*, is of course elliptical for:

(10) H is false for S.

Falsity—and truth—is, like everything else, a relative and subjective manner. No doubt H is false for some men. But that hardly refutes H; for H remains true; true, that is to say, for other men; and in particular, true for Protagoras. 'But then *nothing* can be refuted, and all judgments are equally true or false.'—'Not exactly: some judgments may have more backers than others, and be truer; and some judgments may have a far better property than truth: they may be advantageous to believe.'

(d) *'Isonomia'*

According to Plutarch, Democritus attacked Protagoras' epistemological stance (**68 B 156**); and we know that he applauded Anaxagoras' empiricist aphorism (Diotimus, **76 A 3**). Yet the fragmentary reports of his attitude to human knowledge, its scope and limits, indicate both that he developed the Protagorean Principle of Equipollence, and also that he toyed with a Pyrrhonian scepticism. Democritus' epistemology is perplexing, paradoxical, and perhaps inconsistent; and Democritus himself was ruefully aware of the fact (**B 125**). Our evidence is, again, a tangled skein; and I do not know how best to unravel it. But here at least there is reason to think that the tangles are original, and not due to the accidents of history.

I begin with what I have called the *Ou Mallon* Principle (it was later called the Principle of *Isonomia*, or Balance).[12] '*Mallon . . . ê . . .*' means 'Rather . . . than . . .'; and '*ou*' (for which '*mê*', '*ouden*', and '*mêden*' are common substitutes) is simply the negation sign. Thus '*Ou mallon P ê Q*' means 'Not rather P than Q'. Properly speaking, 'Not rather P than Q' is compatible with 'Q rather than P'; but in Greek idiom *ou mallon* appears to ascribe an equal status to P and to Q, so that '*ou mallon P ê Q*' marks a sort of indifference, equipollence, or equivalence between P and Q.

According to Sextus, '*ou mallon*' was a constant refrain (*epiphthegma*) in the Abderite song (*Pyrr Hyp* I.213). And we have already heard the refrain thrice. First, in **238** (above, p. 61):

If the region outside the heavens is unlimited, so too, it seems, are body and the worlds; for why should it be here rather than here (*entautha mallon ê entautha*) in the void?

Second, in **236** (above, p. 59):

. . . the unlimited quantity of the shapes among [the atoms] because nothing is rather such than such (*ouden mallon toiouton ê toiouton*).

And third, in **297** (above, p. 100):

The thing exists no more than (*ou mallon*) the nothing.

The first argument is ascribed to Democritus. The second is given to Leucippus in **236**; but Simplicius attributes it to Democritus too (**68 A 38**). **297** is a Democritean fragment: its argument is given to Leucippus by Aristotle (*Met* 985b8 = **67 A 6**) and by Simplicius (**67 A 7**).

Aristotle reports a fourth occurrence of the refrain. Our senses, he observes, are at odds with one another in a variety of familiar ways; and the variations in our sense experience may well lead us to conclude that

which of them is true or false is unclear; for the ones are no more (*ouden mallon*) true than the others but to a similar degree; that is why Democritus says that either none is true or it is unclear to us (**501**: *Met* 1009b9–12 = **68 A 112**).

Nausiphanes, pupil of Democritus and teacher of Epicurus, said much the same:

Of the things which seem to be, none is rather than is not (**502**: Seneca, **75 B 4**).

Seneca's Latin phrase '*nihil magis*' translates the Greek '*ouden mallon*'.

That last application of the *Ou Mallon* Principle perhaps suggests an epistemological interpretation of the 'equivalence' involved in *ou mallon*. One perceptual judgment is 'no more true' than another just in so far as the *evidence* for each judgment is equally good; '*ou mallon P ê Q*' will be true, then, just in case any evidence in favour of

P is matched by evidence in favour of Q, and vice versa. Let us abbreviate '*ou mallon P ê Q*' to '$E(P, Q)$', where 'E' may be imagined to stand for 'equivalent' or 'equipollent'. Then Protagoras' Principle of Equipollence can be written compendiously as:

(1) For any proposition P, $E(P, \text{not-}P)$.

And in **501** and **502** we may discern a restricted version of (1). If S is any sensible property (redness, roughness, roundness), then Democritus and Nausiphanes hold:

(2) For any object x, $E(x$ has S, x does not have $S)$.

Consider Protagoras' sentence, 'The wind is cold'. Democritus, I imagine, thought that the only evidence I could have for the truth of that sentence must consist in the fact that the wind seems cold to me or makes me shiver. But what seems cold to me, seems warm to you; so my evidence for thinking that the wind is cold is balanced by your evidence for asserting that it is not. Hence E (the wind is cold, the wind is not cold). I ignore the incautious assumptions made in that argument in order to concentrate on its logical form. Let $R(P)$ abbreviate 'there is sufficient evidence to believe that P'; and let 'P' here stand for 'the wind is cold'. Then my shivering testimony gives Democritus:

(3) $R(P)$,

and your stoical report allows him to hold:

(4) $E(P, \text{not-}P)$.

But it seems to be true that:

(5) It is impossible that both P and not-P:

Now that triad of propositions, (3)–(5), is not formally inconsistent; but an inconsistency can be derived if it is enlarged by two additions:

(6) If $R(P)$ and $R(Q)$, then $R(P$ and $Q)$.

(7) If it is impossible that P, then not-$R(P)$.

For (3) and (4) yield:

(8) $R(\text{not-}P)$.

And (3), (8) and (6) give;

(9) $R(P$ and not-$P)$.

But (5) and (7) give:

(10) not-$R(P$ and not-$P)$.

That schematic argument represents the background both to Protagoras and to Democritus: both men accepted (4); and they would doubtless have accepted (6) and (7). (6) is evidently true; (7) is, I think, false as it stands; for we can have sufficient reason for believing false mathematical propositions. But some suitable modification of (7) will surmount that difficulty: we surely cannot have sufficient reason to believe overt impossibilities. Protagoras, accepting (3), rejected (5) and safeguarded his reputation for consistency by reinterpreting '*P*' by way of his Relativity Thesis. What did Democritus do?

According to Aristotle, 'he says that either none is true or it is unclear to us' (**501**). Did Democritus give that disjunctive conclusion, or did he rather plump for one of the disjuncts? Some scholars argue as follows: 'Presumably Democritus holds that not both *P* and not-*P*; for he will not reject (5) and the Principle of Contradiction. Consequently, he must either reject both *P* and not-*P*, or else come to the sceptical conclusion that we cannot tell which of *P* and not-*P* is true. Now Democritus cannot have been prepared to countenance "neither *P* nor not-*P*" but not "both *P* and not-*P*"; for those two propositions are logically equivalent. And it is charitable to infer that Democritus in fact mentioned the first of Aristotle's disjuncts only as an evident impossibility, and intended to commit himself to the second, sceptical disjunct.'[13]

If that is true, it is strange. According to Sextus,

> [Protagoras] says that the explanations (*logoi*) of all the
> appearances lie in the matter, so that the matter is capable in itself
> of being everything which it seems to anyone (**503: 80 A 14**).

Sextus' account is an implausible interpretation rather than a report; but the account might well have been given by Democritus. For according to the Atomists,

> The truth is in the appearing (**504**: Aristotle, *GC* 315b8 =
> **67 A 9**).[14]

That is to say, all the diverse phenomena are explicable in terms of the atomic structure of matter: their *logoi* 'lie in the matter'. Thus if the wind feels cold to me, that is because certain constituents in the air react in certain ways with some of my constituent atoms; and its feeling warm to you is explained by the different reaction that occurs between the air's atoms and yours. Protagoras accepts (5) and gives a relativistic interpretation to 'cold'. We might expect Democritus to have done exactly the same: temperature is not an intrinsic property of atoms or atomic conglomerates, and *P*, scientifically construed, is after all compatible with not-*P*.

Perhaps, then, Democritus does want to conclude that 'none is true', that neither *P* nor not-*P*. The grass looks green to you, brown to me: which colour is it really? Neither: for colours exist only *nomôi*, nothing is intrinsically coloured. The wine tastes corked to me, clear to you: it is neither, for savours exist *nomôi*. But not all qualities exist only *nomôi*: shape is real; and so are size and motion. If the wind seems a light breeze to you and a gale to me, at most one of us can be right; for the wind, or the atomic conglomerate which forms it, really does have an intrinsic velocity.

I conclude that Aristotle means what he says: Democritus asserted a disjunction: 'Either both P and not-P are false (if P involves a *nomôi* quality),[15] or else we cannot know which, if either, of P and not-P is true (if P involves an *eteêi* quality).' Thus Democritus differs from Protagoras at two points: first, he admits scepticism in certain cases;[16] second, he refuses to relativize sensible qualities.[17] The former difference is more significant than the latter.

The details of that argument should not obscure its essential structure: whatever may be thought about Democritus' attitude to sensible qualities, his use of the *Ou Mallon* Principle displays a subtle and conscious appreciation of a central feature of the notion of rational belief: if $E\ (P,\ Q)$, then it is unreasonable to accept one and reject the other of P and Q.

So far, '*ou mallon*' has shown itself as a destructive weapon. Its more interesting applications are constructive; and I shall now turn to them. Suppose that for some pair of propositions, P and Q, we have:

(11) $R\ (P)$.

(12) $E\ (P,\ Q,)$.

(13) Possibly both P and Q.

That triad threatens no inconsistency; and indeed, given (11), we should believe that P; and given (12), that Q. Consider, then, the application of *ou mallon* to the problem of atomic shapes. There is an infinity of possible shapes, S_1, S_2, ... Let P_i represent the proposition that there are atoms of shape S_i; then the infinite conjunction of the P_is is a logical possibility. But we have (let us grant) sufficient reason to believe that there are atoms; and since every atom has some shape, we have reason to believe that there are atoms of some shape. But we have no reason to believe in, say, spherical atoms rather than in, say, cubic atoms; hence all the P_is are rationally on a par; hence we have reason to believe that there are atoms of every shape.

The argument is confused. The Abderites need the following two premisses:

(14) There is some atomic shape, S_i, such that $R\ (P_i)$.

(15) $E\ (P_1,\ P_2,\ .\ .\ .)$.

But they have not established a title to (14); for the argument I assigned to them yields only:

(16) R (there is some shape S_i, such that P_i).

But (16) does not imply (14). Indeed, the Atomists have no reason for believing in atoms of any particular shape; they may be saddled with the contradictory of (14), viz.:

(17) For no atomic shape, S_i, R (P_i).

And even though (17) yields (15), that will not, so far as I can see, give them their desired conclusion, that there are atoms of every shape.

The second constructive use of *ou mallon* fares no better. Let 'P' now represent 'there are atoms'; 'Q', 'there is void'. And suppose (what again was not uncontroversial) that (13) is true. The Abderites then require both (12) and also either R (P) or R (Q). No doubt they claimed R (P). Yet how are they entitled to E (P, Q)? No Atomist text gives any grounds for holding E (P, Q), nor can I invent any.

Perhaps this interpretation construes *ou mallon* in too narrowly epistemological a fashion: a broader interpretation may be thought to serve the two positive applications better. First, let 'E (P, Q)' represent not epistemological, but what we might call nomological equivalence: 'Necessarily, P if and only if Q'. Then it might seem that the existence of atoms and the existence of void are mutually implicative; there cannot physically be atoms unless there is void, and vice versa. Thus 'E (P, Q)' yields 'if P, necessarily Q'; and that, with R (P), does lead to R (Q). The inference is, I think, again a valid one; but again I do not think that the Atomists are entitled to E (P, Q). Nor will this version of *ou mallon* apply to the case of atomic shapes.

Second, let 'E (P, Q)' embrace what I may call explanatory equivalence: 'For any R, P because R if and only if Q because R'. Consider again the atomic shapes. We have granted the Atomists' proposition (16). Now a generous interpretation of text **309** (Leucippus, **67 B 2**), will give us:

(18) For any proposition P: if P, then there is some proposition Q such that P because Q.

We may now infer to:

(19) R (there is some Q, and some atomic shape S_i, such that P_i because Q).

And then, given (15) and the explanatory reading of 'E', we may conclude to:

(20) R (for any atomic shape S_i, P_i).

It is reasonable to believe in an infinity of atomic shapes.

The inferential apparatus here is interestingly complex; and I am inclined to think that it is valid. But, again, E $(P_1, P_2, \ldots)$ still seems a groundless hypothesis: why on earth suppose that all atomic shapes are explanatorily equivalent? Plato would urge that some shapes are physically and theologically superior to others; a modern atomist, if he allowed his atoms shape at all, would prefer a single atomic shape, and probably deny the need to explain why that shape alone should exist.

I shall not pursue these matters further. In conclusion, I say first, that the epistemological *Ou Mallon* Principle is a sound and important principle of reasoning; second, that certain other *Ou Mallon* Principles, which the Atomists may possibly have confused with it, are equally interesting, though more in need of elucidation; and thirdly, that the few verses of the *ou mallon* song which we possess are less melodious than the refrain which punctuated them.

(e) *Democritean scepticism*

Metrodorus of Chios, a pupil of Democritus (e.g., Clement, **70 A 1**) who held solidly to the main tenets of atomism (e.g., Theophrastus, **A 3**), purveys an extreme scepticism which foreshadows, in its ingenious comprehensiveness, the most extravagant claims of Pyrrho: at the beginning of his book *Concerning Nature* Metrodorus said:

> None of us knows anything, not even that very fact whether we
> know or do not know; nor do we know what not to know and to
> know are, nor, in general, whether anything is or is not
> (**505: B 1**).[18]

Of Metrodorus' book little else survives and nothing tells us what his scepticism rested upon, or why he wrote *Concerning Nature* at all. His scepticism, however, like his atomism, was inherited. For according to Democritus,

> In reality (*eteêi*) we know nothing; for truth is in a pit (**506:**
> **68 B 117**).

Our main source for Democritus' scepticism is Sextus; and I quote the chief Democritean fragments in their Sextan setting:

> Democritus sometimes does away with what appears to the
> senses. . . . In the *Cratunteria*, though he had promised to ascribe
> the power of conviction to the senses, he is none the less found
> condemning them; for he says:
> > We in actuality grasp nothing firm, but what changes
> > (*metapipton*) in accordance with the contact (*diathigên**)[19]
> > between our body and the things which enter into it and the
> > things which strike against it [= **B 9**].
> And again he says:
> > Now that in reality (*eteêi*) we do not grasp of what sort each
> > thing is or is not, has been made clear in many ways [= **B 10**].

And in *Concerning Forms* he says:

A man must know by this rule that he is separated from reality (*eteê*) [= **B 6**].

And again:

This argument too makes it clear that in reality (*eteêi*) we know nothing about anything; but belief (*doxis*) for each group of men is a reshaping (*epirhusmiê*) [= **B 7**].

And again:

Yet it will be clear that to know what sort each thing is in reality (*eteêi*) is inaccessible [= **B 8**].

In those passages he pretty well destroys apprehension in its entirety, even if he explicitly attacks only the senses. But in the *Canons* he says that there are two kinds of knowing (*gnôseis*), one via the senses, one via the intellect (*dianoia*); he calls the one via the intellect 'legitimate (*gnêsiê*)', ascribing to it reliability for the judgment of truth, and he names that via the senses 'bastard (*skotiê*)', denying it inerrancy in the discrimination of what is true. These are his words:

Of knowledge (*gnômê*) there are two forms, the one legitimate, the other bastard; and to the bastard belong all these: sight, hearing, smell, taste, touch. And the other is legitimate, and separated from that.

Then, preferring the legitimate to the bastard, he continues:

When the bastard can no longer see anything smaller, or hear, or smell, or taste, or perceive by touch, † but more fine † [= **B 11**].

Thus according to him too, reason, which he calls legitimate knowledge, is a criterion (**507**: *adv Math* VII. 135–9).

Fragments **B 7** and **B 10** show that Democritus' scepticism was not merely a glum asseveration of intellectual impotence, but the melancholy conclusion of a set of arguments. Two of Democritus' arguments can, I think, be reconstructed.

First, there is *doxis epirhusmiê* of **B 7**. I suppose that '*doxis epirhusmiê*' means 'belief is a rearrangement of our constituent atoms', i.e. 'coming to believe that *P* is having certain parts (e.g., cerebral parts) of one's atomic substructure rearranged' (cf. Theophrastus, *Sens* §58 = **A 135**).[20] Belief, then, cannot ever amount to knowledge, because it is never anything more than an atomic rearrangement. I guess that Democritus is supposing, if only tacitly, that knowledge is essentially reasoned belief: opinion not arrived at by rational considerations cannot qualify as knowledge. But if every belief is simply a cerebral alteration (caused, no doubt, by our changing relation with other atomic conglomerates), then no belief can be rational. To put it crudely, causally determined cerebral mutations cannot be identical with rationally accepted beliefs.

The argument has connexions with Xenophanes (vol. 1, p. 142); but it is less subtle and less persuasive than Xenophanes' argument. According to Xenophanes, certain types of causal chain prevent a caused belief from counting as knowledge; according to Democritus, any belief, being the physical result of a causal chain, is disqualified from knowledge. Democritus, I think, is simply wrong: my belief that P may constitute knowledge even if it is itself a physical state (a state of my nervous system) and even if it stands at the end of a causal chain (as surely it does). Roughly speaking, the belief is knowledge if the physical state which embodies it was caused, mediately or immediately by the fact that P (i.e., if it is true that because P I believe that P); and the belief is rational if the physical state which embodies it was caused by certain other beliefs (i.e., if because I believe that Q I believe that P, where Q in fact gives good grounds for P). If a causal theory of knowledge can be worked out in detail, then Democritus' argument for scepticism in **B 7** must be rejected.

Second, there is **B 9**. Sextus evidently thinks that Democritus means 'perceive' by 'grasp (*sunienai*)'; and he may be right. But Democritus is not simply 'condemning' the senses: he is offering an argument. The point, I think, is this: cognitive processes are interactions between observers and objects of observation; the processes, atomically construed, consist in the impingement of atoms from the object on the body of the observer. Now any such process involves a change in the object; for it loses at least those atoms which impinge upon the observer. Consequently, we can never know the state of any object; for any attempt to discover it thereby changes it. We grasp nothing 'firm'; for our very grip disturbs. Knowledge alters the known; and therefore knowledge is impossible.

According to modern physical theory, we discover the position and characteristics of an object by way of some physical interaction with it: in the simplest case, I see where the cat is by shining a torch on it and receiving the reflected rays. What goes for cats goes for sub-atomic particles; to tell where a particle is I must fire a ray at it and receive it on the rebound. But sub-atomic particles are delicate things, and when a ray hits them they are shaken; thus the reflected ray will not give me the information I want. It cannot tell me where the particle is and how it is travelling; for the impact, without which I can know nothing of the particle, will change the particle's trajectory. (That is meant as a kindergarten version of the reasoning behind Heisenberg's Indeterminacy Principle; science for the infant is usually bad science,

259

but I hope that the point of my parallel is not wholly blunted by my puerile exposition.)

Atomic structures cannot be known; for the process of acquiring knowledge necessarily distorts those structures. The quest for knowledge is like the search for the end of the rainbow: we can never discover the pot of gold; for our journey towards the rainbow's end in itself moves the rainbow to a different and ever distant location.

The argument that I have dredged from **B 9** is not *a priori*: it depends on Democritean physics and psychology. I guess that it may present a plausible deduction from those Atomist theories, though I doubt if there is enough evidence for us to test its validity. In any case, there is no philosophical way of attacking it: it fails if the physics and psychology are false (and I assume that they are).

> Metrodorus of Chios said that no one knows anything: the things we believe we know we do not strictly (*akribôs*) know; nor should we attend to our senses. For everything is by belief (**508**: Epiphanius, **70 A 23**).

Leucippus insists that we have belief, but no more (Epiphanius, **67 A 33**); and in many of the fragments I have quoted, Democritus denies that we have genuine knowledge. Many sceptical philosophers seem to be making what is little more than a verbal point: we do not, strictly speaking, *know* anything, but we can, of course, have reasonable beliefs. Such thinkers set the canons of knowledge artificially high: knowledge must be certain, or infallible, or necessary, or indubitable, or whatever. If the canons are set high, then knowledge is indeed beyond us; but ordinary men are quite happy with relaxed canons, and those sceptics who allow reasonable belief in fact allow precisely the thing that ordinary men call knowledge.

The Atomists, however, do not even allow reasonable belief: their arguments against knowledge, in so far as we know them, are equally arguments against reasonable belief. We have beliefs: that is an incontestable empirical fact. Our beliefs do not amount to knowledge: that is the argument of the Abderites. Yet our beliefs are not even reasonable: being atomically caused, they are not founded on reason; and the physics of the cognitive processes assures us that no impressions of external reality are accurate. If there is no room for knowledge, by the same token there is no room for reasoned belief: 'everything is by belief'—but that, far from being a consolation, is only a cause for despair. The urbane scepticism of Locke allows a decent wattage to the human candle: our light extends as far as we need, but not as far as we like to boast. Abderite scepticism is Pyrrhonian: the light of the mind is an *ignis fatuus*.

That conclusion did not please Democritus; indeed, as Sextus observes, his fragments do not exhibit consistency. Fragment **B 11** tails off into corruption; but the general sense of Democritus' remarks is clear enough: 'the bastard way of knowing (*skotiê gnôsis*)' will not carry us to the finest or ultimate constituents of stuff; for that, 'the legitimate way of knowing (*gnêsiê gnôsis*)' is needed. That coheres with Democritus' approval of the Anaxagorean slogan: *opsis tôn adêlôn ta phainomena*—what the senses cannot apprehend must be grasped by the intellect. There seems, then, to be an empiricist Democritus rising in revolt against the sceptic.

And perhaps the sceptical fragments have been misread: the Heisenbergian argument, after all, at most shows that we cannot directly apprehend the atomic elements of things; it does not show that we may make no inferences from perceptible things to their elemental structure. **B 9** and **B 10** consistently say that we cannot 'grasp' things in their reality; but that only means that atoms are not open to perceptual knowledge.[21] Thus we may find a positive epistemology for Democritus: 'All knowledge rests on perception: and perception will not, directly, yield knowledge of what exists *eteêi*. But by perception we may come to know about what is *nomôi*, and intellectual attention to those sensual pronouncements will enable us to procure an inferential knowledge of genuine reality.'

Alas, that happy picture is mistaken. The *doxis epirhusmiê* argument is resolutely sceptical; and **B 6**, **B 7**, **B 8**, and **B 117** leave no room for any knowledge at all. Moreover, Democritus recognized that the empiricist intimations of **B 11** were misleading:

> Having slandered the phenomena . . . he makes the senses address the intellect thus: 'Wretched mind! Do you take your evidence from us and then overthrow us? Our overthrow is your downfall' (**509: B 125**).

In a puckish mood, Russell once observed that naive realism leads us to accept the assertions of modern science; and that modern science then proves realism false. Realism is false if it is true; hence it is false. And if science rests on realism, then it is built upon sand. The parallel with Democritus is plain: the observations of the senses give us a set of facts upon which an atomistic science is reared; the science then proves the irrationality of all belief and the unreliability of the senses. If the senses are to be trusted, they are not to be trusted; hence they are not to be trusted. And if atomism rests upon the senses, then atomism is ill founded.

Did the mind answer the senses? Had Democritus any solution to the problem which **509** candidly poses? There is no evidence that he had; and I am inclined to think that he had not. It is, I suppose, a tribute to Democritus' honesty that he acknowledged his plight; but it derogates somewhat from his philosophical reputation that he made no move to escape from the *impasse* he found himself in.

EPILOGUE

XI

The Last of the Line

(a) Diogenes the eclectic

Diogenes of Apollonia was no great original. He was a medical man whose views appear to have had some considerable influence on his contemporaries and successors; and Aristotle has preserved for us his detailed account of the human blood vessels (64 B 6; cf. B 9). Like earlier doctors, he engaged in natural philosophy, writing, by his own account, a work *Concerning Nature*, a *Meteorology*, a treatise *On the Nature of Man*, and a book, *Against the Sophists* (Simplicius, A 4).[1] The philosophy he expounded was conceived on the old Ionian pattern; and Theophrastus held him to be the last of the *phusiologoi* (Simplicius, A 5). By common scholarly consent, he was least as well as last: he worked eclectically rather than creatively, and 'does not seem to have attempted original thought'; indeed, he represents a positive regression, for his 'general level of philosophical awareness suggests the age of Anaximenes, not that of Anaxagoras and the sophists'.[2]

A few voices have spoken for Diogenes: he was affected by Heraclitus, a pupil of Leucippus and Anaxagoras, and a significant influence on Melissus—in short, a man of some historical importance. Or he was a teleologist, and indeed the inventor of teleological explanation; or else, *pace* Aristotle, he was the first 'material monist'. But those voices do not convince. Chronologically, the first suggestion is implausible; Anaxagoras was a teleologist before ever Diogenes wrote; and the Milesians were, as Aristotle says, material monists. In the last quarter of the fifth century Diogenes appears to have stood in Athenian estimation as the very type and paradigm of Ionian *phusiologia*: he is a common butt of comedy and he had an influence on Euripidean tragedy.[3] Such a reputation

265

implies not stature and novelty but rather the reverse; it is unoriginal men who are thus representative.

Three reasons, I think, justify the expense of a few pages on this essentially second-rate man: first, though aware of Eleatic arguments he remained a material monist, evidently thinking that the pluralistic accounts of his fellow neo-Ionians were not necessary to evade the Eleatic snares; second, we know far more of him than of the Milesian monists, and in his fragments we find arguments which have not come down to us under any earlier name; third, our knowledge of his teleology is much fuller than our knowledge of Anaxagoras' earlier theory. If the man was a bore, his fragments (partly for accidental and extrinsic reasons) still command interest.

Diogenes was aware of Eleatic metaphysics, and defended an old Milesian monism in its face. The evidence for the first part of that statement is in fact thin, though it will hardly be imagined that a *phusiologos* writing at the end of the fifth century could have been unaware of Parmenides' writings. Diogenes Laertius reports:

> He held that . . . nothing comes into being from what does not exist, nor perishes into what does not exist (**510**: IX.57 = **A 1**).

The report is perfunctory and formulaic, but there is no reason to doubt its accuracy, or to reject the obvious suggestion that it states an acceptance of the Eleatic position on generation and corruption.

Diogenes' adherence to a Milesian monism is attested in his own words. *Concerning Nature* began, according to Diogenes Laertius, thus:

> When beginning any account, one must, it seems to me, provide an indisputable starting point (*archê*) and write in a simple and noble style (**511: B 1**).

It is not, perhaps, entirely fanciful to see a serious methodological point here: in the second half of the fifth century, the Greek geometers had been developing an axiomatic way of presenting their study; and Diogenes, in requiring an 'indisputable starting point', is, I imagine, striving to imitate the geometers and to found something like an axiomatized physics. But it would be foolish to lay much weight on that; and my present interest is in the content of Diogenes' *archê*. 'Immediately after the preface', Simplicius says, 'he writes thus:

> It seems to me, to state it comprehensively, that all existing things change from the same thing and are the same thing (see **515: B 2**).

266

That this is material monism is clear enough; and most of the doxographers identify Diogenes' *Urstoff* as air.

From the *Urstoff* Diogenes developed the world. We have no first-hand fragments; but the doxography supplies the want:

> He says that the nature of the whole is air, unlimited and eternal; and from it, as it is condensed and rarefied and changed in its affections, the form of other things comes into being (512: Simplicius, A 5).

> He makes the cosmos thus: as the whole is moved, and becomes rare here and dense there . . . (513: pseudo-Plutarch, A 6).

Motion of the original stuff introduces variation in density; and those variations account for the different forms that the world assumes. The system is traditional; indeed, it is so far indistinguishable from Anaximenes' cosmogony.

How did Diogenes reconcile an Anaximenean cosmogony with an Eleatic denial of generation?

> The others say that perceptible things are by nature (*phusei*); but Leucippus and Democritus and Diogenes say that they are by convention (*nomôi*), i.e. in opinion (*doxêi*) and in our affections (*pathesi*) (514: Aëtius, A 23).

Aëtius is not the best of authorities; and his testimony is isolated.[4] Yet it can, I think, be supported from B 2. After the general assertion of monism that I have already quoted, Diogenes proceeds thus:

> And that is quite clear; for if the things that now exist in this universe—earth and water and air and fire and the other things which appear (*phainetai*) as existing in this universe—if any of these were different from the others (different in its proper nature) and were not the same as they changed in many ways and altered, they could in no way mingle with one another (see 515: B 2).

The 'proper nature (*idia phusis*)' of any stuff is the same as that of every other stuff; and a proper nature cannot change. Everything is, really, the same; nothing, really, changes. What, then, are the alterations to which 515 refers? Some of them are specified in B 5; speaking of air Diogenes says:

> It is changed in many ways (*polutropos*)—hotter and colder, drier and moister, stabler and having a sharper motion; and there are many other alterations in it, both of taste and of colour, unlimitedly many (see 527).

515 implies that cosmic change is somehow extrinsic to things; the examples of **527** confirm the implication; they are all alterations which can comfortably be construed as relational: if air becomes hotter, that is only to say that it appears differently to us; if the air moves faster, that is only to say that its parts alter their spatial relations to one another. Such changes are extrinsic or relational; they are not intrinsic or real.[5]

Change is a matter of gain and loss: we change by gaining one property and losing another; and a simple-minded definition of change might read thus:

(D) a changes at t if and only if for some ϕ a is not-ϕ before t and a is after t.

But (D), as Plato realized, will not do: if Cebes grows until he overtops Socrates, then according to (D) Socrates, as well as Cebes, has changed; for the predicate 'is shorter than Cebes' comes to be true of him. Cebes, no doubt, has changed; and as a result of Cebes' change a new predicate comes to hold of Socrates. But that is not enough to make us say that Socrates has changed; and definition (D) must be abandoned.

Occurrences which count as changes by (D) but which are not genuine changes have been called Cambridge changes. In the example of Socrates and Cebes, Socrates undergoes a Cambridge change because Cebes suffers a genuine change. But Cambridge change is not always parasitic upon genuine change: if Socrates is alone in his room until Cebes enters, then at the time of Cebes' entry the predicate 'shorter than someone in the room' comes to hold of Socrates. But neither Socrates nor Cebes (nor the room) has changed.

Diogenes, I suggest, wanted us to regard all apparent alterations in the world as Cambridge changes. He adopted the Abderite account of *nomôi* qualities, making them relational and mind-dependent; and he developed that account in an intelligible way. There is reason to think that he borrowed the void from Leucippus (cf. Diogenes Laertius IX.57 = **A 1**); and that the void allowed him locomotion, and condensation and rarefaction. Those operations will explain all apparent changes: yet they do not constitute intrinsic or real change in the *Urstoff*, for they are essentially relational operations. Things alter only in the sense that there are appearances of alteration to be accounted for. Similarly, locomotion, condensation and rarefaction underlie all generation; yet they do not constitute any intrinsic or real generation of things or stuff, for they are essentially relational operations. Things are generated only in the sense that there are appearances of generation to be explained. And the appearances, both of alteration and of generation, can be explained in a way that does no violence to Eleatic logic.

(b) *Monism revived*

Diogenes argued for his monism; he did not merely assert it. I begin by copying out the whole of **B 2**, the first half of which I have already quoted.

> It seems to me, to state it comprehensively, that all existing things change from the same thing and are the same thing. And that is quite clear; for if the things that now exist in this universe—earth and water and air and fire and the other things which appear as existing in this universe—if any of these were different from the others (different in its proper nature) and were not the same as they changed in many ways and altered, they could in no way mingle with one another, nor would advantage and harm come to one from another, nor would plants grow from the earth, nor animals, nor anything else be born, if things were not so put together as to be the same. But all these things, being alterations from the same thing, become different at different times and return to the same thing (**515**).

Theophrastus sums the fragment up in a sentence:

> There would be no acting or being acted upon if everything were not from one thing (**516**: *Sens* §39 = **A 19**).

Material monism is necessary to account for change: if everything is not at bottom one substance, then alteration is not possible. That is, at first blush, an implausible assertion. How can Diogenes have defended it? I offer two interpretations.

First, consider the following reports about Democritus:

> He says that what acts and what is acted upon must be the same or similar; for it is not possible for distinct and different things to be acted upon by one another; but if they *are* distinct and act in some way upon one another, that happens to them not in so far as they are distinct but in so far as some one thing belongs to them both (**517**: Aristotle, *GC* 323b11–15 = **68 A 63**).

> It is impossible, he says, for things which are not the same to be acted upon [by one another]; but if though different they actually act [on one another], they do so not in so far as they are different, but in so far as some one thing belongs to them both (**518**: Theophrastus, *Sens* §49 = **A 135**).

If X and Y interact, then X and Y must be somehow 'the same'. Classical dualism discovered a problem in the interaction between body and soul: how, they wondered, can a corporeal stuff act upon a spiritual, or a spiritual upon a corporeal? Descartes asserted that interaction occurred but was inexplicable. Leibniz allowed that '*the way of influence* [i.e. of interaction] is that of the common philosophy; but as we cannot conceive material particles or immaterial species or qualities which can pass from one of these substances into another, we are obliged to give up this opinion'; and Leibniz advances instead his own theory of the 'pre-established harmony'.[6]

Descartes' difficulty and Leibniz' argument rest upon a specification of the Democritean Principle:

(1) If a acts upon b, then a is of the same stuff as b.

Since soul and body have no stuff in common, soul and body cannot interact. Was this classical application of the Democritean principle also its original application? The Abderite world is homogeneous— all agents are indifferent atoms; but the neo-Ionian world of Anaxagoras is not. In Anaxagorean physics, mind is the supreme agent, and mind is distinct in nature from all other stuffs. I wonder if Democritus had Anaxagoras in his sights when he formulated principle (1).

However that may be, the first interpretation of **515** bases monism on the Democritean Principle. In addition to that Principle, Diogenes needs a premiss to the effect that all things interact with one another. That premiss requires a precise statement. Let us say that a interacts with b if either a acts upon b or b acts upon a; and let us say that a is linked to b if there is some ordered set of objects, $\langle c_1, c_2, \ldots, c_{n|} \rangle$, such that a interacts with c_1, c_1 interacts with c_2, $\ldots$, c_n interacts with b. Then Diogenes' premiss is:

(2) For any objects x and y, either x interacts with y or x is linked to y.

From (1) and (2) we can readily infer monism. Take any two objects, a and b. By (2) either a and b interact or they are linked. If they interact, then by (1) they are of the same stuff; if they are linked, then a is of the same stuff as c_1, c_1 as c_2, $\ldots$, c_n as b; so that, again, a is of the same stuff as b. Generalize the argument, and you have material monism.

Assumption (2) is, I think, a highly plausible hypothesis. Diogenes' argument fails if the Democritean principle is false. And although that principle has been immensely popular, I know of no argument in its favour: the principle is not (as far as I can see) a logical truth; and I do not think that it is confirmed by empirical observation.

I find a different interpretation of **515** in Aristotle:

> Diogenes rightly says that if everything were not from one thing, then things would not act and be acted upon by one another; e.g., the hot become cold, and this again become hot. For it is not the heat and the coldness that change into one another, but

(evidently) the underlying subject (**519**: *GC* 322b12–17 = **A** 7).

Aristotle is not thinking of the Democritean principle, but of a theorem on change which he himself accepts: if at *t* an *F* becomes a *G*, then there must be some one thing, persisting from some time before *t* to some time after *t*, which is first *F* and later *G*. Change is change *in* or *of* something; it requires a unity in diversity; it occurs when some one thing assumes (or appears to assume) different aspects at different times.

The Aristotelian principle may be written as:

(3) If an *F* becomes a *G* at *t*, then there is something which was *F* before *t* and *G* after *t*.

Diogenes, I think, needs a strong version of (3), viz.:

(4) If an *F* becomes a *G* at *t*, then there is some stuff *S* such that a piece of *S* was an *F* before *t* and a *G* after *t*.

In addition to the Aristotelian principle, Diogenes requires a premiss to the effect that everything becomes everything. In order to state that premiss precisely, let us say that *F*s connect with *G*s if either some *F* becomes a *G* or there is an ordered set $\langle H_1, H_2, \ldots, H \rangle$ such that some *F* becomes an H_1, some H_1 an H_2, ..., some H_n a *G*. Diogenes' premiss then is:

(5) For any ϕ and ψ, ϕs connect with ψs.

The parallelism between linking and connecting, between (2) and (5) is evident.

Take any two properties, *F*ness and *G*ness. By (5), *F*s and *G*s connect. Hence either some *F* becomes a *G*, in which case (by (4)) *F*s and *G*s are made of the same stuff; or else some *F* becomes an H_1, some H_1 an H_2 . . ., in which case *F*s and H_1s are of the same stuff, H_1s and H_2s are the same stuff . . ., so that again *F*s and *G*s are of the same stuff. Generalize the argument, and again you have monism.

Assumption (5) is less plausible than assumption (2); but it has evident connexions with Anaxagorean physics (above, p. 28), and I imagine that Diogenes may have adopted it from his neo-Ionian predecessor. Aristotle's principle (3) is surely true—indeed, it is a logical truth about alteration. It may be expressed by saying that alteration implies a persistent substrate; and in a trivial sense any such substrate is an Aristotelian 'matter' or *hulê*—if '*hulê*' is defined as that which persists through change (cf. *Met* 1042a32–b8). But must *hulê* then be a stuff or material? Lot's wife changed into a pillar of salt and Niobe was turned into stone: if we regard those phenomena as alterations, then the persistent substrate is form, not stuff. What links Lot's wife and the pillar, Niobe and the rock, is the shape or form of their different constituent stuffs. Normally, perhaps, a material continuity underlies formal alteration; but in odd cases formal continuity may underpin material change. And if that is so, it is neither a necessary nor even a contingent truth that alteration presupposes some persisting stuff, and proposition (4)—Diogenes' version of the Aristotelian principle—is false.

In any case, as I have stated the argument it contains a logical flaw: given that an F becomes a G, we can infer, by (4), that *that F* and *that G* are made of the same stuff; but we cannot infer—as the argument would have us do—that *all F*s and *all G*s are made of the same stuff. In order to reach that universal conclusion we must supplement the argument with a further premiss, a Principle of Homogeneity:

(6) If any F is made of a stuff S, then every F is made of S.

Now that Principle is perhaps Diogenean; for Diogenes supposes that everything that is F must have some one 'proper nature'; and may not that 'proper nature' consist in, or at least include, being constituted by some stuff, S^F? But the 'proper nature' of Lot's wife or of Niobe does not include a constituent stuff; and in general, if alteration can occur by formal rather than material change, then 'natures' do not determine stuffs. Nor need we look to such *outré* occurrences: it is plainly untrue that everything F ('humaniform', 'green', 'sour', 'six feet long') is made of a single stuff S^F.

Neither interpretation of Diogenes' fragment gives him a sound argument for monism; and that is hardly surprising. Yet **516** indicates some cogitation on the logical features of alteration; and from it we may elicit plausible and influential propositions. The fragment is not devoid of philosophical charm.

(c) *The matter of the universe*

If there is a single stuff, what is it?

> And [Diogenes] too says that the nature of the whole is air, unlimited and eternal. . . . That is what Theophrastus reports about Diogenes; and the book of his entitled *Concerning Nature* which has come into my hands clearly names as air that from which all other things come to be (**520**: Simplicius, A 5).

Theophrastus' account is repeated by the doxographers (Diogenes

Laertius, IX. 57 = **A 1**; pseudo-Plutarch, **A 6**; Aëtius, **A 7**); and it accounts for the tradition that Diogenes was a follower of Anaximenes (Simplicius, **A 4**; cf. Antisthenes, *apud* Diogenes Laertius, IX. 57 = **A 1**). Theophrastus, however, did not win universal support.

> The research of the majority asserts that Diogenes of Apollonia, like Anaximenes, makes the primary element air; but Nicolaus in his book *On Gods* reports that he takes as his principle something between fire and air (**521**: Simplicius, **A 4**).

Simplicius notes that Porphyry adhered to Nicolaus' interpretation (cf. **63 A 1**) and he says that:

> I too, on reading these initial remarks [i.e. **515**], thought that [Diogenes] took the common substrate to be something other than the four elements [and hence something distinct from air] (**522**: *ad* **64 B 2**).

Simplicius offers an argument for taking air as the material *archê*: 'These men thought that the ease with which air is acted upon and altered (*to eupathes kai eualloiôton*) made it susceptible to change' (**A 5**); but he does not ascribe that to Diogenes by name, and he produces no textual evidence to support such an ascription. He does, however, quote from Diogenes to prove Theophrastus' opinion right and Nicolaus' wrong: after copying the passages we list as **B 3**, **B 4** and **B 5** he says:

> Here, then, [Diogenes] evidently says quite clearly that the stuff which men call air is the principle (**523**: *ad* **B 6**).

Simplicius is out to make a case, and he possessed Diogenes' treatise: if we cannot find in **B 3–5** the statement that air is the *archê*, we shall have no reason to ascribe it to Diogenes at all.

I shall later quote those three fragments in full. Here it is enough to say that **B 3** does not mention air at all; and that while **B 4** proclaims that 'men and the other animals that breathe live by air; and this is both soul and thought for them', it makes no mention of an *archê*. It is, I suppose, the following sentence from **B 5** on which Simplicius principally relies: 'And there is not a single thing which does not share in this [sc. air]; but there are many types both of air itself and of thought. For it [i.e. air] is of many types . . .'. Diogenes is not doing cosmology here; nor is he talking of a material substrate. Rather, he is concerned with psychology: that air is 'of many types (*polutropos*)' is advanced to show not that it is a suitable substratum, but that it can constitute souls and thoughts of radically different varieties.

There is, then, no evidence for Theophrastus' interpretation of Diogenes' *archê*; and there is some evidence against it. **515** lists air alongside earth, water, fire and the rest; the collocation implies that air is non-elemental just as they are, and nothing is done to cancel that implication. Nicolaus' assertion that the *archê* is 'something between fire and air' fares no better than Theophrastus: there is no textual evidence in its favour. Yet if we reject both Theophrastus and Nicolaus, what remains? Only, I think, **B 7**:

> And this itself is a body, both eternal and deathless; and of the
> rest, some come into being, others depart (**524**).[7]

Is that Diogenes' final characterization of his material substrate? Is it simply body (*sôma*)—'stuff' or, in the Scholastic jargon, 'prime matter'?

Since water visibly changes into air, and the change is an alteration not a destruction-*cum*-generation, both water and air are modifications of some underlying stuff. But that underlying stuff cannot be characterized by any perceptible properties; for any such characterization would identify it with one of the four elements, or with an elemental compound. Consequently, it is pure, unqualified, stuff. The conclusion will offend philosophers as a nonsense (did not Locke unwittingly explode the notion of 'substance in general', that 'something we know not what'?); and it will offend scholars as an anachronism (prime matter was invented by Aristotle, if not by later Aristotelians). Neither offence is justified, and a single argument will do for both: Diogenes is applying to Milesian stuff precisely the account which the Abderites gave to their atoms. Atoms are bodies (*sômata*); they occupy space and they have motive powers; but they have no perceptible qualities, they are *apoia*, without qualities (above, pp. 66–8). That is a coherent notion; and it is virtually identical with the notion of 'prime matter'. Diogenes. I suggest, married Anaximenes with Leucippus; and the marriage produced an Aristotelian offspring: his *archê* is not air, and it is not a mysterious fifth element between air and fire; it is matter, stuff.

(d) *Immanent will and its designs*

For things could not have been parcelled out (*dedasthai*) in this
way without thought (*noêsis*), so that there are measures of
everything: of winter and of summer, of night and of day, of rains
and of winds and of fine weather. And the other things, if one
wishes to think about them, one would find to have been disposed
in the finest (*kallista*) way possible (**525**: **B 3**).

In this brief fragment we find the first extant exposition of the Teleological Argument for the existence of God, or the Argument from Design. We may conjecture that Anaxagoras had employed it, though no evidence directly supports the conjecture; and we find it elaborated in two passages in Xenophon's *Memorabilia*;[8] but if it was current at the end of the fifth century and not an innovation of Diogenes, it is to the despised Diogenes that we must now look for its first statement.

The Argument was canonized by Aquinas as the fifth of his Five Ways to God. According to Kant, it 'is the oldest, the clearest, and the most accordant with the common reason of mankind. It enlivens the study of nature, just as it itself derives its existence and gains ever new vigour from that source. . . . It would . . . not only be uncomforting but utterly vain to attempt to diminish in any way the authority of this argument. Reason, constantly upheld by this ever-increasing evidence, which, though empirical, is yet so powerful, cannot be so depressed through doubts suggested by subtle and abstruse speculation that it is not at once aroused from the indecision of all melancholy reflection, as from a dream, by one glance at the wonders of nature and the majesty of the universe—ascending from height to height up to the all-highest, from the conditioned to its conditions, up to the supreme and unconditioned Author' (*Critique of Pure Reason*, A 624).

Kant's high praise for the Argument derives from Hume; in Hume's *Dialogues on Natural Religion*, Cleanthes advances the Argument and asserts that 'it requires time, reflection and study, to summon up those frivolous, though abstruse objections, which can support Infidelity. . . . To what degree . . . of blind dogmatism must one have attained, to reject such natural and such convincing arguments?' I am, I confess, a blind dogmatist by Cleanthes' reckoning; but I shall not try here to justify my dogmatism, limiting my task to the exposition and criticism of Diogenes' version of the Argument.

Diogenes' argument is splendidly simple. He starts from the premiss:
(1) Everything is arranged in the finest possible way;
and he concludes to:
(2) There is an intelligent arranger of everything.
The premiss is a truth of experience: we observe that 'there are measures of everything'; and the conclusion follows at once. From the conclusion it is easy to infer the existence of an almighty, everlasting, and merciful God.

I shall ignore the final, theogonical, step in the argument. Hume demonstrated with wit and cogency that the Argument from Design cannot establish the existence of a god with the traditional Christian attributes: infinity, eternity and benevolence cannot be squeezed from the Argument. But Diogenes was not a Christian; and he does not claim that his designing intelligence has the Christian attributes. In any case, the argument from (1) to (2) is interesting in its own right.

The premiss (1) contains two uncertainties. First, the word 'everything' can be taken either collectively ('the whole sum of things') or distributively ('each thing'). The latter sense seems intended in **526**, and it is certainly suggested by Xenophon and by most of the orthodox modern versions of the argument. Suppose, now, that we accept the principle:

(3) If a is finely arranged, then there is an intelligent arranger of a.
Even so, we cannot infer (2) from (1). The premiss entails that everything has its arranger, i.e.:

(4) $(\forall x)\,(\exists y)\,(y$ is the arranger of $x)$;
but it does not entail that there is an arranger of everything, i.e.:

(5) $(\exists y)\,(\forall x)\,(y$ is the arranger of $x)$.

Kant anticipated the objection: having concluded that 'there exists, therefore, a sublime and wise cause (or more than one)', he proceeds to argue that 'the unity of this cause may be inferred from the unity of the reciprocal relations existing between the parts of the world, as members of an artfully arranged structure'. Kant's recipe, in effect, is to read 'everything' in (1) in the collective and not the distributive sense; and (5) rather than (4) is the result. But Hume had already countered that move: 'And what shadow of an argument . . . can you produce, from your hypothesis, to prove the unity of the Deity? A great number of men join in building a house, or ship, in rearing a city, in framing a commonwealth: why may not several deities combine in contriving and framing a world?'

That criticism is, I think, fatal to any Christian use of the Argument; yet it is not so damaging to Diogenes, who does not seem to have shown any particular interest in proving a unique deity. The second uncertainty in (1) brings us nearer to a fatal blow. The traditional Argument speaks of order or design; Diogenes talks of a fine parcelling out or arrangement. These terms may cover two distinct notions. First, the underlying notion may be aesthetic: order, thus construed, is pattern, regularity, symmetry, or in general some aesthetically satisfying and economical arrangement of things. Second, the underlying notion may be one of purpose or plan: order, thus construed, is the appearance of direction, of intention, of purposed or planned progress. A snowflake and the solar system show aesthetic order (of different magnitude and to different degrees): they are intricately patterned, arranged in simple and satisfying regularities. The human digestive track and the maggot show purposive order: their activities appear directed to some goal or end. Snowflakes do not appear to have a purpose; and the intestines are aesthetically disgusting: pattern and purpose regularly fall apart (functional architecture is almost invariably ugly); but they sometimes combine, in the spider's web, the bee's honeycomb, or the elegant root of the parsnip.

Does everything exhibit pattern? does everything exhibit purpose? do we find things 'to have been disposed in the finest way possible'? Let me be brutally dogmatic. First, not all features of the world exhibit the beauty of the snowflake; even in the natural world, untouched by human hand, there is much that is messy, crude, and ugly. Nor, in my judgment, is the universe as a whole a thing of aesthetic value. Second, the universe as a whole does not seem, to me at any rate, to evince or exhibit purpose; it does not look as though it were planned or contrived for some end. And if some of the parts of the natural world do seem purposive, most of inanimate nature does not: there is no appearance of intention in the course of the comets, no goal in the ebb and flow of the tides.

But those reflexions are perhaps a trifle subjective; others may spy pattern and purpose where all I see is heartless, witless Nature. Third, then, I assert that (3) is false. It is certainly not a *logical* truth that patterned objects were planned by a designer or that the apparent goals of natural processes are the actual goals of some instigator of those processes. Nor is (3) a well-grounded empirical hypothesis. Defenders of the Argument regularly call upon analogy: the eye has the same pattern and appearance of function as the telescope; the latter was designed by a human artificer; hence the former was designed by a divine artificer. The analogy is frail: it starts from a very small number of cases, and it implies a false degree of similarity between natural objects and artefacts. Every day we are faced with a thousand attractive or purposive things, none of which bears any mark of the designer's hand. Proposition (3) is grotesquely implausible: experience suggests something quite different: that fine arrangements arise, for the most part, without the plan or intervention of any fine arranger.

The Argument from Design is, I guess, the most appealing of all the traditional arguments for the existence of God; and of all those arguments it is (in my view) the least plausible. At any event, Diogenes' version of it has no probative force.

Having argued for a cosmic intelligence, Diogenes proceeds to inquire into its nature. He argues that it is air; and he implies that it is divine. For that conclusion, which delighted the comic poets (e.g., Philemon, **C 4**) and is frequently reported in the doxography,[9] we have Diogenes' own words:

> Again, in addition to this there are these great signs too: man and the other animals that breathe live by air; and this is both soul (*psuchê*) and thought (*noêsis*) for them (as will clearly be shown in this treatise), and if this is taken away they die and thought leaves them (**526: B 4**).

The promise of **526** is fulfilled in **B 5**, which I here quote in full:

> [i] And it seems to me that what has thought is that which men call air; and that by this all are governed, and it controls all. For (?) the custom of this very thing seems to me to be (?) to have penetrated everything, and to dispose everything, and to be in everything. [ii] And there is not a single thing which does not share in this; but no one thing shares in the same way as another, but there are many types both of air itself and of thought. For it is of many types—hotter and colder, drier and moister, stabler and having a sharper motion; and there are many other alterations in it both of taste and of colour, unlimitedly many. [iii] And the soul of all animals is the same: air, hotter than the external air in which we exist but much colder than the air by the sun. And this warmth is not alike in any of the animals (since not even in men is it the same from one to another), but it differs—not greatly but in such a way as to be similar. [iv] Now none of the things that change can become utterly similar to another, without becoming identical. Thus inasmuch as the alteration is of many types, animals too are of many forms, and many, alike one another neither in form nor in way of life nor in thought, because of the quantity of the alterations. Nevertheless it is by the same thing that all live and see and hear, and all have their other thought from the same thing (**527**).

The argument of this long fragment is far from clear in detail; and I shall not attempt a full exegesis. The chief *probandum*, I take it, is the identification of air as the medium of thought, and in general of life; and part [i] offers the argument for that conclusion: air is the penetrating oil *par excellence*; it is therefore the stuff that can govern and control; and hence it is to be identified as the bearer of thought. The argument is thoroughly Anaxagorean; and it requires no special commentary here.

The function of parts [ii]–[iv] is negative. It seems an objection to Diogenes that there is so vast a variety of life and intelligence; for how can one stuff, air, underlie so many thoughts? Part [ii] answers this by reference to the vast variety of forms of air; and [iii] states how thought can indeed be 'the same' in all animals, and yet 'different'. (In [iv] Diogenes adduces a logical principle which seems to amount to:

(6) If for any ϕ, if a is ϕ then b comes to be ϕ, then b comes to be a. The principle has evident affinities with Leibniz' doctrine of the Identity of Indiscernibles; but it is not the same as that doctrine, and I do not understand how Diogenes intends it to be applied.)

527 has Anaxagorean connexions. The doxographers notice the fact (cf. Simplicius, **A 5**), but they do not make Diogenes a 'pupil' of Anaxagoras: Anaxagoras' pupil, in the standard histories, is Archelaus (e.g., Simplicius, **60 A 5**), the first Athenian philosopher. Archelaus followed Anaxagoras' physics on most points, but on the status of *nous* he differed:

> He says that some mixture inheres in mind essentially (**528:** Hippolytus, **60 A 4**).

> [He held that] air and mind are god—but not the cosmogonical mind (**529:** Aëtius, **60 A 12**).

Anaxagoras' mind is 'pure': Archelaus identifies it with air; and hence he is obliged to treat it as a stuff alongside other stuffs, containing a 'mixture' or a portion of everything. And, being a stuff, mind too will be in everything:

> He thought that everything was constituted in such a way that mind too, he said, inhered (**530:** Augustine, **60 A 10**).

The authorities are late and confused; yet the picture they present is not wholly implausible: in much the same way as Anaximenes gave substantial form to Anaximander's abstract *apeiron*, Archelaus made Anaxagoras' *nous* an intelligible part of the cosmos by identifying it as ordinary air, a familiar stuff capable of figuring in hard-headed physics. If *nous* is divine, and *nous* penetrates everything, then Archelaus has on his hands a panpsychism and a pantheism; and Augustine perhaps indicates as much.

Many scholars find Archelaus' view in Diogenes: 527 contains in [i] a statement that air is god; and in [ii] an assertion of panpsychism. From those two premisses, pantheism follows immediately. The relative chronology of Diogenes and Archelaus is unknown; but whether Diogenes borrowed from Archelaus or Archelaus from Diogenes, both men propounded the same revision of Anaxagoras' doctrine of *nous*.

That view may well be correct; but it rests on insecure foundations. First, the reader may well wonder how god is discovered in [i]: the answer is, by scholarly conjecture. The clause that I have embraced with question marks is textually corrupt; the most popular emendation makes it read: 'And this very thing seems to me to be god'.[10] Palaeographically the suggestion is neat; yet it does not fit particularly well into the argument of 527, and other emendations which ignore god are possible. But however that may be, air is certainly divinized in the doxography; and that does give some force to the first premiss in the argument for Diogenean pantheism.

What of the second premiss, panpsychism? 527 says in [vi] that 'there is not a single thing which does not share in this [i.e. in air]'; and in [i], air is 'in everything'. That amounts to panpsychism provided that 'everything' means literally everything, and that air always bestows thought or intelligence. The first proviso may be true; but it is possible that 'all' and 'everything' are throughout 527 limited to animate objects. (In the clause 'all are governed', 'all' is restricted to men, as its gender shows.) The second proviso is almost certainly false: thought, according to 527, is carried by fairly hot, moist air. To say that 'what has thought is that which men call air' is not to say that every bit of air is intelligent: air is the stuff of thought; but only in one of its modifications does air actually support thinking.

On the orthodox view of Diogenes' philosophy, air is both the omnipresent substratum of change and the omnipresent divinity: stuff and creator coincide, and material monism becomes a form of pantheism. I have preferred to separate both the substratum and god from air: the substratum is 'body' (*sôma*), and air is just one of its forms; the creative intelligence is not air as such, but a modification of air.[11] Diogenes' philosophy may thus be outlined as follows: the phenomena of change show that there is an underlying substrate more primitive than earth or water or fire or even air; it is pure stuff or 'body', and it has the essential characteristics of Abderite atoms. But the substratum logically required by change need not be identified with the *Urstoff* physically employed in cosmogony. It is possible that the cosmogonic *Urstoff* is air, one of the manifestations of body: in Diogenes' thought, as in that of Anaxagoras (59 B 1) and of Archelaus (Sextus, 60 A 7), air plays an important role in cosmogony without being the general fundament of change. The *Urstoff* is moved, and the cosmogonical processes are begun, by the action of thought. And since what thinks is air, the cosmos is thus, in the final analysis, self-starting and self-created.

Diogenes of Apollonia was not a thinker of vast innovatory power:

the monistic insight of the early Milesians, the bold and intricate physics of Anaxagoras, and the profoundly influential speculations of the Atomists, cannot be matched by any grand Apolloniate thought. Diogenes was an eclectic and a synthesizer. Yet to say that is not to damn him: he was, I think, a judicious eclectic and a bold synthesizer. He ignored the intricacies of Anaxagorean mixture, but accepted the simple thesis of *nous*, supporting it by what was destined to become a classic argument; he ignored the untestable hypothesis of the Atomists and did not speak of minute corpuscles swimming in the void, but he took from them their characterization of stuff, and perhaps their account of change. He was conscious of the Eleatic pother and familiar with the neo-Ionian solutions. His own attempt at a solution is in many respects primitive: he does indeed breathe the air of Anaximenes. His primitiveness, however, is neither a weakness nor an indication of ignorance. Rather, grasping the importance of the central Milesian structure of material monism, he attempted to defend it against Eleatic assault, to buttress it with a few neo-Ionian stones, and to reveal its intrinsic strength and majesty.

After Diogenes, science and philosophy took a new turn; and the achievements of Plato, and then of Aristotle, temporarily eclipsed the light of Presocratic thought. For us that light is fitful but not dim: few rays emerge from the clouds of time; but they are brilliant and penetrating. And they will, I think, convince any doubters of the truth of the old platitude, that the history of thought begins with Thales and his Presocratic successors. Those ancient thinkers understood the nature of man long before Aristotle expounded it to the world at large; and they acted upon their understanding. For

> What is a man,
> If his chief good and market of his time
> Be but to sleep and feed? A beast, no more.
> Sure he that made us with such large discourse,
> Looking before and after, gave us not
> That capability and god-like reason
> To fust in us unus'd.

Appendix A Sources

Our knowledge of the Presocratic philosophers is almost entirely indirect; for even where we possess their actual words, those words are preserved, fragmentarily, as quotations in the works of later authors. The sources we rely upon for *testimonia* and fragments span two millennia: they differ widely, one from another, in their literary aims, their historical competence, and their philosophical interests.

This appendix lists *in chronological order* the ancient authors I have quoted from or alluded to in the text and the notes. Some of the authors are (from a Presocratic point of view) of minor or minimal importance. A single asterisk is prefixed to the names of the more freely flowing sources; and those few gushing streams are marked by a pair of stars. Each name is followed by a date, often roundly given, and the briefest of biographical sentences. When a 'principal work' is named, that is not necessarily the author's major *opus*, but rather the book which holds most interest for students of the Presocratics.

Where no edition of the ancient text is mentioned, the reader may assume that I have used only the excerpts printed in Diels-Kranz. In citing editions I use these abbreviations:

CIAG *Commentaria in Aristotelem Graeca* (Berlin, 1881–1909)
OCT Oxford Classical Texts
SdA *Die Schule des Aristoteles*, ed. F. Wehrli (Basel, 1967–9²)

HERODOTUS: *c*.485–*c*.430; the father of history. Edition: OCT, Hude.

HIPPOCRATES: *c*.480–*c*.400. The Hippocratic *corpus* is a compilation of works of various dates and of a medical character; perhaps none of them was written by the great Hippocrates himself. Abbreviations: *cord de corde*

morb   de morbo
morb sacr   de morbo sacro
nat puer   de natura puerorum
vet med   de vetere medicina (ed. Festugière [218])
vict   de victu
Edition: Littré, Paris, 1839–61.
ISOCRATES: 436–338; orator, statesman, and opponent of the Academy. Edition: Teubner, Benseler and Blass.
XENOPHON: *c*.430–*c*.355; general, historian, and pupil of Socrates. Principal work: *Memorabilia*. Edition: OCT, Marchant.
*PLATO: 427–347; his dialogues contain numerous references to his Presocratic predecessors. Edition: OCT, Burnet.
SPEUSIPPUS: d.340; Plato's nephew and successor as head of the Academy; only fragments of his writings survive. Edition: Lang, Bonn, 1911.
XENOCRATES: fl. second half of fourth century; pupil of Plato who succeeded Speusippus as head of the Academy. Only fragments remain. Edition: Heinze [311].
**ARISTOTLE: 384–322; son of a doctor, pupil of Plato, and master of those who know. Abbreviations and editions:
An   de Anima (OCT, Ross)
APst   Posterior Analytics (OCT, Ross)
Cael   de Caelo (OCT, Allan)
EE   Eudemian Ethics (Teubner, Susemihl)
EN   Nicomachean Ethics (OCT, Bywater)
fr.   *Fragmenta* (Teubner, Rose)
GA   de Generatione Animalium (OCT, Drossaart Lulofs)
GC   de Generatione et Corruptione (Joachim, Oxford, 1922)
HA   Historia Animalium (Louis, Paris, 1964–9)
Met   Metaphysics (OCT, Jaeger)
Meteor   Meteorologica (Fobes, Cambridge Mass, 1919)
PA   de Partibus Animalium (Loeb, Peck)
Phys   Physics (OCT, Ross)
Poet   Poetics (OCT, Kassel)
Pol   Politics (OCT, Ross)
Resp   de Respiratione (in *Parva Naturalia*, Ross, Oxford, 1955)
Rhet   Rhetoric (OCT, Ross)
Sens   de Sensu (in *Parva Naturalia*, Ross, Oxford, 1955)
Top   Topics, including *Sophistici Elenchi* (OCT, Ross)
Pseudo-Aristotelian works:
lin insec de lineis insecabilibus (Timpanaro Cardini, Milan, 1970)
MM   Magna Moralia (Teubner, Susemihl)
MXG   de Melisso, Xenophane, Gorgia (Teubner, Apelt)

Prob   Problems (Teubner, Ruelle)

HERACLIDES PONTICUS: *c.*390–*c.*310; Platonist and Pythagorean, renowned as a dandy. Only fragments survive. Edition: SdA VII.

*THEOPHRASTUS: 371–287; Aristotle's greatest pupil and his successor. Only fragments survive. Abbreviation:
Sens   de Sensu
Edition: Diels [4].

ARISTOXENUS: b. *c.*370; musical theorist with Pythagorean interests. Edition: SdA II.

DICAEARCHUS: b. *c.*340; Aristotelian philosopher, only fragments of whose writings are preserved. Edition: SdA I.

*EUDEMUS: fourth century; pupil of Aristotle, philosopher, and historian of mathematics. Edition: SdA VIII.

MENO: fourth century; pupil of Aristotle, and author of history of medicine.

EPICURUS: 342–270; founder and eponym of Epicureanism, a philosophy strongly influenced by Democritus. Principal work: *Letter to Herodotus*. Abbreviations:
ad Hdt   Letter to Herodotus
ad Men   Letter to Menoeceus
Edition: Arrighetti, Turin, 1960.

HERMIPPUS: third century BC, follower of Callimachus; sensational biographer.

SATYRUS: third century BC, peripatetic biographer.

TIMON: 320–230; sceptic philosopher and poet. Edition: Diels [3].

ERATOSTHENES: *c.*280–200; geographer, scholar, and librarian at Alexandria.

CRATES OF MALLOS: mid-second century; scholar and librarian at Pergamum.

SOTION: second century BC, peripatetic historian of philosophy.

ARIUS DIDYMUS: first century BC; Stoic philosopher, teacher of Augustus.

ALEXANDER POLYHISTOR: *c.*105–*c.*25 BC; a Greek who became a Roman prisoner of war and then a polymath. Principal work: *Hypomnemata Pythagorica*.

DEMETRIUS OF MAGNESIA: flourished *c.*50 BC; a source for Diogenes Laertius.

CICERO: 106–43 BC: statesman, orator, master of prose, poet *manqué*, and amateur philosopher.

LUCRETIUS: 97–55 BC; Roman interpreter of Epicureanism in rough hexameters. Work: *de Rerum Natura*. Edition: OCT, Bailey.

PHILODEMUS: *c.*80–*c.*35 BC; Epicurean philosopher, fragments of whose works were discovered in the lava of Vesuvius.

NICOLAUS OF DAMASCUS: fl. second half of first century BC; historian and polymath, who wrote commentaries on Aristotle.

DIODORUS SICULUS: fl. *c*.35 BC; author of a *Universal History*. Edition: Teubner, Vogel and Fischer.

DIONYSIUS OF HALICARNASSUS: fl. end of first century BC; historian, and leading literary critic.

STRABO: 64 BC–AD 20; Romanophile Greek geographer.

AGATHEMERUS: first century AD; geographer.

OVID: 43 BC–AD 18; amatory poet. Principal work: *Metamorphoses*. Abbreviation and edition:

Metam   Metamorphoses (Ehwald and Albrecht, Zürich, 1966)

PHILO: *c*.10 BC–*c*.AD 40. Jewish theologian and philosopher.

VITRUVIUS: fl. *c*.AD 30; leading Roman authority on architecture.

SENECA THE YOUNGER: AD 4–65: politician, Stoic philosopher, playwright. Principal works: *Quaestiones Naturales; Letters*.

PLINY THE ELDER: 23–79: minor politician and omnivorous observer, killed while scrutinizing the eruption of Vesuvius. Work: *Naturalis Historia*.

*PLUTARCH: 45–*c*.120. Biographer and philosopher, whose numerous philosophical essays are known collectively as the *Moralia*. Abbreviations and editions:

adv Col   adversus Colotem (Teubner, Pohlenz and Westman)

aud poet   de audiendis poetis (Teubner, Bernardakis)

comm not   de communibus notitiis (Teubner, Pohlenz)

exil   de exilio (Teubner, Bernardakis)

Plat quaest   Platonicae quaestiones (Teubner, Hubert)

soll anim   de sollertia animalium (Teubner, Hubert)

tranq   de tranquillitate animae (Teubner, Bernardakis)

*AËTIUS: fl. *c*.100. Eclectic philosopher, whose doxography (the *Placita* or *Opinions*) was reconstructed by Diels from Stobaeus and pseudo-Plutarch (2). Edition: Diels [4].

NICOMACHUS OF GERASA: *c*.100; Neoplatonist mathematician.

FAVORINUS: *c*.80–*c*.150, hermaphrodite, favourite of Hadrian, friend of Plutarch, polymath.

JULIUS SORANUS: fl. 100–140; leading physician and author of history of medicine.

PTOLEMY: fl. *c*.140. Geographer, mathematician and astronomer. Principal work: *Syntaxis mathematica*—the '*Almagest*'. Edition: Teubner, Heiberg.

THEON OF SMYRNA: first half of second century; Platonist mathematician.

ARISTOCLES: second century, teacher of Alexander of Aphrodisias and historian of philosophy.

GALEN: 129–199; the most celebrated doctor of the age, and a copious author.

HERMOGENES: b. *c.*150; orator and rhetorician.

TERTULLIAN: 160–220; Christian theologian with rhetorical and legal interests.

AULUS GELLIUS: second century, antiquarian and grammarian; his *Noctes Atticae* is a philosophico-legal miscellany.

JULIUS POLLUX: second century; successful teacher of rhetoric. Work: *Onomasticon.*

DIOGENES OF OENOANDA: second century; Epicurean, who had his philosophy inscribed on stone. Edition: Teubner, Chilton (several new fragments not yet collectively published).

HARPOCRATION: ? second-century lexicographer.

PSEUDO-PLUTARCH (1): mid-second century, author of *Stromateis*, a doxographical compilation. Edition: Diels [4].

*PSEUDO-PLUTARCH (2): mid-second century, author of an *Epitome* of the *Placita* (see Aëtius). Edition: Diels [4].

TATIAN: second half of second century, Christian apologist and rhetorician.

*CLEMENT OF ALEXANDRIA: *c.*150–215, the first major Christian philosopher. Principal work: *Stromateis.*

AELIAN: fl. second half of second century, author of miscellaneous natural histories.

ATHENAGORAS: fl. *c.*180, Athenian philosopher and Christian apologist.

**DIOGENES LAERTIUS: ? third century; scissors and paste historian of philosophy. Work: *Lives of the Philosophers*. Edition: OCT, Long.

PHILOSTRATUS: third-century sophist and author of *Lives of the Sophists.*

CENSORINUS: third-century Roman grammarian. Principal work: *de die natali.*

HERMIAS: ? third to sixth century, author of *Gentilium Philosophorum Irrisio*. Edition: Diels [4].

*SEXTUS EMPIRICUS: fl. 180–200, massive compiler of sceptical *topoi* and our main source for ancient scepticism. Abbreviations and Editions:

adv Math   *Against the Mathematicians* (Teubner, Mau)
Pyrr Hyp   *Outlines of Pyrrhonism* (Teubner, Mau).

ALEXANDER OF APHRODISIAS: fl. *c.*200, seminal commentator on the works of Aristotle. Abbreviation:

quaest nat   *quaestiones naturales*
Edition: CIAG.

ATHENAEUS: fl. *c*.200, author of the anecdotal miscellany, *Deipnosophistae*.

*HIPPOLYTUS: d. 235: presbyter of Rome, opposed to the Establishment. Principal work: *Refutatio Omnium Haeresium (Ref. Haer)*. Edition: Diels [4].

PLOTINUS: 205–70, the principal philosopher of the period between Aristotle and Aquinas. Work: *Enneads*.

DIONYSIUS OF ALEXANDRIA: flourished *c*. 250, episcopal opponent of atomism.

PORPHYRY: 234–303, Neoplatonist pupil of Plotinus. Abbreviations and editions:

de Abst   de Abstinentia (Teubner, Nauck)

VP   Vita Pythagorae (Teubner, Nauck)

ACHILLES: third-century astronomer and mathematician.

EUSEBIUS: *c*.260–340, bishop of Caesarea and leading churchman; principal work: *Praeparatio Evangelica (PE)*.

ANATOLIUS: fl. 270. Bishop of Laodicea, saint, Aristotelian, and mathematician.

CHALCIDIUS: 256–357, Christian philosopher; his Latin commentary on Plato's *Timaeus* had enormous influence on later ages.

IAMBLICHUS: fourth-century pupil of Porphyry. Abbreviations and editions:

comm math sc   de communi mathematica scientia (Teubner, Festa)

VP   de Vita Pythagorica (Teubner, Deubner)

LACTANTIUS: fl. *c*.320, prolific Christian author, influenced by the Platonic and hermetic traditions. Principal work: *de Ira*.

THEMISTIUS: 317–388, Constantinopolitan orator and philosopher, who paraphrased Aristotle's works.

EPIPHANIUS: *c*.315–403, bishop of Salamis. Edition: Diels [4].

AUGUSTINE: 354–428, saint and church father, author of *Confessions* and *City of God*.

SERVIUS: fl. *c*.400, grammarian and author of celebrated commentary on Vergil.

MACROBIUS: early fifth century, author of the literary symposium, *Saturnalia*.

*STOBAEUS: early fifth-century excerptor with particular interest in philosophy. Work: *Florilegium*. Edition: Diels [4].

HESYCHIUS: fifth-century lexicographer.

THEODORETUS: 393–466, Bishop of Cyrrhus, Christian apologist.

BOETHIUS: d. 480, the last of the Romans; author of the *Consolatio Philosophiae* and numerous more professional works.

CLAUDIANUS MAMERTINUS: d. 474, Neoplatonist. Principal work: *de statu animae*.

PROCLUS: *c*.410–485, leading Neoplatonist philosopher and author of valuable commentaries on Plato's dialogues. Abbreviations and editions:

in Parm   *Commentary on the Parmenides* (Cousin, Paris, 1864)
in Tim   *Commentary on the Timaeus* (Teubner, Diehl)

PSEUDO-GALEN: *c*.500, author of *Historia Philosopha*. Edition: Diels [4].

EUTOCIUS: *c*.500, Byzantine mathematician who wrote commentaries on Apollonius and Archimedes.

AMMONIUS: *c*.440–520. A pupil of Proclus and leading Platonist of the Alexandrian school; commentator on Aristotle and influential teacher. Edition: CIAG.

PHILOPONUS: *c*.490–570, Christian pupil of Ammonius; author of commentaries on Aristotle. Edition: CIAG.

**SIMPLICIUS: fl. *c*.550, Ammonius' greatest pupil, and a major source for early Greek philosophy. Edition: CIAG.

OLYMPIODORUS: second half of sixth century, pupil of Ammonius and commentator on Plato.

ELIAS: end of sixth century, pupil of Olympiodorus and commentator on Aristotle. Edition: CIAG.

SUDA: tenth-century, a large Byzantine lexicon, formerly known as Suidas.

HISDOSUS: fl. *c*.1100, wrote on Plato's psychology.

TZETZES: *c*.1110–85, leading Byzantine scholar.

ALBERTUS MAGNUS: *c*.1200–80; St Albert the Great, teacher of Aquinas and Parisian exponent of Aristotle.

SCHOLIASTS on various authors: the margins of many ancient manuscripts contain notes or 'scholia'; the dates and identities of most scholiasts are unknown.

Appendix B   Chronology

Our evidence for Presocratic chronology is scrappy, confused and unreliable: few thinkers can be dated with any precision; and monumental dispute governs all. My chronological table, then, has no high aspirations: its sole aim is to provide the reader with a rough and approximate idea of the temporal relationships that hold among the Presocratic philosophers. The table is tentative (broken lines indicate uncertainty); and it represents orthodoxy (in so far as any view here is orthodox). The reader who is hungry for more information should begin by consulting the relevant pages of Guthrie [25] or of Zeller-Mondolfo [26].

Thales
Anaximander
Pherecydes
Anaximenes
Pythagoras
Heraclitus
Parmenides
Epicharmus
Hippasus
Xenophanes
Alcmeon
Anaxagoras
Empedocles
Zeno
Protagoras
Gorgias
Archelaus
Melissus
Antiphon the Orator
Hippon
Socrates
Antiphon the Sophist
Thrasymachus
Lycophron
Hippias
Ion of Chios
Philolaus
Diogenes of Apollonia
Leucippus
Democritus
Prodicus
Critias
Diagoras
Eurytus
Cratylus
Plato
Archytas

Notes

The text of the book is intended to be self-sufficient; and the reader who ignores these notes should not find the main narrative broken or its arguments enthymematic. The notes are designed to serve four subsidiary functions.

First, they supply additional references to the ancient texts. (For the abbreviations used see the Note on Citations, and Appendix A.)

Second, the notes broach issues too technical or too narrow to justify inclusion in the body of the book.

Third, they explain (and sometimes attempt to justify) disputed readings, translations, or interpretations which the main narrative adopts without comment.

Fourth, there are some selected references to the secondary literature. (References consist of the author's name; a numeral, in square brackets, keying the work to the Bibliography; and, usually, a page or chapter number.) It is customary in scholarly works to compile references, pious and polemical, to authors who agree and disagree with a given interpretation. That practice is a pedantic pleasantry, of little value to the reader; and, apart from acknowledgments of direct quotations, I only provide references where they are likely to yield a useful supplement to my own remarks. The reader who seeks bibliographical assistance will find it, I hope, in the Bibliography.

I The Ionian Revival

1 For Anaxagoras' dates see especially Diogenes Laertius, II.7 = **59 A 1** (cf. Guthrie [25], II.322-3). Euripides: Strabo, **A 7**; Diodorus, **A 62**; etc.; Pericles: Isocrates, **A 15**; Plutarch **A 16**; etc. For the trial see, e.g., Plutarch, **A 17**, **A 18**

(see Derenne [345], 13–41). Gershenson-Greenburg [361], 346–8, argue that the whole story of the trial is an invention based on Plato, *Apology* 26D = **A 35** (see also Jacoby [457], 41, n. 159).

2 On *Met* 984a11 see esp. O'Brien [348], with copious references.

3 See also Diogenes Laertius, VIII.46 = **44 A 4**; IX.38 = **A 2** (see, e.g., Burkert [173], 228–9).

4 He is also called an Abderite (e.g., Diogenes Laertius, IX.30 = **67 A 1**). Probably Miletus was his birthplace; 'Eleatic' and 'Abderite' were applied to him for his philosophical connexions (see Bailey [383], 66–7). For convenience I shall frequently refer to Democritus and Leucippus as 'the Abderites'.

5 The Greeks dated the fall of Troy variously between 1334 and 1136 (see F. Jacoby, *Das Marmor Parium* (Berlin, 1904), 146–9); we cannot tell what date Democritus favoured. The only other publication date for a Presocratic that we possess is given by Olympiodorus, who asserts that Gorgias wrote his treatise *Concerning Nature* in the 84th Olympiad, 444–1 BC (**82 A 10**). If we believe Olympiodorus, we shall date Melissus' treatise to the early 440s at latest; unless, of course, we hold that Melissus was defending Parmenides against the ridicule of Gorgias (see Nestle [260], 561). In any case, Olympiodorus' report is suspect: see Untersteiner [434], 100, n. 96 = [435], I.167, n. 98. Democritus was a widely travelled polymath: on his travels see Guthrie [25], II.387, n. 1; on his learning, see Steckel [385], 212–21.

6 See especially O'Brien [351], 129–44; Bollack [349], III.49–80. Hölscher [356], 201–9, makes **194** a biological fragment; Mansfeld [357] offers a heterodox reading of lines 3–5.

7 I.e. 'the elements' (see line 18); but Bollack [349], III.50 offers a different construe.

8 I.e. 'the one type of generation and destruction': see especially Stokes [56], 154–5 (but *contra*: Bollack [349], III.53–4).

9 Accepting Panzerbieter's palmary emendation ('*threphtheisa*' for '*thruphtheisa*'): see Bollack [349], III.55–7 (who, however, makes a different proposal).

10 Line 9 is interpolated from **B 26**.8: both sense and syntax require it (but see Bollack [349], III.59–60).

11 On Empedoclean atomism see Aristotle, *GC* 334a18–25 = **A 43**; *Cael* 305a1 = **A 43a**; Aëtius, **A 43**, **A 44**. Atomism is accepted by Longrigg [359]; but it was clearly disposed of by Reinhardt [491], 111–13.

12 On the problems caused by these appellations see especially Bollack [349], III.169–85, who quotes a host of doxographical texts omitted from Diels-Kranz.

13 It is hotly disputed whether there were periods of rest between worlds. In the end, everything turns on **B 27**.4 = **B 28**.2: 'a round Sphere, exulting in its joyful (?) *moniê*'. Some connect *moniê* with *monos* ('alone') and translate 'solitariness' (e.g., Bollack [349], III.137–8); others—to whose view I subscribe —connect *moniê* with *menein* ('rest') and translate 'rest' (e.g., Jaeger [48], 237, nn. 56–9).

14 Aristotle praised Empedocles' poetry in his early work, *On Poets* (fr. 70 R³ = **A 1**), but later denied him the title of poet (*Poet* 1447b18 = **A 22**). The later judgment became canonical (e.g., Dionysius, **A 25**).

15 Millerd [352], 21.

16 Already noted by Theophrastus (Diogenes Laertius, VIII.55 = **A 1**); according to Alcidamas, Parmenides 'taught' Empedocles (Diogenes Laertius, VIII.56 = **A 1**).

17 So Aristotle, *Phys* 187a25 = **59 A 46**; Simplicius, **A 64**; Aëtius, **A 63** (see, e.g.,

Guthrie [25], II.313-15). Two fragments have been thought to bear on the question. In **B 8** Anaxagoras says that:

> The things in the one world (*ta en tôi heni kosmôi*) have not been separated from one another.

That has been taken to *prove* that Anaxagoras believes in a unique cosmos. I doubt if the phrase will bear that weight; but I am not sure what precisely it does mean.

Second, there are the references to what happens 'elsewhere' in **B 4** (quoted above, p. 17, as texts **199-201**). **B 4** has been taken to imply: (a) the coexistence of many—perhaps infinitely many—different worlds (e.g., Gigon [364], 25-6); (b) different stages in the development of the unique world (e.g., Simplicius, *in Phys* 157.17); (c) different inhabited parts of the earth's surface, as in Plato, *Phaedo* 109B (e.g., Kahn [90], 52-3); (d) an inhabited moon (cf. Diogenes Laertius, II.8 = **A 1**; Aëtius, **A 77**); (e) another inhabited earth (see references in Burkert [173], 345-8); (f) the counterfactual hypothesis that in every cosmogony there *would* be an inhabited world like ours (Fränkel [362], 288-91). I think that (b), (c), (d) and (f) can be ruled out: they do not fit the text closely enough. (e) is less ambitious than (a); but Democritus embraced (a), and the fact that he explicitly denied that all the other worlds have a sun and a moon suggests that Anaxagoras had asserted that they did (Hippolytus, **68 A 40**). See Vlastos [372], 53-4.

18 O'Brien [351], 244; see especially Bollack [349], I.169-73.
19 Guthrie [25], II.140; see especially Cornford [231], 15. The view is found in Nietzsche [28], 395-6.

II *Anaxagoras and the Nature of Stuffs*

1 Lanza [360], 187.
2 I should perhaps mention the heterodox opinion of Gershenson-Greenburg [361], 378: 'these so-called fragments cannot be used as the basis of a reconstruction of Anaxagoras' theory. . . . They can be assigned no more importance than their late chronological position relative to the time of Anaxagoras indicates. . . . The so-called fragments are assuredly far from direct quotes from Anaxagoras' book'. That view is deliciously wicked, but quite implausible; and the arguments on which it rests are worthless. It must be admitted, however, that the texts in Diels-Kranz are tidier than they should be: some of the fragments are patch-worked from various pages of Simplicius (see below, n. 5), and the text of none is wholly free from doubt.
3 I take 'quantity (*plêthos*)' in a numerical sense: Lanza [360], 190-1, construes it as 'mass'; but that loses the contrast with *megethos* in **196**.
4 'Contained' renders *kateichen*: see Guthrie [25], II.294, n. 1; Lanza [360], 191-3. I construe 'contain' metaphorically, to amount to 'predominate over' (above, p. 23).
5 Diels-Kranz print **199**, **200** and **201** continuously. Burnet [31], 259, n. 1, claims responsibility, falsely stating that Simplicius thrice quotes the remarks continuously. The true situation is set out by Fränkel [362], 287, n. 1; but it is worth repeating the salient facts. *In Phys* 34.21-6 quotes '*prin . . . chrêmata*' (Diels-Kranz, II.34.17-35.5); *in Phys* 34.29-35.9 quotes '*toutôn . . . allêi*' (II.34.5-16); *in Phys* 156.2-4 quotes '*toutôn . . . hêdonas*' (II.34.5-8); *in Phys* 156.4-9 quotes '*prin . . . heterôi*' (II.34.17-35.3); *in Phys* 157.9-16 quotes

'*eneinai . . . chrôntai*' (II.34.5–14); *in Cael* 608.24 quotes '*en tôi sumpanti . . . chrêmata*' (II.35.4–5); *in Cael* 609.5–11 quotes '*toutôn . . . hêmin*' (II.34.5–12).

I doubt if we can make any safe inferences about the arrangements of Anaxagoras' words in the text which Simplicius used; and there is in any case a general opinion that Simplicius was using not a complete text of Anaxagoras but an epitome first prepared by Theophrastus (see Lanza [360], VIII–IX). Fränkel, *loc. cit.*, finds three separate fragments: (a) II.34.5–16; (b) II.34.17–35.3 (*heterôi*); (c) II.35.4–5 (according to Fränkel, the phrase '*toutôn de houtôs echontôn*' at II.35.3 belongs to Simplicius, not to Anaxagoras). My three fragments run thus: **199**: II.34.5–8; **200**: II.34.8–16; **201**: II.34.17–35.5. For other suggestions see Lanza [360], 199–200.

6 Aëtius, **A 46**, gives an unorthodox sense to *homoiomereia* (accepted by, e.g., Bailey [383], 554–5; Peck [376], 62); but I do not think that we can get anywhere by abandoning the Aristotelian notion of homoiomereity.

7 See, e.g., Guthrie [25], II.325–6.

8 See, e.g., Peck [371], 28–31; Reesor [367], 33, n. 3; but I see no reason to restrict the stuffs to 'organic' stuffs (Peck), or even to natural stuffs (Reesor).

9 Why not simply say that Anaxagorean things are both stuffs and qualities? (So Peck [371], 31–3; Reesor [366], 4, relying on *Phys* 187a24, b4–7 = **A 52**). But then Anaxagoras' theory is inelegant; and *he* gives no hint that his 'things' fall into two classes. No doubt the qualities (and the stuffs proper?) were conceived of in terms of 'powers' or *dunameis* (see especially Vlastos [372], 470–3).

10 I ignore the term '*panspermia*' (*GC* 314a29 = **A 46**); its sense and origin are alike obscure (see Lanza [360], 77).

11 There is a massive literature on *spermata*: see especially Vlastos [372], 461–5.

12 **201** speaks of 'seeds unlimited in quantity and not like one another'. Cornford [369], 22, glosses: 'there is a large number of different *kinds* of seeds' (but Anaxagoras says 'unlimited' not 'large'). I prefer to read 'unlimited in quantity' in the same way as I read the phrase in **197**.

13 According to some scholars, *apokrinesthai* is a biological term, referring to organic growth or formation (see Lanza [360], 195).

14 The particulate interpretation comes from Aristotle; he says that things are generated 'from what exists and inheres but which, because of the smallness of the bodies (*onkoi*), is imperceptible to us' (*Phys* 187a36–b1). The word *onkoi* commits Aristotle to a particulate interpretation of Anaxagoras (*pace* Lanza [360], 104—but the word may only be a carelessness); and the passage is a prime source for the doxography.

15 An *atomist* theory is, of course, immediately ruled out by (B); but you can, I suppose, be a corpuscularian without being an atomist.

16 'Anaxagoras was really striving after the idea of a union closer than mere mechanical juxtaposition, and more like our notion of chemical fusion, a union in which things are not merely placed side by side, but are, as it were, completely merged in a new substance' (Bailey [383], 545; Bailey owes the view to J. A. Smith).

17 Cornford [369], 14; *contra*: see especially Kerferd [378], whose main aim is to show that 'there is no logical inconsistency between the major doctrines attributed to Anaxagoras in antiquity' (129).

18 Aristotle is defended by, e.g., Raven [373], 132–3; Kerferd [378], 134–6. **B 15** is sometimes taken to show that earth is non-elemental; but that construe depends upon an uncertain emendation (see Lanza [360], 237; Stokes [365],

218–21). Simplicius, *ad* **B 16**, tries to find a distinction between element and compound in that fragment; but see, e.g., Stokes [365] 16–19.

19 Thus in the view of Vlastos [372], 484–6, *x* contains *S* if and only if *x* possesses all those powers that are constitutive of *S*.

20 What of allomorphs? Anaximenes in effect treats all stuffs as allomorphs of air; and Empedocles is the first man explicitly to introduce the notion of a compound: the element/allomorph distinction is different from the element/ compound distinction; but there is no evidence that Anaxagoras heeded the difference.

21 Charges of incoherence in, e.g., Cornford [369], 91; Guthrie [25], II.290.

22 The MSS. read '*ouden estin homoion oudeni* (nothing is like anything else)'. Wasserstein [363] excises *oudeni*, rightly. (The verbal parallel to the MSS. text at **201** is no use, *pace* Guthrie [25], II.274, n. 1; Lanza [360], 232; the contexts of the two fragments are quite different.)

23 'We have to assume that Anaxagoras' substance words, both particular and generic, are systematically ambiguous' (Strang [374], 102; *contra*: Stokes [365], 2–4). Strang fears an infinite regress: 'Suppose *x* is predominantly *S*. Consider that predominant *S*-portion: presumably *it* is *S* only because *S* predominates in it; then consider *that* predominant *S*-portion . . .' (cf. Cornford [369], 93; Vlastos [372], 51). The regress does not arise once we distinguish carefully between *pieces* of *S* and *portions* of *S*.

24 'The "portions" must be thought of as proportions that cannot be directly located or directly measured' (Hussey [34], 137; cf. Strang [374], 102–3): they cannot be located at all, since they have no location; they can be measured, but only indirectly.

25 Cornford [369], 90, observes that at *Phys* 203a23 Aristotle signals (by the word *eoike*, 'it seems') that his argument for (A) is a conjecture; and Cornford adds that 'Simplicius, after loyally searching Anaxagoras' book for every text that could support the interpretation based upon it by Aristotle, ends by rejecting that interpretation'. As for Simplicius, he may not have had a complete text of Anaxagoras (above, n. 5); and in any event, he does not reject Aristotle's interpretation but only modifies it. Nor, I think, does Aristotle indicate that (1) is conjecturally ascribed to Anaxagoras: what was unclear was the precise connexion between (1) and (A). Finally, (A) is indubitably Anaxagorean; and if we drop (1) we leave (A) unsupported.

26 The last clause is obscure, and no satisfactory account of *ekchôreousi* is to hand (see Guthrie [25], II.301, n. 1). I agree with Stokes [365], 229–44, that **211** deals with changes in the present world and not with cosmogony.

27 See especially Kucharski [379]; Longrigg [63]; Müller [52], 69–72, 126–37. Jaeger [48], 156–7, stresses Anaxagoras' empiricism; but there is nothing innovatory about that. The connexions between the *vet med* and Anaxagoras are especially strong: see Longrigg [63], 158–67.

28 Cornford [369], 18, finds (1) 'grotesquely superfluous and uneconomical'—and he would no doubt say the same for (C). 'Economical' is a slippery word: it seems to me that in a fairly clear sense (C) is the *most* economical hypothesis that Anaxagoras could have excogitated to explain the facts he observed.

29 See especially Schofield [380], 14–24, who suggests Eudemus as the ultimate source of the scholion.

30 Fraser, quoted with reference to Anaxagoras by West [23], 323.

31 Raven [373], 129 (cf. Strang [374], 102, n. 8) stresses the word *moira*, 'portion', which he contrasts to *meros*, 'part'; unfortunately, *moira* in Greek may mean

'part' as well as 'portion' (see Stokes [365], 12–13).

32 Guthrie [25], II.289. But later, 298, n. 2, Guthrie suggests that if we ascribe an understanding of infinite divisibility to Anaxagoras we will 'look back at Anaxagoras from Aristotle, whereas he was starting from Parmenides and Zeno'.

33 So Gigon [364], 14–15, who likewise connects sentence [iii] to Zeno. B 1. A verbal similarity: much of Anaxagoras' language 'echoes' that of Zeno; it does not follow, and I do not think it is true, that Anaxagoras is trying to answer— or even thinking of—Zeno's arguments.

34 Reesor [366], 2; Guthrie [25], II.289, n. 2.

35 The proper comparison is not with Zeno but with Parmenides, 151.1. Zeller's conjecture in [ii] (*tomêi* for *to mê*: 'for what is cannot not be by cutting') gives the wrong sense; and it is in any case poorer grammar than the MS. text whose grammar it was designed to improve.

36 This interpretation was suggested to me by John Guiniven.

37 E.g.: 'A large portion of S and a small portion of S contain as many stuffs—for they contain all the stuffs' (Burnet [31], 260); 'A large portion of S and a small portion of S contain stuffs in the same ratio' (Vlastos [372], 46, n. 64); 'For every larger there is also a smaller' (Reesor [366], 2); 'A large portion of S and a small portion of S are equal in extent, for size is relative' (Lanza [360], 199).

38 An understanding beyond the reach of Plutarch, who argued that if $a > b$, then a must have more parts than b (*comm not* 1079AB). But what of the end of 197? 'These are *the greatest . . . in quantity*': if air is greater in quantity than anything else, how can everything be infinite in quantity? We must assume a slight infelicity of expression here: Anaxagoras means, I suppose, that in the present world there are more discrete, macroscopic, portions of air than of anything else; there are lungfuls of air in every creature, bubbles of air in the water, pockets of air underground, and so on. In any case, the weight of the argument falls on the last phrase: 'These are the greatest . . . *in magnitude*'.

39 I take *dunaito* impersonally (Lanza [360], 214): it is implausible to make 'the least' its subject.

40 *Kai* means 'even' here (*pace* Lanza [360], 214–15): the translation 'and' gives a strange syntax and an odd argument.

41 Reesor [367], 30; cf. [366], 3.

42 It is worth listing Anaxagoras' vocabulary:
apokrinesthai: 197, 200 (twice), 201, 202, B 7, B 9, B 12 (five times), B 13, B 14, 211 (twice).
perichôrein: B 9, B 12 (eight times), B 13.
diakrinesthai: B 5, B 12 (twice), B 13 (twice), B 17.
kinein: B 13 (four times).
summignusthai: B 12 (twice), B 17.
sumpêgnusthai: 200, 211 (twice).
sunkrinesthai: 199.
proskrinesthai: B 14.
sunchôrein: B 15.

43 Anaxagoras' cosmogony and cosmology, which I shall not itemize, was wholly Milesian in spirit: see especially Stokes [365], 217–50 (a heterodox view in Bargrave-Weaver [368]).

III The Corpuscularian Hypothesis

1 Heisenberg [394], 7, 32.

2 I speak usually of 'the Atomists', not distinguishing between the views of Leucippus and those of Democritus. I doubt if our texts will sustain any systematic distinction: the best attempt to make it remains Bailey [383].

3 But McDiarmid [395], 293, n. 1, holds that this comes from Aristotle, *Phys* 265b25, and is not genuinely Abderite.

4 The doxography regularly uses *sômata* or *prôta sômata* ('bodies', 'primary bodies') to refer to the atoms (**68 B 141**; **B 156**; *Phys* 203a33 = **A 41**; and see Diels-Kranz, III.419a15–27). Epicurus states the first axiom of his philosophy by way of *sôma*: '. . . the universe is body (*sôma*) and place' (*ad Hdt* §39). He says that *perception* shows there are bodies (*ad Hdt* §39); but nothing we perceive has those properties (e.g., solidity, immutability) which are characteristic of the Atomists' bodies. Perhaps we perceive *sômata*: we surely do not perceive *prôta sômata*.

5 But Epicurus appears to have adhered to the Eleatic argument (*ad Hdt* §§54–5).

6 Cf. Theophrastus, **68 A 132**; Simplicius, **67 A 13**; *in Phys* 82.1–3; Diogenes Laertius, IX.44 = **68 A 1**. In **68 A 49** Galen appears to assimilate impassivity to indivisibility, and to sever it from immutability. On the sense of '*apatheia*' see, e.g., Aristotle, *Met* 1019a26–32, 1073a11–3.

7 It is often said, vaguely enough, that Atomism is Elea minus monism (see, e.g., Burnet [31], 328; Bailey [383], 45, 71); but see Guthrie [25], II.392, for some apposite qualifications.

8 Simplicius, *in Cael* 609.17, probably means to ascribe both (C) and (D) both to Leucippus and to Democritus. Galen, **68 A 49**, ascribes (C) to the Epicureans and (D) to the Leucippans, and he implies that Leucippus did not use (C); but the passage is muddled.

9 So, e.g., Bailey [383], 204. But Furley [387], 95–6, suggests that the ascription of large atoms to Democritus is a careless inference from this text of Epicurus (cf. Lucretius, II.481–521).

10 Reading '*ho*' for '*hon*' (see Ross [11], II.211).

11 Cf. Lucretius, I.599–634; and see, e.g., Vlastos [401]; Furley [387], 7–43.

12 So, e.g., Furley [387], 97–9; *contra*: Luria [398], 172–80 (but Luria is driven to the unpalatable conclusion that Democritus recognized two different sorts of atom).

13 See especially Furley [387], 81–2 (see vol. 1, p. 337, n. 26).

14 Atoms are also said to be 'partless' (*amerê*) by Aëtius, **68 A 48**; cf. [Aristotle] *lin insec* 969a21.

15 Repeated by Simplicius, *in Cael* 649.1–9; 665.6–8; Philoponus, *in GC* 164.20–4.

16 Democritus was 'too good a mathematician' to believe in mathematically indivisible atoms, according to Heath [19], I.181; other scholars assert that if atoms have magnitude they cannot be mathematically indivisible (e.g., Burnet [31], 336). Heath echoes the reaction of Philoponus to Plato's geometrical atomism (*in GC* 210.12) and of Simplicius to Xenocrates' (*in Phys* 142.16). On Democritean mathematics see Guthrie [25], II.484–8.

17 For *minima* see, e.g., Luria [398], 138–41; against: e.g., Nicol [312], 120. On **233** see especially Hahm [403], with references at 206, n. 3.

18 *Contra*: Luria [398], 145–6; he quotes Plutarch, *Plat quaest* 1003F, which shows that, in the view of the ancient commentators, Plato held that a sphere was compounded of cubes.

19 Furley [387], 102, n. 17, concedes that 'Aristotle seems to have believed that the infinite divisibility of the geometrical continuum entails the infinite divisibility

of matter'. But he adds: (a) that theoretical divisibility is definitely needed if Democritus is to counter Zeno's arguments; (b) that Aristotle cannot simply have overlooked a Democritean distinction between physical and theoretical indivisibility; and (c) that Democritus was probably 'no clearer' about the relation between physical and theoretical indivisibility than Aristotle was. I answer (a) later. On (b), I do not suppose that Democritus ever made the distinction; rather, the question of theoretical divisibility never explicitly arose for him. And as to (c), Democritus may have been as unclear as Aristotle without sharing Aristotle's views.

20 Furley [387], 95, dismisses Simplicius' mention of the parts of Democritean atoms (*in Phys* 82.1) as a 'hasty inference': I should as soon see a hasty inference in **229**.

21 See especially Mau [399], 25–6; *contra*: Luria [398], 129, who thinks that the *GC* contains 'a genuine fragment of Democritus'. That Philoponus calls the argument 'Democritean' (*in GC* 38.28, etc.) is neither surprising nor significant.

22 Furley [400], 92–3. The argument is accepted by Locke, *Essay* II.xiii.20.

23 Furley [400], 92–3, conflates this argument with Archytas' argument and also with Aristotle's fifth argument (*Phys* 203b22–5); and he ascribes the amalgam to Democritus.

24 Cf. Lucretius, I.1014–20; Diogenes of Oenoanda, fr. 19 Ch.

25 Simplicius, *in Phys* 467.16; Philoponus, *in Phys* 405.23; cf. Lactantius, *de Ira* X, 10. See especially Luria [398], 37–40.

26 'Now logically, of course, infinite differences in shape imply infinite differences in size' (Bailey [383], 127; cf. Marx [388], 56). Bailey wrongly ascribes his own error to Epicurus. Klowski [424], 232, argues that if there are infinitely many phenomena and only finitely many possible combinations of atoms, then there must be infinitely many atomic shapes. But why suppose the combinations finite?

27 See especially Müller [52], 85–90, with references. To say that atoms have weight is not to say that they have a 'natural' motion 'downwards': that view is Epicurean, not Abderite.

28 '*eikontos kai mê antitupountos*': cf. Plato, *Cratylus* 420D. Sambursky [396], argues that the phrase is Democritean: it is more likely that Simplicius is echoing—consciously or unconsciously—the Platonic phrase. (*Antitupos* was an Epicurean and Stoic technical term for the resistance or solidity essential to body.)

29 *Peripalassesthai* has been restored at Theophrastus, *Sens* §66 = 68 A 135; *peripalaxis* ibid.; Aristotle, *Cael* 303a8; Simplicius, *in Cael* 609.25 (where two MSS. give it). McDiarmid [395] rejects all those emendations, and prefers *periplekesthai* in **246**; Brunschwig [397], 38–42, allows the term only in **246**. The translation 'vibrate' is favoured, e.g., by Bailey [383], 88; Liddell and Scott give 'collide' (following Hesychius); Brunschwig [397], 42, prefers 'éclabousser': the atoms are 'spattered about in the void' as the brains of a dead warrior spatter the ground. Epicurean atoms vibrate (*ad Hdt* §§43, 50). The Epicurean term is '*palmos*'; and Aëtius reports that:

Democritus maintained one sort of motion to be that by *palmos* (68 A 47).

It is possible that a Democritean theory of atomic vibration lies behind Aëtius' report, but Aëtius may merely be reading an Epicurean idea into Democritus.

30 In the third clause, editors restore the old form of zeta, '𝈋' and consequently

read 'H' for 'N'; then we should read 'H', 'HA' and 'AH' earlier in the sentence. In the Roman alphabet, 'N' is required.

31 The MSS. of Plutarch, *adv Col* 1110F = **68 A 57**, read '*ousias atomous kai diaphorous*'; Diels-Kranz print the emendation '*kadiaphorous*' ('and indifferent'), which makes Plutarch report the view I am describing. But Westman [15], 266-7, plausibly prefers '*kai adiaphthorous*' ('and indestructible').

32 For the text see Westman [15], 253-4. The saying is also quoted by Sextus (**B 9**), Galen (**B 125**; **A 49**), and by Diogenes Laertius (IX.72, *ad* **B 117**); cf. Diogenes Laertius, IX.45; Diogenes of Oenoanda, fr. 6 Ch. The differences among these quotations all lie in the listing of the *nomôi* items.

33 I follow the text and interpretation of McDiarmid [404]; the controversy is about details, and the general point I am illustrating is not in doubt. If 'to us the whole theory seems almost a play of fantasy; yet we must not forget that to its author it was a serious attempt, on the most scientific and common-sense lines at that time known, to account physically for these sensations' (Beare [39], 164).

IV *Philolaus and the Formal Cause*

1 For the text of Diogenes see Burkert [173], 241 n. 10.

2 The evidence is dissected by Burkert [173], 224-7; von Fritz [411], 456-60.

3 I follow, in almost all respects, the masterly account of Burkert [173], ch. III.

4 Philip [180], 116, 32.

5 Many scholars have tried to reconstruct Pythagoreanism from its conjectured influence on other fifth-century philosophies; I agree with Burkert [173], ch. III.3, that all such attempts are doomed to failure.

6 See, e.g., Guthrie [25], I.232-3.

7 See especially Burkert [173], ch. III.1 (cf. 234, n. 83); Burns [412]; *contra*: e.g., Philip [180], 121-2; de Vogel [181], 84-5.

8 For this meaning of *mathêma* see Burkert [173], 207, n. 80. Plutarch continues in a Platonizing vein, and his anecdote is not wholly trustworthy.

9 Burkert [173], 427; cf. especially Heidel [406]. On the other side see especially van der Waerden [58], 92-105; [408], 271-300.

10 On Hippasus see the classic paper by von Fritz [407]—rejected (rightly) by Burkert [173], 456-65. Archytas worked at arithmetic (Boethius, **47 A 19**) and geometry (Diogenes Laertius, VIII.82 = **A 1**; Proclus, **A 6**; Eutocius, **A 14**); and he more or less invented mechanics (Diogenes Laertius, VIII.82 = **A 1**; Eratosthenes, **A 15**, Vitruvius, **B 7**: see Burkert [173], 331). He built a child's rattle (Aristotle, *Pol* 1340b26 = **A 11**) and a mechanical dove (Gellius, **A 10a**). On Archytas' contribution to harmonics see **B 2**; Ptolemy, **A 16**; Porphyry, **A 17**; etc. cf. Burkert [173], 379-80. It is surely significant that Proclus, in his epitomic history of early Greek mathematics, mentions no Pythagorean prior to Archytas.

11 Iamblichus, *comm math sc* 78.8-18: Burkert [173], 50, n. 112, convincingly argues that this comes from Aristotle's *Protrepticus*.

12 Burkert [173], 399.

13 (a) *proêgagon* is usually taken to mean that they 'advanced' mathematics, in a technical way; that goes against the facts, and fits Aristotle's argument ill. (b) *prôtoi* is often taken with *hapsamenoi*: that gives quite the wrong sense.

14 I agree with Burkert [173], 44-5, that there is no significant difference between these two ways of specifying the relation between numbers and things.

15 See **B 5**; **B 7**; **B 19**; pseudo-Iamblichus, **A 12** (but see Burkert [173], 247); Proclus, **A 14**; etc.

16 But the report is rejected by Burkert [173], 461, n. 71.
17 See the elaborations in Speusippus, fr. 4 = **44 A 13** (Burkert [173], 246); Theo of Smyrna, 93.17–99.23; Sextus, *adv Math* IV.3; Aëtius, I.3.8; [Aristotle], *Problems* 910b36 = **58 B 16**.
18 On the *Hypomnemata* see especially Festugière [410]; Burkert [173], ch.I.3. Burkert concludes (82) that 'the "derivation system" is an achievement of Plato and the Academy, a genuine *transposition platonicienne* of an older, Pythagorean number philosophy'. I prefer to believe in a pre-Platonic system, later modified by the Platonists. On the 'derivation system' see especially Raven [178], chh. X–XI; Guthrie [25], I.240–82.
19 Cf. pseudo-Galen, 71. Perhaps moon creatures do not excrete because they live off smells (Aristotle, *Sens* 445a16 = **58 B 43**). Pythagoras did not excrete (Diogenes Laertius, VIII.19). For an inhabited moon see also Xenophanes, **21 A 47**), and perhaps Anaxagoras (above, p. 294, n. 17).
20 Burkert [173], 342, 350; von Fritz [411], 474.
21 Van der Waerden [408], 293–4, ascribes the Philolaic system to Hiketas, because 'Philolaus was . . . no logical mathematician'. The little we know of Hiketas' astronomy precludes that suggestion.
22 Anticipated, perhaps, by Hippasus, a Pythagorean who adopted a *phusiologia* in the Milesian style (Simplicius, **18 A 7**). But we know virtually nothing about Hippasus.
23 Retaining '*en tôi kosmôi*' (Burkert [173], 250, n. 58): Heidel proposed '*tô kosmô*' ('the nature of the universe').
24 **277** continues with an analysis of the musical intervals: two independent passages from Philolaus have been fortuitously conjoined in our source. For the text see Burkert [173], 250–1, nn. 59–65. I follow him on all but two points. (a) He defends *isotachê* ('of equal speed'); but I can make no sense of that, and I adopt Heidel's emendation *isotagê* ('of the same order'). (b) In the last sentence I translate Burkert's text, but prefer a slight anacoluthon to his proposal to begin a new sentence at '*ananka*'.
25 'Being (*estô*) is a condition not of knowledge, but of the origin of this world of ours' (Burkert [173], 251, n. 62). The text of sentence [ii] is usually emended to read: *ouch hoion t' ên ouden tôn eontôn kai gignôskomenon huph' hamôn ga genesthai* ('none of the things that exist could even become known, by us at least, if . . .'). The emendation makes Philolaus' argument epistemological; but it is unnecessary.
26 Why did Philolaus not say, more simply, that what is known is limited, and that what is limited must consist of a limiting and an unlimited component? Perhaps he did not believe that everything that is known is limited. The Pythagoreans held that 'entities can neither exist apart from number not in general be known, but numbers are known even apart from the other things' (Aristotle, fr. 203): Philolaus' limiters will turn out to be shapes, and hence numbers; so that he may have held that only limiters and limiteds, numbers and numbered things (*arithmoi* in both senses of the word) can be known.
27 I take '*erga*' quite generally: other interpretations in Burkert [173], 254, n. 79.
28 See especially *Philebus* 23C; cf. Raven [178], 180–6.
29 See Cornford [231], 3. Burkert [173], 255–6, rejects the attempt to find an Aristotelian form/matter distinction in Philolaus. Some scholars identify the being (*estô*) of things with 'the unlimited' and hence with matter, and they assimilate limit, form and harmony. Others identify the unlimited matter with the even numbers, and the limiting form with the odd numbers. Burkert rightly

rejects these views; but they are distinct from the interpretation I offer, and I do not think that Burkert's objections tell against it.

30 The same thought is embroidered in **B 11**; but the fragment is probably spurious (Burkert [173], 273-5; *contra*: de Vogel [181], 43-54).

31 According to one definition, a number is even if it is divisible into equal parts, odd if it is divisible only into unequal parts: the number 1, not being divisible at all, is thus neither odd nor even, but falls into a kind of its own: the 'even-odd' (see Aristotle, *Met* 986a20; fr. 199; fr. 203; cf. Raven [178], 116-18). There is no evidence that Philolaus adopted those definitions of even and odd; the 'third kind' of number plays no part in his system; and the phrase I translate 'of each kind' (*hekaterô eideos*) means literally 'of each-of-the-two-kinds'. I conclude that the clause introducing the even-odd into Philolaus' text is a later interpolation.

32 See, e.g., Burkert [173], 32-4, 51-2.

33 **A 3** may be 'of dubious authenticity' (Burkert [173], 41, n. 69); but it is surely a fair representation of what Eurytus did. 'Plaster' translates *asbestos*, more suitable for sticking pebbles on than Guthrie's 'whitewash'. 'Sketching' is *skiagraphein*: Guthrie [25], I.274, n. 1, thinks that the sense is 'do a shaded drawing' (to give an illusion of solidity) rather than 'do an outline drawing'.

34 Guthrie [25], I.274; cf. Raven [178], chapter VIII.

35 The 'hearth' is the central fire of Philolaic astronomy (Aristotle, fr. 203; Aëtius, **A 16**). The text of **284** reads: *to praton harmosthen to hen* . . . ('the first thing to be harmonized, the one . . .'). I think that *to hen* is a dittography (see Burkert [173], 255, n. 83); but it is perhaps defended by **B 8**: 'He says that the one is a principle of everything' (i.e., 'cosmogony starts from the central fire, or the One'); and by Aristotle, *Met* 1080b20; 1091a15 (see de Vogel [181], 40-2). **B 8**, however, is hardly genuine; and Aristotle's Pythagoreans may be an orthodoxy from which Philolaus deviated. Even if *to hen* is retained, we cannot infer that 'the number one is itself a *harmosthen*, and is therefore not simply *perainon*' (Burkert [173], 255); for if things are determined by their numerical shape, they may clearly be designated by the names of their shapes: Eurytus might have said 'And then man, 250, is generated', without implying that the *number* 250 is not a limiter.

36 On text and translation of **285** see Burkert [173], 268-9; *achri tou mesou* is hard, but the sense must surely be: 'the cosmos began to be formed at the middle'.

37 De Vogel [181], 33, judges that the limited/unlimited theory described by Aristotle is older than Philolaus' view (cf. perhaps Alcman's *poros* and *tekmôr*: vol. 1, p. 12); von Fritz [411], 230, takes the opposite view. The important point is that they are quite different theories: more evidence that Philolaus' book was not Aristotle's prime source on Pythagoreanism.

V The Logic of Locomotion

1 *MXG* 976b26 = fr. 96 Bollack. Diels-Kranz amalgamate this with fr. 48 Bollack to make their **B 14**; but see Bollack [349], III.84-5, 140-1.

2 See the illustrations on plates 4 and 5 of Bollack [349], III.

3 **B 100** is 'one of the most important discoveries in the history of science' (Burnet [31], 229); it gives an 'implicit proof of the corporeality of the air', even though Empedocles 'knew nothing of the experimental method as it is now understood'

(Kirk-Raven [33], 342). O'Brien [417], 168–9, and Furley [415], 34, show clearly that there is no trace of an 'experiment' in **B 100**; see also Guthrie [25], II.224–6.

4 So Gigon [364], 21, rightly comparing Hippolytus, **A 42**.

5 Gigon [364], 20–2 (cf. Stokes [56], 337–8, n. 14) implies that the problem simply did not arise; for Melissus wrote after Empedocles and Anaxagoras, and before him no one had connected motion with the void. But why then should Empedocles and Anaxagoras have bothered to reject the void?

6 The *MXG* probably means to ascribe *antiperistasis* to Anaxagoras too; and that may be right. But I find no other evidence to support the ascription.

7 Aristotle frequently refers to the theory (see H. Bonitz, *Index Aristotelicus*, 65a19–21, a57–b24); on the later history of the theory see, e.g., Bailey [383], 658–9.

8 *Principles of Philosophy* II.33; cf. Leibniz, *Nouveaux Essais*, preface; see Capek [390], 111–17.

9 Russell, *The Philosophy of Leibniz*, 93 n. (quoted by Capek [390], 112); Capek [390], 113. The objections in Lucretius, I.370–97, are feeble.

10 See, e.g., Diogenes Laertius, IX.31 = **67 A 1**; IX.44 = **68 A 1**; Aristotle, *Met* 985b5 = **67 A 6**; *Phys* 265b24 = **68 A 58**; Alexander, **68 A 165**; Simplicius, **67 A 8**. See also Metrodorus of Chios **70 A 2** (Aëtius), **A 3** (Theophrastus), etc; Epicurus, *ad Hdt* §§39–40; fr. 75 Us.

11 'Thing' is not wholly satisfactory, since (unlike *den*) it is not a rare word; but had Democritus written in English he would certainly have used it, playing on 'thing' and 'no-thing'.

12 See, e.g., Ross [12], 582–3, who vainly refers to *GC* 325a23–32.

13 *Pace* Diogenes, these words are not taken verbatim from Anaxagoras.

14 Zeller proposed *haploon* ('simple') or *amoiron* ('portionless') for *apeiron*; Lanza [360], 226, renders *apeiron* as 'unlimited by anything else'. But if mind is everywhere (**B 14**), then it will be *apeiron* in the ordinary sense.

15 The text of **303** is hopelessly corrupt. Diels-Kranz print: *Ho de nous, hos aei esti, to karta* . . . ('Mind, which always is, in truth now is where . . .'); Sider [422] proposes: *Ho de nous hosa estin ekratêse,* . . . ('Mind controls the things that are, and now is where . . .'); Marcovich [423] suggests: *Ho de nous, hos aei ên kai estai, karta* . . . ('Mind, which always was and will be, in truth now is where . . .').

16 For Anaxagoras, as for Plato and Aristotle, plants have souls: [Aristotle] *de plantis* 815a15 = **A 117**.

17 The first sentence of **204** is ambiguous between: (a) 'All stuffs contain a portion of every stuff other than mind', and (b) 'All stuffs other than mind contain a portion of every other stuff'. I prefer (b).

18 I.e. the 'efficient' cause; but some take Simplicius to mean the 'final' cause (see Lanza [360], 47).

19 Aëtius (**A 48**) identifies mind as God (accepted, e.g., by Vlastos [161], 114, n. 76); but the testimony is frail.

20 See B 11b–11i: eight book titles, *Aitiai Ouraniai, Aitiai Aerioi*, etc.

21 Fr. [34] [30] (p. 352.3–15) Arr (I translate Arrighetti's text, which differs substantially from that in Diels-Kranz).

22 Gigon [364], 150, says of **309** that 'this sentence . . . can only mean the following: The activity of *nous* is rejected'. But **309** neither says nor implies that. On the Principle of Causality see especially Klowski [424]; but he denies the Principle to Anaximander (ignoring **12 A 11**), and to Parmenides (ignoring

156.10); he also denies the Atomists the notion of natural regularities (228–40).

23 Already in Nietzsche [28], 412–3.

24 Some infer from Aristotle, *Phys* 252a27–32, that Empedocles used an inductive argument to show that Love and Strife are the twin forces of nature. But the induction is Aristotle's and he does not ascribe it to Empedocles (though he may well have B 17.22 in mind, as Hölscher [356], 184, believes).

25 For the varied nomenclature of Love and Strife see especially Jaeger [48], 235, nn. 38–9.

26 Cf. *MM* 1208b11 = A 20a; Plato, *Lysis* 214B. At *GC* 334a5, Aristotle repeats his ascription; but his quotation of B 54 is hardly apposite.

27 Cf. Aristotle, *Phys* 198b12; Hippolytus, *ad* B 115; Aëtius, A 32, A 35; Philo, A 49; Cicero, *de Fato* XVII.39; Plutarch, *soll anim* 964DE; Simplicius, *in Phys* 465.12, 1184.5.

28 Simplicius, *in Phys* 1184.9–10, quotes two verses: the second is B 115.2, and the first is very similar to B 115.1. Most scholars plausibly suppose that Simplicius' first verse is in fact a slight garbling of B 115.1; Bollack [349], I.153, n. 6, III.151–2, thinks it a distinct fragment, and he thus finds two separate appeals to necessity in Empedocles' fragments.

29 Simplicius quotes, in order: B 59.2 (but Bollack [349], III.226, sees a separate fragment here); B 98.1; B 85; B 75.2; B 103; B 104. Cf. pseudo-Plutarch, A 30; Philoponus, *in An* 261.17.

30 But Plutarch, A 45, says that Necessity is simply the union of Love and Strife (cf. Hippolytus, *ad* B 115).

31 That, and not the use of *sunkurein*, is why Aristotle quotes the line.

32 Bollack [349], III.453, says that *Tuchê* or Chance here stands for 'le bonheur de Philotès'; he has no argument for that strange suggestion.

33 The full text reads: '. . . are made not by any compelling nature (*nulla cogente natura*), but by a certain chance concurrence': either Cicero is confused, or else '*nulla cogente natura*' means 'without the compulsion of any natural agent'.

34 The point was firmly grasped by Marx [388], 43–5.

35 On **340** see vol. 1, p. 322, n. 22. On the equation of chance and necessity see also Gorgias, **82 B 11**, §§6, 19 (cf. Immisch [472], 16–19); and see Guthrie [25], II.415, n. 1.

VI The Neo-Ionian World Picture

1 I ignore Aristotle's other criticisms of Love and Strife: they are petty (see, e.g., *Met* 985a21–31 = **31 A 37**; *Cael* 295a29–61; and especially *GC* B6, on which see Bollack [349], I.43–8).

2 Simplicius suggests that the ordering of the world by *nous* is not a cosmogonical event but a pedagogical device (**59 A 64**: compare the similar interpretation of the *Timaeus*); Lanza [360], 114, 235, agrees that the activity of mind is extra-temporal. That is very far-fetched.

3 Strictly speaking, the Atomists need not posit eternal motion: they could, in logic, hold that there was no first moment of motion, even though motion has not gone on for ever (see vol. 1, p. 271).

4 E.g., Lanza [360], 102–3; Schofield [380], 17, n. 59; cf. *Phys* 187a29–30 = A 52.

5 On the text of **355** see Bollack [349], III.81–2: I translate his text; but the only significant problems are in the last line which is in any event incomprehensible.

6 Kirk-Raven [33], 329, mark a lacuna after line 32.

7 But the point was perhaps implicit in Parmenides' Way of Opinion: see Reinhardt [30], 75; Kahn [90], 154, n. 2.

8 *Ouk orthôs nomizousin*: many scholars say that *nomizein* here refers to the use of language (see Heinimann [445], 49; Fahr [163], 22-3). But Anaxagoras is saying not that the Greeks misuse words, but that they misdescribe events.

9 On *phusis* meaning 'birth' see, e.g., Guthrie [25], II.140, n. 1. For the contrary view, that *phusis* here means *ousia* or 'essence' see Aristotle, *Met* 1015a1 (cf. Burnet [31], 205, n. 4). Bollack [349], III.88, n. 1, has an idiosyncratic interpretation. See also Ovid, *Metamorphoses* XV.254-7.

10 For the text see Bollack [349], III.92-5. In the last line we should probably read *hê themis, ou kaleousi* . . . (see West [23], 274).

11 Müller [52], 167-73, argues that the neo-Ionian view of generation and destruction was not so far removed from ordinary conceptions of birth and death. See, e.g., Euripides, fr. 839: 'None of the things that come into being dies; but they are dissociated (*diakrinomenon*) one from another, and reveal a different form' (further references at 168, nn. 48-51).

12 Anaxagoras holds that:

> All the stuffs come into being and are destroyed in this way only; by association and dissociation. They neither come into being nor are destroyed in any other way, but persist, eternal (Aristotle, *Met* 984a14-6 = **59 A 43**; cf. Simplicius, **A 41**).

That is not a careful paraphrase of **359**: Aristotle assimilates Anaxagoras to the Atomists.

13 So, e.g., Kirk-Raven [33], 329; Guthrie [25] II.153. Different versions in O'Brien [351], 324, n. 1; Long [358], 404, n. 11, who holds that the 'roots' are not immortal.

14 On the text of **366** see von Blumenthal [427], 18-19. The 'three things' were air, fire and earth (Philoponus, **36 A 6**); and the *Triagmos* was a cosmological work (Scholiast to Aristophanes, **A 2**). Philosophically, Ion may have been close to Empedocles.

15 J. Bennett, *Kant's Dialectic* (Cambridge, 1974), 40; in these paragraphs I am indebted to Bennett's discussion (see especially, 54-6).

VII The Sophists

1 On the history of the word '*sophistês*' see, e.g., Grant [208], 106-15; Guthrie [25], III.27-34. For the fees charged by sophists see Harrison [437], 191, n. 44.

2 If they were not primarily natural scientists in the Ionian tradition, the Sophists had certainly studied science: see, e.g., Prodicus, **84 B 3-4**; Hippias, **86 A 2** (Philostratus); Antiphon, **87 B 22**. Gomperz [433], especially ch. II, states in its most extreme form the thesis that the Sophists were above all interested in rhetoric.

3 I translate the text of **371** as it appears in Diogenes Laertius, IX.51 = **A 1**; other authors append to the first sentence the clause 'nor what they are like in form'. The addition is accepted by Diels-Kranz; but see Gomperz [439]. Versions of **371** appear in Plato, *Theaetetus* 162D = **A 23**; Timon, fr. 5 = **A 12**; Cicero, **A 23**; Sextus, **A 12**; Eusebius, *ad* **B 4** (see further Müller [440], 148, n. 4). On Protagoras' condemnation and the burning of his book see also Hesychius,

A **3**; Eusebius, *ad* **B 4**; Sextus, **A 12**. Von Fritz [438], 910 (comparing Plato, *Meno* 91E) and Müller [440], 149–51, judge the whole tale a fabrication.

4 The continuation of Diogenes' text is uncertain (see Chilton [441]; [22], 56–7); but there is no way of getting Diogenes off the hook. His *gaucherie* is repeated by Epiphanius, III.2.9.

5 Müller [440], 144–7, suggests: 'Of the gods I *know* nothing, but this is what I *believe*: . . .' (cf. Fahr [163], 94–6); and he notes that Diogenes Laertius (IX.54 = **A 1**) and Eusebius (*ad* **B 4**) speak of a Protagorean work *Concerning the Gods*. There have been fanciful attempts to reconstruct Protagoras' *Peri Theôn* (see Untersteiner [434], 38, n. 47 = [435], I.69, n. 47); but I doubt if Protagoras ever wrote a theology. There is no evidence beyond the title in Eusebius and Diogenes; and Diogenes and Eusebius are simply using the first two words of **371** as a title for the work they begin (as we use *Pater Noster* or *Ave Maria*).

6 References to the discussion of this passage in Untersteiner [434], 72, n. 24 = [435], I.118.24; Guthrie [25], III.64, n. 1.

7 The main texts, apart from Democritus and Protagoras, are: Hesiod, *Works and Days* 109–201 (see Kleingünther [444], 11–15); Aeschylus, *Prometheus* 436–506 (see ibid. 66–90); Xenophanes, **21 B 18** (see especially Edelstein [446], 3–11); Hecataeus, *FGrH* F 15; Euripides, *Supplices* 195–249; [Hippocrates], *vet med* 1; Anaxagoras, **59 B 4**, **B 21a**, **A 102** (Aristotle); Archelaus, **60 A 4**; Xenophon, *Memorabilia* I.iv; IV.iii.

8 See, e.g., *Odyssey* XVII.485–7; Aeschylus, *Supplices* 381–6; *Persae* 827–8; fr. 530 M; Euripides, *Heraclides* 387–8; fr. 506; fr. 1131.

9 When the plague struck Athens in 430 BC, 'no fear of god or law of man restrained the people, who judged worship and no worship to be indifferent because they saw that all perished equally' (Thucydides, II.53.4).

10 Cf. *Phoenissae* 1726; *Hercules* 346–7; fr. 645. On Euripidean theology see Guthrie [25], III.232–4; and especially Nestle [459], 87–151. Thrasymachus' view is stated again by Aristodemus in Xenophon, *Memorabilia* I.iv.11; it is reported by Plato at *Laws* 885B and 888C, and argued against at 899E–903A.

11 On the list see Diels [4], 58–9; Müller [440], 151, n. 4.

12 Numerals followed by 'J' refer to the arrangement in Jacoby [457] (Diagoras does not appear in Diels-Kranz). Diagoras is regularly called '*ho atheos*': e.g., Scholiast to Aristophanes, II.2 J; Suda, III.3 J; Cicero, *de natura deorum* I.63 = V.6 J. The explicit statement of atheism in Athenagoras is found again in Diogenes of Oenoanda, fr. 11 Ch. Editors of Diogenes restore his text so as to ascribe the statement about Diagoras to Eudemus; but the stone is fragmentary, and no letter of Eudemus' name appears on it.

13 'Sensational pamphlet': Jacoby [457], 25; no book: Woodbury [458], 207–8 (see Aristoxenus, fr. 127a W; Philodemus, III.5 J); no 'intellectual defence': ibid. 208 (cf. Guthrie [25], III.236); *atheos* means 'ungodly': ibid. 208–9; 'leader of progressive thought': Dodds [43], 189.

14 Following Jacoby [457], 37, n. 106, Woodbury [458] thinks that the anecdotes point to 'a problem of popular belief', not a philosophical issue; and they compare Solon, fr. 1.25–32; Hesiod, *Works and Days* 267–73; Aeschylus, *Prometheus* 1093; Theognis, 731–52. It is doubtless a popular puzzle that the good gods apparently let evil prosper; but Diagoras, I hope, raised that banal puzzlement to an intellectual level and used it to ground an argument for atheism.

15 Cole [448], 153–63, suggests that the later aetiologies of Euhemerus, Diodorus,

and Leo originate from a Democritean model; but those later views are perhaps closer to Prodicus than to Democritus.

16 On the text see Kahn [90], xiv; 148, n. 3. Air is perhaps divinized by Diogenes of Apollonia, **64 B 5** (below, p. 278); cf. the Derveni papyrus (quoted below, p. 316, n. 11); Aeschylus, fr. 70; Epicharmus, **23 B 53**. With **381** compare especially Herodotus, I.131; Euripides, fr. 941 (cf. fr. 877).

17 The Suda (III.3 J) says that Democritus bought Diagoras as a slave. Derenne [345], 59, believes the story and thinks that Diagoras caught atheism from Democritus.

18 In line 13, *exheurein* might mean 'discover' rather than 'invent'; in line 26 *pseudês* might mean 'insincere' rather than 'false'. But no candid reader will seriously dispute my translations.

19 On Prodicus' religious views see also Sextus, *adv Math* IX.39, 41; Epiphanius, III.21 (see, e.g., Gomperz [433], 238-42; Untersteiner [434], 221, n. 9 and 222, n. 27 = [435] II.30, n. 9 and 32, n. 27).

20 Or 'wished': there is a long and somewhat pointless debate over the sense of *eucheto*: in the vernacular, even atheists pray that good will come to them.

21 For the text see J. Blomqvist, *Eranos* 66, 1968, 90-2.

22 See new fr. 1 (Chilton [22], 124-7) and new fr. 12 (see M. F. Smith, *American Journal of Archaeology* 75, 1971, 376-8): fr. 12 appears to link with **388**, and it may upbraid Democritus for giving truth and substance to empty *eidôla*; but (as so often) the crucial words of the fragment are scholarly restorations.

23 So Bicknell [464], 321-6.

24 Luria [514], 4-5, judges that **389** is spurious; Eisenberger [463], 150-2, makes it a politico-ethical fragment.

25 Scholars divide over the question of whether this definition is Gorgias' own; references in Untersteiner [434], 202, n. 7 = [435], I.312, n. 7.

26 On the pre-sophistic rhetoricians, Corax and Teisias, see Radermacher [471], 28-35 (texts on the rhetorical activities of the Sophists are conveniently assembled, ibid. 35-106). Note that Gorgias' teacher Empedocles was called the founder of rhetoric by Aristotle (fr. 65 = **82 A 1**; cf. Sextus, **31 A 19**). Literary studies began with Theagenes of Rhegium, a contemporary of Xenophanes, who wrote about Homer (Tatian, **8 A 1**; Scholiasts on Dionysius Thrax and Homer, **A 2a, A 3**). In the fifth century, Stesimbrotus and Glaucus followed Theagenes (e.g., Plato, *Ion* 530C = **61 A 1**), and so too did Anaxagoras (Diogenes Laertius, II.11 = **59 A 1**). See also the evidence on Anaxagoras' pupil, Metrodorus of Lampsacus: Plato, loc. cit.; Diogenes Laertius, loc. cit.; Porphyry, **61 A 5**.

27 Protagoras

> was the first to divide utterance (*logos*) into four types: prayer, question, answer, command . . . which he called the foundations of utterances (Diogenes Laertius, IX.53 = **80 A 1**).

Again:

> He divided up the types of names: male, female, and chattel (Aristotle, *Rhet* 1407b6 = **80 A 27**).

Both 'divisions' enabled him to criticize Homer for solecism (Aristotle, *Poet* 1456b15 = **A 29**; *Top* 173b18 = **A 28**), criticisms which delighted Aristophanes (*Clouds* 658-79 = **C 3**). Protagoras' thoughts are not syntax in any technical sense; but they do mark the beginning of syntactical studies.

28 Pfeiffer [24], 37; cf. Classen [466], 34–6. Mayer [469], 18, exaggerates when he says that Prodicus 'was the first to attempt consciously to give *a logical analysis* of the meanings of terms in ordinary language'.

29 Cf. Plutarch, *aud poet* 15D. The anecdote about Simonides ('Why don't you deceive the Thessalians?—They're too stupid': ibid. 15C) is ascribed to Gorgias by Untersteiner, on the authority of Wilamowitz; but see Rosenmeyer [474], 233.

30 See, e.g., Pindar, *Olympian* I.28–33; Parmenides, **28 B 8**.52; Aristophanes, *Frogs* 910 (but see *Aeschyli Vita* 7); Aristotle, *Poet* 1460a18–9. Reference to an aesthetic *theory* may perhaps be seen at: Plato, *Republic* 598E; Ephorus, *FGrH* 70 F 8; Polybius, II.56.11; Horace, *Epistles* II.1, 211; Josephus, *IA* VIII.56; Epictetus, I.iv.26. On *apatê* in general see especially Pohlenz [473], 154–62; Rosenmeyer [474]; Segar [475].

31 Prodicus objected to the Greek use of *phlegma* for 'mucus': *phlegma* is cognate with *phlegein*, 'to burn', but mucus is moist and wet (**84 B 5**; cf. Soranus, **68 A 159**). For Democritus' etymologizing see, e.g., Cole [448], 68, n. 17; for early essays in the same genre see Pfeiffer [24], 4–5.

32 These paragraphs draw heavily on H. P. Grice, 'Meaning', *PR* 66, 1957, 377–88.

VIII De Anima

1 Anaximander's name is omitted in Stobaeus' version of Aëtius, and none of the three versions of the report inspires much confidence (but see Kahn [90], 114).

2 **21 A 50** is probably an inference from **21 B 33**; it is contradicted by Diogenes Laertius, IX.19 = **21 A 1** ('soul is breath (*pneuma*)'). **28 A 45** (Macrobius) conflicts with **399**.

3 But see Tugwell [479]. Perhaps compare **22 B 85** = **70 M** ('It is hard to fight with spirit (*thumos*); for whatever it wishes, it buys at the cost of soul'); cf. Verdenius [478]. See also vol. 1, p. 325, n. 9.

4 Cf. Aristotle, *Resp* 471b30–472a25 = **68 A 106**; *An* 406b15–22 = **A 104**; Aëtius, **A 102**.

5 On *asômatos* see vol. 1, p. 335, n. 34.

6 On Iamblichus' different report of Hippasus' psychology (**18 A 11**), which is also wrong, see Burkert [173], 249, n. 50.

7 See Burkert [173], 247–8 (and above, pp. 186–90). **44 B 21** is spurious (ibid. 242–3); on later Academico-Pythagorean psychology, see ibid. 73–5.

8 Burkert [173], 73, n. 130, compares Alexander Polyhistor: 'The whole air is full of souls' (Diogenes Laertius, VIII.32 = **58 B 1a**); and he observes that mote-souls are 'rather compatible than otherwise with metempsychosis' (121, n. 3).

9 See also Alexander, **67 A 29**. Most scholars say that the eye of *a* emits effluences, and that the conjunction of eye-effluences with effluences of *b* compresses the air midway between *a* and *b*; the mid-air compression then causes *a* to see *b*. But our evidence does not support that bizarre theory (see Baldes [480]).

10 See Beare [39], 93, n. 2.

11 Note that Gorgias claims to have been present at Empedocles' magical operations (Diogenes Laertius, VIII.59 = **31 A 1**).

12 Alcmaeon used *poroi*, and some think that Empedocles borrowed them from him. But Alcmaeon's pores lead from the sense organs to the brain (e.g., Theophrastus, *Sens* §26 = **24 A 5**); Empedocles' lead from the surface of the body to the sensitive interior of ear and eye.

13 Aristotle read a theory of vision into **B 84** (*Sens* 437b23–438a5; cf. Alexander, *ad* **B 84**); and so he saddles Empedocles with two theories:

Sometimes he says we see in this way [i.e. by rays leaving the eye], sometimes by effluences from the seen objects (*Sens* 438a4–5).

Some scholars follow Aristotle's interpretation of **B 84**, but attempt to construct a unified theory from the two theories which Aristotle distinguishes; and they thus make Empedocles anticipate the view of *Timaeus* 45B. But once we realize that **B 84** deals with the structure of the eye and not with vision (see especially O'Brien [417], 140–6, with full bibliography at 157–9), we may be sure that there are neither two theories nor one *Timaeus* theory in Empedocles. (Theophrastus probably grasped the matter aright: *Sens* §§7–8 = **31 A 86**).

14 Sextus, *adv Math* VIII.286, quotes line 10 by itself; Bollack [349], III.512, characteristically and implausibly supposes that the line occurred twice in Empedocles' poem. Note that according to Democritus, 'everything has a share in soul of some sort' (Aëtius, **68 A 117**; cf. Albertus Magnus, **A 164**).

15 Differing attempts to unravel the knots of **B 77** and **B 78** in Bollack [349], III.513–7, and Zuntz [193], 209–11.

16 For the translation of **B 108**.2 see Bollack [349], III.458–9. Simplicius and Philoponus (*ad* **B 108**) explain the fragment as an account of dreaming; but see Verdenius [233], 20.

17 Hence *opôpamen* ('we see') in **425**.1 is metaphorical for 'we think' (so Aristotle, *Met* 1000b5), and the fragment has nothing to do with perception. That reading is confirmed by **B 17**.21: 'Gaze at it [sc. Love] with your mind (*noôi*), and do not sit gawping with your eyes.'

18 'Turned', *tetrammena*, is the MSS. reading, accepted by Bollack [349], III.444–6, who takes the four roots to be the subject. Most scholars prefer the emendation *tethrammenê* ('nourished'), and suppose that *hê kardia* ('the heart') is the lost subject.

19 So Bollack [349], III.576–85. For different interpretations of **430** see especially Long [494], 269–73; Schwabl [486].

20 See Theophrastus, *Sens* §10 = **A 86**. Bollack [349], III.447, paraphrases **429**.2 by: 'where especially, but misleadingly, men call the elements thought'. Hardly plausible. On the importance of the heart in thinking see, e.g., [Hippocrates], *morb sacr* VI.392 L; *cord* IX.88 L.

21 I read *hekastot'*, not *hekastos*; *periplanktôn*, not *perikamptôn*; *krasis*, not *krasin*; *parestêken*, not *paristatai*. For discussion see, e.g., Müller [52], 18–25, with references.

22 Fr. 68.3 D. Fr. 68. 1–2 D is a version of *Odyssey* XVIII.130–7, but its connexion with fr. 68.3 is uncertain. On the related fragment of Heraclitus, **B 17** = **3 M**, see vol. 1, p. 144.

23 This interpretation is elegantly argued for by Popper [35], 408–13.

24 Popper argues (i) that Parmenides had no *general* word for 'sense-organ', and so had to invent or adopt one; and (ii) that *guia* which, like *melea*, means literally 'limbs', was used by Empedocles to refer to the sense-organs. Point (i) is true and interesting (cf. Burkert [173], 270, n. 154); point (ii) is false: *guia* at **31 B 2**.1 and **B 3**.13 refers to the body as a whole (*palamai*, literally 'hands', is Empedocles' word for 'sense-organs': **B 2**.1; **B 3**.9).

25 'Body', e.g., Guthrie [25], II.67; 'elements', e.g., Bollack [284], 67 (referring to **31 B 27a**, **B 30**.1, **B 35**.11).

26 So Loenen [238], 53; for further references see, e.g., Bollack [284].

27 *'noêma'* here means 'instrument of thought', as it does at Empedocles, **429**.3.

28 Hicks [10], 221; cf. e.g., Wilamowitz [194], 658–9.

29 E.g., Aristotle, *An* 404b8–15; Porphyry, *ad* **B 126**; Diogenes Laertius, VIII.77 = **A 1**; Hippolytus, **A 31**; Aëtius, **A 32**.

30 Unless he was thinking of medical men: cf. [Hippocrates] *morb* I.30; *morb sacr* 17. Critias held that the *psuchê* is blood (e.g., Aristotle *An* 405b5 = **88 A 23**); and Philoponus, **88 A 23**, quotes Empedocles **429**.3 as a line of Critias. Philoponus may simply have bungled; but it is possible that Critias quoted Empedocles, taking him to have said that the *psuchê* was blood.

31 The reference to *harmonia* is unwanted: I take *harmonia* to be a gloss on *logos tês mixeôs*.

32 I.e., 'or is it rather some substance distinct from the elements?' Aristotle may be thinking of the *daimôn*. But the phrase 'as something else' (*heteron ti ousa*) is Aristotle's normal way of talking about non-substances; does he mean here: 'Is the *psuchê* not a *logos* but some other non-substantial being'?

33 Plotinus, *Ennead* IV.7.8⁴; Olympiodorus, *in Phaedonem* 57.17; Philoponus, *in An* 70.5.

34 **44 B 13** is defended by Burkert [173], 269–70. **44 B 22** is spurious (Burkert [173], 247; *contra*: Gladigow [187], 417–18).

35 *Contra*: see especially Gottschalk [490]. Gottschalk objects (a) that the source ascribing *harmonia* to Philolaus is late; (b) that Aristotle shows an 'inability to name a single adherent' of the doctrine, and that the anonymity of his reference 'looks deliberate and pointed'; and (c) that the doctrine is inconsistent with metempsychosis. I shall deal with (c) later. There is no force in (b): anonymous references are frequent in Aristotle; they are not 'pointed' but merely assume an ordinary knowledge of history in their audience.

Point (a) is stronger: we may well suppose that all the later references to the Pythagoreans as *harmonia* theorists derive from the *Phaedo*, and that the *Phaedo* is no history book. The question then is this: does the *Phaedo* give us reason to ascribe *harmonia* to Philolaus? Well, Plato does, I think, strongly imply that the doctrine was Philolaic; he has no motive for falsification; and the ascription is inherently plausible. And after all, who else can have propounded the doctrine?

36 There is, of course, no question of a harmony of *psychic* parts, as Cornford [405], 146–9, supposed.

37 Athenagoras ascribes the *mot* to Philolaus (**B 15**); but he is merely confused. Clement, **408**, claims to be quoting Philolaus:

> The old theologians and seers also bear witness that as a punishment the soul is yoked to the body and has been buried in it as in a tomb.

Is Clement quoting a Philolaic forgery? Or did Philolaus report the views of the 'old theologians and seers' without assenting to them?

38 Burkert [173], 272; cf. Cornford [405], 146.

39 There is a helpful survey of opinions in Guthrie [25], II.124–8.

40 I quote, in order: Vlastos [161], 125; 93; Burnet [31], 250; Jaeger [47], I.295.

41 See especially Zuntz [193], 236–43, who argues cogently that by and large the arrangement in Diels-Kranz is correct and well grounded.

42 See especially Reinhardt [491], 104–11; Zuntz [193], 211–13, 241–2.

43 Cf. Jaeger [48], 132: 'We ought to be no more surprised [by Empedocles] than when we come upon a purely scientific rationalism combined with the religious spirit of Christianity in a man of our own times.'

44 Westman [15], 247, thinks Empedocles means that human *bodies* do not simply fail to exist before and after life; but he is hardly making that banal point.

Bollack [349], III.98–100, takes the subject of **439** to be the elements; but the mistaken beliefs described in lines 2–3 apply not to the elements but to people. **B 111**.9 promises Pausanias that: 'You will bring the strength of a dead man back from Hades.' Is that a metaphorical way of saying that Pausanias will be able to show people their immortality, or just the implausible promise that Pausanias will raise the dead? **B 2**.8 reads: 'You, then, since you have come here, will learn . . .' Zuntz [193], 406–7, glosses 'since you have come to earth as a man'; and thus he finds another reference to metempsychosis in *Nature* (but see Bollack [349], III.16–17).

45 At **440**.2 I read *hêper*, with the MSS. for Diels-Kranz' *hêiper*; at **441**.3. I follow Zuntz [193], 216, in preferring *stêthea* to *mêdea*.

46 Line 1: *chrêma* probably means 'pronouncement' (Bollack [349], III.151). Between lines 3 and 4 Diels-Kranz print an invented line: it should be omitted (Zuntz [193], 194–6). Line 5: *hôrai* ('seasons') probably means 'years', and the figure 30,000 simply marks a very long period of time (see, e.g., Zuntz [193], 197). Line 10: I read *akamantos*, not *phaethontos*. Line 12: for the reading *tên kai egô nun eimi* see Zuntz [193], 198.

47 Empedocles surely ascribed the tailoring to a female *daimôn*; and that was later (rightly?) interpreted as 'nature' or 'fate'. On clothes of flesh see Zuntz [193], 405–6.

48 **B 59** begins: 'But when to a greater extent *daimôn* mingled with *daimôn* . . .' Simplicius (*ad* **B 59**) says that the *daimones* are Love and Strife; some scholars think they are the four roots; O'Brien [351], 325–36, implausibly argues that they are to be identified with the *daimones* of **442**.

49 So Guthrie [25], II.254, n. 1. Cf. **B 148**: Empedocles called 'the body surrounding the soul "man-encircling earth "'.

50 In favour of the view, O'Brien [351], 328–36, cites **442**; Aristotle, *An* 408a18–23; Plutarch, *exil* 607CE; *tranq* 474B. But I fear I can see nothing in any of those passages which supports him. Some scholars have the *daimôn* of **442** enter the world of Love and Strife from a higher, incorporeal realm (see, e.g., Zuntz [193], 252–8); but that is incredible: Empedocles knows no world beyond that of the four roots.

51 Main texts on the Great Year are Censorinus, *de die natali* 18; Aëtius, II.32; cf. Plato, *Politicus* 269C–271C; *Timaeus* 39CD. See especially van der Waerden [496].

52 The argument is adapted from Nietzsche: see especially I. Soll, 'Reflexions on Recurrence: a Re-Examination of Nietzsche's Doctrine, *die Ewige Wiederkehr des Gleiches*', in *Nietzsche*, ed. R. C. Solomon (New York, 1973).

53 Lactantius, *SVF* II.623; Simplicius, *in Phys* 886.12 = *SVF* II.627; Alexander, *SVF* II.624; cf. *SVF* II.625–31; I.109. See also Hume, *Dialogues concerning Natural Religion*, ch. VIII.

54 Soll, op. cit. 339–40, argues that 'there can be no accumulation of experience from one recurrence to the next. A person can have no direct memories of earlier recurrences'; and he infers that Pythagoras₁ is not identical with Pythagoras₂. But Soll's second statement does not follow from his first.

IX *Conduct Unbecoming*

1 **448** and **449** are fragments 1 and 2 of Pap. Oxy. 1364 (fragments 3–13 contain only a few letters each); **450** is Pap. Oxy. 1797. Harpocration proves that **448**.

and hence (presumably) **449**, belong to Antiphon (see Diels-Kranz, II.346, n.); on the ascription of **450** see, e.g., Guthrie [25] III.110, n. 1.

2 The papyrus has many lacunae; I translate the restorations accepted by Diels-Kranz, except where noted.
448: I.1: Diels reads *ou*]*n* ('justice, therefore, . . .'); Schöne proposed *d' ê*]*n* ('justice, we said, was . . .'). I.12: 'deal with' translates *chrêsthai*; the word is hard to render, but 'manipulate' (Guthrie [25], III.108) gives the wrong idea. I.25: *epith*]*eta*—perhaps rather *sunth*]*eta*, 'conventional' (but see Untersteiner [430], IV.76). II.13: for *para to dunaton* some give *per impossibile*, others 'as far as possible', others 'more than it [sc. nature] can bear'. No translation is wholly agreeable, and I do not know what to make of the phrase. II.24: reading *pantôn heneka toutôn*: see Kerferd [502], 28. III.25: reading *t*[*o gar*] (Hunt), rather than Diels-Kranz' *t*[*o d' au*] ('but'). III.30: I make *apo* partitive, with Guthrie [25], III.109, n. 1. IV.24: lines 25–31 are beyond restoration; for 30–31 Heinimann [445], 138, n. 48, proposes:

. . .*di*] *kaioi* [*no
mizo*] *ntai ka*]*i*

'. . . are thought to be just; and so are those who . . .'. That gives what is surely the right sense. VI.1–5 is fragmentary; but the sense of the lines is clear. VI.19: the text is not in doubt; but I cannot make any sense of it. VI.25–30: the text is again fragmentary: I translate Diels-Kranz' text, which gives a tolerable sense; see further Untersteiner [430], IV.89. Col. VII probably continues the catalogue of injustices begun at VI.25; but the papyrus is too lacunose to translate.
449: Only *frustulae* of col. I survive. II.10: Guthrie [25] III.153, translates: 'since by nature we are all made to be alike in all respects, both barbarians and Greeks'; but he allows that 'the Greek is rather unusual', and considers the translation I adopt to be 'more accurate'. II.16–20: the text is reasonably plain, but the sense is obscure; perhaps a line has been omitted after 16. II.20–2 are too fragmentary to translate.
450: I.12: reading *eipe*]*r* (Diels) for Diels-Kranz' *epeipe*]*r* (Hunt proposed *kai ga*]*r*). I.20: reading *eikos de*] (Hunt) for Diels-Kranz *kai hama*] ('and at the same time'). I.21: reading *eis* [*huste/ro*]*n · ene*[*sti gar* (Hunt-Crönert), for Diels-Kranz' [*husteron/hô*]*n hene*[*ka eipen* ('. . . later on, on account of what he said'). II.20: As Kranz observes, we expect not *mêde auton adikeisthai* but *mêden auton adikoumenon* ('and for not wronging at all when one has not oneself been wronged at all . . .'). Perhaps the text is in error.

3 Untersteiner [434] 267, n. 127 = [435]. II.98, n. 127, places **450** between **448** and **449**; in [430], IV.91, he inserts Pap. Oxy. 414 between **450** and **449**. But see Guthrie [25] III.110, n. 1.

4 'Not everything that is *phusei* is advantageous, and Antiphon's norm must be restricted to *ta phusei xumpheronta*' (Kerferd [502], 31. He translates *ta phusei xumpheronta* by 'what is advantageous *to* human nature'). But there is no 'norm' laid down in **448**; *ta phusei xumpheronta* contrast with the artificial advantages brought by *nomima*.

5 'The principal argument to be extracted with certainty from the fragments is a criticism of *nomos* that is essentially ethical, not anarchistic' (Moulton [504], 331); see ibid. 329, n. 1, for references to those scholars who find a 'radical critique' of morality in **448–50**.

6 Euripides, *Hecuba* 799–801; Lysias, II.19; Xenophon, *Memorabilia* IV.iv.12–3;

312

Aristotle, *EN* 1129a32–4; cf. Pindar, fr. 169; Plato, *Theaetetus*, 172A; Chrysippus, *SVF* III.314.

7 See especially Kerferd [525]; *contra*: e.g., McDowell [526], 172–3. I pass by the question whether Protagoras is presented as a moral relativist in the *Protagoras*: see Moser-Kustas [507].

8 **90 A 1** §8 says that the Peloponnesian War is the most recent war. The text is emended; the reference hardly does the chronological work required of it; and a detailed commentary is required before the piece can be dated with any certainty.

9 'The author places side by side, without connecting them organically, elements borrowed from different sophists, among whom Protagoras is pre-eminent both as to thought and as to the methods employed' (Levi [511], 302; cf. Gomperz [433], 138–92).

10 Reading *all' allo hekateron* (Blass; cf. §11; **A 2** §12), for the MSS. *all' hekateron*.

11 See, e.g., Adkins [207], 124–7 (who strangely states that 'the concept of moral responsibility is . . . unimportant to the Greek', ibid. 3). Compare Euripides' defence of Helen in *Troades* 914–1059.

12 A. J. Ayer, *Philosophical Essays* (London, 1954), 275. (For Greek attitudes to chance and responsibility see especially Dover [206], 138–41).

13 Ayer, op. cit., 279.

14 I translate *kai gar horômen echontes opsin ouch* . . . (Immisch); the text is very uncertain.

15 Immisch [472], 22.

16 The text is too corrupt for restoration (see Immisch [472], 39, n. 1); but it is clear enough that *logos* is assimilated to *bia*.

17 130 in Stobaeus, 80 under the name of 'Democrates': the authenticity of both sets of fragments has been doubted; see especially Guthrie [25], II.489–92.

18 Luria [514], 6–7, refers to **B 299** and holds that the trivial *gnômai* are translations from Achikar. On early Greek gnomic moralizing see Grant [208], 86–97. Nestle [460], 589–93, finds numerous parallels between Democritus' *gnômai* and the *sententiae* of Euripides' characters.

19 'A democrat' (Bailey [383], 211); cf. **B 251**. *Contra*: Aalders [518] (cf., e.g., **B 49**, **B 75**, **B 254**, **B 266**, **B 267**). If the Anonymus Iamblichi (**89 A 1**) is Democritean (see Cole [519]), then there is more evidence available to decide the dispute.

20 Democritus propounds 'the first rigorously naturalistic ethics in Greek thought' (Vlastos [513], 62); see Guthrie [25], II.492, n. 1, for other attempts to find an ethical system in Democritus. But 'Democritus' "ethics" hardly amounts to a moral theory; there is no effort to set the picture of the "cheerful" man on a firm philosophical basis' (Bailey [383], 522).

21 Scholars usually see an apparent contradiction between **478** and **479**, which they try in various fashions to reconcile. The contradiction arises from the standard mistranslation of **479** as: 'Accept nothing pleasant unless it is advantageous'.

22 References in Luria [514], 3–4.

23 So Luria [514], 9–13; cf. Aelian, **A 150a**; Stobaeus, **C 7** §3; Aristotle, *HA* 630b31; [Aristotle], *Mirabilia* 830b1; Xenophon, *Memorabilia* IV.iv.20; see further Heinimann [445], 145–7.

24 See Taylor [517], 16–27, who also refers to Diotimus, **76 A 1** (but see Bailey [383], 188–9).

25 Bailey [383], 188; cf. Luria [514], 7.

26 Bailey, loc. cit.

X *The Bounds of Knowledge*

1 Line 3: I read *athroisantes* (*athrêsantes*, Diels-Kranz; *athroisantos* or *athrêsantos*, MSS.); and I accept, with little confidence *en zôêsi biou* (see Bollack [349], III.11). Line 6: the MSS. read, unmetrically, *to d' holon euchetai einai*; I translate Fränkel's *to d' holon tis ar' euchetai einai*; (Diels-Kranz prefer to insert *pas* after *holon* ('but everyone boasts . . .'): Bollack reads *ta d' hol' oudeis* . . . ('but no one boasts he has found the wholes'). No emendation is wholly satisfactory; but the import of the line is plain enough. Line 9: retain *ou pleion ge* (MSS.). Diels-Kranz read *ou pleon êe*, with no stop before *ou* ('you will learn no more than human wit achieves'). The emendation is needless, and it produces bathos.

2 Line 2: translation as in Bollack [349], II.8. Line 6: 'you' probably refers to the Muse of line 3; Pausanias is not addressed until line 9. But the sentiments of lines 6–8 are odd if put to a Muse: some scholars refer 'you' to Pausanias, and posit a lacuna before line 6.

3 *Contra*: Bollack [349], III.8, who refers to Empedocles' alleged theory that vision involves the eye in sending out rays and 'grasping' its object. But that theory is not Empedoclean (above, p. 308, n. 13).

4 Bollack [349], III.19–22, rightly connects **B 2** with the promise of **B 111**.

5 The Greek of **487** is, unfortunately, not unambiguous. Thus Mourelatos [245], 347, translates: 'What manifests itself to us is the look of things which are not themselves perceptible'; Gomperz [521], 342, gives: 'For the appearances are only the way in which what is unperceived presents itself to us'. Those readings are, of course, thoroughly consonant with Anaxagorean physics; and we can understand Democritus' admiration for the fragment. But Epicurus understood the apophthegm according to the orthodox interpretation which I follow in the text (Diogenes Laertius, X.32); and no doubt Democritus did too.

6 *hôs* means 'that', not 'how'. For excellent notes on text and translation see Guthrie [25] III.188–92.

7 So, e.g., McDowell [526], 118, who thinks that 152A6–8 may be a quotation from Protagoras; *contra*: e.g., Versenyi [522], 181 (who wrongly cites *Theaetetus* 170A, 170E, 171AC, in support of the collective sense).

8 McDowell [526], 120, takes 167A8 to imply that Protagoras 'denies the possibility of non-perceptual judgments'; that is implausible in itself, and it does not follow from the distinction between judgmental and phenomenological seeming.

9 'Man is the measure of "all things" (*pantôn chrêmatôn*)': *chrêma* means, quite generally, 'thing'; it is fashionable but futile to recall its etymological connection with *chrêsthai* 'use', and to talk of 'things with a special relation to our involvement with them' (Versenyi [522], 182).

10 Democritus perhaps attacked Protagoras at this point: see **68 B 11** .

11 A papyrus fragment refers the thesis to Prodicus (see Binder-Lieseborghs [530]); Isocrates refers to it (*Helen* 1); and cf. Plato, *Cratylus* 429DE.

12 The *Ou Mallon* Principle had a long history; but I ignore later uses of the Principle, which seem to me to differ considerably from the Abderite use.

13 So Weiss [538], 49, n. 1; von Fritz [438], 916.

14 [Democritus] says that soul and mind are simply the same; for what is true is what appears (Aristotle, *An* 404a28 = **68 A 101**).

Presumably that has to be explained by way of **504** (see Kapp [537], 166–7).

15 Cf. Sextus, **A 59**, **A 110**, **A 134**.
16 The 'new fragment' of Protagoras (see Gronewald [528]) makes him a sceptic:

> e.g., I see the moon, another man does not: it is unclear (*adêlon*) whether it exists or not.

But the 'fragment' is full of Stoic terminology and has no authority.
17 Plutarch distressingly contradicts Aristotle's report. Colotes, it seems, had ascribed to Democritus the restricted Principle of Equipollence; Plutarch vehemently retorts:

> So far is Democritus from thinking that each thing is no more (*mê mallon*) thus than thus, that he attacked Protagoras the sophist when he said this, and wrote many convincing things against him (**68 B 156**).

We know nothing more of Democritus' attack on Protagoras than the *peritropê*. Democritus attacked Protagoras on matters intimately connected to the Principle of Equipollence, and he drew quite un-Protagorean conclusions from the Principle: Plutarch, who is engaged in heated polemic, may have wrongly inferred that Democritus rejected the Principle outright. In any event, I prefer the testimony of Aristotle and Colotes to that of Plutarch.
18 Cf. Sextus, **70 A 25**; Philodemus, **A 25**; Epiphanius, **A 23**; Diogenes Laertius, IX.58 = **72 A 1**. The text of **505** is reconstructed in part from Cicero's translation, and the details are far from certain.
19 The MSS. read *diathêkên* ('disposition'); for the emendation see, e.g., Steckel [385], 207.
20 The word '*epirhusmiê*' itself has foxed the scholars; de Ley [539] plausibly suggests *ameipsirhusmiê* (cf. **B 139**), which would have the sense I give to *epirhusmiê*.
21 And some translate *idmen* in **506** as 'know by experience' (see especially Cleve [37], 428–31). Compare Fränkel's version of Xenophanes' sceptical fragment (vol. 1, p. 138). But *idmen* means no more than 'know'; and **B 7** and **B 8** are more than enough to impose a scepticism on Democritus.

XI The Last of the Line

1 Diels-Kranz, II.59, think that these are different titles for (parts of) a single work; *contra*: Theiler [541], 6–7.
2 Hussey [34], 141.
3 See, e.g., Aristophanes, *Clouds* 225–36 = **C 1**; *Frogs* 892; Euripides, *Troades* 884–9 = **C 2**. And perhaps the pseudo-Hippocratic *de natura hominis* singles out Diogenes as the representative of Ionian science (see Jouanna [270], 307–14).
4 Some may suspect that **514** refers to Diogenes of Smyrna, who 'believed the same things as Protagoras' (Epiphanius, **71 A 2**).
5 'Diogenes agreed with the atomists in holding that sensations were subjective and relative', but 'this subjectivity . . . did not for him carry with it the denial of sensible qualities to the primary substance itself, as the atomic theory demanded' (Guthrie [25], II.377 and n. 3). That ascribes a strange view to Diogenes; and there is no textual evidence to show that he did not agree with the Atomists on both counts.
6 'Third Explanation of the New System', in Leibniz, *The Monadology*, ed. R. Latta (Oxford, 1898), p. 333.

7 Diogenes is presumably 'speaking with the vulgar', if he really denies generation and destruction.
8 The source of the passages (I.iv and IV.iii) is much debated: see especially Theiler [541], 14–54, who argues that they are in part based on Diogenes; Huffmeier [542], who strangely denies any teleological thoughts to Diogenes.
9 Air and thought: e.g., Theophrastus, *Sens* §§39, 44 = **A 19**; Aristotle, *An* 405a21 = **A 20**; cf. Aëtius, **A 30**. Divine air. e.g., Philodemus, Cicero, Aëtius, Augustine, **A 8**.
10 The MSS. read *apo gar moi touto ethos*, which makes no sense. Diels-Kranz, and most scholars, accept Usener's emendation: *auto gar moi touto theos*. I translate, hesitantly, Panzerbieter's: *auto gar moi toutou ethos*.
11 Two fragments tell against that interpretation:

And this itself is a body, both eternal and deathless; and of the rest, some come into being, others depart (**525**).

But this seems to me to be clear, that it is both great and strong and eternal and immortal and multiscient (**B 8**).

Simplicius quotes **B 8** immediately after **525**, and he takes the subject of both fragments to be the *archê*. Hence the *archê* is multiscient, and therefore (by the argument of **528**) it is air—and presumably also the divinity. But Simplicius found **B 8** 'elsewhere', i.e., not in the same context as **525**; and we are not obliged to associate the two fragments as he does. Compare also column 15, lines 1–3 of the Derveni papyrus:

And since the things that exist are, each one, called after that which predominates (*epikratountos*), everything by that same argument was called Zeus; for the air predominates over everything to the extent that it wishes.

(Text in G. S. Kapsomenos, *Archaiologikon Deltion* 19, 1964, 17–25; discussion in Burkert [67]). Air is the divinity and the predominant element: and the connexions between this fragment and Anaxagoras and Diogenes are not far to seek. But there is no suggestion that air is also the *Urstoff* or material *archê*.

Bibliography

The bibliography has two functions: it gives detailed references to the various books and articles cited in the Notes; and it attempts to provide an intelligible and articulated guide to the vast modern literature on the Presocratics. The second aim accounts for the arrangement of the bibliography; the first explains the inclusion of some fairly minor items.

I use the following abbreviations:

ABG *Archiv für Begriffsgeschichte*
AC *Acta Classica*
AGP *Archiv für Geschichte der Philosophie*
AJP *American Journal of Philology*
An *Analysis*
APQ *American Philosophical Quarterly*
BICS *Bulletin of the Institute of Classical Studies*
BJPS *British Journal for the Philosophy of Science*
CP *Classical Philology*
CQ *Classical Quarterly*
CR *Classical Review*
H *Hermes*
HSCP *Harvard Studies in Classical Philology*
JHI *Journal of the History of Ideas*
JHP *Journal of the History of Philosophy*
JHS *Journal of Hellenic Studies*
JP *Journal of Philosophy*
M *Mind*
MH *Museum Helveticum*
Mnem *Mnemosyne*
NGG *Nachrichten von der Gesellschaft der Wissenschaft zu Göttingen*
PAS *Proceedings of the Aristotelian Society*
PCPS *Proceedings of the Cambridge Philological Society*
Phlg *Philologus*
Phron *Phronesis*
PQ *Philosophical Quarterly*
PR *Philosophical Review*

317

BIBLIOGRAPHY

QSGM   Quellen und Studien zur Geschichte der Mathematik
RE   Pauly-Wissowa's Realenkyklopädie der klassischen Altertumswissenschaft
REA   Revue des Études Anciennes
REG   Revue des Études Grècques
RhM   Rheinisches Museum
RM   Review of Metaphysics
SO   Symbolae Osloenses
TAPA   Transactions of the American Philological Association
WS   Wiener Studien

A: GENERAL

I: Texts

The standard work on the Presocratics, a monument to scholarship and an indispensable aid, is:
[1] H. Diels and W. Kranz: *Die Fragmente der Vorsokratiker* (Berlin, 1960[10])
The fragments, but not the *testimonia*, are Englished in:
[2] K. Freeman: *The Pre-Socratic Philosophers* (Oxford, 1946)
For the poetical Presocratics it is worth consulting:
[3] H. Diels: *Poetarum Philosophorum Fragmenta* (Berlin, 1901)
   The doxography is finely discussed, and the main texts printed, in another magisterial work by Diels:
[4] H. Diels: *Doxographi Graeci* (Berlin, 1879)
   Editions of texts of individual Presocratics are listed under the appropriate heading in part B of the bibliography; editions of certain other ancient authors are mentioned in the next section, and in Appendix A.

II: Source Criticism

Most scholars accept the reconstruction of the doxographical tradition which Diels established in [4]; but there are some important qualifications in:
[5] P. Steinmetz: *Die Physik des Theophrasts*, Palingenesia I, Bad Homburg, 1964)
and some intemperate disagreements in Gershenson-Greenberg [361].
   The historical value of the doxography is a matter of grave dispute. A lengthy denunciation of Aristotle was made in:
[6] H. F. Cherniss: *Aristotle's Criticism of Presocratic Philosophy* (Baltimore, 1935)
and Theophrastus was attacked in similar vein by:
[7] J. B. McDiarmid: 'Theophrastus on the Presocratic Causes', *HSCP* 61, 1953, 85–156 = Furley-Allen [70]
Most books on the Presocratics contain appreciations of the doxography. Against Cherniss see especially: ·
[8] W. K. C. Guthrie: 'Aristotle as an Historian of Philosophy', *JHS* 77, 1957, 35–41 = Furley-Allen [70]
Guthrie's paper has been examined in turn by:
[9] J. G. Stevenson: 'Aristotle as Historian of Philosophy', *JHS* 94, 1974, 138–43
A wealth of relevant material can be found in the classic commentaries of:
[10] R. D. Hicks: *Aristotle: de Anima* (Cambridge, 1907)
[11] W. D. Ross: *Aristotle's Metaphysics* (Oxford, 1924)
[12] W. D. Ross: *Aristotle's Physics* (Oxford, 1936)

And there is a brilliant paper on a nice detail by:

[13] B. Snell: 'Die Nachrichten über die Lehre des Thales und die Anfänge der griechischen Philosophie- und Literaturgeschichte', *Phlg* 96, 1944, 170–82 = Snell [82]

On Theophrastus see Steinmetz [5], and the Introduction to:

[14] G. M. Stratton: *Theophrastus and the Greek Physiological Psychology before Aristotle* (London, 1917)

Plutarch's testimony is analysed by:

[15] R. Westman: *Plutarch gegen Colotes*, Acta Philosophica Fennica VII (Helsinki, 1955)

[16] J. P. Hershbell: 'Plutarch as a Source for Empedocles Re-examined', *AJP* 92, 1971, 156–84

And on Hippolytus consult:

[17] J. P. Hershbell: 'Hippolytus' *Elenchos* as a Source for Empedocles Re-examined', *Phron* 18, 1973, 97–114

The major commentaries on the classical authors frequently shed incidental light on the Presocratics; I have found myself most often helped by:

[18] U. von Wilamowitz-Moellendorf: *Euripides: Herakles* (Berlin, 1895)

[19] T. L. Heath: *The Thirteen Books of Euclid's Elements* (Cambridge, 1926²)

[20] C. Bailey: *Epicurus* (Oxford, 1926)

[21] C. Bailey: *Lucretius: de Rerum Natura* (Oxford, 1947)

[22] C. W. Chilton: *Diogenes of Oenoanda* (London, 1971)

[23] M. L. West: *Hesiod: Theogony* (Oxford, 1966)

Finally, no one should fail to peruse the opening chapters of:

[24] R. Pfeiffer: *A History of Classical Scholarship*, I (Oxford, 1968)

III: General Histories

English readers will find a treasury of humane scholarship in the first three volumes of:

[25] W. K. C. Guthrie: *A History of Greek Philosophy* (Cambridge, 1962, 1965, 1969)

Zeller's handbook, *Die Philosophie der Griechen*, has undergone several revisions since its first appearance in 1892; the fullest and most recent edition—still incomplete—is:

[26] E. Zeller and R. Mondolfo: *La Filosofia dei Greci nel suo sviluppo storico* (Florence, 1932–   )

Philosophers will enjoy the relevant chapters of:

[27] G. W. F. Hegel: *Lectures on the History of Philosophy*, trans. E. S. Haldane and F. H. Simson (London, 1892; first publishing of German text, 1840)

and also:

[28] F. Nietzsche: *Die Philosophie im tragischen Zeitalter der Griechen*, in vol. III of Nietzsche's *Werke*, ed. K. Schlechta (Munich, 1956; first published in 1872)

Of other general accounts of Presocratic thought, the most influential have been:

[29] P. Tannery: *Pour l' histoire de la science Hellène* (Paris, 1887)

[30] K. Reinhardt: *Parmenides und die Geschichte der griechischen Philosophie* (Bonn, 1916)

([30] is, for my money, the most sparkling book in the whole field)

[31] J. Burnet: *Early Greek Philosophy* (London, 1930⁴)

[32] H. F. Cherniss: 'Characteristics and Effects of Presocratic Philosophy', *JHI* 12, 1951, 319–45 = Furley-Allen [70]

There are sober introductions in:

[33] G. S. Kirk and J. E. Raven: *The Presocratic Philosophers* (Cambridge, 1962⁴)

[34] E. Hussey: *The Presocratics* (London, 1972)

And a spirited introduction in:

[35] K. R. Popper: 'Back to the Presocratics', *PAS* 59, 1958/9, 1–24 = K. R. Popper: *Conjectures and Refutations* (London, 1969³) = Furley-Allen [70]

See also:

[36] T. Gomperz: *Greek Thinkers* (London, 1901–12)

[37] F. M. Cleve: *The Giants of Pre-Sophistic Greek Philosophy* (The Hague, 1965)

[38] G. Calogero: *Storia della logica antica* (Bari, 1967)

IV: Monographs

I list here a number of books which bear upon particular aspects of early Greek thought: their titles on the whole are adequate guides to their contents.

[39] J. I. Beare: *Greek Theories of Elementary Cognition* (Oxford, 1906)

[40] F. M. Cornford: *The Laws of Motion in Ancient Thought* (Cambridge, 1931)

[41] F. M. Cornford: *Principium Sapientiae* (Cambridge, 1952)

[42] D. R. Dicks: *Early Greek Astronomy to Aristotle* (London, 1970)

[43] E. R. Dodds: *The Greeks and the Irrational* (Berkeley, Cal., 1951)

[44] H. Fränkel: *Early Greek Poetry and Philosophy*, trans. M. Hadas and J. Willis (Oxford, 1975)

[45] T. L. Heath: *Aristarchus of Samos* (Oxford, 1913)

[46] T. L. Heath: *A History of Greek Mathematics* (Oxford, 1921)

[47] W. W. Jaeger: *Paideia* (Oxford, 1939–45)

[48] W. W. Jaeger: *The Theology of the Early Greek Philosophers* (Oxford, 1947)

[49] W. H. S. Jones: *Philosophy and Medicine in Ancient Greece* (Baltimore, 1946)

[50] G. E. R. Lloyd: *Polarity and Analogy* (Cambridge, 1966)

[51] H. Lloyd-Jones: *The Justice of Zeus* (Berkeley, Cal., 1971)

[52] C. W. Müller: *Gleiches zu Gleichen—ein Prinzip frühgriechischen Denkens* (Wiesbaden, 1965)

[53] S. Sambursky: *The Physical World of the Greeks* (London, 1956)

[54] B. Snell: *Die Ausdrücke für den Begriff des Wissens in der vorplatonischen Philosophie*, Philologische Untersuchungen 29 (Berlin, 1924)

[55] B. Snell: *The Discovery of Mind* (Oxford, 1953)

[56] M. C. Stokes: *One and Many in Presocratic Philosophy* (Washington, DC, 1971)

[57] L. Sweeney: *Infinity in the Presocratics* (The Hague, 1972)

[58] B. L. van der Waerden: *Science Awakening*, trans. A. Dresden (New York, 1961)

[59] M. L. West: *Early Greek Philosophy and the Orient* (Oxford, 1971)

I append to this section a number of articles of a general scope. The first two are seminal pieces:

[60] W. A. Heidel: 'Qualitative Change in Pre-Socratic Philosophy', *AGP* 19, 1906, 333–79 = Mourelatos [72]

[61] W. A. Heidel: 'Περὶ Φυσέως:|A Study of the Conception of Nature among the Pre-Socratics', *Proceedings of the American Academy of Arts and Sciences* 45, 1910, 77–133

The next article is of wider scope than its title suggests, being a comprehensive account of early notions of cognition:

[62] K. von Fritz: 'Νοῦς, νοεῖν and their Derivatives in Presocratic Philosophy', *CP* 40, 1945, 223–42 and 41, 1946, 12–34 = Mourelatos [72] = Gadamer [71]
With Jones [49], compare:
[63] J. Longrigg: 'Philosophy and Medicine: some early Interactions', *HSCP* 67, 1963, 147–76
With Lloyd [50], compare:
[64] G. E. R. Lloyd: 'Hot and Cold, Dry and Wet, in early Greek Thought', *JHS* 84, 1964, 92–106 = Furley-Allen [70]
With Dicks [42], compare:
[65] D. R. Dicks: 'Solstices, Equinoxes and the Presocratics', *JHS* 86, 1966, 26–40
and the reply by:
[66] C. H. Kahn: 'On Early Greek Astronomy', *JHS* 90, 1970, 99–116
Finally, note the interesting piece on the Derveni papyrus by:
[67] W. Burkert: 'Orpheus und der Vorsokratiker', *Antike und Abendland* 14, 1968, 93–114

V: Anthologies

[68] V. E. Alfieri and M. Untersteiner (eds): *Studi di Filosofia Greca* (Bari, 1950)
[69] J. P. Anton and G. L. Kustas (eds): *Essays in Ancient Greek Philosophy* (Albany, New York, 1971)
[70] D. J. Furley and R. E. Allen (eds): *Studies in Presocratic Philosophy* (London, 1970, 1975)
[71] H. G. Gadamer (ed.): *Um die Begriffswelt der Vorsokratiker* (Darmstadt, 1968)
[72] A. P. D. Mourelatos (ed.): *The Presocratics* (Garden City, New York, 1974)

VI: Collected Papers

[73] J. Bernays: *Gesammelte Abhandlungen* (Berlin, 1885)
[74] F. M. Cornford: *The Unwritten Philosophy* (Cambridge, 1950)
[75] H. Diller: *Kleine Schriften zur antiken Literatur* (Munich, 1971)
[76] H. Fränkel: *Wege und Formen frühgriechischen Denkens* (Munich, 1960²)
[77] K. von Fritz: *Grundprobleme der Geschichte der antiken Wissenschaft* (Berlin, 1971)
[78] O. Gigon: *Studien zur antiken Philosophie* (Berlin, 1972)
[79] U. Hölscher: *Anfängliches Fragen* (Göttingen, 1968)
[80] W. Nestle: *Griechische Studien* (Stuttgart, 1948)
[81] K. Reinhardt: *Vermächtnis der Antike* (Göttingen, 1966²)
[82] B. Snell: *Gesammelte Schriften* (Göttingen, 1966)
[83] F. Solmsen: *Kleine Schriften* (Hildesheim, 1968)
[84] M. Untersteiner: *Scritti Minori* (Brescia, 1971)

VII: Bibliography

There are excellent bibliographies in Guthrie [25], Sweeney [57], and Mourelatos [72]; see also:
[85] G. B. Kerferd: 'Recent Work on Presocratic Philosophy', *APQ* 2, 1965, 130–40
And of course most of the books and papers I list here contain a multitude of further references.
   Bibliographies date quickly. The reader may keep abreast of the tide by consulting

BIBLIOGRAPHY

L'Année Philologique, Repertoire bibliographique de la Philosophie de Louvain, and *The Philosophers Index*, periodicals which, taken together, catch all the new literature on the subject.

B: PARTICULAR

The second half of the bibliography is divided into sections that correspond to the chapters of the book. Items referred to in one section will often contain material relevant to other sections; and many of the works listed in part *A*—notably Guthrie [25]—will profitably be consulted in connexion with every chapter.

Chapter I

Neo-Ionian history and chronology are discussed in all the General Histories; see also:

[343] A. E. Taylor: 'On the Date of the Trial of Anaxagoras', *CQ* 11, 1917, 81–7
[344] J. A. Davison: 'Protagoras, Democritus and Anaxagoras', *CQ* n.s. 3, 1953, 33–45
[345] E. Derenne: *Les Procès d' Impiété intentés aux philosophes à Athènes au Vme et au IVme siècles avant J.C.* (Liège, 1930)
[346] J. Ferguson: 'On the Date of Democritus', *SO* 40, 1965, 17–26
[347] H. de Ley: 'Democritus and Leucippus: two notes on ancient Atomism', *L' Antiquité classique* 37, 1968, 620–33
[348] D. O'Brien: 'The Relation of Anaxagoras and Empedocles', *JHS* 88, 1968, 93–114

For Anaxagoras, the Atomists and Philolaus see the bibliographies to Chapters II, III and IV.

The most recent edition of Empedocles' poem *Concerning Nature* is:
[349] J. Bollack: *Empédocle* (Paris, 1965–9)
The classic study is:
[350] E. Bignone: *Empedocle* (Turin, 1916)
And there is a full-scale treatment in:
[351] D. O'Brien: *Empedocles' Cosmic Cycle* (Cambridge, 1969)
See also:
[352] C. E. Millerd: *On the Interpretation of Empedocles* (Chicago, 1908)

The orthodox account of the cosmic cycle is stated at length in Bignone [349] and O'Brien [351], and more concisely by:
[353] D. O'Brien: 'Empedocles' Cosmic Cycle', *CQ* n.s. 17, 1967, 29–40
For various heterodoxies see Bollack [349]; and also
[354] E. Minar: 'Cosmic Periods in the Philosophy of Empedocles', *Phron* 8, 1963, 127–45 = Anton-Kustas [69]
[335] F. Solmsen: 'Love and Strife in Empedocles' Cosmology', *Phron* 10, 1965, 109–48 = Furley-Allen [70]
[356] U. Hölscher: 'Weltzeiten und Lebenzyklus', *H* 93, 1965, 7–33 = Hölscher [79]
[357] J. Mansfeld: 'Ambiguity in Empedocles B 17.3–5', *Phron* 17, 1972, 17–40
There is a judicious survey by:
[358] A. A. Long: 'Empedocles' Cosmic Cycle in the 'Sixties', in Mourelatos [72]
Finally, on Empedoclean atomism see Reinhardt [491], and:
[359] J. Longrigg: 'Roots', *CR* n.s. 17, 1967, 1–5

322

Chapter II

There is an edition of Anaxagorean texts by:
[360] D. Lanza: *Anassagora—testimonianze e frammenti* (Florence, 1966)
and the Greek is Englished in:
[361] D. E. Gershenson and D. A. Greenberg: *Anaxagoras and the Birth of Physics* (New York, 1964)
On textual matters see also:
[362] H. Fränkel: review of Ciurnelli, *La Filosofia di Anassagora*, *CP* 45, 1950, 187–91 = Fränkel [76]
[363] A. Wasserstein: 'A note on fragment 12 of Anaxagoras', *CR* n.s. 10, 1960, 4–6
    There are comprehensive papers on Anaxagoras' thought by:
[364] O. Gigon: 'Zu Anaxagoras', *Phlg* 91, 1936, 1–41 = Gigon [78]
[365] M. C. Stokes: 'On Anaxagoras', *AGP* 47, 1965, 1–19 and 217–50
See also:
[366] M. E. Reesor: 'The Meaning of Anaxagoras', *CP* 55, 1960, 1–8
[367] M. E. Reesor: 'The Problem of Anaxagoras', *CP* 58, 1963, 29–33 = Anton-Kustas [69]
[368] D. Bargrave-Weaver: 'The Cosmogony of Anaxagoras', *Phron* 4, 1959, 77–91
    The problem of Anaxagoras' ontology has aroused a massive literature; see the Appendix to Bailey [383]; and:
[369] F. M. Cornford: 'Anaxagoras' Theory of Matter', *CQ* 24, 1930, 14–30 and 83–95
[370] I. R. Mathewson: 'Aristotle and Anaxagoras: An Examination of F. M. Cornford's Interpretation', *CQ* n.s. 8, 1958, 67–81
[371] A. L. Peck: 'Anaxagoras: Predication as a Problem in Physics', *CQ* 25, 1931, 27–37 and 112–20
[372] G. Vlastos: 'The Physical Theory of Anaxagoras', *PR* 59, 1950, 31–57 = Furley-Allen [70] = Mourelatos [72]
[373] J. E. Raven: 'The Basis of Anaxagoras' Cosmology', *CQ* n.s. 4, 1954, 123–37
[374] C. Strang: 'The Physical Theory of Anaxagoras', *AGP* 45, 1963, 101–18 = Furley-Allen [70]
[375] W. Schwabe: 'Welches sind die materiellen Elements bei Anaxagoras?', *Phron* 20, 1975, 1–10
On homoiomeries in particular see:
[376] A. L. Peck: 'Anaxagoras and the Parts', *CQ* 20, 1926, 57–62
[377] D. Lanza: 'Le Omeomerie nella tradizione dossografica Anassagorea', *Parole del Passato* 18, 1963, 256–93
But the clearest and the best paper on the whole topic is:
[378] G. B. Kerferd: 'Anaxagoras and the Concept of Matter before Aristotle', *Bulletin of the John Rylands Library* 52, 1969, 129–43 = Mourelatos [72]
    The biological slant of Anaxagoras' thought has often been remarked upon; see Vlastos [372], Müller [52], Longrigg [63];
[379] P. Kucharski: 'Anaxagore et les idées biologiques de son siècle', *Revue philosophique de la France et de l' Étranger* 89, 1964, 137–66
    Finally note the detailed study of **B 10** by:
[380] M. Schofield: 'Doxographica Anaxagorea', *H* 103, 1975, 1–24
    On *nous* see under Chapter V below.

Chapter III

Atomist texts have been edited (with a Russian commentary which may be of more use to some readers than it is to me) in:

[381] S. Luria: *Demokrit* (Leningrad, 1970)

On the vocabulary and style of Atomism see:

[382] K. von Fritz: *Philosophie und sprachlicher Ausdruck bei Demokrit, Platon und Aristoteles* (New York, n.d.)

There are general surveys of atomism by:

[383] C. Bailey: *The Greek Atomists and Epicurus* (Oxford, 1928)

[384] V. E. Alfieri: *Atomos Idea* (Florence, 1953)

[385] H. Steckel: 'Demokritos', *RE* suppt 12, 1970, 191–223

See also chapter 5 of Sambursky [53]; and:

[386] H. Langerbeck: Δόξις ἐπιρρυσμίη. Neue Philologische Untersuchungen (Berlin, 1935)

[387] D. J. Furley: *Two Studies in the Greek Atomists* (Princeton, NJ, 1967) = (in part) Mourelatos [72]

And it is still worth reading:

[388] K. Marx: *The difference between the Democritean and the Epicurean Philosophy of Nature*, in K. Marx and F. Engels, *Collected Works*, I (London, 1975)

On Abderite cosmology see:

[389] J. Kerschensteiner: 'Zu Leukippos A 1', *H* 87, 1959, 444–8

On the historical continuity of the philosophy of atomism see especially:

[390] M. Capek: *The Philosophical Impact of Contemporary Physics* (Princeton, NJ, 1961)

There is fascinating historical matter in:

[391] A. van Melsen: *From Atomos to Atom* (Pittsburgh, Pa., 1952)

[392] D. M. Knight: *Atoms and Elements* (London, 1967)

[393] R. H. Kargon: *Atomism in England from Hariot to Newton* (Oxford, 1966)

And read the essay by an eminent modern physicist:

[394] W. Heisenberg: *Natural Law and the Structure of Matter* (London, 1970)

Atomic motions are discussed by:

[395] J. B. McDiarmid: 'Phantoms in Democritean Terminology: περιπαλάξις and περιπαλάσεσθαι', *H* 86, 1958, 291–8

[396] S. Sambursky: 'A Democritean Metaphor in Plato's Kratylos', *Phron* 4, 1959, 1–4

[397] J. Brunschwig: 'Deux figures principales de l' atomisme d' après Aristote: l' entrecroisement des atomes et la sphère du feu', in I. During (ed.), *Naturphilosophie bei Aristoteles und Theophrast* (Heidelberg, 1969)

The issue of theoretical indivisibility is subtly treated by:

[398] S. Luria: 'Die Infinitesimaltheorie der antiken Atomisten', *QSGM* B 2, 1932, 106–85

and the discussion was advanced by:

[399] J. Mau: *Zum Problem des Infinitesimalen bei den antiken Atomisten* (Berlin, 1954)

and by Furley [387], and:

[400] D. J. Furley: 'Aristotle and the Atomists on Infinity', in I. During (ed.), *Naturphilosophie bei Aristoteles und Theophrast* (Heidelberg, 1969)

See also Heinze [311], Nicol [312]; also

[401] G. Vlastos: 'Minimal Parts in Epicurean Atomism', *Isis* 56, 1965, 121–47

[402] J. Mau: 'Was there a Special Epicurean Mathematics?', in E. N. Lee, A. P. D.

Mourelatos and R. Rorty (eds) *Exegesis and Argument: Studies in Greek Philosophy presented to Gregory Vlastos, Phron* suppt 1, 1973

[403] D. E. Hahm: 'Chrysippus' Solution to the Democritean Dilemma of the Cone', *Isis* 63, 1972, 205–20

Finally, for a special study of one Abderite account of a sensible quality see:

[404] J. B. McDiarmid: 'Theophrastus *de Sensibus* 66: Democritus' Explanation of Salinity', *AJP* 80, 1959, 56–66

Later pages give reading on the Atomists' account of explanation (see Chapter V), of anthropology (VI), of the soul (VIII), of morals (IX) and of knowledge (X).

Chapter IV

Of the scientific achievements—or alleged achievements—of the Pythagoreans by far the best account is that in Burkert [173]. There is also much of value in Heath [45], chapters 6 and 12; in Heath [46], chapter 5; in van der Waerden [58], and in:

[405] F. M. Cornford: 'Mysticism and Science in the Pythagorean Tradition', *CQ* 16, 1922, 137–50 and 17, 1923, 1–12 = (in part) Mourelatos [72]

[406] W. A. Heidel: 'The Pythagoreans and Greek Mathematics', *AJP* 61, 1940, 1–33 = Furley-Allen [70]

[407] K. von Fritz: 'The Discovery of Incommensurability by Hippasus of Metapontum', *Annals of Mathematics* 46, 1945, 242–64 = von Fritz [77] = Furley-Allen [70]

[408] B. L. van der Waerden: 'Pythagoreische Wissenschaft', *RE* 24, 1963, 277–300

There is a clear account of 'number philosophy' in chapter 5 of volume I of Guthrie [25], a somewhat credulous account in Raven [178], and a hard-headed account in Burkert [173]. See also:

[409] A. Delatte: *Études sur la littérature pythagoricienne* (Paris, 1915)

[410] A. J. Festugière: 'Les mémoires pythagoriques cités par Alexandre Polyhistor', *REG* 58, 1945, 1–65

On Philolaus see, again, Burkert [173]; and also de Vogel [181], Kahn [177], and

[411] K. von Fritz: 'Philolaus', *RE* suppt. 13, 1973, 453–84

[412] A. Burns: 'The Fragments of Philolaus', *Classica et Mediaevalia* 25, 1964, 93–128

[413] J. A. Philip: 'Aristotle's Source for Pythagorean Doctrine', *Phoenix* 17, 1963, 251–65

Chapter V

Most of the literature relevant to this Chapter has already been cited under Chapters I–III.

On the central and fascinating notion of *antiperistasis* I know of no special literature; but the minor matter of Empedocles' account of the clepsydra has been massively studied. See, e.g.:

[414] H. Last: 'Empedocles and his Clepsydra Again', *CQ* 18, 1924, 169–74

[415] D. J. Furley: 'Empedocles and the Clepsydra', *JHS* 77, 1957, 31–5

[416] N. B. Booth: 'Empedocles' Account of Breathing', *JHS* 80, 1960, 10–6

[417] D. O'Brien: 'The Effect of a Simile: Empedocles' theories of seeing and breathing', *JHS* 90, 1970, 140–80

The void, and motion therein, has been scarcely better treated than *antiperistasis*. See:

[418] A. C. Moorhouse: 'Δεν in Classical Greek', *CQ* n.s. 12, 1962, 235–8
[419] W. I. Matson: 'Democritus, fragment 156', *CQ* n.s. 13, 1963, 26–30
[420] D. McGibbon: 'The Atomists and Melissus', *Mnem* s.4, 17, 1964, 248–55
And consult Klowski [271] and Jouanna [270].
    The standard piece on Anaxagoras' *nous* is:
[421] K. von Fritz: 'Der νοῦς des Anaxagoras', *ABG* 9, 1964, 87–102 = von Fritz [77]
On the textual problem of **B 14** see:
[422] D. Sider: 'Anaxagoras Fr 14 DK', *H* 102, 1974, 365–7
[423] M. Marcovich: 'Anaxagoras B 14 DK', *H* 104, 1976, 240–1
    The Atomists' notion of causation, and their adherence to the Principle of Causality, are discussed by:
[424] J. Klowski: 'Die historische Ursprung des Kausalprinzips', *AGP* 48, 1966, 225–66
And the roles of chance and necessity in Abderite physics is examined in:
[425] L. Edmunds: 'Necessity, Chance and Freedom in the Early Atomists', *Phoenix* 26, 1972, 342–57

Chapter VI

I have already listed items that bear upon the neo-Ionian accounts of explanation, locomotion, alteration, and generation. On Empedoclean ontology I may add:
[426] F. Solmsen: 'Eternal and Temporal Beings in Empedocles' Physical Poem', *AGP* 57, 1955, 123–45
    For Ion of Chios see:
[427] A. von Blumenthal: *Ion von Chios: die Reste seiner Werke* (Stuttgart, 1939)
[428] F. Jacoby: 'Some Remarks on Ion of Chios', *CQ* 41, 1947, 1–17
[429] G. Huxley: 'Ion of Chios', *Greek, Roman and Byzantine Studies* 6, 1965, 29–46

Chapter VII

Texts bearing upon the Sophists have been edited by:
[430] M. Untersteiner: *Sofisti—testimonianze e frammenti* (Florence, 1949–62)
And they are translated in:
[431] R. K. Sprague: *The Older Sophists* (Columbia, SC, 1972)
    The most celebrated account of the sophistic movement is the one in Chapter 67 of volume 7 of:
[432] G. Grote: *A History of Greece* (London, 1888)
There are two full-length studies, each somewhat bizarre in its general conclusions:
[433] H. Gomperz: *Sophistik und Rhetorik* (Leipzig, 1912)
[434] M. Untersteiner: *The Sophists*, trans. K. Freeman (Oxford, 1954)
There is an expanded version of [434]:
[435] M. Untersteiner: *I Sofisti* (Milan, 1967²)
For a full and sober description of the Sophists consult the second half of volume III of Guthrie [25]; and see the notes by:
[436] G. B. Kerferd: 'The First Greek Sophists', *CR* n.s. 64, 1950, 8–10
[437] E. L. Harrison: 'Was Gorgias a Sophist?' *Phoenix* 18, 1964, 183–92
    On Protagoras in general see:
[438] K. von Fritz: 'Protagoras', *RE* 23, 1957, 908–23
And on his attitude to the gods:

[439] T. Gomperz: 'Das Götterbruchstück des Protagoras', *WS* 32, 1910, 4–6
[440] C. W. Müller: 'Protagoras über die Götter', *H* 95, 1967, 140–59
[441] C. W. Chilton: 'An Epicurean View of Protagoras', *Phron* 7, 1962, 105–9
There is much excellent matter on early anthropology:
[442] E. Norden: *Agnostos Theos* (Leipzig, 1913)
[443] W. von Uxkull-Gyllenband: *Griechische Kulturentstehungslehre* (Berlin, 1924)
[444] A. Kleingünther: Πρῶτος Εὑρετής *Phlg* suppt 26, 1933
[445] F. Heinimann: *Nomos und Phusis* (Basle, 1945)
[446] L. Edelstein: *The Idea of Progress in Classical Antiquity* (Baltimore, 1967)
[447] E. R. Dodds: *The Ancient Concept of Progress* (Oxford, 1973)
Democritus' views on the origins of man and the growth of civilization are expansively analysed in:
[448] T. Cole: *Democritus and the Sources of Greek Anthropology*, Philological Monographs 25 (n.p., 1967)
And on Protagoras see the notes in:
[449] C. C. W. Taylor: *Plato: Protagoras* (Oxford, 1976)
The special issue of the Diodoran anthropology has aroused passionate controversy; the most interesting items are:
[450] K. Reinhardt: 'Hekataios von Abdera und Demokrit', *H* 47, 1912, 492–513 = Reinhardt [81]
[451] G. Vlastos: 'On the Pre-History of Diodorus', *AJP* 67, 1946, 51–9
[452] W. Spoerri: *Späthellenistische Berichte über Welt, Kultur und Götter* (Basle, 1959)
[453] W. Spoerri: 'Zu Diodor von Sizilien I.7–8', *MH* 18, 1961, 63–82
[454] A. Burton: *Diodorus Siculus, Book I* (Leiden, 1972)
On Critias there is a rare but good book by:
[455] D. Stephans: *Critias, his Life and Literary Remains* (Cincinnati Ohio, 1939)
and a useful article by:
[456] A. Battegazzore: 'Influssi e polemiche nel fr (DK) 25 di Crizia', *Dioniso* 21, 1958, 45–58
The texts bearing on Diagoras of Melos are splendidly edited by:
[457] F. Jacoby: *Diagoras ὁ Ἄθεος*, Abhandlungen der Akademie der Wissenschaften, Berlin, 3, 1959
And Diagoran problems are discussed by:
[458] L. Woodbury: 'Diagoras of Melos', *Phoenix* 19, 1965, 178–213
On Euripides' theology there are two informative studies by Wilhelm Nestle:
[459] W. Nestle: *Euripides der Dichter der griechischen Erklärung* (Stuttgart, 1901)
[460] W. Nestle: *Untersuchungen über die philosophischen Quellen des Euripides*, *Phlg* suppt 8, 1900
Some reading on ancient atheism has already been given in vol. 1, under Chapter V: see especially Drachmann [164], Fahr [163], and De Mahieu [168].
Finally, on Democritus' attitude to the gods see:
[461] V. E. Alfieri: 'Il concetto del divino in Democrito e in Epicuro', in Alfieri-Untersteiner [68]
[462] D. McGibbon: 'The Religious Thought of Democritus', *H* 93, 1965, 385–97
[463] H. Eisenberger: 'Demokrits Vorstellung vom Sein und Wirken der Götter', *RhM* 113, 1970, 141–58
And, on a related issue:
[464] P. J. Bicknell: 'Democritus' Theory of Precognition', *REG* 82, 1969, 318–26

BIBLIOGRAPHY

The linguistic studies of the Sophists are the subject of a delightful paper by Hermann Diels:

[465] H. Diels: 'Die Anfänge der Philologie bei den Griechen', *Neue Jahrbuch für Philologie* 25, 1910, 1–25

More recent papers include:

[466] J. C. Classen: 'The Study of Language among Socrates' Contemporaries', *Proceedings of the African Classical Association* 2, 1959, 33–49

[467] D. Fehling: 'Zwei Untersuchungen zur griechischen Sprachphilosophie', *RhM* 108, 1965, 212–29

[468] W. Burkert: 'La genèse des choses et des mots', *Les études philosophiques* 1970, 443–55

And see also the early pages of Pfeiffer [24].

On Prodicus' invention of 'semantics' there are some helpful remarks in Taylor [449], and a monograph by:

[469] H. Mayer: *Prodikos von Keos und die Anfänge der Synonymik bei den Griechen* (Paderborn, 1913)

See also:

[470] K. von Fritz: 'Prodikos', *RE* 23, 1957, 85–9

Early rhetorical fragments are collected and edited in:

[471] L. Radermacher: *Artium Scriptores*, Sitzungberichte der österreichische Akademie der Wissenschaft, 227, 1951

In vol. 1 under Chapter IX I listed some items touching on Gorgias' metaphysics, or antimetaphysics; his *Helen* is admirably edited by:

[472] O. Immisch: *Gorgiae Helena* (Berlin, 1927)

On the aesthetic theory of *apatê* see especially:

[473] M. Pohlenz: 'Die Anfänge der griechischer Poetik', *NGG* 1920, 142–78

Compare:

[474] T. G. Rosenmeyer: 'Gorgias, Aeschylus and ἀπατή', *AJP* 76, 1955, 225–60

[475] C. P. Segal: 'Gorgias and the Psychology of the Logos', *HSCP* 66, 1962, 99–156

Finally, on Democritus **B 26**, on meaning, see:

[476] R. Philippson: 'Platons Kratylos und Demokrit', *Philologische Wochenshcrift* 49, 1929, 923–7

Chapter VIII

Some bibliography on Presocratic psychology has already been given in vol. 1 under Chapter VI; and the book by Beare [39] is uniformly informative.

There is a fine paper on Heraclitus by:

[477] M. C. Nussbaum: 'Ψυχή in Heraclitus', *Phron* 17, 1972, 1–16 and 153–70

On two points of detail see:

[478] W. J. Verdenius: 'A Psychological Statement of Heraclitus', *Mnem* s.3, 11, 1943, 115–21

[479] S. Tugwell: 'Heraclitus: fragment 98 (DK)', *CQ* n.s. 21, 1971, 32

Democritus' theory of perception is discussed by:

[480] R. W. Baldes: 'Democritus on Visual Perception: Two Theories or One?', *Phron* 20, 1975, 93–105

[481] K. von Fritz: 'Democritus' Theory of Vision', in E. A. Underwood (ed.), *Science, Medicine and History* (Oxford, 1953) = von Fritz [77]

And on Democritean thought see:

[482] P. J. Bicknell: 'The Seat of the Mind in Democritus', *Eranos* 66, 1968, 10–23

Alcmeon, Empedocles and Parmenides may be taken together. On their physiological psychology see:

[483] F. Solmsen: 'Greek Philosophy and the Discovery of the Nerves', *MH* 18, 1961, 150–97 = Solmsen [83]
[484] J. Mansfeld: 'Alcmaeon: "Physikos" or Physician? With some remarks on Calcidius' "On Vision" compared to Galen, Plac. Hipp. Plat. VII', in J. Mansfeld and L. M. de Rijk (eds), *Kephalaion: Studies in Greek Philosophy and its continuation offered to Professor C. J. de Vogel* (Assen, 1975)
[485] W. J. Verdenius: 'Empedocles' Doctrine of Sight', in *Studia Carolo Guglielmo Vollgraff Oblata* (Amsterdam, 1948)
—but consult O'Brien [417]. On Empedocles **B 110** see in particular:
[486] H. Schwabl: 'Empedokles Fr B 110', *WS* 69, 1956, 49–56
And on Parmenides **B 16**:
[487] G. Vlastos: 'Parmenides' Theory of Knowledge', *TAPA* 77, 1946, 66–77
[488] J. A. Philip: 'Parmenides' Theory of Knowledge', *Phoenix* 12, 1958, 63–6
[489] J. P. Hershbell: 'Parmenides' Way of Truth and B 16', *Apeiron* 4, 1970, 1–23
And also Bollack [284]

For literature on Philolaus see above, under Chapter IV. The *harmonia* theory of the soul is discussed by:
[490] H. B. Gottschalk: 'Soul as Harmonia', *Phron* 16, 1971, 179–98
The commentaries of Hicks [10] and Bailey [21] contain remarks on the objections to the theory put forward by Aristotle and by Lucretius; see too Gladigow [187] and Gomperz [288].

Empedocles' intellectual schizophrenia has been widely discussed:
[491] K. Reinhardt: 'Empedokles, Orphiker und Physiker', *CP* 45, 1950, 170–9 = Reinhardt [81] = Gadamer [71]
[492] H. S. Long: 'The Unity of Empedocles' Thought', *AJP* 70, 1949, 142–58
[493] C. H. Kahn: 'Religion and Natural Philosophy in Empedocles' Doctrine of the Soul', *AGP* 42, 1960, 3–35 = Anton-Kustas [69] = Mourelatos [72]
[494] A. A. Long: 'Thinking and Sense-Perception in Empedocles: Mysticism or Materialism?', *CQ* n.s. 16, 1966, 256–76
See also Wilamowitz-Moellendorf [194], and chapter 8 of Jaeger [48].

Empedocles' theology and 'demonology' is treated in several of the studies I have just listed; in addition see:
[495] M. Detienne: 'La "Démonologie" d' Empédocle', *REG* 72, 1959, 1–17
The accounts of the Cosmic Cycle catalogued on p. 322 will contain matter touching on the theory of Eternal Recurrence; for more detailed studies see:
[496] B. L. van der Waerden: 'Das Grosse Jahr und die ewige Wiederkehr', *H* 80, 1952, 129–55
[497] M. Capek: 'The theory of Eternal Recurrence in Modern Philosophy of Science', *JP* 57, 1960, 289–96
[498] M. Capek: 'Eternal Return', in P. Edwards (ed.), *Encyclopaedia of Philosophy* (New York, 1967)

Chapter IX

Various studies in early Greek ethical theory have been given in vol. 1 under Chapter VII: in particular, see Dover [206], Adkins [207], and Grant [208]. Chapter 6 of Lloyd-Jones [51] is useful too.

On Antiphon's personal problems see:
[499] J. Stenzel: 'Antiphon', *RE* suppt 4, 1924, 33–43

[500] J. S. Morrison: 'Antiphon', *PCPS* n.s. 7, 1961, 49–58

[501] S. Luria: 'Antiphon der Sophist', *Eos* 53, 1963, 63–7

Antiphon's moral—or amoral—doctrines are examined by:

[502] G. B. Kerferd: 'The Moral and Political Doctrines of Antiphon the Sophist', *PCPS* n.s. 4, 1956/7, 26–32

[503] J. S. Morrison: 'The *Truth* of Antiphon', *Phron* 8, 1963, 35–49

[504] C. Moulton: 'Antiphon the Sophist, *On Truth*', *TAPA* 103, 1972, 329–66

And a connexion between Antiphon and Democritus is discerned by:

[505] C. Moulton: 'Antiphon the Sophist and Democritus', *MH* 31, 1974, 129–39

On the alleged moral relativism of Prodicus see:

[506] G. B. Kerferd: 'The "Relativism" of Prodicus', *Bulletin of the John Rylands Library* 37, 1954, 249–56

On the moral relativism of Protagoras see:

[507] S. Moser and G. L. Kustas: 'A Comment on the "Relativism" of the *Protagoras*', *Phoenix* 20, 1966, 111–15

and refer to the general literature on Protagorean relativism cited under Chapter X.

Out of various articles on the *Dissoi Logoi* I select:

[508] C. Trieber: 'Die Διαλέξεις', *H* 27, 1892, 210–48

[509] W. Kranz: 'Vorsokratisches IV', *H* 72, 1937, 223–32

[510] A. E. Taylor: 'The *Dissoi Logoi*', in his *Varia Socratica* (Oxford, 1911)

[511] A. Levi: 'On Twofold Statements', *AJP* 61, 1940, 292–306

There is an edition of the tract in Untersteiner [430], and a translation in Sprague [431].

There are helpful remarks on Gorgias' account of responsibility in Immisch [472]; and it is worth consulting the relevant pages of Adkins [207]. See also:

[512] G. Calogero: 'Gorgias and the Socratic Principle *Nemo sua sponte peccat*', *JHS* 77, 1957, 12–17 = Anton-Kustas [69]

Democritean ethics are treated in Bailey [383], and in Langerbeck [386]; and there is a classic paper by:

[513] G. Vlastos: 'Ethics and Physics in Democritus', *PR* 54, 1945, 578–92 and 55, 1946, 53–64 = Furley-Allen [70]

and a monograph by:

[514] S. Luria: *Zur Frage der materialistischen Begründung der Ethik bei Demokrit* (Berlin, 1964)

See also:

[515] D. McGibbon: 'Pleasure as the "Criterion" in Democritus', *Phron* 5, 1960, 75–7

[516] S. Luria: 'Heraklit und Demokrit', *Das Altertum* 9, 1963, 195–200

[517] C. C. W. Taylor: 'Pleasure, Knowledge and Sensation in Democritus', *Phron* 12, 1967, 6–27

And on Democritus' political viewpoint:

[518] G. J. D. Aalders: 'The Political Faith of Democritus', *Mnem* s.4, 3, 1950, 302–13

[519] A. T. Cole: 'The Anonymus Iamblichi', *HSCP* 65, 1961, 127–63

Chapter X

Anaxagoras' 'methodology', *opsis adêlôn*, is treated in two classic papers: Diller [120] and:

[520] O. Regenbogen: 'Eine Forschungsmethode antiker Naturwissenschaft', *QSGM* B 2, 1930, 131–82

See also:

[521] H. Gomperz: 'ὄψις τῶν ἀδήλων τὰ φαινόμενα', H 68, 1933, 341–3
and Lloyd [50], part II.
On Protagoras' slogan, 'Man the Measure', consult:
[522] L. Versenyi: 'Protagoras' Man-Measure Fragment', AJP 83, 1962, 178–84
[523] D. K. Glidden: 'Protagorean Relativism and the Cyrenaics', APQ monograph 9, 1975
[524] D. K. Glidden: 'Protagorean Relativism and Physis', Phron 20, 1975, 209–27
The reliability of Plato's report of Protagoras' views is discussed in:
[525] G. B. Kerferd: 'Plato's Account of the Relativism of Protagoras', Durham University Journal n.s. 11, 1949/50, 20–6
[526] J. McDowell: Plato: Theaetetus (Oxford, 1973)
[527] J. P. Maguire: 'Protagoras or Plato?', Phron 18, 1973, 115–39
On the 'new fragment' of Protagoras see:
[528] M. Gronewald: 'Ein neues Protagoras-Fragment', Zeitschrift für Papyrologie und Epigraphik 2, 1968, 1–2
[529] J. Mejer: 'The Alleged New Fragment of Protagoras', H 100, 1972, 175–8
On the Impossibility of Contradiction consult:
[530] G. Binder and L. Lieseborghs: 'Eine Zuweisung der Sentenz οὐκ ἔστιν ἀντιλέγειν an Prodikos von Keos', MH 23, 1966, 37–43
And on the peritropê or 'about-turn' see:
[531] M. F. Burnyeat: 'Protagoras and Self-Refutation in Later Greek Philosophy', PR 85, 1976, 44–69
[532] M. F. Burnyeat: 'Protagoras and Self-Refutation in Plato's Theaetetus', PR 85, 1976, 172–95
The Democritean Ou Mallon Principle is treated in:
[533] S. Luria: 'Zwei Demokrit-Studien', in J. Mau and E. G. Schmidt (eds), Isonomia (Berlin, 1964)
[534] C. Diano: 'Mallon Hetton e Isonomia', in J. Mau and E. G. Schmidt (eds), Isonomia (Berlin, 1964)
[535] P. de Lacey: 'οὐ μᾶλλον and the Antecedents of Ancient Scepticism', Phron 3, 1958, 59–71
[536] P. de Lacey: 'Colotes' First Criticism of Democritus', in J. Mau and E. G. Schmidt (eds), Isonomia (Berlin, 1964)
Democritus' epistemology is discussed in the general studies of his thought. See in particular Langerbeck [386], and the criticisms in:
[537] E. Kapp: review of Langerbeck [386], Gnomon 12, 1936, 65–77 and 158–69 = E. Kapp, Ausgewählte Schriften (Berlin, 1968)
See also:
[538] H. Weiss: 'Democritus' Theory of Cognition', CQ 32, 1938, 47–56
[539] H. de Ley: 'Δόξις ἐπιρυσμίη—a critical note on Democritus Fr. 7', H 97, 1969, 497–8

Chapter XI

Diogenes of Apollonia has not excited the scholars. But he is given a decent place in history by Jouanna [270] and by:

[540] H. Diller: 'Die philosophiegeschichtliche Stellung des Diogenes von Apollonia', H 76, 1941, 359–81 = Diller [75]

And his teleology is debated in Chapter 9 of Jaeger [48], and by:

[541] W. Theiler: Zur Geschichte der teleologischen Naturbetrachtung bis auf

Aristoteles (Zurich, 1925)
[542] F. Huffmeier: 'Teleologische Weltbetrachtung bei Diogenes von Apollonia?', *Phlg* 107, 1963, 131-8

C: APPENDIX

The following works which bear primarily on the subject matter of volume 1 are also referred to in the present volume:

[90] C. H. Kahn: *Anaximander and the Origins of Greek Cosmology* (New York, 1960)
[120] H. Diller: 'ὄψις ἀδήλων τὰ φαινόμενα', *H* 67, 1932, 14–42 = Diller [75]
[161] G. Vlastos: 'Theology and Philosophy in Early Greek Thought', *PQ* 2, 1952, 97-123 = Furley-Allen [70]
[163] W. Fahr: 'Θεοὺς νομίζειν', Spudasmata 26 (Hildesheim, 1969)
[164] A. B Drachmann: *Atheism in Pagan Antiquity* (London, 1922)
[168] W. de Mahieu: 'La doctrine des Athées au xᵉ livre des Lois de Platon', *Revue belge de philologie et d'histoire* 41, 1963, 5-24; and 42, 1964, 16-47
[173] W. Burkert: *Lore and Science in Ancient Pythagoreanism* (Cambridge, Mass., 1972; first German edition, 1962)
[177] C. H. Kahn: 'Pythagorean Philosophy before Plato', in Mourelatos [72]
[178] J. E. Raven: *Pythagoreans and Eleatics* (Cambridge, 1948)
[180] J. A. Philip: *Pythagoras and Early Pythagoreanism* (Toronto, 1966)
[181] C. J. de Vogel: *Pythagoras and Early Pythagoreanism* (Assen, 1966)
[187] B. Gladigow: 'Zum Makarismos des Weisen', *H* 95, 1967, 404-33
[193] G. Zuntz: *Persephone* (Oxford, 1971)
[194] U. von Wilamowitz-Moellendorf: 'Die καθαρμοί des Empedokles', *Sitzungsberichte der preussichen Akadamie*, 1929, 626-61 = Wilamowitz-Moellendorf, *Kleine Schriften* I (Berlin, 1935)
[206] K. J. Dover: *Greek Popular Morality in the Time of Plato and Aristotle* (Oxford, 1974)
[207] A. W. H. Adkins: *Merit and Responsibility* (Oxford, 1960)
[208] A. Grant: *The Ethics of Aristotle* (Oxford, 1885⁴)
[218] A. J. Festugière: *Hippocrate: L'Ancienne Médicine* (Paris, 1948)
[231] F. M. Cornford: *Plato and Parmenides* (London, 1939)
[233] W. J. Verdenius: *Parmenides* (Groningen, 1942)
[238] J. H. M. M. Loenen: *Parmenides, Melissus, Gorgias* (Assen, 1959)
[245] A. P. D. Mourelatos: 'The Real, Appearances and Human Error in Early Greek Philosophy', *RM* 19, 1965, 346-65
[260] W. Nestle: 'Die Schrift des Gorgias "Ueber die Natur oder über das Nichtseiende",' *H* 57, 1922, 551-62 = Nestle [80]
[270] J. Jouanna: 'Rapports entre Mélissos de Samos et Diogène d'Apollonie, à la lumière du traité hippocratique de natura hominis', *REA* 67, 1965, 306-23
[271] J. Klowski: 'Antwortete Leukipp Melissos oder Melissos Leukipp?', *MH* 28, 1971, 65-71
[284] J. Bollack: 'Sur deux fragments de Parménide (4 et 16)', *REG* 70, 1957, 56-71
[288] H. Gomperz: 'ἀσώματος', *H* 67, 1932, 155-67
[311] R. Heinze: *Xenokrates* (Leipzig, 1892)
[312] A. T. Nicol: 'Indivisible Lines', *CQ* 30, 1936, 120-6.

D: ADDENDA (1978)

Several valuable studies in Presocratic philosophy have appeared since my typescript was submitted to the publishers in August 1976. I mention here a small selection.

To section *A V* add:

[72A] C. J. Classen (ed.): *Sophistik* (Darmstadt, 1976)

[72B] R. A. Shiner and J. King-Farlow (eds): *New Essays on Plato and the Presocratics, Canadian Journal of Philosophy* suppt 2 (Guelph, 1976)

Classen's volume includes Snell [13], Müller [440], Classen [466], Fehling [467], Luria [501], Morrison [503], Kranz [509], Calogero [512], Versenyi [522], Mejer [529], Binder-Liesenborghs [530]; it also contains an excellent bibliography.

To section *B*, *Chapter II*, add a major study by:

[368A] D. J. Furley: 'Anaxagoras in Response to Parmenides', in Shiner-King-Farlow [72B]

On atoms and *minima, Chapter III*, see now:

[403A] D. Sedley: 'Epicurus and the Mathematicians of Cyzicus', *Cronache Ercolanesi* 6, 1976, 23–54

New light has been shed on a subject of *Chapter VII* by:

[463A] A. Henrichs: 'Two Doxographical Notes: Democritus and Prodicus on Religion', *HSCP* 79, 1975, 93–123

—a study of far wider scope than its title suggests. Finally, on the whirligig of time, *Chapter VIII*, I may be allowed a reference to:

[498A] J. Barnes: 'La doctrine du retour éternel', in J. Brunschwig (ed.), *Les stoiciens et leur logique* (Paris, 1978)

Indexes

Compiled by Ian Arthur

(i) *Passages*

(ii) *Persons*

(iii) *Topics*

Concordance

Barnes	Diels-Kranz		Barnes	Diels-Kranz
193	67 A 8		224	(Aristotle, *GC* 326a1–3)
194	31 B 17.1–13		225	(Alexander, *in Met*
195	31 B 21.9–12			36.25–7)
196	31 B 23		226	(Aristotle, *Phys* 187a1)
197	59 B 1		227	(Aristotle, *GC* 316a10–14)
198	59 B 3		228	(Aristotle, *GC*
199	59 B 4			316b28–317a2)
200	59 B 4		229	67 A 13
201	59 B 4		230	68 A 48a
202	59 B 6		231	(Aristotle, *Cael* 271a9–11)
203	59 B 8		232	(Aristotle, *Cael* 303a20–4)
204	59 B 11		233	68 B 155
205	59 A 43		234	68 B 155a
206	59 A 46		235	68 A 38
207	59 B 12		236	67 A 8
208	59 B 7		237	(Aristotle, *Phys* 203b20–2)
209	59 A 52		238	(Aristotle, *Phys* 203b25–8)
210	59 A 45		239	67 A 9
211	59 B 16		240	68 A 60
212	59 B 10		241	68 A 61
213	68 A 37		242	68 A 135
214	68 A 71		243	68 A 47
215	68 A 57		244	67 A 10
216	67 A 13		245	(Lucretius II.114–22)
217	67 A 14		246	68 A 58
218	68 A 1		247	68 A 47
219	68 A 43		248	68 A 47
220	68 A 47		249	67 A 6
221	67 A 7		250	67 A 6
222	67 A 7		251	(Aristotle, *GC* 326a1–3)
223	68 A 42		252	67 A 19

Barnes	Diels-Kranz	Barnes	Diels-Kranz
253	68 A 135	300	59 A 58
254	(Plutarch, *adv Col* 1110E)	301	59 B 12
255	68 A 125	302	59 B 13
256	68 A 126	303	59 B 14
257	68 A 135	304	68 B 118
258	67 A 32	305	68 A 69
259	68 A 49	306	68 A 6
260	68 B 9	307	68 A 66
261	68 A 49	308	68 A 1
262	68 A 64	309	67 B 2
263	68 A 123	310	67 A 22
264	67 A 32	311	68 A 70
265	68 A 48	312	59 A 47
266	68 A 135	313	59 A 47
267	44 A 29	314	59 A 102
268	44 A 7a	315	59 A 16
269	47 B 1	316	59 A 45
270	58 B 4	317	31 B 17.19–20
271	(Iamblichus, *comm math sc* 78.8–18)	318	31 B 17.22–4
		319	31 B 27.8
272	(Aristotle, *Met* 1090a20–2)	320	31 B 33
273	58 B 4	321	31 B 86
274	58 B 4	322	31 B 95
275	58 B 1a	323	31 B 35.9
276	44 B 1	324	31 A 70
277	44 B 6	325	31 A 20a
278	44 B 3	326	31 B 62.6
279	44 B 2	327	31 B 90
280	44 B 4	328	31 A 38
281	44 B 5	329	31 B 115.1–2
282	58 B 5	330	(Aristotle, *Phys* 196a19–24)
283	45 A 3	331	31 B 22.4–5
284	44 B 7	332	31 B 30
285	44 B 17	333	31 B 103
286	58 B 8	334	67 A 11
287	58 B 5	335	68 B 118
288	31 B 13	336	68 A 67
289	(Aristotle, *MXG* 976b26)	337	68 A 68
290	59 A 68	338	68 A 69
291	30 A 5	339	68 A 68
292	31 A 35	340	31 A 48
293	31 A 35	341	59 A 59
294	67 A 20	342	67 A 6
295	67 A 6	343	67 A 10
296	67 A 8	344	67 A 16
297	68 B 156	345	67 A 16
298	70 B 2	346	67 A 18
299	59 A 1	347	68 A 65

CONCORDANCE

Barnes	Diels-Kranz	Barnes	Diels-Kranz
348	59 A 52	396	68 B 26
349	67 A 9	397	82 B 3
350	68 A 58	398	12 A 29
351	31 B 21.13–14	399	18 A 9
352	31 B 17.34–5	400	22 B 36
353	31 A 41	401	22 B 118
354	31 B 11	402	22 B 98
355	31 B 12	403	22 B 115
356	59 A 52	404	22 B 67a
357	59 B 5	405	64 A 20
358	31 B 17.30–3	406	67 A 28
359	59 B 17	407	18 A 10
360	31 B 8	408	44 B 14
361	31 B 9	409	58 B 40
362	67 A 7	410	67 A 30
363	67 A 37	411	68 A 119
364	67 A 14	412	68 A 135
365	31 B 17.34	413	68 A 135
366	36 B 1	414	24 A 5
367	68 A 57	415	31 B 111.1–2
368	62 A 1	416	31 B 112.10–12
369	67 A 33	417	31 A 92
370	79 A 2a	418	31 A 86
371	80 B 4	419	31 B 89
372	80 A 23	420	31 B 101
373	68 B 144	421	31 A 86
374	68 B 154	422	31 B 102
375	88 B 25	423	31 B 110.10
376	85 B 8	424	31 A 86
377	(Euripides, fr.286)	425	31 B 109
378	84 B 5	426	31 A 86
379	68 A 75	427	31 B 106 + B 108
380	68 B 297	428	31 A 86
381	68 B 30	429	31 B 105
382	84 B 5	430	31 B 110
383	68 B 37	431	28 B 16
384	68 B 189	432	31 A 30
385	68 B 217	433	31 A 78
386	68 A 74	434	44 A 23
387	68 A 74	435	58 B 41
388	68 B 166	436	(Plato, *Phaedo* 86B)
389	68 B 175	437	44 A 23
390	82 B 23	438	31 B 131
391	82 B 11.9	439	31 B 15
392	90 A 3.10	440	31 B 133
393	90 A 3.17	441	31 B 134
394	68 B 5	442	31 B 115
395	68 B 145	443	31 B 126

Barnes	Diels-Kranz	Barnes	Diels-Kranz
444	31 B 128	488	59 B 21
445	31 B 112.$_4$	489	59 A 97
446	31 B 146.$_3$ + B 147.$_1$	490	59 A 28
447	58 B 34	491	80 B 1
448	88 B 44	492	80 B 1
449	88 B 44	493	80 A 14
450	88 B 44	494	68 A 114
451	60 A 2	495	80 B 1
452	90 A 1.$_1$	496	80 A 19
453	90 A 1.$_{17}$	497	80 A 1
454	90 A 1.$_3$	498	80 A 20
455	90 A 2.$_{9-10}$	499	80 A 1
456	90 A 3.$_{2-3}$	500	80 A 19
457	90 A 1.$_{12}$	501	68 A 112
458	90 A 2.$_{25}$	502	75 B 4
459	90 A 3.$_{16}$	503	80 A 14
460	80 A 10	504	67 A 9
461	82 B 11.$_2$	505	70 B 1
462	82 B 11.$_6$	506	68 B 117
463	82 B 11.$_{20}$	507	68 B 6–11
464	82 B 11.$_{21}$	508	70 A 23
465	82 B 11.$_{17}$	509	68 B 125
466	82 B 11.$_{15}$	510	64 A 1
467	82 B 11.$_{12}$	511	64 B 1
468	68 B 35	512	64 A 5
469	68 B 37	513	64 A 6
470	68 B 39	514	64 A 23
471	68 B 62	515	64 B 2
472	68 B 102	516	64 A 10
473	68 B 274	517	68 A 63
474	68 B 260	518	68 A 135
475	68 B 53	519	64 A 7
476	68 B 4	520	64 A 5
477	68 A 1	521	64 A 4
478	68 B 188	522	64 B 2
479	68 B 74	523	64 B 6
480	68 B 71	524	64 B 7
481	68 B 211	525	64 B 3
482	68 B 194	526	64 B 4
483	68 B 207	527	64 B 5
484	68 B 230	528	60 A 4
485	68 A 30	529	60 A 12
486	31 B 3	530	60 A 10
487	59 B 21a		

Diels-Kranz	Barnes	Diels-Kranz	Barnes
12 A 29	398	31 B 109	425
18 A 9	399	31 B 110	423, 430
18 A 10	407	31 B 111	415
22 B 36	400	31 B 112	416, 445
22 B 67a	404	31 B 115	329, 442
22 B 98	402	31 B 126	443
22 B 115	403	31 B 128	444
22 B 118	401	31 B 131	438
24 A 5	414	31 B 133	440
28 A 16	431	31 B 134	441
30 A 5	291	31 B 146	446
31 A 20a	325	31 B 147	446
31 A 30	432	36 B 1	366
31 A 35	292, 293	44 A 7a	268
31 A 38	328	44 A 23	434, 437
31 A 41	353	44 A 29	267
31 A 48	340	44 B 1	276
31 A 70	324	44 B 2	279
31 A 78	433	44 B 3	278
31 A 86	418, 421, 424, 426, 428	44 B 4	280
		44 B 5	281
31 A 92	417	44 B 6	277
31 B 3	486	44 B 7	284
31 B 8	360	44 B 14	408
31 B 9	361	44 B 17	285
31 B 11	354	45 A 3	283
31 B 12	355	47 B 1	269
31 B 13	288	58 B 1a	275
31 B 15	439	58 B 4	270, 273, 274
31 B 17	194, 317, 318, 352, 358, 365	58 B 5	282, 287
		58 B 8	286
31 B 21	195, 351	58 B 34	447
31 B 22	331	58 B 40	409
31 B 23	196	58 B 41	435
31 B 27	319	59 A 1	299
31 B 33	320	59 A 16	315
31 B 35	323	59 A 28	490
31 B 62	326	59 A 43	205
31 B 86	321	59 A 45	210, 316
31 B 89	419	59 A 46	206
31 B 90	327	59 A 47	312, 313
31 B 95	322	59 A 52	209, 348, 356
31 B 101	420	59 A 58	300
31 B 102	422	59 A 59	341
31 B 103	333	59 A 68	290
31 B 105	429	59 A 97	489
31 B 106	427	59 A 102	314
31 B 108	427	59 B 1	197

Diels-Kranz	Barnes	Diels-Kranz	Barnes
59 B 3	198	67 A 28	406
59 B 4	199, 200, 201	67 A 30	410
59 B 5	357	67 A 32	258, 264
59 B 6	202	67 A 33	369
59 B 7	208	67 A 37	363
59 B 8	203	67 A 47	247, 248
59 B 10	212	67 B 2	309
59 B 11	204	68 A 1	218, 308, 477
59 B 12	207, 301	68 A 6	306
59 B 13	302	68 A 37	213
59 B 14	303	68 A 38	235
59 B 16	211	68 A 42	223
59 B 17	359	68 A 43	219
59 B 21	488	68 A 47	220, 243
59 B 21a	487	68 A 48	265
60 A 2	451	68 A 48a	230
60 A 4	528	68 A 49	259, 261
60 A 10	530	68 A 50	485
60 A 12	529	68 A 57	215, 367
62 A 1	368	68 A 58	246, 350
64 A 1	510	68 A 60	240
64 A 4	521	68 A 61	241
64 A 5	512, 520	68 A 63	517
64 A 6	513	68 A 64	262
64 A 7	519	68 A 65	347
64 A 10	516	68 A 66	307
64 A 20	405	68 A 67	336
64 A 23	514	68 A 68	337, 339
64 B 1	511	68 A 69	305, 338
64 B 2	515, 522	68 A 70	311
64 B 3	525	68 A 71	214
64 B 4	526	68 A 74	386, 387
64 B 5	527	68 A 75	379
64 B 6	523	68 A 112	501
64 B 7	524	68 A 114	494
67 A 6	249, 250, 295, 342	68 A 117	506
67 A 7	222, 362	68 A 119	411
67 A 8	193, 236, 296	68 A 123	263
67 A 9	239, 349, 504	68 A 125	255
67 A 10	244, 343	68 A 126	256
67 A 11	334	68 A 135	242, 253, 257, 268,
67 A 13	216, 229		412, 413, 518
67 A 14	217, 364	68 B 4	476
67 A 16	344, 345	68 B 5	394
67 A 18	346	68 B 6–11	507
67 A 19	252	68 B 9	260
67 A 20	294	68 B 26	396
67 A 22	310	68 B 30	381

CONCORDANCE

Diels-Kranz	Barnes		Diels-Kranz	Barnes
68 B 35	468		68 B 260	474
68 B 37	383, 469		68 B 274	473
68 B 39	470		68 B 297	380
68 B 53	475		70 A 23	508
68 B 62	471		70 B 1	505
68 B 71	480		70 B 2	298
68 B 74	479		75 B 4	502
68 B 102	472		79 A 2a	370
68 B 118	304, 335		80 A 1	497, 499
68 B 125	509		80 A 10	460
68 B 144	373		80 A 14	493, 503
68 B 145	395		80 A 19	496, 500
68 B 154	374		80 A 20	498
68 B 155	233		80 A 23	372
68 B 155a	234		80 B 1	491, 492, 495
68 B 156	297		80 B 4	371
68 B 166	388		82 B 3	397
68 B 175	389		82 B 11	391, 461–7
68 B 188	478		82 B 23	390
68 B 189	384		84 B 5	378, 382
68 B 194	482		85 B 8	376
68 B 207	483		87 B 44	448–450
68 B 211	481		88 B 25	375
68 B 217	385		90 A 1	452, 453, 454, 457
68 B 230	484		90 A 2	455, 458
			90 A 3	392, 393, 456, 459